The Collected Works of
James M. Buchanan

VOLUME 18
Federalism, Liberty, and the Law

From left: Bruno Leoni, James M. Buchanan, unknown,
Sylvana Leoni, Ursula Hicks, unknown, Stresa, Italy, 1961

The Collected Works of

James M. Buchanan

VOLUME 18

Federalism, Liberty,
and the Law

LIBERTY FUND

Indianapolis

This book is published by Liberty Fund, Inc., a foundation
established to encourage study of the ideal of a society of free
and responsible individuals.

The cuneiform inscription that serves as our logo and as the design
motif for our endpapers is the earliest-known written appearance
of the word "freedom" (*amagi*), or "liberty." It is taken from a clay
document written about 2300 B.C. in the Sumerian city-state of Lagash.

Library of Congress Cataloging-in-Publication Data
Buchanan, James M.
Federalism, liberty, and the law / James M. Buchanan.
p.   cm. — (The collected works of James M. Buchanan ; v. 18)
Includes bibliographical references and index.
ISBN 0-86597-247-8 (hc. : alk. paper). — ISBN 0-86597-248-6 (pbk. : alk. paper)
1. Federal government.   2. Liberty.   I. Title.   II. Series : Buchanan,
James M.   Works.   1999 ; v.18.
JC355.B89   2001
321.02—dc21   99-42628

LIBERTY FUND, INC.
8335 Allison Pointe Trail, Suite 300
Indianapolis, IN 46250-1684

Contents

3. Liberty, Man, and the State

4. The Constitution of Markets

5. Economists, Efficiency, and the Law

6. Law, Money, and Crime

Foreword

The papers reprinted in this eighteenth volume of the Collected Works are less diverse than they may seem initially. All of them at least implicitly touch on two characteristic James Buchanan concerns: on the one hand, the desire that individual sovereignty be respected in society and, on the other, that monopoly power as a threat to individual sovereignty be controlled.[1]

Since the state is the greatest threat to individual sovereignty, why not eliminate this threat completely and try to do away with the state altogether? Anarchism, in this sense, appeals to Buchanan, as it must to all who value liberty. But, as opposed to more extreme and more utopian libertarians, he well understands that in our world it takes a state to defend the individual against the state. Buchanan, therefore, is not an anarchist but, rather, what may be called a "reluctant anarchist" who accepts both that the state is the greatest threat to individual sovereignty and that without some statelike monopoly, individual sovereignty cannot be protected.

Obviously, for Buchanan, founding a state is not intrinsically desirable. But at least under modern conditions of population density and organizational skills, there is no way to prevent a state or a statelike monopoly organization from emerging in any given territory. Once the state is invented, there is no longer a "stateless" equilibrium in the game of life.

Maximizing liberty, or freedom from political power, would inevitably lead to the precept that one should strive to reach an anarchistic situation without any monopoly over the use of power in any territory. However, be-

---

1. On the concept of interindividual respect, see the introduction to volume 17 in the Collected Works, *Moral Science and Moral Order*, as well as some of the essays in part 1 of that volume, "Methods and Models." On the theory of monopoly, see volume 17, part 3, "Moral Community and Moral Order."

cause anarchy is not among the options of constitutional choice, the maximization of liberty must be rejected.[2] As is argued in "Federalism and Individual Sovereignty," the maximand of a rational libertarian can be individual sovereignty only within the constraints of a system of law backed by the political power of a state.

But even if some degree of statelike monopoly power seems unavoidable, there are, of course, several ways to control and contain monopoly power. Besides the separation of powers in society and the assignment of offices by periodic elections, federalism, for Buchanan, is of particular importance. He imagines a federation as an organizational structure characterized by competition among several states.

Competition among states is desirable provided that such harmful forms of anarchic competition such as arms races or outright war are controlled. For Buchanan, therefore, the first function of the central authority of a federation is to prevent states from harmful ways of competing with each other. A second function of the central federal authority is to provide the basic "traffic rules" for the interaction of individuals living in the federation. More specifically, it has to lay down the basic rules of the game such that the free movement of capital, goods, and, most important, people among states is guaranteed.

If freedom of movement of capital, goods, and people is guaranteed, then the power of the collective decision-making bodies of the several states over the individual members of the states is limited. Not only freedom of exit but also freedom of entry must be guaranteed by the central structure of the federation. These twin guarantees and the related suppression of the harmful forms of competition mentioned previously create a competitive system in which individuals can freely utilize the protection of one state against exploitation by another. It is not required that everyone be potentially mobile for freedom of movement to constrain the conduct of state governments. The mere possibility of some citizens leaving and taking their taxable capacity with them can serve as a protection for all.

Because of his fundamental quasi-Kantian respect for the individual, Bu-

---

2. On this see, in particular, James M. Buchanan, "Federalism and Individual Sovereignty," *Cato Journal* 15 (Fall/Winter 1995/96): 259–68, reprinted in part 2 of this volume, "Federalism and Freedom."

chanan thinks of competitive federalism as a universal principle of social organization rather than a specific American achievement.[3] Ideas such as those expressed in the preceding paragraph seem so simple and almost self-evident for Buchanan that he deems it surprising that so few social philosophers and scholars of jurisprudence and political economy seem to be adherents of true, or competitive, federalism.

At least two factors may explain why competitive federalism is not more popular. First, there are those social theorists and ordinary citizens who imagine themselves as sitting in the driver's seat when forming their political opinions. They imagine that they decide for the collective as a whole and, therefore, quite naturally tend to conceive of decision making for the collective in terms of a benevolent despot. But if the decision maker is imagined as a benevolent despot, why divert his powers by competitive federal structures? It seems quite plausible indeed that a benevolent decision maker should be endowed with monopoly power. For then he certainly can do most good. Then there are those who are totally disillusioned with the state in general. They are immune to falling into the benevolent despot trap. Rather they feel that the state is so dangerous that no good can be expected from federal state structures as well. For them, the devolution of a unitary state into a federal one is not worth the effort. Adding another layer of state organization to an existing structure of independent states is, at best, futile but can make things worse.

As far as the first view is concerned, nothing needs to be added to Buchanan's thorough rejection of the model of the benevolent despot in all its forms. With respect to the latter view, it may be helpful to recall the original American dispute about reforming the first American constitution. In this dispute between the so-called Federalists, who in fact were favoring quite strong central structures, and the so-called Anti-Federalists, who, arguably, were the true adherents of competitive federalism, the Federalists won the day. But the Anti-Federalists' prediction that the constitution envisioned by the Federalists and later adopted by the American people would eventually

---

3. On this see, in particular, some of the papers reprinted in part 1, "Methods and Models," of volume 17 of the Collected Works, *Moral Science and Moral Order*, and, for additional remarks, see also the introduction to that volume.

lead to a unitary or quasi-unitary state was proved right in the course of history.[4] Studying American constitutional history might, therefore, teach Europeans some lessons about the risks of European integration. But Buchanan thinks that American history can teach the Europeans some lessons about their federative opportunities as well.

Those Europeans who, like the British, have been living under free institutions for an extended period of time may feel that giving up parts of their sovereignty in a European federation might not be a price worth paying. Evidently, the danger of creating a super-Leviathan must be taken seriously whenever we merge several states into a federation. And Buchanan himself is well aware of the omnipresent threat of Leviathan.[5] Yet, in view of Buchanan's arguments, even the British might want to give federal structures some second thought. In the Buchanan framework, giving up national sovereignty is desirable if this can help to protect individual sovereignty. In particular, if such constitutional options as a well-specified secession clause and a well-specified fiscal constitution for the European Union are taken into account, Buchanan would insist that there is such a thing as Europe's constitutional opportunity which to seize might, in fact, be favorable for European citizens.[6]

In a characteristically Buchanan-like move, Buchanan insists on comparative institutional analysis in which likely developments under a European competitive federal structure should be compared with realistic predictions of the likely future if present structures remain in place. As far as the likely

---

4. The Federalist Papers are so well-known and so easily available that any specific reference seems to be superfluous; but attention might be drawn to the work of the Anti-Federalists as, for instance, selected by Murray Dry from *The Complete Anti-Federalist,* ed. Herbert J. Storing (Chicago and London: University of Chicago Press, 1981).

5. The title of one of the papers reprinted in volume 1, "Socialism Is Dead, but Leviathan Lives On," says it all (the John Bonython Lecture, CIS Occasional Paper 30 [Sydney: Centre for Independent Studies, 1990], 1–9). For more on postsocialist political economy, see part 3, "Economics in the Post-Socialist Century," of volume 19 of the series, *Ideas, Persons, and Events.*

6. In this volume, see James M. Buchanan and Roger L. Faith, "Secession and the Limits of Taxation: Toward a Theory of Internal Exit," *American Economic Review* 77 (December 1987): 1023–31; James M. Buchanan and Dwight R. Lee, "On a Fiscal Constitution for the European Union," *Journal des Economistes et des Etudes Humaines* 5 (June/September 1994): 219–32; and James M. Buchanan, "Europe's Constitutional Opportunity," in *Europe's Constitutional Future* (London: Institute of Economic Affairs, 1990): 1–20.

course of events under present political efforts of European integration is concerned, Buchanan would certainly be as skeptical as the British critics of Europe. He would insist only that a better federal future for Europe can be imagined. If the right constitutional measures were adopted, this would have overall beneficial effects and would, predictably, lead to a constitutional future superior to the likely course of events without such federal structures. In fact, the observable effects of the freedom of movement of capital, goods, and people realized in present-day Europe make it hard to deny that the sovereignty of the individual citizen as opposed to his national (Leviathan) government has been enlarged by federal structures. So, why not try to move in this direction?

The first part of this volume, "The Analytics of Federalism," contains highly influential papers of a more technical nature. They provide important analytical insights into the workings of federal structures. Certainly Buchanan's views on more practical policy issues, in particular with regard to European federalism, are much more contested. But regardless of this, the papers reprinted in the second part, "Federalism and Freedom," should make fascinating reading for anyone who is interested in the subject of securing individual sovereignty by means of federal safeguards. The same holds true for the papers reprinted in the third part, "Liberty, Man, and the State." These papers basically speak for themselves. It might be noted in passing, though, that the concern with the monopoly power of the state, if often implicit, is always distinct. This holds good also for the essay "Property as a Guarantor of Liberty," even though here the concern is with society rather than the state as exerting power over the individual.[7] In the form of a conjectural history, this extended essay provides a theory of economic cooperation which brings together many of Buchanan's basic ideas and ideals.

Creating and protecting the sovereignty of the individual is central also to the papers reprinted in the next part, "The Constitution of Markets." Somewhat more extended comments on the fifth part, "Economists, Efficiency, and the Law," may be in order, however. At first glance, the relationship to individual sovereignty, on the one hand, and the state monopoly to the legitimate use of power, on the other, seems quite weak. But Buchanan is still

---

7. James M. Buchanan, "Property as a Guarantor of Liberty," *The Shaftesbury Papers*, vol. 1 (Hants, England: Edward Elgar, 1993), 1–64.

dealing with potential abuses of the monopoly power of the state. For instance, Buchanan criticizes those who suggest that judges rather than seeking for the right answer to a problem within the limits of the law should act as law makers and solve the problem according to some extralegal standard. He feels that acting that way amounts to an abuse of the discretionary power that is granted to those who are involved in the enforcement of law.

Now Buchanan acknowledges that all law is in need of interpretation, but for him, it makes a huge difference whether we approach the law from the point of view of someone who, to the best of his knowledge, intends to interpret the law as is or as someone who feels entitled to make it what it should be. Even if the law per se leaves quite a bit of scope for maneuvering, it makes a difference to a judge's behavior whether he feels entitled to decide things according to extralegal standards of right and wrong or whether he imagines himself as being bound by the law as he sees it. Adopting the attitude of someone who perceives himself as bound by the law, a judge will try to find out what the law of the land is, while a judge who feels entitled to take resort to extralegal standards will search for the "right answer" somewhere outside the "constitutional contract."[8] And, what the judge is looking for will at least, in part, influence what he finds—and how he "finds."

Obviously Buchanan rejects the view of many jurists who believe that law is so open to interpretation that virtually "anything goes." In support of Buchanan's position, it might be added here that the lawyers' view of the law tends to be distorted precisely because it is the view of lawyers. Their perception of the law is, to a large extent, determined by cases that go to court. Yet, forming a theory of the workings of the law on the basis of such cases is as if a management scientist would form a theory of the firm based on a sample of firms that have gone bankrupt. For our understanding of how the law, in fact, works in social reality, it is at least as important to look at those dealings that do not go to court as at those that do. Taking this into account, speaking of "the law as is" becomes much more plausible, and consequently, Buchanan's insistence on the distinction between within-law choices and the choice of law becomes more plausible too.

We must be content to let the discussion of law rest with that, since this is certainly not the appropriate occasion to enter into a debate about some of

---

8. For the related discussion of the separation of law and morals, see Herbert Hart, *The Concept of Law* (Oxford: Oxford University Press, 1961).

the deeper issues of the philosophy of law and the methodology of jurisprudence. Suffice it to note that in a somewhat less philosophical vein, two contributions in part 5 are intriguing too. The piece "In Defense of *Caveat Emptor*" is a strikingly clear and relevant contractarian contribution to the ongoing debate on "risk management" in society, while "Notes on Irrelevant Externalities, Enforcement Costs and the Atrophy of Property Rights" takes us, at least in a way, to "the edge of the jungle."[9] The former paper concerns the defense of individual sovereignty in the domain of decisions about risk taking. The second connects the idea of individual sovereignty to the issue of state monopoly. This issue of state monopoly is a central one in the two papers that make up part 6 of this volume, "Law, Money, and Crime." The problem of controlling the discretionary powers of those who are themselves in charge of controlling money in society is obvious.[10] That nonstate monopoly is perhaps not always a bad thing and may even be deemed desirable in a comparative institutions approach as a second-best solution is made clear in the very last paper, "A Defense of Organized Crime?"[11]

Although monopoly and its control are central topics in all the pieces reprinted here, "monopoly" does not appear in the title of this volume. This fact reflects our view that titles should have a positive cast. We have judged it better to direct attention to those mechanisms that protect individual sovereignty than to those that assault it. On this basis, *Federalism, Liberty, and the Law* seemed an appropriate title for this volume.

Harmut Kliemt

University of Duisburg

1998

9. "In Defense of *Caveat Emptor*," *University of Chicago Law Review* 38 (Fall 1970): 64–73, and "Notes on Irrelevant Externalities, Enforcement Costs and the Atrophy of Property Rights," in *Explorations in the Theory of Anarchy*, ed. Gordon Tullock (Blacksburg, Va.: Center for Study of Public Choice, 1972), 77–86. The term is, of course, borrowed from Gordon Tullock, "The Edge of the Jungle," in *Explorations in the Theory of Anarchy*, 65–75.

10. It may useful also to consult the paper "Predictability: The Criterion for a Monetary Constitution" (James M. Buchanan, in *In Search of a Monetary Constitution*, ed. Leland B. Yeager (Cambridge: Harvard University Press, 1962), 155–83 in volume 1 of the series, *The Logical Foundations of Constitutional Liberty*.

11. James M. Buchanan, "A Defense of Organized Crime?" in *The Economics of Crime and Punishment*, ed. Simon Rottenberg (Washington, D.C.: American Enterprise Institute, 1973), 119–32.

PART ONE

The Analytics of Federalism

Federalism and Fiscal Equity

Fiscal relations between central and subordinate units of government have become an important problem area in the United States during the last two decades.[1] Increasing attention has been, and is being, given to the more practical policy proposals aimed at accomplishing specific short-run objectives. While this may have been necessary, perhaps too little attention has been placed upon the study and the formulation of the long-run objectives of an inter-governmental fiscal structure.[2] This paper seeks to formulate a specific long-run goal for policy and will discuss the advantages which might be expected to arise from its general acceptance.

I

A distinct group of problems inherently arises when a single political unit possessing financial authority in its own right contains within its geographical limits smaller political units also possessing financial authority.[3] These

From *American Economic Review* 40 (September 1950): 583–99. Reprinted by permission of the publisher.

1. The most general survey of the whole field published to date is: U.S. Congress, Senate, *Federal, State and Local Government Fiscal Relations*, Sen. Doc. 69, 78th Cong., 1st Sess. (Washington, Government Printing Office, 1943). Other competent works include: J. A. Maxwell, *The Fiscal Impact of Federalism in the United States* (Cambridge, Harvard University Press, 1946); Jane P. Clark, *The Rise of a New Federalism* (New York, Columbia University Press, 1938); G. C. S. Benson, *The New Centralization* (New York, Farrar and Rinehart, 1941).

2. One important work in the field is concerned with this aspect: B. P. Adarkar, *The Principles and Problems of Federal Finance* (London, P. S. King and Sons, 1933).

3. Financial authority may be defined as the power of a governmental unit to collect revenues from contained fiscal resources and to expend such revenues in the performance of governmental functions. See Adarkar, op. cit., 31.

problems become especially important in a federal polity since the financial authority of the subordinate units is constitutionally independent of that of the central government. In a federalism, two constitutionally independent fiscal systems operate upon the fiscal resources of individual citizens.[4]

The fiscal system of each unit of government is limited in its operation by the geographical boundaries of that unit; it can withdraw resources for the financing of public services only from those available within this area. If the subordinate units are required independently to finance certain traditionally assigned functions, fiscal inequalities among these units will be present unless the fiscal capacities are equivalent. There will be differences in the number and/or the standard of the public services performed for, and/or the burden of taxes levied upon, the owners of economic resources within the separate units. The nature and the extent of these differences, and the difficulties involved in their elimination, constitute the elements of the over-all fiscal problem of the federal polity.

The situation has grown progressively more acute in the United States. This can be attributed largely to the three following parallel historical trends: First, the continual industrialization, specialization, and integration of the economy on a national scale have tended to concentrate high income receivers in specific geographical areas. Second, there has been an extension of the range of governmental activity at all levels in the political hierarchy. This has required the diversion of greater and greater shares of the total of economic resources through the fiscal mechanism. Third, this extension of governmental activity at the lower levels of government (and in peacetime at the top level) has taken place largely through the increase in the provision of the social services. This when coupled with the type of tax structure prevailing has increased the amount of real income redistribution accomplished by the operation of the fiscal system.

In 1789, a significant share of economic activity was limited to local markets; there was relatively little areal specialization of production. Govern-

4. The individual must deal with three or more fiscal systems, federal, state, and one or more local units. Local financial authority is, however, derivative from that of the state, and for present purposes, the combined state-local fiscal system will be considered as one unit.

mental services were performed predominantly by the local units which were drawn up roughly to correspond in area to the extent of the local markets. Rapid developments in transportation and communication led to an ever-increasing specialization of resources. The economy grew more productive, but the inequalities in personal incomes and wealth increased. This emerging inequality was both inter-personal and inter-regional; expanding individual differences were accompanied by closer concentration of the higher-income recipients in the more favored areas. This created disparities among the states in their capacities to support public services.

These fiscal divergencies were not conspicuous, however, until the extension of governmental activity caused the traditional sources of revenue to become inadequate. As greater amounts of revenue were required at all levels, conflicts over revenue sources among state units, and between states and the central government, arose.

The form which the extension of governmental activity took was an important determining factor in making the problem more difficult. Even with the increasing costs of government, inter-regional disparities in fiscal capacity would not have been accentuated had not the extension taken place largely through the expanded provision of the social services. Had the rôle of government remained "protective," and thus the fiscal system conformed more closely to the benefit or *quid pro quo* principle, richer units would have needed greater governmental expenditures. Only when the "social" state appeared did the divergency between need and capacity become clear. As more government services were provided equally to all citizens, or upon some basis of personal need, the discrepancies between the capacities and needs of the subordinate units arose.

The emerging fiscal problem has been only one of many created by the progressive national integration of the economic system within a decentralized political structure. This development has caused many students to view the political structure as outmoded, and the federal spirit as a thing of the past.[5] The federal polity has outlived its usefulness, and the conditions which made it necessary as a stage in the process of political development no longer

5. See Roy F. Nichols, "Federalism vs. Democracy," *Federalism as a Democratic Process* (New Brunswick, Rutgers University Press, 1942), 50.

prevail.[6] It is true that complete political centralization would resolve the peculiar fiscal problem of federalism. If there were only one fiscal system, as there would be in a unitary form of government, regional differences in standards of public services and/or burdens of taxation would not exist.[7] But political centralization as a proposal for solution is precluded if we accept the desirability of maintaining the federal form. The approach taken in this paper accepts the federal political structure, with the existence of the states as constitutionally independent units sovereign within specified areas. Thus, the problem is reduced to that of formulating a solution within this given framework.

The same problem of fiscal inequality is, of course, present among local units of government within the same state unit. However, the scope for adjustment by non-fiscal means, through political or administrative devices (local government consolidation, state assumption of local functions, etc.), seems broader in state-local relations. The policy proposals stemming from the analysis which follows presume a fixed political structure. But it should be emphasized that both the analysis and the policy implications can be extended to inter-local unit fiscal adjustment as well as to inter-state fiscal adjustment. Subsequent discussion will, however, be limited to the latter.

II

The ideal type adjustment can be presented in reference to the relative fiscal systems of different state units which possess the same fiscal capacity. If all states were approximately identical in per capita incomes and wealth, the burden of taxation upon resources would not necessarily be equal in all. Neither would the general level nor the distribution of public services be equivalent. Some states might choose to tax more heavily and thus provide a higher level of public services than other units equal in fiscal potential. The criterion of comparison must be some balance between the two sides. Both

6. Gordon Greenwood, *The Future of Australian Federalism* (Melbourne, Melbourne University Press, 1946), viii.

7. The proposal for integration and unification of the fiscal systems at different levels has been excellently presented by Professor S. E. Leland. See, for example, his "The Relations of Federal, State, and Local Finance," *Proceedings, National Tax Association*, 23 (1930), 94–106.

the level of tax burden and the range of publicly provided services must be included. Units of equal fiscal capacity should be able to provide equivalent services at equivalent tax burdens.

An inter-governmental transfer system can be worked out which would allow state units originally unequal in fiscal capacity to provide equal services at equal rates of taxation. The explicit objective of such a system would be the placing of all state units in a position which would allow them to provide a national average level of public services at average tax rates.[8] Immediately there arises the difficult task of determining average rates of taxation and average standards of public service. A more important objection to the statement of the policy goal in this form is that it appears in terms of adjustment among organic state units. Equality in terms of states is difficult to comprehend,[9] and it carries with it little ethical force for its policy implementation. And, is there any ethical precept which implies that states should be placed in positions of equal fiscal ability through a system of inter-governmental transfers?

If the inter-state differences in fiscal capacity can be traced through to their ultimate impact upon individuals, and a policy objective formulated in inter-personal terms, it would seem that greater support could be marshalled for inter-state fiscal equalization. Any discussion of the operations of a fiscal system or systems upon different individuals or families must be centered around some concept of fiscal justice. And although fiscal justice in its all-inclusive sense is illusory and almost purely relative to the particular social environment considered, there has been contained in all formulations the central tenet of equity in the sense of "equal treatment for equals" or equal treatment for persons dissimilar in no relevant respect.[10] This basic principle has been so widely recognized that it has not been expressly stated at all times, but rather implicitly assumed. Whether or not this principle is consis-

8. This is the policy objective of the National Adjustment Grants proposed by the Royal Commission on Dominion-Provincial Relations after a study of the problem in Canada. See *Report of the Royal Commission on Dominion-Provincial Relations,* Book 2, *Recommendations* (1940).

9. See R. McQueen, "Economic Aspects of Federalism: A Prairie View," *Canadian Journal of Economics and Political Science,* 1 (1935), 353.

10. "Different persons should be treated similarly unless they are dissimilar in some relevant respect." (A. C. Pigou, *A Study in Public Finance* [London, Macmillan, 1929], 9.)

tent with maximizing social utility,[11] it is essential as a guide to the operations of a liberal democratic state, stemming from the same base as the principle of the equality of individuals before the law.[12]

The statement of "equal treatment for equals" as a central principle immediately raises the question of defining precisely the conditions of equality which are relevant in fiscal policy, and more especially inter-governmental fiscal policy. Traditionally, rather objective measures or standards have been accepted, and the divergency between the equality represented in these and subjective or psychic quality has been neglected. Money income and estimated property values in money have therefore been used as the bases for judging individual standing for tax purposes. Some allowance has been made for family size, for income source, and for other differences generating real income effects, but differences in geographical location have not been held to warrant differences in tax treatment.[13] There seems no special reason why inter-governmental fiscal adjustment policy should be set apart in this regard from national government tax policy. Thus, "equals" in the following analysis are individuals equal in those objective economic circumstances traditionally employed in the calculation of national government tax burdens.[14] Through the use of this definition of equals and the adoption of the equity principle, a formal solution to the fiscal problem of federalism can be worked out. This allows the problem to be isolated and separated from the much more difficult one of the distribution of fiscal

11. If all aspects of equality, including utility or pleasure creation, are included in the definition of "equals," then the principle will be directed toward maximum social utility but will be useless due to the impossibility of application. This would be true because any application would require some inter-personal comparison of utility. Any realistic definition of "equals" must omit subjective attributes of equality; therefore, the application of the principle does not necessarily maximize social utility.

12. See J. S. Mill, *Principles of Political Economy* (Boston, Charles C. Little and James Brown, 1848), Vol. 2, 352.

13. Differences in geographical location perhaps cause significant differences in real incomes among particular individuals, but these would seem to be offsetting when large numbers of individuals are considered. If the real incomes of all, or large numbers of, individuals were increased or decreased by location in particular geographical areas, then these differences would become relevant for fiscal policy.

14. This analysis does not require any particular set of attributes of equality. All that is required is that geographical location not be included.

burdens and benefits among unequals, in which an explicit formulation of "justice" is impossible.

III

What is equal fiscal treatment for equals? The orthodox answer has been almost wholly in reference to the tax side alone, the implication being that if tax burdens of similarly situated individuals were identical, the equity criterion would be satisfied. The necessity of including the benefit side of the fiscal account has been overlooked completely in many cases, and understressed in all.[15] The object of comparison should be the aggregate fiscal pressure upon the individual or family, not tax treatment alone. The balance between the contributions made and the value of public services returned to the individual should be the relevant figure. This "fiscal residuum" can be negative or positive. The fiscal structure is equitable in this primary sense only if the fiscal residua of similarly situated individuals are equivalent.

It is next necessary to define the appropriate political structure to be considered in its relative impact on individuals. In a federal polity, the individual has a plurality of political units with which to deal fiscally. Two or more independent fiscal systems act upon his economic resources, subtract from those resources through compulsory taxation, and provide in return certain public services. In this situation, what becomes of the criterion of equity postulated? Each political unit may treat equals equally.[16] If this were done, individuals similarly situated would be subjected to equal fiscal treatment only if they were citizens of the same subordinate unit of government. There would be no guarantee that equals living in different subordinate units would be equally treated at all. Therefore, the principle of equity must

15. For a further elaboration on this and related points, see the writer's "The Pure Theory of Government Finance: A Suggested Approach," *Journal of Political Economy,* 57 (1949), 496–505.

16. This requirement has been expressly stated by one student of the problem. "In a democratic society considerations of equity demand that governmental programs *at each level* treat all citizens in similar circumstances uniformly" (italics supplied). (Byron L. Johnson, *The Principle of Equalization Applied to the Allocation of Grants in Aid,* Bureau of Research and Statistics Memo No. 66 [Washington, Social Security Administration, 1947], 88.)

be extended to something other than individual governmental units to be of use in solving the fiscal problem of federalism.

The limitation of the application of the equity principle to single fiscal systems within a federal polity can be questioned. It can be plausibly established that the appropriate unit should be the combined "fisc," including all the units in the political hierarchy. The argument can take either or both of two forms.

(a) In the United States, the economy, for all practical purposes, is national in scope. In large part, resources are allocated in response to incentives provided in a nationwide market both for final products and for productive services. Goods are sold and equities are traded nationally. The fiscal system represents the political unit in its direct impact upon the economy. Therefore, since the economy is national, the matching political structure must be considered as one unit in its operations upon that economy.[17] If it be accepted that one of the guiding principles in the operation of a fiscal system should be that of "least price distortion,"[18] or least interference with efficient resource allocation consistent with the attainment of other specific objectives, the necessity of this approach becomes clear. The principle of equal treatment of equals is consistent with that of least price distortion only if the "treatment" refers to that imposed by a political unit coincident in area with the economic entity. This is, in the United States, the whole political structure, central and local. For, in a federal structure with economically heterogeneous subordinate units, some interference with the proper resource allocation necessarily arises, unless some inter-area fiscal transfers are made.

Fiscal pressures are economic in nature, whether expressed as net burdens or net benefits. If states are not identical in fiscal capacity, the people in the low-capacity (low-income) states must be subjected to greater fiscal pressure (higher taxation and/or lower value of public services) than people in high-capacity states. If "equals" are thus pressed more in one area than in another, there will be provided an incentive for migration of both human and non-

17. Accepting this does not imply that the political structure should be one unit as has been proposed. There may be, and in my opinion are, definite values to be gained in maintaining a decentralized political structure. The purpose of this paper is that of showing how this decentralization might be retained while still solving the fiscal problem.

18. F. C. Benham, "What Is the Best Tax System?" *Economica*, 9 (1942), 116.

human resources into the areas of least fiscal pressures. Resources respond to market-determined economic reward, plus fiscal balance. If the fiscal balance for equals is not made equivalent for all areas of the economy, a considerable distortion of resources from the allocation arising as a result of economic criteria alone might result. The whole fiscal structure should be as neutral as is possible in a geographic sense.[19] An individual should have the assurance that wherever he should desire to reside in the nation, the overall fiscal treatment which he receives will be approximately the same.

It seems somewhat anomalous that states are forced through constitutional provision to remain parts of a national economy in the market sense and yet are forced to act as if they were completely independent economic units in their fiscal operations. This was recognized by William H. Jones in 1887, when he proposed a system of centrally collected taxes shared equally per head among states.[20] Requiring state areas to remain integrated in the national economy is inconsistent with the forcing of the governmental units of these areas to act as if the economies were fiscally separate and independent. This inconsistency can be removed only by centralization of fiscal authority or by the provision of some inter-governmental fiscal adjustment.

(b) The appropriateness of using the whole political structure as the unit in fiscal equity considerations can be justified in another way. Prior to the impact of the fiscal system, the income distribution arises largely as a result of the payment for resources in accordance with productivity criteria and competitive conditions established on a national basis. The fiscal system is the major means through which this income distribution is redressed toward

---

19. This should not be taken to imply that complete neutrality in this sense could ever be reached. Even with a transfer system worked out along the proposed lines, differences among states would always be present to provide some distortionary effects. In the nongeographic sense, the fiscal structure will, and should, have some distortionary effects, if the whole system is redistributive.

20. ". . . so long as we persist in applying the principle of autonomous State taxation under Federal forms, and Federal principles of trade and intercourse for purposes of Federal autonomy, the malady will stick to the patient.

"This mingling of autonomous State taxes and Federal principles of free interstate trade and citizenship for purposes of Federal autonomy, is contrary to both the letter and spirit of the Federal Constitution." (William H. Jones, *Federal Taxes and State Expenses* [New York, G. P. Putnam's Sons, 1887], 86–87.)

one which is more ethically acceptable. It follows, then, that the fiscal system, in carrying out this function, should operate in a general manner over the whole area of the economy determining the original distribution. The generality with which the "fisc" can be operated has been held to be one of its important advantages over redistribution methods which entail particularistic or discriminatory interference with the economic mechanism. But unless the fiscal system is considered that of the whole hierarchy, this advantage of generality is lost, and the system necessarily operates in a geographically discriminatory fashion.

The application of the equity principle on the basis of considering the whole political hierarchy as the appropriate unit will yield substantially different results from its application on the basis of considering separate governmental units in isolation. If there are subordinate units of varying economic characteristics within the central government area, the equity principle applied to the whole hierarchy will require that the central government take some action to transfer funds from one area to another. Thus, the central government, considered alone, must violate the orthodox equity precept since it must favor the equals residing in the low-capacity units. The central financial authority must enter the process and treat equals unequally in order to offset the divergencies in the income and wealth levels of the subordinate units.[21]

The necessity of assigning this rôle to the central unit in no way implies that the over-all fiscal system be unified in the sense that all financial decisions be made by one authority. Subordinate units should be able to retain complete authority. Neither the tax burdens nor the standards of public service need be equal for "equals" in any of the states. Satisfaction of the equity criterion requires only that the residua be substantially the same.

The policy objective for inter-governmental transfers then becomes one, reduced to individual terms, of providing or ensuring "equal fiscal treatment for equals." If this objective is attained, the individual's place of residence will no longer have a significant effect upon his fiscal position. Persons earning the same income and possessing the same amount of property will no longer

---

21. "The position that the federal government would occupy in the scheme is that of filling in the gaps of unevenness as between one state and another." (Adarkar, op. cit., 195.)

be subjected to a much greater fiscal pressure in Mississippi than in New York, solely because of residence in Mississippi.

That a much greater and more effective force can be mustered in support of a transfer system worked out on this basis does not seem open to question. Reduced in this way to a problem of fiscal equity among individuals, the need for inter-area transfers becomes meaningful. Although the results of the working out of such a proposed system would perhaps differ little, if at all, from those forthcoming from a system based upon equalizing the fiscal capacities of the state units, the former carries with it considerable ethical force for its implementation while the latter does not. The ideal of "equal treatment for equals" is superior to that of equalization among organic state units.

IV

The following arithmetical illustration is presented to show how the use of the equity principle can lead to a determinate system of transfers in a simplified model. Assume that in a hypothetical federal government, X, there are two states, A and B. The total population of X is six citizens, with three residing in each state. Their names are A-1, A-2, A-3, B-1, B-2, B-3. The economic characteristics of X are such that in A, two skilled workers and one unskilled worker can be employed, while in B, one skilled worker and two unskilled workers can be employed. Differences in the natural abilities of the six men are such that only three are equipped to do the skilled work, A-1, A-2, and B-1. The other three must do unskilled work. There are no non-pecuniary advantages to employment in either state. The six men are substantially similar in all other respects. The relative money incomes for the two groups are $10,000 per year for the skilled workers, and $1,000 per year for the unskilled. Therefore, A has two citizens receiving $10,000 and one receiving $1,000, while B has one $10,000 man and two $1,000 men.

Let it be assumed further that the central government imposes a progressive income tax amounting to 10 per cent of the higher incomes and 5 per cent of the lower incomes. All of its revenue is derived from this source. States A and B impose proportional taxes at the rate of 10 per cent on incomes. All their revenue is derived from this source. The tax liability of each of the citizens then is as follows:

Name	Collected by X	Collected by A or B	Total
A-1	$1,000	$1,000	$2,000
A-2	1,000	1,000	2,000
A-3	50	100	150
B-1	1,000	1,000	2,000
B-2	50	100	150
B-3	50	100	150

It can be easily seen that if tax liability alone is considered, the over-all fiscal structure is equitable in the primary sense. Equals are treated equally. But if both sides of the fiscal account are included, glaring inequities in the treatment of equals appear.

Now, let it be assumed that both the central government, X, and states A and B expend funds in such a manner that all citizens within their respective jurisdictions benefit equally from publicly provided services. The central government collects a total of $3,150, and when it is expended each citizen gets a value benefit of $525 from services provided by that unit. State A collects $2,100 from its three citizens, and each gets in return a value benefit of $700 from public services provided by A. State B collects $1,200, and each citizen thus receives only $400 in value benefit from public services provided by B. The final fiscal position of each of the citizens is represented in the following:

Name	Total Taxes	Total Benefits	Fiscal Residuum
A-1	$2,000	$1,225	$ 775
A-2	2,000	1,225	775
A-3	150	1,225	− 1,075
B-1	2,000	925	1,075
B-2	150	925	− 775
B-3	150	925	− 775

B-1 is taxed at equal rates with his equals, A-1 and A-2, by both the central government and the state, and receives the same benefits from the central unit, but he receives $300 less in benefits from his state. His fiscal residuum is $1,075 (taxes over benefits) as compared with $775 for his equals. Likewise, the fiscal residuum of B-2 and B-3 is a negative $775 (benefits over taxes), while that of their equal, A-3, is a negative $1,075.

If a transfer of $200 were made among the set of high-income equals in this model, from State A to State B, thus reducing the residuum or net tax of B-1 by $200 and increasing that of A-1 and A-2 by $100 each, then each of this group would end up with a residuum of $875. A further transfer of $200 from A-3 to B-2 and B-3 would equalize the negative residua of the low-income equals at $875. Thus, a total transfer of $400 from A to B would enable the equals to be placed in identical fiscal positions.

This model presents the use of the equity principle in its most favorable abstraction. Certain major qualifications must be made if the principle is to be universally applicable even in such structurally simple models. In the above model, both state units imposed taxes at the same flat proportional rate and distributed benefits equally per head, while the central government imposed progressive tax rates and distributed benefits equally among its citizens. It is necessary to examine these conditions and trace through the effects of possible changes upon the results. First of all, it can be shown that the central government acting alone can vary the progressiveness or redistributiveness of its fiscal system (on either the tax or the expenditure side, or both) without in any way affecting the resulting transfer total.[22] This is, of course, due to the fact that the central government system, in principle at least, treats equals equally, and thus no action carried out by this system alone would affect the existing inequalities among equals.

Second, it can be shown that the transfer total is not changed by a simple increase (decrease) in the desires of the citizens of one state for public services. The result will be changed only if, in the process of providing the in-

---

22. This can be illustrated by changing the above model to one in which the central government collects all its tax revenues from the three high-income receivers. The resulting individual fiscal positions are then as follows:

Name	Total Tax	Total Benefit	Residuum
A-1	$2,050	$1,225	$ 825
A-2	2,050	1,225	825
A-3	100	1,225	− 1,125
B-1	2,050	925	1,125
B-2	100	925	− 825
B-3	100	925	− 825

It can be seen that a transfer of $400 will again place equals in identical fiscal positions. Absolute differences among equals have not been changed by the increase in the progression of the central government tax structure. It will be noted, however, that the fiscal positions of the citizens of B have been improved relative to those of A's citizens.

creased (decreased) services, the redistributiveness of the state fiscal system is affected. For example, either of the states in the above model, desiring to provide additional services, could levy equal per head poll taxes of any amount without changing the required transfer total at all.

This is not the case, however, when the amount of redistribution carried out in the operation of either or both of the state fiscal systems is changed. Such a change can be carried out by shifts in the allocation of tax burdens or benefits among the different income classes, or through altering the total amounts of economic resources entering the fiscal systems. The limiting case is that in which neither state system is at all redistributive, both operating on purely benefit principles.[23] In this case, each individual receives in value benefits the equivalence of contributions made, i.e., has a zero residuum. Thus, whatever the income differences among the units, equals are equally treated, and no required transfer is indicated. Thus, it can be stated that as the fiscal system of either of the state units is shifted more toward operation on a benefit basis, i.e., is made less redistributive, the required transfer between the high-income state and the low-income state is reduced. Conversely, as either system is made more redistributive, a greater transfer is necessary to satisfy the equity criterion.[24] This dependence of the resulting transfer total upon the redistributiveness of the state fiscal systems creates

23. A special form of this limiting case is that in which neither state levies taxes or provides public services.

24. These effects can easily be seen by imposing changed conditions in the original model. Assume now that State A, instead of levying proportional tax rates, adopts a progressive income tax which increases the tax burden on its high-income citizens, A-1 and A-2, to $1,050 each and reduces the tax burden on A-3 to zero. Assume that the distribution of benefits in both states and B's tax rates remain the same as before. The fiscal positions then are as follows:

Name	Total Taxes	Total Benefits	Fiscal Residuum
A-1	$2,050	$1,225	$ 825
A-2	2,050	1,225	825
A-3	50	1,225	− 1,175
B-1	2,000	925	1,075
B-2	150	925	− 775
B-3	150	925	− 775

In this model, a transfer of $166.67 among the three high-income individuals and $266.67 among the low-income individuals is required, or a total of $433.34, as compared with the total of $400 before the change in A's tax structure was made.

difficult problems in the use of the principle as a direct guide for policy. Since a state unit can by its own action in shifting its internal fiscal structure affect the amount of funds transferred to or away from that state, the practical working out of the transfer system would make necessary some determination of a standard state fiscal structure as the basis for calculation.[25] It is also noted that the transfers are among equals; bloc transfers among states will satisfy the equity criterion only if made in a specific fashion. These and many other more technical problems make a precise application of the equity principle in the real world extremely difficult, but should not serve to prevent its use as a proximate standard for inter-governmental fiscal policy.

A specific type or method of inter-governmental fiscal adjustment is suggested from the above analysis. This is geographically discriminatory central government personal income taxation. Central government income tax rates could be made to vary from state to state so as to offset differences in state fiscal capacities.[26] This method of adjustment, by varying personal income tax rates among equals, could come closest to achieving the equity goal. In effect, it would limit the transfers to those among "equals." In the first model above, central government taxes on A-1 and A-2 would be increased from \$1,000 to \$1,100, while those on B-1 would be reduced from \$1,000 to \$800. Central government income taxes on A-3 would be increased from \$50 to \$250, while those on B-2 and B-3 would be reduced from \$50 to a negative tax of \$50.

Adjustment through the central governmental personal income tax system has another major advantage in that it allows the necessary inter-area transfer of funds to take place without any necessary increase in the total amount of federal revenue. This is an important feature in this era of big central government. Any other transfer method, either in the form of grants to states or geographically discriminatory central government expenditure, requires, initially at least, that a greater share of economic resources be diverted to flow through the central government fiscal mechanism. A further

25. Applied to the existing structure in the United States this would not present serious difficulties, since various state fiscal structures are substantially similar on both the tax and the expenditure side.

26. Adarkar included both geographically discriminatory central government taxation and geographically discriminatory central government expenditure as appropriate adjusting devices. (Op. cit., 195.)

advantage of this adjustment system is that it does not conflict with either the revered principle of financial responsibility or that of state fiscal independence, both of which are so often encountered in discussions of grant-in-aid policy.[27]

Geographically discriminatory personal income taxation by the central government probably would, however, have to hurdle a very significant constitutional barrier before coming into existence in the United States. The courts have held repeatedly that the constitutional uniformity of taxation required was geographical in nature.[28] Although accomplishing the same purpose as a system of positive revenue transfers, this method would appear more violative of traditional, though erroneous, equity precepts.[29] A more practical objection to this method is that individuals probably respond more quickly to tax burden differentials (especially direct taxes) than to differentials in public service standards. Therefore, if income tax rates vary from state to state in some direct correlation with per capita incomes, even though the system of rates was calculated so as to provide exact equality (to equals) in all states in over-all fiscal treatment, there might still be distortionary resource allocative effects due to this "tax illusion."

Any method of adjustment which involves the federal collection of revenue and subsequent transfer to state governmental units via specific or bloc grants is inferior to the tax adjustment method insofar as the equity criterion alone is considered. A system of grants based upon the equity principle could do little more than utilize the Canadian proposals. States could be placed in a position to treat citizens in the same manner fiscalwise as their equals in all other states. But states would not necessarily, or probably, choose to do so. Differences in the allocation of both burdens and benefits would be present. Nevertheless, the resultant inequities in the treatment of "equals" would be due to state political decisions, not to the fact that citizens were resident of

27. See the following section.

28. See *Head Money Cases* 112 US 580; *Knowlton* v. *Moore* 178 US 41; *Flint* v. *Stone Tracy Co.* 220 US 107.

29. The apparent anomaly here can be attributed in large part to the doctrinal errors made in economic and fiscal theory which have caused the expenditure side to be treated as an area of study less important than the tax side. Differing rates of federal taxation in different states would probably be declared unconstitutional. Arbitrarily differing amounts of federal expenditures per capita among states are not questioned.

the state *per se*. The differences in the treatment of equals could be reduced to insignificance in comparison with those now present.

V

The mere acceptance of the equity principle in discussions concerning the fiscal problem of federalism can yield important results. First of all, upon its acceptance inter-area transfers do not represent outright subsidization of the poorer areas, do not represent charitable contributions from the rich to the poor, and are not analogous to the concept of ability to pay in the inter-personal sense. The principle establishes a firm basis for the claim that the citizens of the low-income states within a national economy possess the "right" that their states receive sums sufficient to enable these citizens to be placed in positions of fiscal equality with their equals in other states. A transfer viewed in this light is in no sense a gift or subsidy from the citizens of the more favored regions. It is no more a gift than that made from the citizens of the community property states to those of the non-community property states when income splitting for tax purposes was extended over the whole nation to make the federal tax system more equitable. After the proposed inter-area transfer of funds, relatively greater fiscal pressure would be imposed upon citizens of the high-income areas and relatively less upon those of the low-income areas in comparison with those now imposed. But tradition gives little ground for continuing inequities, and we normally give short shrift to the individual who has continued to escape a share of his fiscal burden.

The policy implications of adopting the equity principle as a long-run goal for adjustment policy are far reaching. Applied to the existing structure of inter-governmental fiscal relations in the United States, several steps are indicated. First, the elimination of the many matching provisions in the present grant-in-aid program is essential before progress can be made in any equalization policy. These provisions have served to prevent the whole grant-in-aid system from accomplishing any fiscal equalization between the rich and poor areas at all.

A second and major implication is that the equity approach provides a justification for inter-area transfers independent of any particular public service or group of services. In the past, the principle of fiscal need has been combined with the principle of national interest with the result that grants have been justified only in specific service areas (highways, vocational education, etc.). There is, of course, legitimate justification for federal grants to states with the objective of furthering certain national interests, for example, minimum standards in educational services. But such grant-in-aid programs should be sharply divorced from the basic equalization policy. It seems highly probable that if an equalization policy of the sort proposed here were carried out national interests would be adequately served without any national government direction of state expenditure. The low-income states provide deficient educational standards largely because of their fiscal plight; remove this, and it seems likely that their service standards would approach those of other states without any restraints upon state budgetary freedom. The acceptance of the equity objective, therefore, could lend support to a policy of broadening the functions for which grants are made and of extending broadened conditional grants to other public service areas.

Ultimately, an essential step, if equalization is to be carried out via grants to states, and one which will not be easy to accomplish, is the elimination of directional conditions entirely in federal grants to states and the substitution of unconditional grants. The equity principle provides an adequate justification for grants wholly unconditional, but traditional barriers against the unconditional inter-governmental transfer of funds, especially in the United States, are likely to loom large. The principle of financial responsibility which says, in effect, that "legislatures can be trusted to spend if required to tax accordingly,"[30] and not otherwise, is strong and has certain intrinsic merit when considered in isolation. But as is the case with the traditional principle of equity, the substitution of a federal political structure for a unitary one transforms the setting within which the principle may be applied. The fact that the central government must enter the adjustment process and transfer funds to effectuate equity in the over-all fiscal system does not therefore imply that the central government should be allowed to direct the recipient states in the allocation of their expenditure. There seems no apparent reason why there should be more central interference or direction in the financial operation of the recipient states than in that of the non-recipient states.

30. Henry C. Simons, "Hansen on Fiscal Policy," *Journal of Political Economy*, 50 (1942), 178.

States are made claimant through no fault of their own or of their respective citizens. They are made claimant by the income distribution arising from a resource allocation and payment in a national economy. Once it is recognized that the transfers are adjustments which are necessary to coordinate the federal political structure with a national economy, and as such are ethically due the citizens of the low-income state units, then the freedom of these citizens to choose the pattern of their states' expenditure follows.

This concept of financial responsibility is, however, so strong that progress will perhaps require some compromise with it. Substantial progress can be made in inter-governmental transfer policy by the gradual substitution of procedural for directional conditions. Movement in this direction can be made while observing the fiscal responsibility principle and still not greatly reducing the budgetary independence of the states.

However, as pointed out above, these problems, which arise in any inter-governmental policy utilizing revenue transfers, disappear when the method of geographically discriminatory personal income taxation is adopted. No governmental unit receives revenue other than what is internally raised within its fiscal system; therefore, neither the principle of financial responsibility nor that of state fiscal independence is violated. This method of adjustment, however, can be expected to become positive policy only after there is a more widespread recognition of the basic elements of the fiscal problem of federalism, and the advantages of this method over others are clearly impressed upon the public by competent authorities.

VI

The fiscal problem of federalism discussed here is not likely to become less acute. As the need for an ever-expanding scope of public services increases, with especial emphasis on the social services, the divergencies in fiscal capacities among state units will be more evidenced. The *laissez-faire* result will be the ultimate centralization of a large share of effective political power, either directly through the assumption by the central government of traditional state and local functions, or indirectly through restraining financial conditions in an expanded grant-in-aid system. Therefore, those who desire to see maintained a truly decentralized political structure in the power sense must take some action in support of proposals aimed at adjusting these inter-state fiscal differences. Heretofore, little progress has been made, although increasing attention has been given to the problem. The failure to take positive steps may, in part, have been due to the lack of a specific long-run objective for policy. The equity principle presented here possibly offers an objective which, if accepted, can serve as the basis for the development of a rational inter-governmental fiscal adjustment system.

An Efficiency Basis for Federal
Fiscal Equalization

James M. Buchanan and Richard E. Wagner

Discussions of the "financial crisis" faced by state and local governments in the United States are continuing, and pressures mount for some form of remedial action. Various bloc-grant and revenue-sharing proposals began to command increasing attention in the mid-1960's. Almost all of the suggested bloc-grant schemes involve the transfer of tax revenues from the federal to the state-local governments with some provision made for equalizing adjustments in state shares.[1]

Strong arguments can be mustered to support tax sharing in a federalist system. In its basic form, however, tax sharing is explicitly nonequalizing as among separate states. We shall neglect this here; our paper is limited to an examination of possible efficiency bases for the introduction of *equalizing* elements into a program of bloc, or unconditional, grants. Several econo-

From *The Analysis of Public Output*, ed. Julius Margolis (New York: National Bureau of Economic Research, 1970), 139–58. Copyright 1970 by the National Bureau of Economic Research, Inc. Reprinted by permission of the publisher.

Wagner's research was supported by a grant from the Relm Foundation.

1. The "Heller-Pechman scheme" is the most familiar of the various plans, especially among economists, although the Pechman Task Force Report in which it was initially outlined was never officially released. Specific proposals are contained in Walter H. Heller, "Strengthening the Fiscal Base of Our Federalism," in his *New Dimensions of Political Economy,* New York, 1966, 117–72; and Joseph A. Pechman, "Financing State and Local Government," *Proceedings of a Symposium on Federal Taxation,* New York, 1965, 71–85. Other proposals, all of which are similar in essential respects, are associated with the names of Congressman William Brock, Secretary of Defense Melvin Laird, and Senators Charles Goodell and Jacob Javits. The Republican Coordinating Committee has also proposed a broadly similar policy scheme.

mists, including one of the authors, have advanced equity arguments to support fiscal equalization. But we propose also to leave this set of issues out of this discussion. Our analysis is confined solely to efficiency considerations relative to equalization.

In Section I, the previous discussion on efficiency and equalization is selectively and briefly reviewed. Section II analyzes fiscal equalization under the assumption that state and local governments provide purely public, or collective, goods, and that they do so efficiently. Section III drops the assumption of the purely public nature of government-provided goods and introduces impure public goods. This change is demonstrated to have significant implications for the analysis and the ultimate set of policy conclusions. Section IV specifically examines some of the more relevant policy suggestions that emerge from the analysis.

I. Some Previous Discussion

Early analyses of federal finance were all grounded in neoclassical orthodoxy. The overriding efficiency norm was summarized in the term "least-price distortion," and there was little or no integration between the tax and the expenditure sides of the fiscal account. In his early work, Buchanan reduced the analysis to interindividual comparisons that allowed both sides of the account to be considered. His predominant concern was, however, the satisfaction of horizontal equity norms, and efficiency considerations were treated as secondary. Buchanan did argue, nonetheless, that the set of interarea fiscal transfers designed to achieve horizontal equity over geographic space in a national economy was defensible on efficiency grounds. If resources are to yield the maximum gross product, defined in price values of privately produced goods and services, differential fiscal treatment of the like resource units must be eliminated.[2]

A. D. Scott independently came to the opposing conclusion about the efficiency effects of equalizing transfers, and several of the fundamental issues here were treated in the Buchanan-Scott exchange that followed.[3] Scott ar-

---

2. James M. Buchanan, "Federalism and Fiscal Equity," *American Economic Review,* 40, September 1950, 583–99.

3. Anthony D. Scott, "A Note on Grants in Federal Countries," *Economica,* 17, November 1950, 416–22; James M. Buchanan, "Federal Grants and Resource Allocation," *Journal*

gued that transfers from richer to poorer areas slow down resource reallo-
cation, thereby reducing national income and its rate of growth. Transfers
were alleged to provide amenities to persons living in states with poor resource endowments, amenities that reduce incentives to migrate to wealthier, more productive areas. Buchanan argued that no generalized conclusions
of this sort were possible, and that different types of transfers exert different
effects on resource shifts. Some grants were alleged to affect potential migration decisions for high productivity families, while others affected low productivity families. Hence, grants for unemployment compensation seemed
likely to be more resource distorting than grants for education. Buchanan's
argument here may be interpreted as a negative basis for equalization; it was
held that a properly designed grant program need not distort the regional
allocation of resources. Buchanan did not, however, emphasize the positive
arguments, implicit in his earlier paper, in demonstrating that some equalization is necessary to prevent regional allocation distortion. In retrospect,
the whole Buchanan-Scott discussion was not so pointed as it might have
been, because each participant employed a different analytical framework.
Scott assumed an economy out of long-run equilibrium whereas Buchanan's
implicit model was one of comparative statics.

Until the mid-1950's, despite some recognition of the inadequacy of existing models, the discussion of federal finance remained strictly neoclassical in
the sense that efficiency in allocation was defined in terms of GNP measured
by market prices of private goods and services. The general inadequacy of the
private-goods, neoclassical orthodoxy was revealed in Paul A. Samuelson's
two fundamental papers on public-goods theory.[4] For the first time, at least
in the English-language tradition, efficiency norms were extended to the
world that included public as well as private goods. The whole notion of allocative efficiency in public finance was modified, and subsequent discussions of federal finance reflected this change in the underlying analytical
framework.

---

of Political Economy, 60, June 1952, 208–17; Scott, "Federal Grants and Resource Allocation," ibid., December 1952, 534–36; Buchanan, "A Reply," ibid., 536–38.

4. Paul A. Samuelson, "The Pure Theory of Public Expenditure," *Review of Economics
and Statistics,* 36, November 1954, 387–89; "Diagrammatic Exposition of a Theory of Public Expenditure," ibid., November 1955, 350–56.

The 1959 Universities–NBER Committee Conference provided the occasion for papers on federal finance by Tiebout and Musgrave.[5] Tiebout incorporated modern public-goods logic in his efficiency examination of multilevel fiscal structures, and his paper contains the seeds of many subsequent and more detailed analyses. The second part of Musgrave's paper contains the material relevant to the question we are trying to analyze here. Musgrave noted that if all states provide public goods efficiently, in terms of the standard public-goods efficiency conditions, net fiscal differentials among separately located equals will be eliminated, and, consequently, Buchanan's earlier joint equity-efficiency argument for the making of equalizing interarea transfers would vanish. In his criticism of the Musgrave paper, Buchanan noted that net fiscal differentials would continue to exist even when all states provide public goods efficiently because of the relevance of total as well as marginal fiscal effects in locational decisions.[6] Richer communities can provide a higher taxpayer's surplus than poorer communities, so movement will take place in response even if the necessary marginal conditions for public-goods efficiency are fully satisfied. To this argument, Musgrave replied that he did not think that

> . . . such influences on the location of X should be classified as "distorting" the regional allocation of resources. Rather it appears that they constitute a given datum for location, just as does the geographical location of natural resource deposits. The fact that the benefit incidence of public services is spatially limited, and that this has a bearing on how people wish to group themselves, is part of the economic map which determines resource allocation. Efficiency is not served by erasing this feature of the map. Indeed, a central policy aimed at nullifying resulting differentials (such as remain with universal benefit taxation) in state finance will interfere with efficiency in the regional structure of public finances.[7]

5. Charles M. Tiebout, "An Economic Theory of Fiscal Decentralization," *Public Finances: Needs, Sources, and Utilization,* New York, NBER, 1961, 79–96; Richard A. Musgrave, "Approaches to a Fiscal Theory of Political Federalism," ibid., 97–122.

6. James M. Buchanan, "Comment," ibid., 122–29; along with Musgrave's "Reply," ibid., 132–33. Much of the literature has been surveyed recently in Anthony D. Scott, "The Economic Goals of Federal Finance," *Public Finance,* 19, 1964, 241–88.

7. Musgrave, op. cit., 133.

In terms of the models presented prior to his contribution, Musgrave's reply seems essentially correct. Within that context, there appeared to be no efficiency basis for fiscal equalization so long as the several states provided public goods efficiently. State-local governments rely, of course, on the traditional tax instruments to finance their outlays; hence, the conditions for allocative efficiency are necessarily violated. This raises the interesting question as to whether efficiency norms can be invoked in support of fiscal equalization when state-local systems are inefficiently organized.[8] But this question is not our primary concern here. Instead, we shall assume in our basic models that state-local governments provide public goods efficiently, and we shall reexamine the efficiency basis for fiscal equalization.

II. Purely Public Goods under State Provision in a Federalism

A CONSTANT-COST, FULL-MOBILITY MODEL

Initially we shall postulate the existence of a wholly closed economy extending over a defined geographic space. All goods and services are fully divisible as among persons; that is, all goods and services are purely private. The economy is perfectly competitive and *all* resources are fully mobile over space. In this initial model, "land," as such, or space itself, is not a productive resource. There are no natural advantages in particular locations.

Under these conditions, resource equilibrium is attained when identical units of resource earn like returns at the several margins of employment.[9] National product will be maximized by the allocation dictated by this equilibrium. Resource units in the broad functional classifications need not be fully homogeneous, of course, and there may exist many different resource categories or classes. Therefore, earnings will vary widely among separate resource classes even though returns are equal for all units within each particular class. In this equilibrium allocation, we should expect to find that dif-

8. See Albert Breton, "A Theory of Government Grants," *Canadian Journal of Economics and Political Science*, 31, May 1965, 175–87. In this paper, Breton supported a system of grants partially on these grounds, but he did not develop the analysis fully.

9. We neglect the possibility of equalizing differences in monetary returns, since this is not directly relevant for our analysis.

ferent areas of the geographic space would be characterized by differing mixes among resource classes. Some such pattern may be generated by assuming random locational shifts, or we may think of spatial clustering in response to differential limits of market specialization. In any case, equilibrium will be characterized by variations in per capita incomes among different areas of the national economy. Some regions will contain relatively more high-income earners than others.

The income structure of the surface will be similar to its central place structure; in both cases a hierarchical ranking in terms of income and order of central place can be formed.[10] The basic idea of central place theory is that there exists a hierarchy of cities and types of goods. A city of order $n + 1$ provides the same activities as cities of order n, plus additional activities, not found in lower order places, that service both the higher order place and its tributary area of lower order places. Likewise, a city of order $n + 2$ provides the same activities as cities of order $n + 1$, plus additional activities not found in the lower order places. A hierarchical order of cities and goods is thus formed. Christaller described a system of central places in terms of the now-familiar geometrical pattern of interlocking regular hexagons. In terms of the strict geometry, the hexagonal-shaped areas and the regular spacing of central places are clearly not accurate descriptions of empirical reality. Central place theory can be viewed much more favorably, however, as a perceptive way of looking at the spatial structure of an economy rather than as an attempted theoretical explanation of reality. In this manner, the notion of higher and lower order goods and places is maintained, but the rigid geometrical patterns are considered only as a way of looking at the spatial structure.[11] Under the postulated conditions of competitive equilibrium, perfect

10. The seminal contribution to central place theory, which attempts to explain the size and geographical distribution of and the functional variation among cities and their tributary areas, is Walter Christaller, *Die zentralen Orte in Süddeutschland,* Jena, 1933, a large part of which has been recently translated by Carlisle W. Baskin, *Central Places in Southern Germany,* Englewood Cliffs, N.J., 1966. For a comprehensive bibliography, see Brian J. L. Berry and Allen Pred, *Central Place Studies: A Bibliography of Theory and Applications,* Philadelphia, 1965.

11. For an excellent criticism of Christaller's geometry along these lines, see Rutledge Vining, "A Description of Certain Spatial Aspects of an Economic System," *Economic Development and Cultural Change,* 3, January 1955, 147–95 (especially 164–66).

resource mobility, and a uniform distribution of resource endowments over the area, regional variation in per capita income will reflect the variation in the central place structure of the area.

We now impose a federalized political structure on this all-private-goods economy. Initially, we assume that the central government, which is coincident in area with the national economy, exists but that it provides no goods and services. Subordinate units of government—states—contain equal populations, and each state provides a single purely public good under ideally neutral conditions. Each citizen pays a marginal tax-price equal to his own marginal evaluation for the good, and the summed marginal evaluations equal marginal cost. The required total conditions are also assumed to be met.[12] Furthermore, we assume that the range of publicness extends only to state boundaries; there are no spillovers beyond these limits.

If this public-goods provision by the separate state governments is suddenly imposed on the pre-existing private-goods equilibrium, the latter no longer holds even when the public goods are, in themselves, supplied efficiently. The higher-income states are able to provide the same quantity of the public good at lower tax rates, or a larger quantity at the same tax rates. The tax-price per unit of public good will, in any case, be lower in the wealthier areas. This provides a strictly fiscal incentive for individuals to migrate to the wealthier regions of the economy.

Under the starkly simple conditions of this model, this resource flow will continue until all persons are located in the single highest-income state. Under the constant-cost assumption, private resources are equally productive in all areas; hence no private goods are sacrificed by resource shifts as among areas. And, since one production unit of a purely public good embodies an unlimited number of potential consumption units within the appropriate geographic limits, residents who move from one area to another secure the full value of this consumption without reducing the public-goods consumption of prior residents. Consequently, resources initially required for public-goods production in the areas of out-migration can be released once

---

12. The significance of the individual and total marginal conditions for the tax-pricing of publicly provided goods is discussed in James M. Buchanan, *The Demand and Supply of Public Goods*, Chicago, 1968.

resources have shifted. Under such conditions as these, total value of output is maximized only when the entire population is located in a single state.[13]

Although the argument here is straightforward, geometrical illustration will prove helpful in providing a framework for later discussion of more complex models. Figure 1 presents a model of population allocation between states *A* and *B* in a two-state federalism. The abscissa measures total population in each state; we assume that the total population in the federalism is fixed. Along the ordinate, we measure the values for both private and public product, as these are related to population, for a single person. Under the assumptions of this model, movement from one region to the other does not affect private-product values. This is reflected in the constant value for the curves of marginal and average private product over all sizes of population.[14]

The curves for public-product value must be more carefully examined. Once each state commences to provide the single public good, efficiently under our assumption, there will arise recognizable differences between the two regions for the individual. The greater per capita income in *A* insures either that the same quantity of the public good can be provided at a lower tax-price than in *B* or that some greater quantity can be provided at the same tax-price. In any event, the individual faces a potential fiscal gain in migrat-

---

13. Some problems of national product accounting might fruitfully be raised here to indicate some of the issues introduced by public goods. The existing convention is to measure private goods at market prices and public goods at cost-outlays. Under these circumstances, it is quite conceivable that current measures for national product would exhibit no change after the movement of all resources to one region. Before movement, the national product of *AB* is the sum of the market values of private goods and the cost-outlays on public goods in the two areas. After all resources shift to *B*, the only difference is in accounting for the resources that were formerly used for public-goods production in *A*. It seems entirely possible that the cost-outlay of this former production in *A* would not differ from the market value of private goods now produced in *B* by the released resources. If so, no change in national product would be reported. Some of the issues raised by public goods for national accounting are examined in Richard A. Musgrave, *The Theory of Public Finance,* New York, 1959, 184–201, and by Francesco Forte and James M. Buchanan, "The Evaluation of Public Services," *Journal of Political Economy,* 69, April 1961, 107–21.

14. Since the product curves are those experienced by a single person, these have a common point on the ordinate. The individual is equally productive in the market economy regardless of his location. The fact that relatively more high-income earners reside in state *A* does not affect the private productivity of any single person in this model.

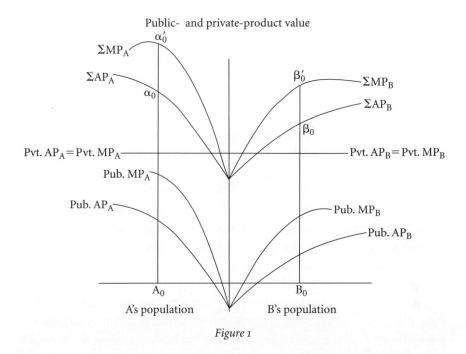

Figure 1

ing from *B* to *A* over reasonable patterns of population distribution. As drawn in Figure 1, the public-product value curves originate along the ordinate at negative values. This indicates that over some initial ranges of population concentration in either state the individual may secure a negative "taxpayer's surplus" because of the relatively small number of taxpayers available to share in the cost of the public facility. As population increases in each state, we assume that the "mix" among income-earning types is representative of that which characterizes the equilibrium pattern. This means that the curve for public-product value in *A*, the state with the relatively higher per capita income, diverges from that in *B* as soon as we depart from the one-person level in each state.

It should be emphasized that the curves for public-product value faced by the individual embody both tax-price and benefit components. In this model, where the goods provided by the two states are, by definition, purely public in the Samuelsonian sense, the individual's evaluation of the service flow received is not directly influenced by the number of persons with whom he shares the benefits. On the tax-price side, however, the individual's net fiscal position is affected. As more persons enter the sharing group, the tax-price to any resident member declines so long as new entrants pay any taxes at all.

If we take the simplest case of equal per capita sharing in costs of the public good, average tax-price declines with in-migration along a rectangular hyperbola, assuming a fixed-size public facility. For almost any other reasonable sharing assumption, and with variability allowed in the size of the public facility, the hyperbolic decline in tax-price remains characteristic, although no particular shapes can be assigned. It is this decline in average tax-price for the individual resident in the state which experiences in-migration that generates the curves of rising average and marginal public-product values as population increases. As the construction indicates, the curves tend asymptotically toward some maximum value equal to the individual's marginal evaluation of the public good. Tax-price to the individual approaches zero as population tends to infinity, leaving only the benefit component.[15]

We can now sum the private- and public-product value curves to show the fiscal pressures that will induce migration away from the purely private-goods population equilibrium, which we can arbitrarily designate as $A_0 = B_0$. As Figure 1 shows, at this initial population allocation the summed product values, in either average or marginal terms, are greater in A than in B.[16] This will induce the individual, whose calculus the figure depicts, to migrate to A. As this sort of movement continues, the differential in product values between the two states for remaining persons will increase. In such a model as this, resource equilibrium is never attained, because this requires an infinite migration. The final position reached is that which is imposed by the constraint of the fixed total population in the economy.[17]

15. It should be noted that our analysis does not assume a fixed-size facility. As the tax-price of the public good falls, more will be demanded so long as the price elasticity of demand exceeds zero. Likewise, less will be demanded in the state where the tax-price increases.

16. In marginal terms $A_0\alpha_0' > B_0\beta_0'$; in average terms $A_0\alpha_0 > B_0\beta_0$.

17. This conclusion is not independent of the initial population distribution assumption. If population differences are sufficiently wide, the fiscally induced migration flows may be reversed. If the initial population in A is sufficiently small relative to that in B, the larger per capita income in A will be more than offset by the larger number of sharers in B, and migration from A to B will occur. The possibility of multiple equilibrium in this

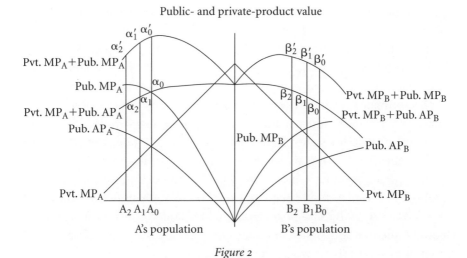

Figure 2

AN INCREASING-COST, RICARDIAN MODEL

"Realism" can be added to the analysis by introducing locational fixity in at least one productive factor, say, "land." The fiscal surplus or public-product value curves are unchanged from those drawn in Figure 1. But curves for private-product values are modified; these no longer are unaffected by population shifts. As the population of a state increases, the marginal productivity of a resource unit, measured in terms of derived private-product valuations, declines. This is indicated by the configuration of the marginal private-product value curves in Figure 2.[18] The purely private-goods equilibrium population allocation is A_0 in A and B_0 in B, where the total population is $A_0 B_0$.

In this Ricardian model, there is a determinate amount of fiscally induced migration, given the initial assumption about the private-goods equilibrium

---

and in subsequent models should be acknowledged. We suggest, however, that the assumptions generating migration to the wealthier state are more reasonable than those generating migration to the poorer state.

18. The possibility of increasing returns over the initial ranges of population growth cannot be excluded, but our abstraction from this possibility does not affect the analysis so long as actual population levels lie beyond any possible range of increasing returns.

population distribution. This is indicated in the construction of Figure 2 where $A_1 - A_0 = B_0 - B_1$ people have shifted from B to A. This equilibrium is attained when the marginal private-product value plus the *average* public-product value is the same in the two states. The position reached by individuals making their own migration decisions will not be Pareto optimal. Optimality would require that resources shift to the point where marginal private-product value plus *marginal* public-product value are identical in the two states. Individuals "should" migrate from B to A so long as the marginal loss in private-product value is less than the marginal gain in public-product value. In the construction of Figure 2, Pareto optimality or efficiency would require a total population shift from B to A of $A_2 - A_0 = B_0 - B_2$. This position could be attained only if property rights could somehow be assigned in public-product values. The establishment of a set of property rights would permit states to set prices upon and require the purchase of the right to migrate to that state. In terms of our illustration, state A could offer subsidies to individuals to migrate from B which B could not match until the A_2, B_2 population distribution is reached. Since such property rights do not exist, and probably would not be desirable if they could be established, individual choices must be analyzed in terms of responses to differentials in average public-product values.[19]

In this Ricardian model in which states provide purely public goods, there will be too little migration from the poorer state, B, to the richer state, A. There is no efficiency argument for fiscal equalization here. In fact, an efficiency case can be made out for disequalizing transfers *from* the poorer state to the richer state so as to induce additional migration sufficient to attain full Pareto optimality in resource location in space. This policy would be based on an acknowledgement that people are allowed to choose on the basis of

---

19. This model is only one among many conceptually interesting and often policy-relevant institutional settings that require an analysis of individual response to differentials in average rather than marginal values. For a closely related discussion, even if on a different problem, see Leland B. Yeager, "Immigration, Trade, and Factor Price Equalization," *Current Economic Comment*, 20, August 1958, 3–8. In this paper, Yeager shows that despite the analytical similarities between trade and immigration they differ precisely because immigration normally allows sharing in socially created values that are not directly related to the marginal productivities of the in-migrants. Trade, of course, does not involve this sort of sharing.

average rather than marginal public-product values, with the change in the results generated by a modification in the levels of these average values themselves.

III. Impurely Public Goods under State Provision in a Federalism

Initially, we assumed full resource mobility along with state provision of purely public goods. In the last part of Section II, we dropped the mobility assumption of the model. In this section, we relax the other restrictive assumption, that of purity in the public good. When we introduce impurely public goods, one production unit no longer embodies an unlimited quantity of consumption units in an area. Each production unit does, however, embody more than one consumption unit, so long as we are not all the way to the other pole, the purely private good. For the impurely public good, given any fixed-size public facility, the addition of one person to a beneficiary group reduces the quantity of consumption units available to other members, although the correspondence is not normally one-to-one. This amounts to saying that as population increases in any given region or area, congestion in the usage of the publicly supplied good sets in ultimately, and, as a result, individual evaluations of the commonly shared facilities fall.[20]

The introduction of impurely public goods significantly modifies our previous analysis. The private-product value curves of Figure 2 remain unchanged, so long as we remain in the Ricardian model, but the fiscal surplus or public-product value curves take on quite different configurations. The tax component is unchanged; the tax-price confronted by the individual declines as the size of the sharing group is increased. The change here comes from the benefit side of the account. Individual evaluation curves for the state-supplied good take on different shapes. With purely public goods, these evaluations remained unaffected by the size of the group.[21] When impurity

20. Complex problems of measurement arise in the model with impurely public goods. Conceptually, it is possible to measure the benefit flows to individuals in physical units, but it is relatively easy to confuse changes in physical service flows with changes in individuals' evaluations of fixed quantity flows.

21. Indirectly, through changes in the quantity supplied, the individual marginal evaluations may be affected by changes in group size, even in the purely public-goods case.

is introduced, individual evaluations of the public good decline with the size of the group once the point of initial congestion is passed. Under the most reasonable assumptions, it seems likely that this decline will be at an increasing rate; successive doublings in the size of the sharing group will tend to yield successively increasing reductions in individual evaluations. In terms of our geometry, this implies that the fiscal surplus or public-product curves no longer rise continually over group size. They will now decline from the point where the negative effects from congestion of the facilities offset the positive effects of the tax-price reductions. The optimality of individual migration decisions under these modified conditions can now be examined.

Social consequences of individual migration adjustment

Individual choice behavior will generate nonoptimal results in this model under the most plausible set of assumptions. In making their private decisions concerning migration, individuals will not take into account the effects of their behavior on others. In this sense, the model is similar to the one previously analyzed; individuals adjust to average rather than marginal fiscal product. The direction or pattern in which the private adjustment equilibrium departs from Pareto optimality may, however, be different in this model. With purely public goods in the Ricardian model, migration to the richer region tends to be less than optimal because individuals do not incorporate the tax-price reductions that their migration generates for other members of the wealthy-state sharing group. With impurely public goods, this effect remains, but it may well be dominated by a second. Individuals will fail to take into account in their decisions the effects that their actions exert on others due to congestion of the publicly supplied facilities. With purely public goods, the individual in-migrant to the richer state exerts an external economy on residents of that state and an external diseconomy on residents of the state which he leaves. With impurely public goods, these tax-side externalities may be swamped and reversed by benefit-side externalities.

For any given quantity, defined in production units, however, the size of the sharing group does not influence the individual's marginal evaluation.

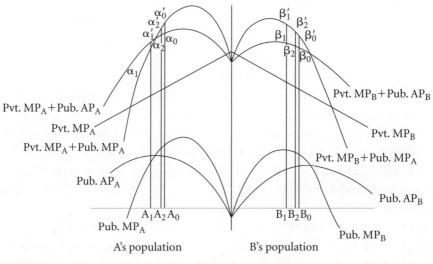

Public- and private-product value

Figure 3

Figure 3 incorporates the changes that are required by the introduction of impurity in the public good. As drawn, the socially optimal amount of migration is $A_2 - A_0 = B_0 - B_2$, where the summed marginal values of private and public goods are equal in the two states, and both are in the declining range. Individual adjustments will, however, lead to an excessive migration, indicated by $A_1 - A_0 = B_0 - B_1$.[22]

22. In this Ricardian model, even with the impure public goods, it is possible that private adjustment will generate a position in the range of increasing marginal public-product value curves. If over-all population levels were sufficiently small to permit this, marginal public-product values would exceed average public-product values, and the analysis of Figure 2 would hold. If population levels are sufficient to allow the declining range of public-product values to be reached, however, the privately determined equilibrium involves an excessive shift of resources into the richer areas. Detailed discussion is limited to this case, which seems the more meaningful in the modern federal setting, especially in the United States.

For completeness, the analysis which assumes full mobility but which incorporates the impurely public good can be briefly discussed with the construction of Figure 3. In this case, curves for marginal private-product value are unaffected by population shifts and would assume the shape of those in Figure 1. Optimal migration levels are indicated by

The situation here is generally equivalent to that discussed by Pigou and Knight in terms of the now-classical crowded good road–uncrowded bad road illustration.[23] Knight showed that individual choice behavior leads to too much traffic on the good road and too little on the bad road only in the absence of established property rights in the good road. Knight's emphasis was that of demonstrating the social function of property rights in allocating scarce resources. The problem that we examine in this paper is fully equivalent to the road illustration. The excessive migration generated by private choice can be mitigated by the granting of property rights to residents of subordinate units of government in the federalism. Practically, this would amount to allowing such political communities the right of excluding in-migrants. Individuals then wishing to migrate would be forced to purchase these rights. Conceptually, this set of institutions would be possible, but, even should the competition among the several states be sufficiently intense, the implied limitations on individuals' freedom of movement seem inimical to the functional values of Western civilization. For this reason, we simply rule out any further consideration of schemes designed to allow states directly to exclude immigrants as a means of correcting spatial resource inefficiencies.

Fiscal equalization as a substitute for exclusion rights

Under the conditions discussed, too many people will migrate to the wealthier political subdivisions of the federalism. National income, appropriately mea-

---

the points where marginal public-product values are equal in both states. But individual adjustment would generate migration to the points where average public-product values are equal, which would imply, of course, excessive migration to the wealthier state, A.

23. The issues are most clearly defined in Frank H. Knight, "Some Fallacies in the Interpretation of Social Cost," *Quarterly Journal of Economics*, 38, 1924, 582–606, originally written as a comment on A. C. Pigou's, *The Economics of Welfare*, London, 1918.

In an important recent paper that, unfortunately, is not known to English-language readers, Francesco Forte discussed the problem of internal migration, with especial reference to the south-north Italian population shifts, in the Pigovian framework. Forte specifically relates his analysis to the Pigou-Knight good road–bad road discussion. See Francesco Forte, "Le migrazioni interne come problema di economia del benessere," *Studi Economici*, 17, March–June 1962, 97–124.

sured to include valuations on public goods, would be higher if the excessive resource shifts could somehow be prevented. Since property-exclusion rights are ruled out as a relevant policy alternative, optimality requires some other institutional means of eliminating the sources for the excessive population flows. This suggests that some means should be found for reducing the fiscal surplus differentials so that individuals in their responses to average differentials will be induced to promote the same outcome that would emerge under their conceptual response to marginal surplus differentials. With reference to Figure 3, this might be achieved if the curve for average public-product value in state A is shifted downward while the curve for average public-product value in state B is shifted upward, such that the sum of private marginal product and public average product becomes equal between A and B at population levels A_2 and B_2. Under these modified conditions, rational individual choice of locations would generate collectively efficient allocations of population.

The institutional embodiment of the process described here is, of course, a transfer of funds from state A to state B, an equalizing grant. After a grant of the appropriate magnitude, state B will be able, at identical rates of tax, to provide a larger quantity of the public good than before, and state A will be able to provide a smaller quantity than before. A partial equalization of fiscal capacities will have taken place.[24]

As our analysis demonstrates, the transfer suggested will be Pareto optimal. Fiscal equalization of the sort described will be to the advantage of citizens of *all* regions. The analysis also indicates that the formula for making the interarea transfers should be based on some appropriate measurement of optimal-sized sharing units. This suggests, in turn, that the size of the required transfers should be directly related to the goods, services, facilities, and "atmosphere" generally that are to be commonly shared. If state-local units provide many goods and services that are quantitatively important, the

---

24. Full equalization of fiscal capacities, defined in terms of fiscal surplus differentials, would eliminate resource flows entirely and would be clearly nonoptimal. In Pareto-optimal conditions, the individual who remains in state B, the poorer of the two in our model, earns a somewhat higher private income and enjoys the benefits of somewhat less congested public facilities than his equal in state A. These two advantages are, however, offset by the fact that he must pay a somewhat higher tax-price for the units of public good that he does receive.

efficiency distortions generated by uncorrected private choice behavior will be greater than in the case where state-local units are less active fiscally. Increasing collectivization at the state-local level in a federalism enhances the efficiency basis for making equalizing fiscal transfers.[25]

There are two characteristics of an optimal equalization program that warrant mention. First, the type of transfer indicated is not, even conceptually, one among individuals but instead is among *collectivities* of individuals. The source of the excessive migration lies in the provision of public goods, which are not fully divisible among persons; corrective measures must work through a similar process.[26] Second, the system of optimal equalizing transfers would be zero sum or purely redistributive as among separate states. No net budgetary activity by the central government would be required.[27]

INEFFICIENCY IN STATE PROVISION OF PUBLIC GOODS

To this point we have deliberately ignored those problems that might be raised by distributional differences among the fiscal structures of the state governments. In one sense this introduces a secondary set of issues, and these should not be allowed to distract attention from the central analysis presented above. In the latter, differential fiscal surpluses generate popula-

---

25. We have wholly neglected central government provision of public goods and services in our analysis. If the central government provides goods and services directly over the whole national economy, whether these be pure or impure, some divorce of the central government tax structure from a measured money income base is indicated in any Ricardian model. Since one of the necessary equilibrating adjustments is in the levels of money earnings for like resource units that are differently located, central government tax adjustments should take this into account. If this proves to be impracticable, as seems to be the case, an additional, if limited, argument for equalizing transfers to the poorer states is provided.

26. This represents a different formulation for equalizing transfers from Buchanan's early proposals which, ideally, called for transfers among individual citizens differently located. See "Federalism and Fiscal Equity," op. cit.

27. This is similar to the West German system for fiscal equalization. This is one of zero-sum transfers, but the effects are secured through variations in the amount of tax collections that each state returns to the federal government. For a recent description, see Emilio Gerelli, "Intergovernmental Financial Relations: The Case of the German Federal Republic," *Weltwirtschaftliches Archiv*, 97, 1966, 273–302.

tion movement even when all states provide public goods efficiently; that is, when all persons in each state pay marginal tax-prices equal to their marginal evaluations of the public goods provided. States probably come much closer to satisfying these extreme efficiency norms than central governments; income-wealth redistribution as an objective explicitly divorced from allocative goals cannot readily be sought by states in a federal system. Nevertheless, states may embody departures from neutrality in their fiscal structures, and it will be useful to examine the effects on the results of our earlier analysis.

Initially, we assume that, even if state-local fiscal systems embody net redistribution at the margins of public-goods provision, the aggregative marginal conditions for efficiency remain satisfied for each state. That is, the summation of marginal tax-prices equals the summation of individual marginal evaluations, but the "rich" pay marginal tax-prices in excess of their own marginal evaluations while the "poor" pay marginal tax-prices offsettingly lower than their marginal evaluations. In this setting, insofar as the separate states attempt roughly the same degree of marginal redistribution, the previous analysis is not significantly modified. All resource owners in states of below-average incomes will have a fiscal incentive to migrate.

The introduction of marginal redistribution becomes important for our purposes only when the separate states differ substantially one from another concerning the amount and direction. Assume, for example, that an above-average-income state tries to accomplish more net income redistribution than its below-average-income counterpart. For a convenient illustration, suppose that California increases its rate of income tax progression to finance an increase in welfare payments. This change will increase the fiscal pressures felt by high-income groups and reduce the fiscal pressures felt by lower-income groups. The effect will be to alter the structure of migration from lower-income states to California in the direction of increasing the proportion of lower-income migrants.

By contrast, if a below-average state attempts to accomplish greater net redistribution than its higher-income counterparts, the initial disparity in income levels will be aggravated by the patterns of migration that this change will produce. A greater proportion of higher-income groups will migrate out, and the remaining population will be changed in the direction of more lower-income earners.

When departures from optimality in the over-all quantity of public goods are introduced (when the aggregative marginal conditions are no longer satisfied), the results depend critically on the effects of the attempted redistribution at the margin on the position of the taxpayers-beneficiaries in the median income ranges. Spending programs may be above or below optimal levels, depending on the coalition structure that is decisive in collective choices and upon the tax institutions that are utilized. If spending programs are reduced below optimal levels, the effects on migration discussed in our general models tend to be less significant; if spending programs are increased above optimal levels, the effects on migration tend to be more significant.

IV. Some Policy Implications

Policy implications have been implicit in the preceding analysis, but it will be useful to discuss these more directly. To the extent that the conditions of the central model are at all descriptive of real-world institutions, an efficiency basis exists for making equalizing fiscal transfers in a federalism. The potential real-world relevance is clear from the simple logic of the analysis; individuals make migrational choices on the basis of marginal private values and *average* public values because of the absence of enforceable property rights in the latter. Only if this essential fact can somehow be denied would the analysis lose its potential relevance. The actual relevance, of course, is an empirical matter that depends upon current congestion levels and interstate population levels. Empirical relevance requires that the largest populations not reside in the poorer states; this requirement is clearly fulfilled. Furthermore, the observed congestion of existing public facilities in areas of population concentration also supports the applicability of the central model in the United States of the late 1960's and 1970's. The argument strongly suggests the desirability of initiating equalizing fiscal transfers aimed at offsetting to some degree the differentials in fiscal surplus that privately motivate excessive resource concentration in space.[28] At current margins of decision, there is likely to be a greater return per dollar invested in keeping a family in

28. Although our analysis has been posed in terms of the efficiency of equalizing *inter-state* transfers, it is equally applicable to the efficiency of equalizing *intrastate* transfers.

Arkansas than in helping Chicago finance a part of the external costs that this family's migration might impose on current Illinois residents.

Perhaps the most significant policy implications currently are negative. The central argument provides a warning against relying too heavily upon the use of massive central government grants to urbanized areas in attempting to improve the urban environment. Such a policy of grants can aggravate existing allocative distortions by providing still further fiscal incentives for individual migration to the high-income, urbanized sectors.[29] The spatial pattern of population distribution that satisfies Pareto-efficiency requirements, including efficiency in the utilization of public goods (including "atmosphere"), surely dictates some slowing down of the continuing flow of population into the areas where public facilities seem currently to be congested. This seems clearly to be an important, and much-neglected, problem where individual or private responses to market forces generate socially inefficient outcomes.[30]

The general problem that we have examined has also been examined recently by Koichi Mera. He, however, failed to escape the shackles of the purely private-goods orthodoxy, so his analysis was irrelevant for the major issues. See "Trade-off Between Aggregate Efficiency and Inter-regional Equity: A Static Analysis," *Quarterly Journal of Economics*, 81, November 1967, 658–74.

29. Any detailed discussion would, of course, have to take into account the different migration patterns for different income groups. But the potential relevance of our analysis can be sufficiently demonstrated by imagining that, through some political "miracle," the cities of the United States were to be suddenly transformed into the crime-free, pollution-free, amenities-bountiful "paradises" envisaged in some of the current discussion. Unless this policy would be accompanied by some limitation on migration, congestion would soon reemerge with little net improvement over the existing situation.

The whole problem here is, of course, identical to the attempt to relieve traffic congestion by the continual construction of larger and better superhighways. Private decisions will insure that traffic flows will ultimately increase to the level of the improved highway capacity and beyond. Economists make vigorous policy proposals in the highway-street case, and they have normally suggested that efficient outcomes can be secured by pricing scarce space in accordance with standard marginal-cost criteria. The full efficiency of this pricing mechanism may be questioned, even in the highway model, and, with the movement of population over space, direct pricing solutions seem to be neither feasible nor desirable.

30. Another policy implication is that attempts to redistribute income in kind through an increased provision of various social services are likely to be significantly dissipated through the additional in-migration induced by their provision.

Efficiency Limits of Fiscal Mobility

An Assessment of the Tiebout Model

James M. Buchanan and Charles J. Goetz

1. Introduction

In 1956, Charles M. Tiebout published "A Pure Theory of Local Government Expenditures,"[1] a paper that has become a classic in the public-finance theory of local government. Perhaps largely in response to practical reality, economists have since devoted increasing attention to the provision of goods and services by local units of government. The traditional discussion has been recognized to be lacking in rigor, consisting as it does in a crude mixture of equity norms and immature analysis. Since the Tiebout model offers something of apparent substance in this confused and complex jungle, it is not surprising that its limits have often been neglected.[2]

From *Journal of Public Economics* 1, no. 1 (1972): 25–43. Copyright 1972. Reprinted with permission from Elsevier Science.

Research on this paper was partially supported under the auspices of a Ford Foundation grant.

1. *Journal of Political Economy* 64 (October 1956), 416–24. Essentially the same analysis was developed, at about the same time but less rigorously, by George J. Stigler. See his "The Tenable Range of Local Government," in *"Federal Expenditure Policy for Economic Growth and Stability* (Joint Economic Committee, 1957), 213–19.

2. For papers that, on balance, stress the explanatory potential of the Tiebout hypothesis rather than its limits, see Bryan Ellickson, "Jurisdictional Fragmentation and Residential Choice," *American Economic Review* 61 (May 1971), 334–39; Martin Mc-Guire, "Group Segregation and Optimal Jurisdictions" (mimeographed paper prepared for meeting of Committee on Urban Economics, Toronto, 1971); Wallace Oates, "The

Our purpose is to provide a critical re-examination of the Tiebout model for local public-goods provision. The efficiency properties of the model are familiar, and these will be noted indirectly here, but the less-familiar efficiency *limits* will be emphasized. We shall demonstrate that there remain inherent inefficiencies in the Tiebout adjustment process, even when this is interpreted in a conceptually idealized form. Specifically, we neglect (1) the problems of fiscal spillovers among local communities and (2) all problems of discreteness that locational groupings almost necessarily introduce.[3] Our aim is to examine the Tiebout adjustment in its most favorable setting.

Tiebout tried to demonstrate that so long as local governmental units are appropriately assigned the task of providing certain public goods and services and so long as individuals retain freedom of personal migration among jurisdictions, there are efficiency-generating processes at work, despite the "publicness" of the goods provided. His analysis was presented in partial but positive response to the negative proposition advanced by Samuelson that with nonexcludable public goods there exists no means of using market-like decentralization to attain tolerably efficient results. Tiebout recognized and acknowledged that institutional rigidities will make the fiscal mobility adjustment process even more imperfect than its market analogue. Nonetheless, he swept these imperfections away in an admittedly extreme model in which the fiscal shopper guarantees that the Pareto efficiency frontier will be reached in equilibrium. Just as the careful shopper of market goods and services tends to insure that the necessary conditions for optimality are met, the careful migrator, in choosing among alternative communities which offer him assorted packages of local public goods and services, tends to insure that

---

Effects of Property Taxes and Local Public Spending in Property Values: An Empirical Study of Tax Capitalization and the Tiebout Hypothesis," *Journal of Political Economy* 77 (December 1969), 957–71.

3. The spillover problems have been widely discussed. On these, see Alan Williams, "The Optimal Provision of Public Goods in a System of Local Government," *Journal of Political Economy* 74 (February 1966), 18–33; Burton Weisbrod, *External Benefits of Education* (Princeton: Princeton University Press, 1964). For a critique of the Tiebout process that calls primary attention to discreteness problems, see Charles J. Goetz, "Fiscal Incentives for the Cities" (mimeographed paper prepared for meeting of Committee of Urban Public Economics, Philadelphia, 1970).

the necessary conditions for Pareto optimality are met in the localized public sector of the economy.

To our knowledge, there has been no exhaustive criticism devoted explicitly to the Tiebout model, and his analysis has secured wide acceptance. In an appendix subsection to a 1958 paper, Paul A. Samuelson briefly discussed "local finance and the mathematics of marriage."[4] Although he acknowledged that Tiebout's solution "goes some way toward solving the problem," Samuelson rejected it in more general terms. He did so in part on the existence of migration thresholds in individual decision-making and in part on the absence of demonstrable nonoptimality under restricted voluntaristic choices. In an interesting potential marriage-partner model, he showed that maximum efficiency need not result from simple pair-wise combinations of ordinally preferred partners. Although his discussion was characteristically cryptic, Samuelson seemed to suggest that fiscally induced migration would amount to marriage of like-with-like, which he apparently rejected on efficiency grounds. It is perhaps unfortunate that this critique was not elaborated either by Samuelson himself, by Tiebout, or by others.

We shall concentrate on two features which eliminate or at least reduce severely the normative efficiency properties from the equilibrium generated by the Tiebout adjustment process. The first is the *fact of location*. Both in the private-goods or market sector of the economy and in the local public-goods sector, spatial dimensions are relevant to any allocation of resources. To ignore these dimensions or to assume that they are nonexistent is to remove a central part of the problem. The second feature is the *absence of proprietary ownership-entrepreneurship* in the spatially defined scarcities relevant for local public goods. As our analysis will demonstrate, local political communities cannot act in the particular profit-maximizing role dictated by allocative efficiency criteria.

2. Locational Fixity

The absence of proprietary entrepreneurship imposes a severe constraint on any adjustment process. Nonetheless if we could disregard locational

4. Paul A. Samuelson, "Aspects of Public Expenditure Theories," *Review of Economics and Statistics* 40 (November 1958), 337–38.

fixity, adjustment toward a market-type equilibrium with optimality properties would take place. In such a model, individuals would make choices
among relevant alternatives which do not embody geographical dimensions.
One way of illustrating an absence of locational fixity would be to introduce
a setting of either consuming or producing clubs.[5] We assume that private
profit-making in the formation or organization of clubs is prohibited. If
there are gains to be secured from either joint consumption or joint production, these must be discovered and exploited by the participating members.
Individuals would, within limits, voluntarily reach agreements on the joint
efforts that efficiency criteria might dictate, and some proximate "clubs"
equilibrium might be attained. In the idealized setting for this model, the individual would find himself confronted with a large number of clubs for each
activity on either the consuming or the producing side.

The characteristics of the conceptual equilibrium approach in this model
are in all respects parallel to those of competitive equilibrium. Different
persons would be charged equivalent "prices" for similar services or facilities. Within each club, payments made by each member would be identical
so long as services provided are identical. The total gains that are potentially realizable from joint or cooperative action would be exhausted in
equilibrium. The necessary conditions for Pareto optimality would be satisfied.

In our view, Tiebout's analysis may best be interpreted as an early and pi-
oneering attempt to describe the adjustment process in an essentially *non-
spatial* world of voluntary clubs. It seems clear that Tiebout did not actually
intend that his analysis of the local public-goods problem be interpreted in
this fashion. He formulated his analysis to be applicable in a local public-
goods setting. Despite this, he sensed the difficulties that locational fixity
would introduce. In his formal model, therefore, he introduced the assump-

---

5. James M. Buchanan has examined the normative efficiency requirements for individual club equilibrium, with his emphasis centered on consuming clubs with congestible
facilities or services. See his "An Economic Theory of Clubs," *Economica* (February 1965),
1–14. Buchanan's model has been interpreted to be applicable to the theory of local public
goods, notably by Mitchell Polinsky. See his "Public Goods in a Setting of Local Governments," Working Paper, 705–777, The Urban Institute, Washington, D.C., October 1970.
As will be noted in this section, the clubs model cannot readily be extended in this fashion, precisely because of the locational fixity problem.

tion that all personal incomes are from dividends. This provides a means of virtually eliminating locational fixity from the model of adjustment. If all income should be received from dividends, the individual's actual choice of location in space would be independent of the allocation of resources in the private sector of the economy. The implications of this interpretation should, however, be noted. In choosing among clubs in this model, the individual presumably is not making a simultaneous locational adjustment in his private-sector activities in the economy. To him, the clubs are means of securing particular services more efficiently, and there is no requirement that he modify his private-sector behavior in any compensating sense. There is no "voting with the feet" in the adjustment, no migration or mobility as such. Demanders of various club services and facilities stratify themselves voluntarily in accordance with their relative preferences for quantity-quality of those services, including preferences for privacy. Geographic stratification or classification is not implied nor is stratification by income and wealth level necessarily embodied, except indirectly. Note that in this world of voluntary clubs individuals can locate in space strictly in accord with criteria of maximal individual productivity in the private-goods sector of the economy. That is to say, there is nothing in the model which prevents the simultaneous maximization of the value of strictly private-goods product and the value of joint-goods product.

The setting within which local governments provide public goods and services to their citizens is quite different, conceptually, from this idealized Tiebout model. Individuals locate themselves in space. Their incomes are not exclusively drawn from dividends, and their allocation over space does influence the total value of private-goods product in the economy. Local governments have geographic as well as membership dimensions. This fact of location along with the absence of proprietary entrepreneurship must be systematically incorporated into any model that purports to represent the forces at work in any adjustment process, even at the most abstract and rarified level of analysis.

3. Models of Migrational Adjustment

Fiscally induced migration of persons among separate communities will take place in a setting where local units of government provide at least some goods and services collectively. Individuals will "vote with their feet," at least within limits, and their choices among locational alternatives involves a Tiebout-like process of adjustment. When locational fixity and the absence of proprietary entrepreneurship are taken into account, however, the equilibrium solution of this interaction is *not* characterized by efficiency properties.

When public goods, which embody jointness efficiencies, are produced along with private goods in an economy, resources should be allocated so that the total value of output, from private *and* public goods, is maximized. The criterion for optimality is that individuals should locate themselves in space in such a fashion that each person's contribution to total value, private and public, is the same in all locations. If all persons are in this situation, gains-from-trade in the most inclusive sense will be fully exhausted. More importantly, in making any movement from a competitive private-goods equilibrium, the individual does not exert an external economy or diseconomy on other persons. In equilibrium, the individual's private returns are identical to his marginal *social* product in all alternatives, including locational ones.

This result does not carry over when we introduce locally provided public goods and services. There will normally be fiscal externalities, both with respect to benefits and costs, involved in any shift of a person between two communities. A person's tax dollars, wherever they are collected and used, generate public-goods inputs for *others* in the appropriate sharing group as well as for himself and allow the per-unit cost of public goods to fall for each individual as group size expands. Hence, any move imposes an external diseconomy on all those who remain in the original sharing group and an external economy on all those in the jurisdiction that the migrant enters. This direction of effect is the same for all cost or tax-side externalities. The benefits side of local fiscal accounts may also become a means through which migration exerts externalities. These may parallel and reinforce the tax-side effects when "publicness" attributes of locally provided goods and services are sufficiently strong so that the addition of an immigrant's demand permits mutual net benefits from some increase in the quantity of the public good. They may, however, offset or oppose tax-side externalities when the local goods exhibit nonpublicness or private-goods features (e.g., congestibility).[6]

---

6. "Publicness" is not an attribute that inheres in the technology of a good or service independent of the numbers of persons who secure benefits. A good that is purely public

The necessary conditions that must be satisfied for Pareto optimality are that for each person i and for each pair of locational alternatives, X and Y,

$$\text{MVP}_X^i + \text{MVG}_X^i = \text{MVP}_Y^i + \text{MVG}_Y^i, \tag{1}$$

where the MVPs refer to marginal private-goods value or product and the MVGs refer to marginal public-goods value or product generated by an individual location in the subscripted community. Designating the number of persons in a local fiscal community by N,[7] the total benefit that the person secures from the public good or service made available by that community by B, and the total tax payment made by the individual by T, the MVG terms may be broken down in detail:

$$
\begin{aligned}
\text{MVP}_X^i + (B_X^i - T_X^i) + \left[\frac{\partial(\Sigma B^j)}{\partial N_X} - \frac{\partial(\Sigma T^j)}{\partial N_X} \right] = \\
\text{MVP}_Y^i + (B_Y^i - T_Y^i) + \left[\frac{\partial(\Sigma B^j)}{\partial N_Y} - \frac{\partial(\Sigma T^j)}{\partial N_Y} \right] \\
i, j = 1, 2, \ldots, N \\
i \neq j.
\end{aligned}
\tag{1a}
$$

As he migrates from one community to the other, or as he considers the locational alternatives, the individual will be cognizant of the benefits and the taxes that he, personally, will share. Just as MVP incorporates the "consumer surplus" achievable through market transactions, the terms in parentheses $(B^i - T^i)$ measure the "fiscal surplus" that the person secures from location in the designated jurisdiction. The fiscal externalities noted earlier are summarized in the bracketed terms in (1a). The individual will *not* take these values into account in his own decision-process.[8] Instead, the

---

for a small group may become effectively private for a larger number of persons. For background discussion of these points, see James M. Buchanan, *The Demand and Supply of Public Goods* (Chicago: Rand McNally, 1968).

7. For expository convenience, we treat the number of individuals at each location as a continuous variable rather than one which may take only integer values. This greatly simplifies the statement of equilibrium conditions without effecting the practical conclusions in any important respect.

8. The explicit role of spatial rents as an equilibrating device should be clarified. In their simplest and most abstract form, our two communities may be thought of as two islands, each of which is sufficiently large to satiate all potential demands for space. This

following conditions will be satisfied in a Tiebout-like adjustment equilibrium:[9]

$$\text{MVP}_X^i + (B_X^i - T_X^i) = \text{MVP}_Y^i + (B_Y^i - T_Y^i), \text{ for all } i. \qquad (2)$$

Model 1. In order to demonstrate the efficiency limitations of fiscal mobility, we may look briefly at several models. Consider a situation where each of two communities, X and Y, provides the *same* quantity of a Samuelson pure public good. Each local unit undergoes the same total outlay. The interesting feature of this model is that the allocation of individuals between communities that satisfies the conditions for optimality remains unchanged

---

extreme case, in which space itself cannot command any positive price is, of course, one model in which spatial rents cannot serve as adjustment devices even though the model incorporates genuine locational differentiation between the two communities. More realistically, however, assume that privacy, the consumption of space, is a scarce good which commands a positive price, a "rent." How does this affect our equations developed above? If we wish to bring space explicitly into the equations, we need only add an additional term both to (1a) and to (2).

Letting S equal a migrant's total evaluation of the space he consumes in a community and R the total rent paid (quantity of space $\times$ rent per unit), it is clear that $(S - R)$, properly subscripted, should be added to both sides of (2) in order to reflect the net benefits of space consumption in each community. In the optimality equation (1a) the change, S, in private values created by the migrant is counterbalanced by one of opposite sign for all other members of the community whose use of space has implicitly been altered. It would seem, then, that

$$\left(S_i - \sum_j \frac{\partial j}{\partial N} \right) \qquad i \neq j$$

should be added to both sides of (1a). Provided that the space consumed by an immigrant is small and the number of pre-existing residents from whom the space is bid away is relatively large, we can say that

$$R \approx \sum_j \frac{\partial S_j}{\partial N} \qquad i \neq j,$$

because the marginal rental rate (marginal evaluation) of the land approaches, in the limit, the average evaluation of the space consumption to those who have surrendered it. Thus, the same $(S - R)$ terms may be added to both (1a) and (2), in which case our results are unaltered. Alternatively, we prefer to regard this effect as being subsumed in the generalized MVP private net product term.

9. Strictly speaking, this condition involves the sign $>$ rather than $=$, assuming the X is the equilibrium location. See the discussion of locational rents in section 4.

with the introduction of local public goods into the economy. That is to say, Pareto optimality is attained when,

$$\text{MVP}^i_X = \text{MVP}^i_Y. \tag{3}$$

This result arises because of the assumption of the fixed and identical quantity of public good provided in each of the two communities. The assumption of pureness not only insures that $B^i_X = B^i_Y$, for any and all allocations of persons, but also guarantees that

$$[\partial(\Sigma B^i_X)]/\partial N_X = [\partial(\Sigma B^i_Y)]/N_Y = 0.$$

Further, we know that in this model

$$T^i_X = [\partial(\Sigma T^i_X)]/\partial N_X, \text{ and that } T^i_Y = [\partial(\Sigma T^i_Y)]/\partial N_Y.$$

Hence, the general statement for optimality (1a) reduces to (3).

In this model, any fiscally induced migration that might be necessary to satisfy (2) will be inefficient.[10] The manner in which the Tiebout mechanism may fail in this model is apparent if the private productivity functions differ at the two public goods provision sites. Then, in order to equalize the marginal private products, as demanded by the optimality condition (3), the values of N_X and N_Y must be unequal. In turn, an implication of the different values of N when $\text{MVP}_X = \text{MVP}_Y$ are equal is that individuals in the larger community enjoy lower tax shares and higher values of the fiscal surplus $(B - T)$. Under these circumstances, the optimality condition (3) is inconsistent with the equilibrium condition (2), and individual migration would have the effect of inducing overconcentration at the site with the more productive private returns function. On the other hand, if the sites are identical in all respects, conditions (2) and (3) will be satisfied simultaneously so that the distribution of people among the two communities will be optimal.[11]

10. This is the model that was implicitly used by Martin Feldstein in his critique of the Buchanan-Wagner analysis, and his conclusions are identical to those reached here. See Martin Feldstein, "Comment," in *The Analysis of Public Output* (New York: National Bureau of Economic Research, 1970), especially p. 160.

11. Note, however, that optimal distribution among clubs does not necessarily imply the correct number of clubs. If the private returns at a site decline very slowly or not at all, then it is perfectly possible that optimality in the most general sense may require that public goods be produced at only one site.

Model 2. Here we retain the assumption of model 1, except that we now allow the communities to adjust their provisions to *differing* levels of the public good or service in accord with the number and preferences of the resident individuals.[12] The general conditions for Pareto optimality or efficiency remain as stated in (1a) above. These conditions cannot now, however, be simplified to (3) as was the case with model 1. The Pareto efficient allocation of persons will not be characterized by the equality of marginal private-goods product. As in model 1, the Tiebout adjustment process will attain an equilibrium when (2) is satisfied. Individuals will neglect the bracketed terms in (1a). The question concerns the direction of the distortion that this neglect will introduce.

Assume that the Tiebout process has produced the equilibrium allocation (2), but that the local units of government, *X* and *Y*, are observed to be offering differing quantities of the public good or service. In both communities, however, the good or service remains within the range of pure "publicness." Consider the shift of a single person from *Y* to *X* in this setting. Will this shift improve or worsen the allocation in accordance with Paretian criteria? This requires an evaluation of the fiscal externalities on each side of (1a).

Under the assumptions of this model an immigrant cannot impose any net costs, and we know that the values for each of the bracketed terms are positive for any increase in population. This means that a shift of a person from *Y* to *X* will exert a net fiscal benefit on the recipient community and a net fiscal harm on the community which loses population. There is no means, however, of specifying relative absolute values for the two bracketed terms in (1a). Although their analysis was concentrated on the situation to be discussed in model 3, Buchanan and Wagner argued that a higher-valued

---

12. The necessary conditions for efficiency in public-goods provision in any single community are

$$\sum_{i=1}^{n} \frac{\partial B}{\partial Q} = \frac{\partial F}{\partial Q};$$

that is, summed marginal evaluations equal marginal cost. But the quantity of the public good (Q) which will satisfy these conditions will itself be dependent on the size of *n*. Immigration will increase the efficient quantity of a pure public good in a community; outmigration will decrease it. See Paul A. Samuelson, "The Pure Theory of Public Expenditure," *Review of Economics and Statistics,* 36 (November 1954), 387–89.

bracketed term for the community with the larger public-goods output would be the normal outcome for model 2. They based their analysis on a geometric construction, and they implicitly assumed that real-world examples would fall within the adjustment ranges generating this result. In this case, the Tiebout adjustment process stops short of inducing an optimal concentration of population in the community that is relatively affluent in public goods and services.[13] In the converse case, where X is observed to be providing a larger quantity of public goods *and* the value of the terms in the X-subscripted bracket is less than that in the Y-subscripted bracket, the Tiebout adjustment mechanism produces an overconcentration of persons in the community with the relatively affluent local government budget.

Model 3. We now drop the restriction that the goods or services provided by local communities must be *purely* "public." These remain "public" in the strict sense of nonexclusion. A unit that is available to any one person in the relevant local community or jurisdiction is available to all persons. But the evaluation that is placed on specific physical quantities of these goods is now allowed to depend on the number of persons with whom the goods are to be shared. This category of "impure" public goods seems descriptively characteristic of many items in local government budgets (e.g., fire protection, police services, health facilities, water and sewage facilities).[14]

The statement for the necessary conditions that must be met for Pareto optimality remains that in (1a) above. This model does, however, modify the fiscal externalities that are included in the bracketed terms. As noted, tax-side externalities always work in the same direction. In-migration must reduce tax-cost per unit of public good to other persons in the community, and out-migration must increase tax-cost per unit of public good to other persons. Benefit-side externalities are unidirectional, however, only under

13. Note that a community would normally be predicted to supply a larger quantity of localized public goods and services under either one or a combination of two conditions, (1) a larger population, and/or (2) higher average incomes and wealth. See James M. Buchanan and Richard E. Wagner, "An Efficiency Basis for Federal Fiscal Equalization," in *The Analysis of Public Output,* edited by Julius Margolis (New York: National Bureau of Economic Research, 1970), especially pp. 148–50.

14. For a general discussion of the taxonomy here, see James M. Buchanan, *The Demand and Supply of Public Goods.*

the strict pure publicness assumptions of model 2.[15] In that setting, the in-migrant's tax share (at any value above zero) produces some public-goods benefits to all other persons in the jurisdiction to which he moves, and, by assumption, these persons are indifferent as to the number of persons in the sharing group. If we introduce impurity, however, this result no longer holds.

Formally, we may state the effects of in-migration on members of the community in the following way. For any person, j, in the community, his public goods benefits function now includes an argument for numbers, that is,

$$B^j = B^j (Q,N),$$

where Q refers to quantity of the public good. The effect of an in-migrant on j's utility becomes,

$$\frac{dB^j}{dN} = \left(\frac{\partial B^j}{\partial Q}\frac{dQ}{dN}\right) + \frac{\partial B^j}{\partial N}. \tag{4}$$

In model 2, there is no explicit argument for numbers in the utility function of j, in which case only the first term on the right-hand side of (4) exists. And, since public goods are presumed to retain positive value over relevant ranges, the effects on j's utility are positive for the benefits side considered in isolation. In model 3, however, the last term in (4) must be evaluated, and this term normally will be negative when congestibility of facilities and services is present. Moreover, the sign of the first term now depends on whether dQ/dN is positive or negative. The negative change in output may occur if the price effect due to increased cost-sharing is swamped by the downward shift in marginal evaluation schedules as the good becomes more congested.

It remains impossible to generalize concerning the direction of distortion that the Tiebout process will produce, even in this model. To the extent that public-goods impurities in the form of congestibility become important, it seems plausible to suggest that the Tiebout process here is likely to lead to an overconcentration of population in those communities where public-goods quantities are large. This would, in turn, suggest that there may be an over-

---

15. Benefit-side externalities are nonexistent in model 1 because of the combined assumptions of pure publicness and unchanged goods quantity.

concentration of persons in the larger communities and in the communities with higher than average income levels.[16]

Our purpose in this paper is not that of deriving policy implications concerning the socially desired direction of adjustments in population distribution among local units of government, important though this may be. As the analysis has indicated, within the descriptively plausible models 2 and 3 no such implications can be derived in the general case. To take this step would require that empirical estimates be made of the actual values for the fiscal externalities that we have identified. Our purpose here is the much more restricted one of assessing the efficiency limits of the Tiebout-like adjustment process. The question we have put is: Does the prospect of "voting with their feet" insure that individuals will locate themselves among local jurisdictions so as to satisfy Pareto efficiency criteria, at least to some close approximation? We have not thrown in the "noise" that distorts any economic adjustment process; we have not incorporated moving costs, search costs, decision thresholds, etc. We have examined the Tiebout process in its conceptually idealized form. As the examination of the models indicates, our answer to this question is negative. Our overall conclusion is, therefore, consistent with that reached by Samuelson in his brief comment. Unfortunately perhaps, the world with local public goods is not an analogue to the competitive market in private goods.

4. The Absence of Proprietary Institutions

In the analysis of section 3, goods and services provided by local governmental units are "public" in the nonexcludability sense. This assumption insures that the B terms in (2) do not change in value for an individual as he might assume different roles in a temporal locational sequence for a community; "pioneers" and "latecomers" enjoy the same benefits. The B terms need not, of course, take on identical values for all persons, but the non-

---

16. This is the conclusion reached by Buchanan and Wagner upon which they placed policy emphasis. While this conclusion seems highly plausible in terms of existing reality in the United States, it depends critically on whether or not the existing population distribution falls within certain ranges. This is at base an empirical question.

excludability requirement guarantees that for any given person his temporal role in the formation of the sharing group is irrelevant.

No assumption was made about the values for the T terms in (2), and, in this respect, the migrational adjustment analysis was deliberately left ambiguous. The necessary conditions stated in (1a) are fully general and involve no ambiguity. But we did not specify the T terms in (2), and we did not say how these were derived. Until we do so, we cannot be sure that Pareto relevant fiscal externalities exist at all.

We showed that, under certain implicitly assumed values, the Tiebout process generates an equilibrium that is not optimal. Gains-from-trade in their most inclusive sense are not exhausted. Will not "trades" emerge to eliminate all potentially realizable gains? Will not the fiscal externalities, if these exist, be internalized?

4.1. A REGIME OF PRIVATE CITIES

Such internalization might, in fact, occur if proprietary ownership arrangements should characterize the institutions through which localized public goods and services are provided. Suppose that persons jointly consuming nonexcludable goods and services, locationally defined, find themselves purchasing these goods and services from private supplying firms, from "private cities."[17] Consider a setting in which all nonexcludable goods are offered privately and assume that the characteristics of model 2 above prevail. Recall that the value of the terms in the brackets are positive in this model. In this case, should we not expect that the firm supplying community X would offer a subsidy to the potential in-migrant, and, in the limit, would we not expect that competition among separate community-supplying firms would equal the value of the externality? This could be treated as a negative item in the value of the T term in the migrant's decision calculus. The firm supplying community Y could, of course, take the same action and offer a subsidy to the potential out-migrant to stay where he is. If this sort of adjustment should take place on both sides of a potential migrant's decision account, his

---

17. Certain retirement and resort communities are organized on proprietary bases.

choice would then be made on the basis of socially correct evaluations, and migrational adjustment would produce Pareto efficient results.

4.2. COLLECTIVE INTERNALIZATION
OF FISCAL EXTERNALITIES

It may seem that a collectivity might similarly differentiate among persons so as to internalize all fiscal externalities. It could do this, however, only if it divorces individual tax shares from all objective criteria that reflect internal demands for the nonexcludable goods. Tax shares would have to be related to the size of the *locational rent* component in individual income receipts. Locational rent is the surplus, if any, that an individual gains from being in his present location as compared to his next most favorable location. The possible existence of such rents requires us to revise slightly the conditions described in section 3 above by substituting $>$ for each $=$ sign in the equations. That is, for a person's efficient location to be community X, his returns in X must be *at least* as high as in any other location Y. In the theory of the firm, such locational rents are eliminated in equilibrium because there are always a large number of identical potential bidders for the locational advantages concerned. In the case of consumers, however, utility functions of individuals may be unique and a person making a locational selection need only pay as much as the next highest bidder.

It is the absorption of locational surpluses through differentially higher tax shares which provides the principal rationale for bargaining over the individual values of T. Under the conditions of model 2, for instance, one would expect the fiscal surpluses in a local jurisdiction to vary *inversely* with the importance of locational rents in individuals' private returns.

Consider a two-person community under model 2 conditions, where there are positive benefit-side as well as positive tax-side external economies derived from in-migration. In the community, one person, A, secures all of his income from locational rents (from "land" or some other spatially defined resource). The second person, B, secures all of his income from wages, no part of which represents locational rents. The income receipts of the two persons are the same, and they hold total assets of equal value. Furthermore, they both have identical preferences for the public good supplied in the community. Under these conditions, simple equity norms would dictate that total tax shares be equal as between the two persons, and standard efficiency norms would dictate that marginal tax rates also be equal. Let us suppose, however, that a potential in-migrant appears, who is himself identical in all respects to B. Both A and B recognize the favorable fiscal externality that this in-migrant would exert on the community, and they agree to share equally in the subsidy required to induce C to move into the community.

Once this move is made, however, B could clearly observe that C, who is in *all* respects his equal, is more favorably treated than himself. Since B is a "marginal" member of the community who secures no locational rents, he can readily threaten to withdraw from the community unless he is treated on equal terms with C. This system becomes completely unstable until and unless A recognizes that his receipt of locational rents is the only source for payment of the subsidy to C. In order to keep both B and C in the community, and on an equal footing, A must agree to bear a larger share in total taxes, despite the identity between his objectively measured income-wealth position and those of B and C, and despite the identity of public-goods preferences over the three persons. A will, however, accept this apparently disadvantageous fiscal treatment since he will secure some net gain under the conditions postulated. Note, however, that no gain would be forthcoming if B and C should be absolved from *all* tax payments. This situation would eliminate all tax-side external economies and A would clearly be in a worsened or at least no better position with a larger than with a smaller community size.

The relationship of total tax shares to locational rents under the model 2 conditions examined here does not modify the criteria for Pareto optimality in the community. Given any size of sharing group, these criteria are summarized in the equality between summed marginal evaluations over all taxpayers-beneficiaries and marginal cost. But this condition for optimality in public-goods quantity must be supplemented by a condition for optimality in the location of persons over space in the world of local public goods, and this second condition may, and normally will, involve differences in *inframarginal* tax shares even when the satisfaction of the standard Samuelson criteria, interpreted in individualistic terms, suggests equality in marginal tax shares.[18]

18. The local public-goods model considered in this paper offers only one of several examples of the failure of orthodox marginal-cost pricing norms to provide complete

The relationship between total tax shares and locational rent shares in personal income receipts is unidirectional only so long as we remain within the pure "publicness" range, as defined for model 2. If we consider the provision of local public goods and services where congestibility is present alongside nonexcludability, the externality terms in (1a) may be negative rather than positive in absolute value. In this case, the recipients of locational rents become residual claimants in this conceptually efficient internalization process, not residual payers as before.

5. The Realities of Fiscal Mobility

The difficulties that a local fiscal unit would face if it tried to follow strict efficiency norms should be apparent from the discussion in section 4. Even if all goods and services remain fully nonexcludable, nondiscriminating taxes would not be suitable to finance their provision. Nor would the common forms of discrimination, based on income, asset, or expenditure criteria, result in efficient tax shares. Total taxes of persons would have to depend on relative fiscal alternatives, and these need bear no relationship to incomes, assets owned, or expenditures on private goods. Indeed, it seems likely that, for many local units, relatively high-income recipients will have more effective fiscal alternatives (will secure less locational rents in a relative sense) than their low-income counterparts.[19] In this instance, total taxes might have to be lower for the high-income, high-demand member of a local fiscal community than for the low-income, low-demand member. (Marginal taxes may, of course, still be higher for the former.)

It should be evident that local governmental units simply do not, and cannot, behave in the manner that efficiency criteria would dictate. The or-

---

prescriptive norms in the presence of nonexcludability in any form. This more detailed analysis, centered on a critique of orthodox marginal-cost pricing discussion, will be developed in a forthcoming paper by James M. Buchanan and Charles J. Goetz, "Limitations of Marginal Cost Pricing for Congestible Facilities."

19. For an elaboration of this possibility in the context of the modern central city-suburban migration problem, see James M. Buchanan, "Principles of Urban Fiscal Strategy," *Public Choice*, 11 (Fall 1971), 1–16.

ganization and operation of a fiscal sharing group on this basis violates the central notion of *free migration,* the notion upon which the models of the Tiebout adjustment process are initially founded. Freedom of migration means that a person may choose among local governmental jurisdictions on the basis of nondiscriminatory fiscal treatment. That is to say, a person is insured that if he moves into a local community he will be allowed equal access to nonexcludable goods and services made available in that jurisdiction and, further, that he will be taxed for these goods and services on the *same* basis as residents of the community who are his equals in an objectively measurable sense. The fiscal discrimination between old residents and in-migrants or new residents that would be required for efficiency violates the central meaning of resource mobility. If nothing else, constitutional provisions would surely prevent local governments from adopting policies that would be aimed exclusively at promoting locational efficiency. Individuals are guaranteed "equality before the law," and as this has been interpreted by the courts, any overt discrimination among persons in taxes that is not directly related to an objectively measurable base such as income or assets would be held illegal.

Quite apart from constitutional issues, the very meaning of local *government* makes efficient fiscal adjustment difficult. If the ultimate franchise is open to all citizens in a local community, it becomes almost impossible to trace out a plausible public-choice sequence that will generate an efficient policy mix. If recipients of locational rents are in the minority, and if the conditions of model 2 hold, it becomes relatively easy to think of a sequence where the sources of fiscal subsidization might be found in locational rents. In such a model, however, there is nothing that insures the utilization of other fiscal sources, without which the appropriate adjustments will not even be proximately realized. If the conditions of model 3 are present, and if these are such as to make for fiscal external diseconomies, efficiency dictates that entry fees be collected. But an open franchise could hardly be expected to limit the rebates of these funds to recipients of locational rents. If we allow for franchises limited to the recipients of locational rents, the opposing results would be predicted for the two cases noted. There seems to be no escaping from the fundamental contradictions between the discriminatory distribution of costs and benefits as between persons who secure locational rents and those that do not, the distribution required for allocative efficiency, and the nonexcludability or genuine "publicness" of goods and services supplied by governmental units.

While we do not emphasize the point in this paper, there remains the final difficulty that even in the absence of any operational limits on a local government's ability to discriminate there is no mechanism from which the government can derive the information upon whose basis the optimal type of discrimination must be calculated. Although we speak of locational rents which accrue to certain individuals, the existence or nonexistence of such rents may be calculable only with considerable knowledge of the utility functions of the individuals involved.[20] A government may know that it can and should discriminate, but against whom and by how much?

Somewhat circuituously, we have arrived at a precise conceptual definition for the T terms in the equations of section 3 above. We would expect the total tax bill for any person to be a pro rata share of the total taxes assessed by the community on all persons in the group who are classified as belonging to the same fiscal category by legally acceptable criteria of equality.[21] This means that individualized tax shares in the real world of local public finance cannot be adjusted to incorporate fiscal externalities. Hence, the analysis of the models in section 3 holds without qualification.

6. Conclusions

If locational rents in the private-goods sector did not exist (Tiebout's model of dividend income), the locational dimension of nonexcludable local public goods would create no problems for migrational adjustments.

---

20. The persistence of the preference-revelation problem is developed at some length by Charles J. Goetz in "Efficient Distribution of Individuals among Alternative Fiscal Clubs" (forthcoming).

21. In terms that are more familiar to economists, we can say that taxes must be assessed in terms of some *average* per person value, whereas efficiency criteria would require that net taxes (and/or benefits) should be assigned in terms of *marginal* values. This is one way of conceptualizing the resource misallocation that free migration among fiscal units generates. This was the approach used by Buchanan and Wagner in their paper. We have avoided using these terms in the discussion here because, as the analysis indicates, the fiscal externalities vary as among different fiscal categories, and any average or marginal value would have to be applied only to members of defined categories.

Individuals with similar demand patterns would simply form themselves into efficient "fiscal clubs." On the other hand, if those goods and services exhibiting nonexcludability did not simultaneously embody locational attributes (the world of voluntary clubs), the presence of locational rents in the private sector of the economy would not be a source of inefficiency in allocation. Individuals would, once again, form themselves into an efficient set of consuming-purchasing units. But locational rents do exist and nonexcludable goods and services carry a locational dimension. Even this combination of circumstances might not, however, generate inefficiency except in the absence of proprietary ownership of locational or spatial scarcities. If all valued "space" should be privately owned, and if competition among proprietary ownership units were effective in all respects, allocational efficiency might emerge. In general, however, internalization of migration-produced externalities requires interpersonal discrimination in tax shares of a type which local governments are unlikely to be able either operationally to impose or even to calculate correctly.

The conclusions of our analysis must be nihilistic. There are elements at work in fiscally induced migration of persons among local communities that are efficiency-generating, and perhaps these dominate those that are efficiency-retarding. If we broaden our objectives somewhat and introduce available but unused options in individual utility functions, the protections offered to the individual in the opportunity of "voting with his feet" have intrinsic value quite apart from the standard efficiency properties examined in this paper.[22] Samuelson said that the Tiebout process "goes some way toward solving the problem." This can surely be accepted if the alternative to fiscal decentralization in the provision of spatially limited nonexcludable goods and services should be increased fiscal concentration at central government levels. But, also with Samuelson, we must conclude that there "remain important analytical problems of public-goods determination that still need investigation at every level of government."[23]

Our analysis is perfectly consistent with the important and relevant hypothesis advanced by Buchanan and Wagner to the effect that fiscally in-

22. See Burton Weisbrod, "Collective-Consumption Services of Individual-Consumption Goods," *Quarterly Journal of Economics* 78 (August 1964), 471–77.

23. Paul A. Samuelson, "Aspects of Public Expenditure Theories," 338.

duced migration is responsible for an undue concentration of persons in the large and growing conurbations of America in 1971. Their particular hypothesis cannot be rigorously supported on analytical grounds in the most general model where the *direction* of the inefficiency is indeterminate. Nonetheless, before meaningful attempts are made to examine the implications of the hypothesis empirically, it seemed necessary to analyze the pseudo-paradigm embodied in the Tiebout hypothesis. There is nothing in the Tiebout solution that rules out the possible validity of the overurbanization hypothesis.

PART TWO

Federalism and Freedom

Federalism as an Ideal Political Order and an Objective for Constitutional Reform

Abstract: Federalism is first examined as an ideal-type political order as possibly emergent from initial constitutional agreement among members of a prospective political community. This abstracted and nonhistorical analysis is followed by an examination of the possible applicability of the federalist ideal as the basis for reform in specific historical-institutional settings. The direction of constitutional change toward effective federalism is discussed, with the devolution of political authority from centralized structures carefully distinguished from the limited concentration of authority from previously autonomous political units.

My aim here is to discuss federalism, as a central element in an inclusive political order, in two, quite different, but ultimately related, conceptual perspectives. First, I examine federalism as an ideal type, as a stylized component of a constitutional structure of governance that might be put in place *ab initio,* as emergent from agreement among citizens of a particular community before that community, as such, has experienced its own history. Second, the discussion shifts dramatically toward reality, and the critical

From *Publius: The Journal of Federalism* 25 (Spring 1995): 19–27. Reprinted by permission of the publisher.

Author's note: An initial version of this paper was prepared for and presented at a conference in Mexico in January 1995, cosponsored by the Fraser Institute and the Instituto Cultural Ludwig von Mises.

importance of defining the historically determined status quo is recognized as a necessary first step toward reform that may be guided by some appreciation of the federalist ideal.

Ideal Theory

FEDERALISM AS AN ANALOGUE TO THE MARKET

An elementary understanding and appreciation of political federalism is facilitated by a comparable understanding and appreciation of the political function of an economy organized on market principles. Quite apart from its ability to produce and distribute a highly valued bundle of "goods," relative to alternative regimes, a market economy serves a critically important political role. To the extent that allocative and distributive choices can be relegated to the workings of markets, the necessity for any politicization of such choices is eliminated.

But why should the politicization of choices be of normative concern? Under the standard assumptions that dominated analysis before the public choice revolution, politics is modeled as the activity of a benevolently despotic and monolithic authority that seeks always and everywhere to promote "the public interest," which is presumed to exist independent of revealed evaluations and which is amenable to discovery or revelation. If this romantic image of politics is discarded and replaced by the empirical reality of politics, any increase in the relative size of the politicized sector of an economy must carry with it an increase in the potential for exploitation.[1] The well-being of citizens becomes vulnerable to the activities of politics, as described in the behavior of other citizens as members of majoritarian coalitions, as elected politicians, and as appointed bureaucrats.

This argument must be supplemented by an understanding of why and how the market, as the alternative to political process, does not also expose the citizen-participant to comparable exploitation. The categorical differ-

---

1. James M. Buchanan, "Politics without Romance: A Sketch of Positive Public Choice Theory and Its Normative Implications," Inaugural Lecture, Institute for Advanced Studies, Vienna, Austria, *IHS-Journal, Zeitschrift des Instituts für Höhere Studien, Wien* 3 (1979): B1–B11.

ence between market and political interaction lies in the continuing presence of an effective exit option in market relationships and in its absence in politics. To the extent that the individual participant in market exchange has available effective alternatives that may be chosen at relatively low cost, any exchange is necessarily voluntary. In its stylized form, the market involves no coercion, no extraction of value from any participant without consent. In dramatic contrast, politics is inherently coercive, independent of the effective decision rules that may be operative.

The potential for the exercise of individual liberty is directly related to the relative size of the market sector in an economy. A market organization does not, however, emerge spontaneously from some imagined state of nature. A market economy must, in one sense, be "laid on" through the design, construction, and implementation of a political-legal framework (i.e., an inclusive constitution) that protects property and enforces voluntary contracts. As Adam Smith emphasized, the market works well only if these parameters, these "laws and institutions," are in place.[2]

Enforceable constitutional restrictions may constrain the domain of politics to some extent, but these restrictions may not offer sufficient protection against the exploitation of citizens through the agencies of governance. That is to say, even if the market economy is allowed to carry out its allocational-distributional role over a significant relative share of the political economy, the remaining domain of actions open to politicization may leave the citizen, both in person and property, vulnerable to the expropriation of value that necessarily accompanies political coercion.

How might the potential for exploitation be reduced or minimized? How might the political sector, in itself, be constitutionally designed so as to offer the citizen more protection?

The principle of federalism emerges directly from the market analogy. The politicized sphere of activity, in itself, may be arranged or organized so as to allow for the workings of competition, which is the flip side of the availability of exit, to become operative. The domain of authority for the central government, which we assume here is coincident in territory and membership with the economic exchange nexus, may be severely limited, while re-

2. Adam Smith, *The Wealth of Nations* (1776; Modern Library ed.; New York: Random House, 1937).

maining political authority is residually assigned to the several "state" units, each of which is smaller in territory and membership than the economy. Under such a federalized political structure, persons, singly and/or in groups, would be guaranteed the liberties of trade, investment, and migration across the inclusive area of the economy. Analogous to the market, persons retain an exit option; at relatively low cost, at least some persons can shift among the separate political jurisdictions. Again analogous to the market, the separate producing units (in this case, the separate state governments) would be forced to compete, one with another, in their offers of publicly provided services. The federalized structure, through the forces of interstate competition, effectively limits the power of the separate political units to extract surplus value from the citizenry.

PRINCIPLES OF COMPETITIVE FEDERALISM

The operating principles of a genuinely competitive federalism can be summarized readily.[3] As noted, the central or federal government would be constitutionally restricted in its domain of action, severely so. Within its assigned sphere, however, the central government would be strong, sufficiently so to allow it to enforce economic freedom or openness over the whole of the territory. The separate states would be prevented, by federal authority, from placing barriers on the free flow of resources and goods across their borders.

The constitutional limits on the domain of the central, or federal, government would not be self-enforcing, and competition could not be made operative in a manner precisely comparable to that which might restrict economic exploitation by the separate states. If the federal (central) government, for any reason, should move beyond its constitutionally dictated mandate of authority, what protection might be granted—to citizens individually or to the separate states—against the extension of federal power?

The exit option is again suggested, although this option necessarily takes on a different form. The separate states, individually or in groups, must be constitutionally empowered to secede from the federalized political struc-

---

3. See Geoffrey Brennan and James M. Buchanan, *The Power to Tax: Analytical Foundations of a Fiscal Constitution* (New York: Cambridge University Press, 1980), 168–86, for more comprehensive treatment.

ture, that is, to form new units of political authority outside of and beyond the reach of the existing federal government. Secession, or the threat thereof, represents the only means through which the ultimate powers of the central government might be held in check. Absent the secession prospect, the federal government may, by overstepping its constitutionally assigned limits, extract surplus value from the citizenry almost at will, because there would exist no effective means of escape.[4]

With an operative secession threat on the part of the separate states, the federal, or central, government could be held roughly to its assigned constitutional limits, while the separate states could be left to compete among themselves in their capacities to meet the demands of citizens for collectively provided services. Locational rents, differential preferences for publicly provided goods and services, scale efficiencies, and the absence of residual claimancy—these and other factors would prevent even the idealized federal structure from attaining overall results that would be comparably efficient to those attained in the market economy, even when one acknowledges the shortfall of the latter from its idealized variant. Nonetheless, an effectively competitive federalism can be imaginatively constructed that is consistent with the observed behavioral regularities of human nature. Such a construction surely belongs in the realm of the "might be" rather than in the realm of science fiction. In such an idealized political order, the individual citizen would be insured against undue fiscal or economic exploitation by either the federal government or the state governments. The exploitation that might occur would be kept within threshold limits determined by the costs of personal and institutional work.

Some observers might be prompted to inquire: What political activities will the separate states perform in an effectively competitive federalism? The asking of such a question as this suggests a basic misunderstanding of the principles sketched out in this section.

Within each separate state of the federal system, both the dividing line between privately and publicly organized production-distribution activity and

4. For formal analysis of secession, see James M. Buchanan and Roger Faith, "Secession and the Limits of Taxation: Towards a Theory of Internal Exit," *American Economic Review* 5 (December 1987): 1023–31; for a more general discussion, see Allen Buchanan, *Secession: The Morality of Political Divorce from Fort Sumter to Lithuania and Quebec* (Boulder, Colo.: Westview, 1991).

the allocational-distributional mix among the items within the publicly organized sector remain to be determined by the interworkings of the preferences of the citizenry and the internal political process. There is no external
constraint that takes explicit shape here, whether emanating from the Constitution, the central government, or anywhere else. The separate states are
free to do "as they please," constrained only by the participation of their own
citizens in the decision processes.

We should predict, of course, that the separate states of a federal system
would be compelled by the forces of competition to offer tolerably "efficient"
mixes of publicly provided goods and services, and, to the extent that citizens
in the different states exhibit roughly similar preferences, the actual budgetary mixes would not be predicted to diverge significantly, one from the other.
However, the point to be emphasized here (and which seems to have been
missed in so much of the discussion about the potential European federalism) is that any such standardization or regularization as might occur, would
itself be an emergent property of competitive federalism rather than a property that might be imposed either by constitutional mandate or by central
government authority.

The Path Dependency of Constitutional Reform

FROM HERE TO THERE: A SCHEMA

The essential principle for meaningful discourse about constitutional-
institutional reform (or, indeed, about any change) is the recognition that
reform involves movement from some "here" toward some "there." The
evaluative comparison of alternative sets of rules and alternative regimes of
political order, as discussed above in the first section, aims exclusively at defining the "there," the idealized objective toward which any change must be
turned. But the direction for effective reform also requires a definition of the
"here." Any reform, constitutional or otherwise, commences from some "here
and now," some status quo that is the existential reality. History matters,
and the historical experience of a political community is beyond any prospect of change; the constitutional-institutional record can be neither ignored nor rewritten. The question for reform is, then: How do we get there
from here?

These prefatory remarks are necessary before any consideration of federalism in discussion of practical reform. The abstracted ideal—a strong but severely limited central authority with the capacity and the will to enforce free trade over the inclusive territory, along with several separate "states," each one of which stands in a competitive relationship with all other such units—of this ideal federal order may be well defined and agreed upon as an objective for change. However, until and unless the "here," the starting point, is identified, not even the direction of change can be known. A simple illustration may be helpful. Suppose that you and I agree that we want to be in Washington, D.C. But, suppose that you are in New York and I am in Atlanta. We must proceed in different directions if we expect to get to the shared or common objective.

Constitutional reform aimed toward an effective competitive federalism may reduce or expand the authority of the central government relative to that of the separate state governments in the inclusive territory of potential political interaction. If the status quo is described as a centralized and unitary political authority, reform must embody devolution, a shift of genuine political power from the center to the separate states. On the other hand, if the status quo is described by a set of autonomous political units that may perhaps be geographically contiguous but which act potentially in independence one from another, reform must involve a centralization of authority, a shift of genuine power to the central government from the separate states.

Figure 1 offers an illustrative schema. Consider a well-defined territory that may be organized politically at any point along the abstracted unidimensional spectrum that measures the extent to which political authority is centralized. At the extreme left of this spectrum, the territory is divided among several fully autonomous political units, each one of which possesses total "sovereignty," and among which any interaction, either by individuals or by political units, must be subjected to specific contractual negotiation and agreement. At the extreme right of this spectrum, the whole of the ter-

Figure 1. A constitutional reform schema

ritory is organized as an inclusive political community, with this authority centralized in a single governmental unit. Individuals and groups may interact, but any such interaction must take place within the uniform limits laid down by the monolithic authority.

An effective federal structure may be located somewhere near the middle of the spectrum, between the regime of fully autonomous localized units on the one hand and the regime of fully centralized authority on the other. This simple illustration makes it easy to see that constitutional reform that is aimed toward the competitive federal structure must be characterized by some increase in centralization if the starting point is on the left, and by some decrease in centralization if the starting point is on the right.

The illustration prompts efforts to locate differing regimes at differing places in their own separate histories on the unidimensional scalar. In 1787, James Madison, who had observed the several former British colonies that had won their independence and organized themselves as a confederation, located the status quo somewhere to the left of the middle of the spectrum, and he sought to secure an effective federalism by establishing a stronger central authority, to which some additional powers should be granted. Reform involved a reduction in the political autonomy of the separate units. In the early post–World War II decades, the status quo exhibits some features that are analogous to those assessed by Madison. They sought reform in the direction of a federalized structure—reform that necessarily involved some establishment of central authority, with some granting of power independent of that historically claimed by the separate nation-states.

By comparison and contrast, consider the United States in 1995, the history of which is surely described as an overshooting of Madison's dreams for the ideal political order. Over the course of two centuries, and especially after the demise of any secession option, as resultant from the great Civil War of the 1860s, the U.S. political order came to be increasingly centralized. The status quo in 1995 lies clearly on the right of the spectrum, and any reform toward a federalist ideal must involve some devolution of central government authority and some increase in the effective independent power of the several states. (The electoral results in November 1994 suggest that the federalist ideal contains considerable popular appeal, and prospects for reform appear better than in many decades.)

Constitutional reform in many countries, as well as in the United States, would presumably involve devolution of authority from the central government to the separate states.

Constitutional strategy and
the federalist ideal

The simple construction of Figure 1 is also helpful in suggesting that it may be difficult to achieve the ideal constitutional structure described as competitive federalism. Whether motivated by direct economic interest, by some failure to understand basic economic and political theory, or by fundamental conservative instincts, specific political coalitions will emerge to oppose any shift from the status quo toward a federal structure, no matter what the starting point. If, for example, the status quo is described by a regime of fully autonomous units (the nation-states of Europe after World War II), political groups within each of these units will object to any sacrifice of national sovereignty that might be required by a shift toward federalism. Additionally, the strategic success of such groups is enhanced to the extent that the effective alternative is presented, not as a federal structure located somewhere in the middle of the spectrum, but as the highly centralized authority at the other extreme. If the anti-federalists raise the specter of central government domination, popular support for the federalist reform necessarily becomes weaker.

Similar comments may be made about the debates mounted from the opposing direction. If a unitary centralized authority describes the status quo ante, its supporters may attempt to and may succeed in conveying the potential for damage through constitutional collapse into a regime of autonomous units, vulnerable to economic and political warfare. The middle way offered by devolution to a competitive federalism may, in this case, find few adherents.[5]

---

5. The theory of agenda-setting in public choice offers analogies. If the agenda can be manipulated in such fashion that the alternatives for choice effectively "bracket" the ideally preferred position, voters are confronted with the selection of one or the other of the extreme alternatives, both of which may be dominated by the preferred option. See Thomas Romer and Howard Rosenthal, "Political Resource Allocation, Controlled Agendas, and the Status Quo," *Public Choice* 33 (Winter 1978): 27–43.

The discussion of steps toward a constitution for the European Union, especially during the period 1989–1995, seems to reinforce the points made above. The discussion appears to have proceeded largely as if the genuine federalist structure is not considered as a constitutional alternative. The position represented by Jacques Delors and much of the Brussels bureaucracy envisages a Europe in which political authority is highly centralized, with the whole economy subjected to uniform regulation. By contrast, the position represented by the Bruges group, and promoted by Margaret Thatcher, more or less accepts the Delors thrust as the only effective alternative to the retention of full national sovereignty. From this base of interpretation, any talk of federalism becomes an anathema.[6]

As the construction in Figure 1 also suggests, however, the fact that the federalist structure is, indeed, "in the middle," at least in the highly stylized sense discussed here, may carry prospects for evolutionary emergence in the conflicts between centralizing and decentralizing pressures. Contrary to the poetic pessimism of William Butler Yeats, the "centre" may hold, if once attained, not because of any intensity of conviction, but rather due to the location of the balance of forces.[7]

Federalism and increasing economic interdependence

In the preceding discussion, I have presumed that the economic benefits of a large economic nexus, defined both in territory and membership, extend at least to and beyond the limits of the political community that may be constitutionally organized anywhere along the spectrum in Figure 1, from a regime of fully autonomous political units to one of centralized political authority. Recall that Adam Smith emphasized that economic prosperity and growth find their origins in the division (specialization) of labor and that this

6. For earlier analyses of the discussion, see my several papers, "Politics without Romance"; "Europe's Constitutional Opportunity," Europe's Constitutional Future (London: Institute of Economic Affairs, 1990), 1–20; "National Politics and Competitive Federalism" (Fairfax, Va.: Center for Study of Public Choice, George Mason University, 1994).

7. William Butler Yeats, "The Second Coming," The Collected Works of W. B. Yeats, vol. 1, The Poems, ed. Richard J. Finneran (New York: Macmillan, 1989), 187.

division, in turn, depends on the extent of the market. Smith placed no limits on the scope for applying this principle. But we know that the economic world of 1995 is dramatically different from that of 1775. Technological development has facilitated a continuing transformation of local to regional to national to international interactions among economic units. Consistently with Smith's insights, economic growth has been more rapid where and when political intrusions have not emerged to prevent entrepreneurs from seizing the advantages offered by the developing technology.

Before the technological revolution in information processing and communication, however, a revolution that has occurred in this half-century, politically motivated efforts to "improve" on the workings of market processes seemed almost a part of institutional reality. In this setting, it seemed to remain of critical economic importance to restrict the intrusiveness of politics, quite apart from the complementary effects on individual liberties. Political federalism, to the extent that its central features were at all descriptive of constitutional history, did serve to facilitate economic growth.

The modern technological revolution in information processing and communications may have transformed, at least to some degree, the setting within which politically motivated obstructions may impact on market forces. This technology may, in itself, have made it more difficult for politicians and governments, at any and all levels, to check or to limit the ubiquitous pressures of economic interdependence.[8] When values can be transferred worldwide at the speed of light and when events everywhere are instantly visible on CNN, there are elements of competitive federalism in play, almost regardless of the particular constitutional regimes in existence.

Finally, the relationship between federalism, as an organizing principle for political structure, and the freedom of trade across political boundaries must be noted. An inclusive political territory, say, the United States or Western Europe, necessarily places limits on its own ability to interfere politically with its own internal market structure to the extent that this structure is, itself, opened to the free workings of international trade, including the movement of capital. On the other hand, to the extent that the internal market is pro-

8. Richard McKenzie and Dwight Lee, *Quicksilver Capital: How the Rapid Movement of Wealth Has Changed the World* (New York: Free Press, 1991).

tected against the forces of international competition, other means, including federalism, become more essential to preserve liberty and to guarantee economic growth.

Conclusion

The United States offers an illustrative example. The United States prospered mightily in the nineteenth century, despite the wall of protectionism that sheltered its internal markets. It did so because political authority, generally, was held in check by a constitutional structure that did contain basic elements of competitive federalism. By comparison, the United States, in this last decade of the twentieth century, is more open to international market forces, but its own constitutional structure has come to be transformed into one approaching a centralized unitary authority.

Devolution toward a competitive federal structure becomes less necessary to the extent that markets are open to external opportunities. However, until and unless effective constitutional guarantees against political measures to choke off external trading relationships are put in place, the more permanent constitutional reform aimed at restoring political authority to the separate states offers a firmer basis for future economic growth along with individual liberty.

The Europe of the 1990s offers a second example. If trade beyond the limits of the European Union's members remains open, the concerns about excessive centralization of political authority may be misplaced. However, to the extent that "fortress Europe" becomes descriptive of political reality, the movement toward a genuinely competitive federalism takes on much more importance.

Federalism and
Individual Sovereignty

I have been both surprised and disturbed by two sources of opposition to efforts to move toward federalist structures in which political authority is divided between levels of government. I refer, first, to the opposition in Europe, mainly in Britain, to movements toward effective European federalism. Second, I refer to the successful agitation that blocked the proposed Conference of the States in the United States in 1995. What is disturbing about these sources of opposition to the very idea of political federalism is that both emerge from groups that are identified variously to be right-wing, conservative, or libertarian. We should not, of course, be surprised at all by socialist-inspired opposition to the federalist idea and ideal. Socialists have been and remain forthright in their desire to extend the range of politicized control over the lives and liberties of persons. But why should conservatives, classical liberals, or libertarians join socialists in opposing structural reforms that embody federalist principles?

I suggest that a coherent classical liberal must be generally supportive of federal political structures, because any division of authority must, necessarily, tend to limit the potential range of political coercion. Those persons and groups who oppose the devolution of authority from the central government to the states in the United States and those who oppose any limits on the separate single nation-states in modern Europe are, by these com-

From *Cato Journal* 15 (Fall/Winter 1995/96): 259–68. Reprinted by permission of the publisher.

This paper is based on a presentation made at the Mont Pèlerin Society's regional meeting in Cancun, Mexico, January 15, 1996.

mitments, placing other values above those of the liberty and sovereignty of individuals.

The incoherence in values that such anti-federalist ambivalence reflects is not widely acknowledged. The relationships between federalist political structure and the sovereignty of the individual must be carefully examined, particularly in terms of the implications for current discussions in Europe, Mexico, and the United States.

In this paper, I shall summarize the theory of competitive federalism and examine the relation between the engagement-participation of the individual in politics and the size of the political unit. The theory of competitive federalism emphasizes the prospects for exit, both internal and external, as constraints on political control over the individual. In contrast, the theory of what we might call "partitioned sovereignty federalism" emphasizes the prospects for the exercise of voice in limiting political excesses.

In addition, I shall introduce moral elements that may emerge in arguments for federal political structures and relate those arguments to observed crises in modern welfare states. Finally, I shall apply the analysis more directly to discussions of movements toward federalist structures in several parts of the world.

The Theory of Competitive Federalism

The normative theory of competitive federalism is congenial to economists in particular because it is simply the extension of the principles of the market economy to the organization of the political structure. The market economy produces high levels of value from which all participants benefit; persons are legally guaranteed rights of entry into and exit from production and exchange relationships one with another. If a good or service offered by a producer-seller is "bad" compared with goods offered by other producers-sellers, the prospective purchaser-consumer simply exercises the exit option and shifts his or her business to an alternative supplier. And the fact that profits are promised by marketing "good goods" rather than "bad goods" ensures that scarce resources will flow toward those uses that yield relatively high values. Suppliers remain always in competition among themselves, faced with the knowledge that demanders have available the continuing prospect of exiting from any ongoing economic relationship.

Normatively, the political structure should complement the market in the sense that the objective for its operation is the generation of results that are valued by citizens. By its nature, however, politics is coercive; all members of a political unit must be subjected to the same decisions. The prospect of exit, which is so important in imposing discipline in market relationships, is absent from politics unless it is deliberately built in by the constitution of a federalized structure.

Consider a large economy, characterized by liberty of resource flow and trade throughout the territory—liberty that is enforced by a political unit, a government, that is coincident in extent with the effective size of the market. If politics could be restricted to the exercise of these minimal or protective state functions (the night watchman state), little or no concern need be expressed about coercive political intrusions on the liberties of citizens. As the experience of this century surely demonstrates, however, politics is almost certain to extend beyond any such limits. (We need not argue here about whether or not and to what extent expansions in the domain of politics are justifiable.) The problem becomes one of organizing the beyond-minimal politics of the "productive" state and the "transfer" state so as to minimize the potential for political coercion or, stated conversely, to maximize the protected sphere of individual sovereignty.

It is here that the prospects for organizing the polity in accordance with federalist principles become exceedingly attractive. Federalism offers a means of introducing essential features of the market into politics. Consider, for example, a setting in which the central, or federal, government is constitutionally restricted to the exercise of minimal or protective state functions, while all other functions are carried out by separated state or provincial units. The availability of the exit option, guaranteed by the central government, would effectively place limits on the ability of state-provincial governments to exploit citizens, quite independent of how political choices within these units might be made. Localized politicians and coalitions would be unable to depart significantly from overall efficiency standards in their taxing, spending, and regulatory politics. And note that the feedback effect of potential exit need exert itself only on a relatively small share of economic decision takers. Even those citizens who might never consider migration in some Tiebout-like regime would be protected by the acknowledged existence of those few citizens who might be marginally sensitive to differential political treatment.

Federalism serves the dual purposes of allowing the range or scope for central government activity to be curtailed and, at the same time, limiting the potential for citizen exploitation by state-provincial units.

Partitioned Sovereignty Federalism: The Exercise of Voice

The efficacy of competitive federalism depends directly on the operative strength of the exit option. The ability of persons to migrate and to shift investment and trade across boundaries serves to limit political exploitation. Recall, however, that in his seminal work, Albert Hirschman placed "voice" alongside "exit" in his examination of control institutions.[1] In the market, exit is the dominant means through which persons indirectly exercise control, and, as indicated earlier, federalism incorporates this means into politics. But the exercise of voice is also important, especially perhaps in politics, and this feature lends independent support for federal structures.

The basic logic is straightforward. If the concern is for the protection and maintenance of individual sovereignty against the potential coercion that may be imposed by political or collective action, the size of the political unit, measured by the number of members, becomes a relevant variable, quite apart from the presence or absence of an exit opportunity. And political authority may be deliberately shared by a central government and component units, with effective sovereignty partitioned among levels.[2]

Consider, again, a large economy in which a central government, coincident in size with the economy, is limited to the carrying out of protective or minimal state functions. How should the extensions of political activity beyond these limits be organized? How should the public-goods and welfare state activities be structurally designed?

Even if citizens are predicted to remain locationally fixed, and hence within a single jurisdiction, so that exit is not a potentially effective means of

1. A. O. Hirschman, *Exit, Voice and Loyalty* (Cambridge, Mass.: Harvard University Press, 1970).

2. R. Vaubel (*The Centralisation of Western Europe*, Hobart Paper No. 127 [London: Institute of Economic Affairs, 1995]) makes several of the same points that I emphasize here. Notably, Vaubel also used the "exit" and "voice" metaphors in the federalist context.

institutional control at all, there remains a strong normative argument to be made for establishing relatively small, and coexisting, political units, all of which may be geographically contained within the boundaries of the economic interaction and the territorial reach of the central government. If persons are, for any reason, either unable or unwilling to exercise the exit option, actually or potentially, they may be able to exercise voice, defined here as activity that is participatory in determining political choices. And voice is more effective in small than in large political units. One vote is more likely to be decisive in an electorate of 100 than in an electorate of 1,000 or 1 million. Also, it is easier for one person or small group to organize a potentially winning political coalition in the localized community than in a large and complex polity.

But voice is more than a vote in some precise mathematical formula for measuring potential influence over political outcomes. Neither the set of alternatives among which political choices are made nor the preferences of citizens-voters are exogenous to the processes of political discussion. And it is self-evident that the influence of any person in a discussion process varies inversely with the size of the group.

Even if exit is nonexistent in reality, what we may label as "virtual exit" may be important and relevant in the internal discussion-choice process. The mere fact that coexisting units of government exist and can be observed to do things differently exerts spillover effects on internal political actions. As a practical example, even though exit was of some importance, especially in Germany, the *observations* of Western economies, culture, and politics by citizens of Central and Eastern Europe were independently critical in effecting the genuine political revolutions that occurred in 1989–91. As an additional conceptual experiment, think about how much less vulnerable the communist regimes would have been if all of Europe had been under communist domination. Or imagine how prospects for the revolution might have fared in a world without television.

Note that the normative arguments for federalizing political authority made so far have not considered the relative economic efficiency of public-goods delivery by the different levels of government. Those arguments suggest that, even if productive welfare state functions could, in some ideal sense, be best carried out by the central government, there are offsetting grounds, based on what we may call "political efficiency," for partitioning political choice.[3]

Homogeneity, Moral Capacity, and Federalization

The effects of community size on the individual's protection against political exploitation discussed so far are independent of any consideration of the homogeneity or heterogeneity of the constituent members of the separated state or provincial units. Even if the inclusive polity is made up of similar persons, there remains a normative argument for partitioning effective political sovereignty between central and state-provincial units of governance. If, however, we now introduce prospects for heterogeneity in the inclusive constituency, the argument for federalization is surely strengthened. Small units, defined geographically or territorially, are likely to be more homogeneous in makeup than larger units, and the individual is more likely to share preferences for political action with his or her peers than would be the case where political interaction must include persons who are considered to be "foreign," whether the lines here be drawn racially, ethnically, religiously, economically, or otherwise. If the objective is the minimization of politically orchestrated coercion, the individual will, personally, feel under less potential threat in a community of similarly situated peers than in a large community that embodies groups with differing characteristics.

Quite apart from the objectively identifiable characteristics that might allow an outside observer to classify persons into groups, the size of the community also becomes relevant in its direct relationship to the moral capacity of the individual to share values with others. That is to say, homogeneity in values among persons may itself be related to social and locational distance. And those values may include community bonding, which may be expressed in terms of utility interdependence. A person may feel genuine empathy for other persons whom he or she classifies, internally, as members of his or her moral community, the boundaries of which are determined, in part, by numbers and by proximity. For example, I may share a common concern for the plight of persons who are citizens of Montgomery County,

---

3. See G. Brennan and J. M. Buchanan, *The Power to Tax: Analytical Foundations of a Fiscal Constitution* (Cambridge: Cambridge University Press, 1980), chap. 9.

Virginia, or, more inclusively, for the plight of the citizens of Virginia, a concern that is either absent or much attenuated with reference to the citizens of Kern County, California, or of California itself.

In a paper that I presented at the American Economic Association meetings several years ago, I argued that each of us has only a limited moral capacity.[4] It is surely easier and more natural to feel sympathy for and to care about others who are members of the same small community than it is to care for members of a large polity. I suggested, further, that a major factor in generating the breakdown of the welfare state was the shift of transfer activities to the central government and away from local communities in which political action might well embody a greater sense of interdependence. I suggested that the shift of political activities that must incorporate moral elements to levels of interaction that extend well beyond our moral capacities can only serve to exacerbate the emergence of raw self-seeking by groups of potential clients on the one hand and by those who feel unduly exploited on the other.

The argument here is, of course, related closely to F. A. Hayek's emphasis on our genetic heritage, which is basically tribal, and leads us to classify other persons into two groups—"us" and "them," or "neighbors" and "strangers." Hayek perceptively noted that only as these genetic dispositions came to be transcended by the culturally evolved norms for generalized reciprocity in interactions did the "great society," defined by the extended market order, become possible.[5] We must recognize, however, that politicization, in itself, explicitly encourages the reemergence of tribal identities. Political action, regardless of how decisions are made, involves choices that are made for, and coercively imposed on, *all* members of the relevant political community. Anyone who is a participant is, almost by necessity, required to classify his or her own interests in juxtaposition to the imagined interests of others in the polity. Federalized structures allow for some partial mapping of politics with tribal identities. At the very least, federalized structures reduce the extent to which tribal identities in politics must be grossly transcended. This consid-

4. J. M. Buchanan, "Markets, States, and the Extent of Morals," *American Economic Review* 68 (May 1978): 364–68.

5. F. A. Hayek, *Law, Legislation and Liberty,* vol. 3, *The Political Order of a Free People* (Chicago: University of Chicago Press, 1979).

Figure 1. A constitutional reform schema

eration assumes relatively more importance if and as the moral linkages are locational, rather than strictly genetic.

Federalism as an Ideal Polity and Federalism in Reality

It is relatively easy to describe the ideal structure of politics for a large community, defined by territory or by numbers of citizens, if the overriding objective is the protection of individual sovereignty against political coercion.[6] A central government authority should be constitutionally restricted to the enforcement of openness of the whole nexus of economic interaction. Within this scope, the central authority must be strong, but it should not be allowed to extend beyond the limits constitutionally defined. Other political-collective activities should be carried out, if at all, by separate state-provincial units that exist side-by-side, as competitors of sorts, in the inclusive polity.

This definition of the idealized federalism is useful only because it offers a concrete objective toward which reforms in political arrangements may be directed. In reality, no existing political structure comes close to the ideal. Any constructive effort must therefore commence with an understanding of and appreciation for the politics that is observed to exist. "We start from here and now." This elementary fact should always be prefatory to any discussion of reform.

With reference to the common federalist ideal, however, we may observe categorically different starting places. The situation may be represented by the spectrum in Figure 1, in which a federal political structure stands halfway

6. The discussion in this section closely parallels that in J. M. Buchanan, "Federalism as an Ideal Political Order and an Objective for Constitutional Reform," *Publius: The Journal of Federalism* 25, no. 2 (1995): 1–9.

between a regime of fully autonomous states on the one hand and a monolithic all-powerful central authority on the other.

Individual protection against political exploitation is increased as we move toward the center of the spectrum from starting points either left or right of center. In 1787, James Madison sought to increase the authority of the central government; he located the status quo under the Articles of Confederation somewhere to the left of center in Figure 1. He sought to increase the authority of the federal government as a means of placing limits on the authority of the separate states. We know now that United States history has destroyed Madison's vision. As a result of the destructive Civil War in the 1860s, secession was permanently eliminated as an effective extra-constitutional check on the progressive increase in central government authority. And, in the 20th century, constitutional guarantees against federal encroachment on the authority of states were undermined by executive, legislative, and judicial departures from established principles. At the century's end, therefore, the status quo is clearly on the right side of the spectrum in Figure 1. Effective reform must embody devolution of power from the central government to the states—change that is in the opposite direction from what Madison accomplished in 1787.

In Mexico, the situation is similar with respect to the direction of change, despite the categorically different history of the country. Reform in the direction of securing effective federalism must incorporate a devolution of authority toward the states and away from the central government.

In Europe, however, matters are quite different. There the status quo exhibits some features that are analogous to those assessed by Madison in 1787. The opportunity has existed, and still exists, to organize European politics so as to put in place a genuine federal structure with many elements of the ideal set out earlier. The Europe-wide economy has been substantially integrated, with historically unprecedented liberties of resource flows and trade across traditional national boundaries. Reform requires the establishment of a strong but limited central authority, empowered to enforce the openness of the economy, along with the other minimal state functions. In this way, and only in this way, can the vulnerability of the individual European to exploitation by national political units be reduced. At the same time, however, the extension of the central authority's powers beyond such minimal limits must be rigidly opposed. The separated nation-states, as members of the federal union, must zealously protect the whole range of subminimal political activities.

Opposition to the federalist idea, especially as expressed in arguments by some U.K. political leaders, stems from an imagined fear of a monolithic central authority in Brussels—a fear that has been fueled, in part, by the residual vestiges of the socialist mentality among some influential nominal supporters of the federal structure. Both attitudes fail to understand that federalism and socialism are contradictory systems of political order. Federalism is a means of reducing political power overall and of dividing the power that exists. Socialism is opposed on both counts.

The opposition to federalism that comes from those who otherwise seem sympathetic to classical liberalism apparently reflects a failure to understand that federalism offers protection against the excesses of the autonomous nation-state. Or could it be that the genuine objective of those who oppose reforms toward federalism is not individual liberty, but rather the preservation of national political sovereignty? It is as if the U.K. anti-federalists are saying, "We do not mind being politically coerced, so long as it is done by the British Parliament."

The position of those zealots in the United States who successfully thwarted the organization of the Conference of the States in 1995 is even more bizarre and surely borders on paranoia. The initiative behind the Conference was aimed almost exclusively toward designing ways and means through which effective political authority could be devolved from the federal government to the separate states. How could those persons and groups who mouth slogans about liberty and oppose such initiatives be other than dishonest or ignorant?

Postscript: Individual Sovereignty and Individual Liberty

Note that my title is "Federalism and Individual Sovereignty" rather than "Federalism and Individual Liberty." It may be useful to clarify the distinction. What is the ultimate maximand when the individual considers the organization of the political structure? Unless he or she is a genuine anarchist who thinks that private and voluntary action can be efficacious over the whole social space (including basic protections to person, property, and contract), this maximand cannot be summarized as the maximization of (equal) individual liberty from political-collective action. Implementation of such an objective would, to many of us, represent a leap backward into the Hobbesian jungle.

A more meaningful maximand is summarized as the maximization of (equal) individual sovereignty. This objective allows for the establishment of political-collective institutions, but implies that these institutions be organized so as to minimize political coercion of the individual. Coercion is defined as being required to do things or to submit to things others do to you, that you do not, or would not, voluntarily agree to do yourself or to have done to you. A person may give up his or her liberty to steal from others and pay taxes to support the enforcement of laws against theft provided others are subjected to the same general constraints. So long as one's agreement to such political action is voluntary, the individual's sovereignty is protected, even though liberty is restricted.[7]

7. J. M. Buchanan and L. Lomasky, "The Matrix of Contractarian Justice," *Social Philosophy* 2 (Autumn 1984): 12–32.

Economic Freedom and Federalism

Prospects for the New Century

I want to commence this lecture with two separate presuppositions upon which we will all agree and about which there should be no dispute. First, the performance of a market economy is superior to that of an economy subject to command and control, with superior being directly measured by the size of the bundle of goods and services produced—goods and services that are valued as end items of consumption and used by participants in the economies themselves. This presupposition is surely confirmed by recent historical experience, but it is also confirmed by scientific analysis which now incorporates recognition of the epistemological as well as the incentive advantages of market or market-like organisation structures.

Second, there is an on-going worldwide process of institutional change that involves depoliticisation of economic activity, a process that appears variously and in separate countries under the several descriptive labels: denationalisation, privatisation, federalism, devolution, deregulation and others. The two presuppositions are, of course, directly related; the institutional process of change, which can be observed to be taking place, occurs as a direct consequence of the near-universal recognition of the validity of the first presupposition stated. The process of institutional change represents a decoupling of the spheres of political and economic interaction. And this decoupling, or divorce, emerges as a necessary consequence of collapse of the central command principle that was the basis of the socialist ideal.

Special contribution to the inaugural issue, *Asian Journal of Business & Information Systems* 1 (Summer 1996): 5–10. Reprinted by permission of the publisher.

This paper was given as a public lecture on 3 June 1996 at The Hong Kong Polytechnic University.

Centralised command and control over the economic activity of a whole national territory requires that the mapping of political authority correspond with the extent of economic interaction. In my own country, the United States, it would make no sense at all for a single state, among the fifty, to try to control the economic activity of its citizens in detail when the state's borders remain open to the free flow of goods and resources across state boundaries throughout the whole national territory. In the American setting, a socialised economy, described in terms of the normative ideals envisaged by the central planners of the early twentieth century, would have demanded the centralisation of political power and authority into the unit of control that is, territorially, correspondent with the limits of economic activity. When we recognise this point, and when we also recognise that the socialist ideology was omnipresent and significant in driving American institutional change during much of this century, we should not really be at all surprised that the central government in the United States (the federal government in our terminology) increased its powers dramatically at the expense of those of the states. A viable federalism, in which political power, or sovereignty, is genuinely shared between the central government and the separate states or provinces, is simply incompatible with the command-control model of socialist economic organisation. The philosophical logic of the socialist century dictated centralised political power.

We can understand why political power came to be centralised, everywhere, both in those nations that were defined to be in either the socialist or nonsocialist camps. With the intellectual-scientific as well as the practicable bankruptcy of the command-control model of economic organisation, we should indeed sense the institutional mismatch that now exists. Institutional conservatives, from all across the ideological spectrum, are reluctant to acknowledge that the historical nation-state has lost its *raison d'être*, at least to the extent that political activity is considered to include directed control and regulation of economic life.

What is the political structure that is appropriate for the national units of the world, when increasingly, internal economies are described by freedom of entry and exit to all markets, both for citizens and for foreigners?

To begin to get at an answer to this critically important question we must, I think, go back to the basic understanding of why the central-command models of economic organisation failed, and why market models are so superior, at least in some comparative sense. As noted, the centrally planned economy failed because it did not, and cannot, utilise either the knowledge of opportunities or the incentive structures that emerge more or less naturally in markets. But why and how do markets use knowledge, and why and how do markets exploit incentives? Is there some central principle that allows markets to be more effective along these dimensions?

The central principle is summarised in the word "competition." Markets work well—they produce large bundles of goods and services wanted by participants—because they exploit the forces of competition. If markets are open to entry and exit, the existence of any potential profit opportunity will attract investment; and note that only one entrepreneur need recognise any opportunity. There is no need that the potential profitability be sensed by a committee, a board or by the whole membership of the political authority. The entrepreneur who first senses knowledge of the profit opportunity can anticipate gains, but his gains will themselves be quite limited by the freedom of entry of imitators and followers. Profits will be dissipated as more and more persons and firms enter the newly opened line of market activity. The initial entrepreneur who discovered the opportunity is restricted by the entry of others in the degree to which he can withdraw profits.

The consumer-user of economic goods and services is thereby protected against undue exploitation by prospective monopolists; he is protected by the competitive process, which insures that profits if and when they appear will quickly be dissipated, and, further, which insures that any available profit opportunity will be discovered. The participant in an effectively functioning market economy can rest assured that there is no major source of current economic value that is mysteriously hidden from sight and waiting to be discovered. The competitive process of the market economy allocates resources to those uses that participants value most highly.

Why is it necessary to go through this lesson in elementary or introductory economic theory in order to get at the question posed above relating to the appropriate political organisation for the nation-state in the post-revolutionary world economy? My answer is succinct. Only a *federalised* political structure can effectively exploit the forces of competition in any manner at all analogous to the market process. The appropriate political structure is one of *competitive federalism,* whether for my own country, the United States, for Europe, for Latin America or for China.

What competitive federalism does is to introduce into political order the disciplinary pressure of competition, analogous to that present in markets, even if necessarily attenuated by the nature of political authority. Note that I am not suggesting here that there is no role for political authority; I am not making a case for limiting political authority to the role sometimes described as the night-watchman, the minimal or the protective state. The point here is quite different. There may well exist goods and services that are desired by participants that cannot be efficiently supplied by markets. "Public goods and services" in the definitional Samuelsonian sense of shared collective consumption may exist, and persons may organise political action to secure these goods through collective agency, through political units or governing bodies. But how can governments, charged with the responsibility of collecting taxes from citizens and using the revenues to supply commonly shared public goods and services, themselves be controlled so as to limit the exploitation of the principals, that is, the people themselves? Again, the answer is *competition*. If the public-goods functions of collective or governmental organisation can be federalised, so that several units coexist, side-by-side in an inclusive but economically open political nexus, no single unit can unduly exploit its monopoly position with respect to its treatment of either taxpayers or consumers-users of public goods. In an integrated economy, persons and capital investment can shift between units, and further, the observations of differential treatment by different units will, itself, exert disciplinary pressure on deviant governmental units in a federalism.

Consider, as a first example, law enforcement of the ordinary sort. Assume that law enforcement is within the responsibility of the local units of government, which includes a territory and a membership that is only a small part of an inclusive open economic nexus. If the local unit operates its law enforcement effort inefficiently, either from localised corruption or from laxness or severity in operation, the community becomes less attractive relative to its neighbours. It will lose members by outmigration as well as capital investment. The threat of this result will put pressure on local agencies to remain roughly efficient, in some comparative sense, in its operation.

Or, as a second example, consider government subsidy (or regulative favours) to a particular industry, that reduces economic productivity. If the political unit that practices such discrimination is integrated in an open trading network with other competing jurisdictions, the effects will be quickly noticed and will be measured by resource migration. Internal political discrimination will be severely constrained.

How far should devolution be carried? Even if the principle of competitive federalism be acknowledged, how much deconcentration or decentralisation of political authority is implied? In one limit, of course, the principle might suggest that all political-collective activity should be privatised, thereby securing the maximal efficiency of competition. But we have suggested that there do exist *genuinely public goods,* for which there are perhaps major efficiency gains to be secured through collective provision. The principle of competitive federalism suggests only that the prospective efficacy of competition be put into the balance when other efficiency considerations are introduced. For example, just because the standard efficiency logic might dictate the financing and supply of a good or service by the central government does not suggest that only the central government should serve this function. To some extent, the advantages from decentralised provision stemming from the competitive process might offset the standard efficiency logic.

A current example comes immediately to mind. Consider the European Union and the prospects for a unified currency in 1999 or so. An argument can, of course, be made that a single European currency unit would increase overall efficiency throughout the territory of the Union. The range of "publicness" is European-wide. But this fact alone does not imply that the optimal monetary arrangements for modern Europe involve a common monetary unit or a single European central bank. My own view is that such arrangements would not be the most preferred at this juncture in history. A regime of separated national currencies, with competing national central banks, each of which remains in competition with others to secure the allegiance and loyalty of Europeans, continent-wide, seems to me to insure greater net efficiency because the danger of centralised monopoly control is mitigated.

As this example perhaps suggests, the particular political arrangements for carrying out the separate public-goods functions may depend on the history that has settled the status quo in being. For any particular function, there is, of course, what may be called a "natural" range of publicness, a "natural" size for the membership of the community of persons who might share in non-excludable benefits. The argument from the principle of competitive federalism suggests that the potential, and dynamic, efficiency to be anticipated from competition always offsets, to a degree, the precise mapping of governmental units and ranges of provision.

Again, an example may be helpful, this time drawn from American experience in this century. On strictly efficiency grounds, an argument can be made that governmentally financed (and possibly provided) educational services might best be organised in large jurisdictional units, perhaps at the level of the separate American states. There is, however, ample empirical evidence now in place to support the finding that as the centralisation and consolidation of educational services has proceeded throughout the last half of the century the delivery of services preferred by the final consumer-user has suffered. Attitudes of experts now suggest that education is best provided at and by local government units, which must operate in settings where competitive pressures are intensified.

We must, of course, remain wary of making evaluative comparisons across separated public functions and especially across national boundaries. Institutional structures of governance differ, and each historical developmental pattern differs from others. Nonetheless, the principle of competitive federalism, as such, can be helpful in any setting, as offering a normatively meaningful guide toward structural reform.

I have left one issue of central importance yet to be discussed. To what extent should the federalised structure of politics in a single large nation embody uniform or standard devolution of political authority and autonomy as among the separate sub-units? Is it desirable to allow some states, provinces or regional units to assume more public-goods autonomy than others within an overall national jurisdiction? Or must a devolution of authority to any one unit necessarily imply devolution of like or similar authority to all other units in the national jurisdiction? Must constitutional separation of powers be uniform or can this separation be discriminatory or differentiated?

Modern Spain offers an example where the federalised structure is highly discriminatory; modern United States offers the converse case, where the granting of authority to one state implies (with some rare exceptions) the granting of comparable autonomy to all states. Consider, first, modern Spain. Confronted with separatist insurgence in the Basque Country, the national government in Spain granted extraordinary powers of autonomy to this region, while keeping the region within the national territory of and under the suzerainty of the nation-state. In separate action, Catalonia was also granted substantial autonomy, but not nearly so extensive as that of the Basque Country. Further, Valencia and other provincial governments were given particular status, with less autonomy than either the Basque Country or Catalonia, but yet more than some other regions in the Spanish national territory. Modern Spain is now best described as a discriminatory competitive federalism, which seems to work so long as the loyalties of citizens are sufficiently localised to forestall demands of equal treatment across all units. Internally, within Spain itself, goods and services and resources flow freely across provincial boundaries; the economic nexus is clearly national in scope. And as Europe opens up its markets generally, extending the market nexus across countries, we may expect that the within-Spain political differentiation among the separate provinces or regions will assume less significance.

In the United States, pressures for devolution from the central government to the separate states is strong and especially for the provision of welfare-state-type services, essentially income transfers to the poor. The historical tradition as well as the institutional status quo suggest that differentiated treatment of the separate states in terms of autonomous authority is unlikely to take place. However, the Spanish example suggests that such differential autonomy is not out of bounds, while adhering to the principle of competitive federalism.

I am not sufficiently familiar with the situation in Hong Kong to comment either positively or normatively on the policy and constitutional alternatives that will be faced in 1997 and beyond. But I should suggest the feasibility of looking to the Spanish model of devolution of political authority as a source of possible instruction and guidance.

In the discussion to this point, I have discussed the possible efficacy of competitive federalism as a means of dividing political authority between central and smaller units of governance in a large territory with an integrated economic nexus. I have not examined the situation confronted by a relatively small state with limited membership and restricted territory. In this setting, the limits to devolution of authority and autonomy to units of government smaller than the central authority are obvious. How, then, can the equivalent of competitive federalism be achieved in such settings?

The smaller the national political unit, the more necessary it becomes to maintain open entry and exit for goods, capital and labour across its borders with other jurisdictions. In an open economic and trading network, the degree to which persons in any country can be politically exploited is severely limited, even in the absence of competition among separate political jurisdictions. In one sense, freedom of international trade does substitute for the competitive discipline imposed by federalised political structures. But history has surely taught us that we cannot depend on the internal politics of any nation, regardless of its ideology, to enforce freedom of trade between its citizens and those of other countries. A small nation must keep its borders open if it expects to maintain its place or to move up in the comparative league tables that measure economic value. A large nation may also insure its own prosperity by free trade; but the large nation can, in addition, use the devolution of political authority within its borders to introduce competitive pressures over and beyond those emerging from international markets.

In concluding this lecture, let me return to the title, "Economic Freedom and Federalism." What does it mean to say that a person has economic freedom? To me, this means that the person has available exit options, that he or she has choices, concerning what to purchase and from whom, concerning what profession or occupation to enter, concerning what new enterprise to start up, concerning what to invest in. So long as, and to the extent that, persons possess these economic freedoms, they are independent of the power of any single person or group. These freedoms are understood to be characteristic features of a functioning market economy. What federalism accomplishes for the political sphere of action is some measure of economic freedom over and beyond those offered by the market in fully partitionable or private goods and services. Insofar as persons combine through political agency to finance and to share the benefits of commonly supplied goods and services, the potential exit option offered in competitive federalism places discipline on exploitation akin to that placed on the private-goods monopolist who must always know that any profit position is strictly temporary.

The second part of my title is "Prospects for the New Century." The thrust toward privatisation, denationalisation and devolution is by no means yet exhausted. It is difficult to predict just what the political equilibrium, in any country, or in the world, will look like in, say, two decades. I am firmly convinced that rapidly developing modern technology insures that markets must be opened up further, not closed, and that political authority must, necessarily, lose out if it engages in belated efforts to re-establish controls over economic life.

I should hope that political leaders, everywhere, will recognise that the constitutional framework can be reformed with an aim of exploiting the competitive forces that only federalised political structures expose and energise. The findings of modern economic science suggest that the wealth of any large nation can be increased by constitutional guarantees that to the extent possible political authority will be devolved from central to several, and competing, quasi-autonomous units integrated economically in a federal structure.

Europe's Constitutional Opportunity

I. Introduction

At a 1986 Cato Institute Conference, I commended Professor Peter Bernholz for opening up a previously unexplored area for constitutional inquiry, an area that involves neither comparative analysis of alternative ideal designs nor attention to current constitutional change.[1] Bernholz focussed on the potential for examining the characteristics of political régimes in the course of their historical development with a view towards identification of circumstances that might bring constitutional reform more closely to the realm of the politically possible. Bernholz suggested that there may exist phases in an historical sequence where a temporary convergence of interests makes a constitutional reform possible, settings that the political economist may identify and exploit in normative discourse.

Bernholz was directly concerned with prospects for reform in the monetary constitution, and I shall return to his more recent proposal in Section V. But my reason for reference to the earlier discussion is by way of introduction to the central thesis of this paper. I shall argue that Europe is now presented with an historically unique opportunity to achieve that greatness which has so long remained unrealised. Quite literally, the 1990s offer Europe

From *Europe's Constitutional Future* (London: The Institute of Economic Affairs, 1990), 1–20. Reprinted by permission of the publisher.

1. P. Bernholz, "The Implementation and Maintenance of a Monetary Constitution," *Cato Journal* 6 (Fall 1986): 477–511; J. M. Buchanan, "The Relevance of Constitutional Strategy," *Cato Journal* 6 (Fall 1986): 513–17.

a *once-in-history* opportunity, which, if seized, can promise greatness as defined in a mutually agreed-on dimensionality, but which, if missed, must promise disaster. I do not use the "once-in-history" appellation carelessly. And it is because of the descriptive accuracy of this appellation that I am optimistic about Europe's future. The opportunity is so clear that the folly reflected in failure to seize it is not included even within my public choice perspective on politics and politicians.

A *constitution* that will embody the terms of the contract that the peoples of Europe must make, one with another, individually and as members of separate national-cultural communities, is a *sine qua non* of the whole enterprise. But there are constitutions and constitutions, and the terms of the contract must match the corresponding historical realities. The contract must be such as to ensure mutual gains-from-trade, the ultimate test for which is voluntary agreement on the terms. And such agreement will be forthcoming only if the parties to the contract (individually, both separately and in groups) are effectively guaranteed or protected against exploitation during periods subsequent to ratification.

Europe has a history of conflict among separately identified nation-states, each of which has commanded the loyalties of individual members. It is folly to expect a simple transference of these loyalties to "Europe," conceptualised and romanticised as a supra-nation-state. The only constitutional structure that is consistent with the historically constrained setting of the 1990s is that of a *federal union,* within which members of the separate units co-operate for the achievement of widely recognised and commonly shared objectives, those of internal (intra-European) peace and economic prosperity, within political arrangements that ensure individual liberties and, at the same time, allow for the maximal practicable achievement of standards of justice.

The Europe of the 1990s can learn lessons from the doomed experience of the USA, as Section II sets out in more detail. Europe can, under properly designed and historically relevant constitutional guarantees, ensure that the continuing advantages of the American structure are implemented and preserved while protecting against the tragically originated sequence of events that have undermined the attainment of the American ideal. In order to accomplish this grand design, which is available to Europe at this historical moment, individual participants must rethink and reformulate their public political philosophy. They must recapture something of the mind-set of the

18th century. They must shed all semblance of the Hegelian mythology in which the individual realised himself/herself fully only in the specific political community defined by the collectivity. This fountainhead of ideas for the socialist century, which spawned the "fatal conceit" that socialism represented,[2] must be categorically refuted, repudiated and rejected.

Fortunately, and here again the circumstances of current history must command attention, the momentous events of the 1980s in Eastern Europe and, indeed, throughout the world have served to shift public attitudes towards the philosophical reversals that seem required here. Section III sets out the argument in somewhat more detail.

As the discussion which follows in Section IV indicates, however, more is needed than the attainment of something akin to the 18th-century scepticism about the efficacy of politicised achievement of individuals' values. Such scepticism, standing alone, opens the door to interest-driven exploitation of the historically developed institutions of modern politics, to the epoch of "politics without principle" or, in de Jasay's terminology, "the churning state."[3] A public rediscovery of the romance of *laissez-faire* might suffice, but in Western Europe and America such a shift in attitudes seems beyond the possible. (Eastern Europe is an altogether different matter, and, indeed, the new-found faith in the efficacy of markets, defined in the negation of politicised direction, may well prove sufficient to ensure dramatic threshold leaps in economic well-being.) Again, however, appropriate constitutional design for a federal union can allow the predicted working of interest-driven utilisation of political agency to proceed so long as the limits to damages are constrained by effective competition among the separated polities of the inclusive federation.

In Section V, I illustrate the whole argument by reference to a European monetary constitution, and here I again build on the suggestions advanced by Bernholz. Section VI addresses some of the more general issues in summary, and, specifically, those that are involved in the German question. Finally, Section VII concludes the chapter with a defence of the prediction that Europe will, in the 1990s, establish an effective federal union.

2. F. A. Hayek, *The Fatal Conceit* (London: Routledge & Kegan Paul; Chicago: University of Chicago Press, 1989).

3. A. de Jasay, *The State* (New York: Basil Blackwell, 1985).

The idea of *federalism,* of diversity among separate co-operative communities, of shared sovereignty, of effective devolution of political authority and, perhaps most importantly, of the *limits on* such authority—this idea, enforced within credible *constitutional* guarantees, can be the European source of a fabulous century.

II. United States, 1787—Europe, 1990[4]

Europe in 1990 finds itself historically positioned in a setting analogous to that of the United States in 1787. There are, of course, major differences as well as similarities, and analogies can always be overdrawn. But if attention is placed on the comparison between the unrealised opportunity that is (was) within the possible and the alternative future that failure to seize the opportunity would represent, the similarities surely overwhelm the differences.

In 1787, the citizens of the separate states in the American confederation shared the common experience of successful conflict with a colonial ruling government and, also, the failed effort at economic integration by the independent sovereign polities. To James Madison and his compatriots at Philadelphia, the confederation among the separate states was not enough, and the future prospect was one of continuing interstate economic conflict, described by economic autarky in a setting of increasing vulnerability of the separated states to external enemies. What was needed was a *constitution,* a set of rules that would restrict the sovereign authority of the states over citizens, and, at the same time, would establish a *central government* that would also command, directly, the loyalties of citizens.

Madison's grand design for the American federal union succeeded in its objective of creating and maintaining an open economy over the whole territory of the several states. The American economy, the effective extent of the market, came to be co-extensive with the external boundaries of the central government. Freedom of trade in goods, freedom of migration of persons, freedom of movement for capital, a common monetary unit—these characteristics ensured that the division of labour would be exploited to an internal maximum. And America, predictably, became rich.

---

4. For a paper that treats the subject matter of this section at length, see P. Aranson, "The European Economic Community: Lessons from America," paper for a conference in Aix-en-Provence (Emory University, Atlanta, Ga., 1989, duplicated).

But Madison's grand design for the federal union failed in its less recognised but ultimately much more important objective, that of limiting the range and scope of political authority over the liberties of citizens. In 1787, concern was centred on the potential abuses of authority by the separated states; the anti-Federalists were unsuccessful in raising effective concerns about the potential authority of the central or federal government. After all, citizens of the states were creating a new government, the delegated powers of which were to be severely circumscribed. And, further, even as it exercised these delegated powers, Montesquieu's separational scheme was expected to provide further checks on over-extension. Madison's philosophy of federalism did not allow him even to dream of a federal Leviathan.

To the Founders in 1787, the fact that the citizens of the separate states were involved in creating a central government that would itself commence to share sovereignty with these creating states more or less carried with it the ultimate right of citizens in the separate units to secede from the federal union so established. And, indeed, had the question of secession been raised at all in the initial debates on the formation of the union, representatives of all the states would have dismissed it since the answer was, to them, self-evident. Without an implicit acceptance of an ultimate right to secede, to opt out, to exercise the exit option, the constitutional agreement hammered out in Philadelphia in the hot summer of 1787 would never have come into being at all.

If the advantages of economic union are so great, why should secession ever come to be in the interests of citizens of particular states in the federation? The potentiality of a viable secessionist threat could emerge only if the central government, through its internal decision structure, should take action that differentially damaged citizens of the separate states or regions within its territory. Should the central authority remain within the limits of actions defined by the "general interest" of all its citizens, an effective argument for secession could never emerge from considerations of economic interest. This relationship may be stated obversely: the threat of potential secession offered a means of ensuring that the central government would, indeed, stay within those boundaries of political action defined by the general interests of all citizens in the inclusive territory.[5]

---

5. For a technical argument, see J. Buchanan and R. Faith, "Secession and the Limits of Taxation: Towards a Theory of Internal Exit," *American Economic Review* 77 (December

We may ask the hypothetical question: If the American constitutional agreement of 1787 should have included an effective guarantee that the economy remain open, *externally* as well as internally, would the secession option have become viable to the coalition of Southern states in 1860? We can agree on the direction of effect. Secession from the federal union would have seemed less desirable to Southerners than, in fact, was the case in the presence of central government restriction on external trade.

I do not neglect the critical importance of the institution of human slavery for American constitutional history. The immorality of slavery provided the impetus for the formation and maintenance of regional coalitions, conflict among which generated both differentially damaging federal government trade restrictions and created the potential for southern secession, both of which may well have been counter to the strict economic interests of supporting citizenry. I emphasise only that this discussion is not an enterprise in American history but is, instead, an interpretation of some of that history that seems relevant to the European position in 1990.

In this context, Lincoln's decision to fight to preserve union can be viewed as a breaking of the implicit contract that had established the federal structure. The ultimate victory ensured that secession was no longer a viable option for citizens of the separate states, individually or in coalition. In the absence of the threat of the exercise of the exit option, there then existed no effective limit to the expansion of the powers of the central government beyond those embodied in the formalised structure of constitutional rules. It was perhaps inevitable that, sooner or later, these formal limits would be violated, although we may speculate on whether or not the Madisonian structure might have survived in a time when there existed no generalised mind-set similar to that which described the socialist century. In any case, the history has been written. It is mockery to use "federalism" or "federal union" in descriptive reference to the United States of 1990, which is, of course, simply a very large nation-state.

The lessons of the American experience for the Europe of 1990 are clear. The citizens of the separated nation-states face an opportunity to enter into a federal union that can be an instrument for achieving the enormous gains

---

1987): 1023–31; for a general philosophical treatment, see A. Buchanan, "Liberalism and the Right to Secede" (University of Arizona, Tucson, 1989, duplicated).

of economic integration. In this respect, the parallel with the America of 1787 is direct. In the process of establishing an effective federal union, a central political authority must come into being with some sovereignty over citizens in all of the nation-states. But the ultimate powers of this central unit must be reckoned with, and checks must be included in the constitutional contract that defines the federal structure. The formal rules of such a contract will not, however, be sufficient, as the American experience so well demonstrates. There must also be some explicit acknowledgement, in the contract of establishment, of the rights of citizens in the separate units to secede from union, upon agreement of some designated supra-majority within the seceding jurisdiction.

As the American experience suggests, the advantages of union should be such that secession should never become a meaningful alternative for the citizenry of any unit or set of units. This result emerges, however, only if the central political authority is constitutionally prohibited from enacting policy measures that are unduly discriminatory in their impacts on the separate units. Recognition of this potentiality suggests, in turn, that the initial contract should provide guarantees of freedom for both internal and external trade, that is, for trade among all citizens and firms within the inclusive territory of union *and* for trade among citizens-firms within the territory of union and all parties outside these limits insofar as internal policy makes this possible.

III. Public Philosophy for Effective Federal Union

If Europe is to seize its opportunity to constitute a genuine federal union, its citizens must arrive at a philosophical understanding of the relationships among themselves, as individuals, and the collectivities in which they participate as members, both those defined as the historically familiar nation-states and the emergent inclusive Europe, a philosophical understanding that is quite different from that which described the public philosophy of the Hegelian-influenced socialist century. By reference to a "philosophical understanding" or "public philosophy" of citizens, I do not suggest that the disputation of those who call themselves philosophers need reach the level of conscious public awareness. I suggest only that observed attitudes of individuals in confrontation with politically orchestrated alternatives find their origins, at least in part, in some abstracted and idealised model of social inter-action, a model which may remain subconscious and which may, of course, contain internal contradictions.

For well over a century, political entrepreneurs found it profitable to ex-ploit the ideological precept that the individual comes to the full realisation of human potentiality only as a sharing participant in a collective, the aims for which are objectively determinate, whether by the working of the laws of history or by the light of scientific reason. That which was "good" for the individual is defined externally to any internal calculus of personal interest or reason. From this precept followed two direct consequences. First, the range and scope for the exercise of individual autonomy through free and voluntary contractual interaction independent of collectivised control was progressively narrowed. Secondly, decision-making procedures for the col-lective were evaluated in terms of their efficacy in identifying the objectively existent "goodness" or "truth" for all participants. In this setting, it is evident that an informed élite may, even if it need not, be superior in its judgement to any majority coalition of the total electorate.

I have deliberately generalised the capsule description of the prevalent public philosophy of the "Hegelian epoch" to include both Marxian and non-Marxian variants of socialism-cum-collectivism. Central to both was the precept that autonomously derived or originated individual values are superseded by the objectively defined ideal that is potentially attainable only by the collective. The public philosophy of the long socialist century was marked by a dramatic loss of the 18th-century faith in the co-operative-contractual potential released by individual autonomy and by an accom-panying acceptance of faith in the working of collective agency. The naïve romanticism of 19th- and 20th-century socialism may be difficult for some historians of the 1990s to understand. But the history of ideas is marked by an epoch during which politics, defined as the total working of collectivities, was assumed to be characterised by both benevolence and omniscience.

The presupposed superiority of collective, over individual, choice and ac-tion necessarily required that there exist some well-defined collective unit. Socialist direction and control of the use of resources could be implemented only through a collective unit that could meaningfully define the effective boundaries of "the economy." And it was perhaps historical accident that caused attention to be focussed, practically, on the emerging nation-states, and particularly as nationalistic sentiments arose to complement the collectivist attitudinal thrust.

The nation-state, through its political agents, was successful in placing individual citizens in a status of dependency, to varying degrees. This loss of independence was necessarily accompanied by the emergence of an artificial loyalty to the collective, which granted any and all access to economic value. So long as the collectivised structure seemed to work within very broad limits of tolerance, the public philosophy of individuals, as subjects, could hardly have been expected to include consideration of alternative arrangements.

As noted, however, the dependency-induced loyalties to collective agencies were, from the start, artificial. Public attitudes towards collectivist experiments had never matched the romanticised models described by the intellectuals and academicians, as promulgated and elaborated by interest-driven political entrepreneurs. Over the long term, a viable public philosophy for collectivism required a demonstration of tolerably successful performance along with an observation of a tolerably efficient bureaucracy. As we know, neither of these conditions was met, and the second half of the 20th century witnessed an erosion in citizen support, both for highly centralised collectivised régimes and for politicised overreaching in those nation-states that continued to allow considerable scope for individual autonomy.

The failure of the experiments in "democratic socialism" in the 1950s, the Khrushchev revelations of Stalinist terror, the flawed welfare-state extensions of the 1960s, the inadequacies of Keynesian macromanagement in the 1970s, the woeful performance of collectivised economies in meeting the minimal demands of citizens—these events compounded to generate the genuine revolutions of the late 1980s, revolutions that surprised even those who had never been deluded by the Hegelian mythology.

In 1990, the public philosophy of collectivism belongs to an historical epoch that is past. Political entrepreneurs can no longer exploit the Hegelian sublimation of the individual to a collective *zeitgeist* or the Marxian dialectic of class conflict. Citizens, in both Western and Eastern nation-states, are sceptical of politicised, collectivised nostrums for alleged societal ills. Political entrepreneurs move now to exploit the rediscovered precepts of liberty and autonomy. Although displaced by two centuries from its origins, the public philosophy that can make European federal union a reality seems well on the way to being in place in 1990, giving credence to my claim that Europe does, indeed, have its once-in-history opportunity.

IV. Politicisation, Profits and Rules for a Competitive Constitutional Game

I have suggested that the public philosophy required for European federal union must embody considerable scepticism about the efficacy of collective arrangements to produce economic value, and notably as authority is lodged in nation-states. A socialist ideology could never countenance the genuine diminution of sovereignty that nation-states must experience, a diminution reflected in some transference to a supra-national central unit, to "Europe," and the more important transference to the free play of competitive forces operating across and beyond national boundaries. I have suggested, in Section III, that such a required shift in public philosophy is well on the way to becoming a reality of the 1990s.

The implementation of this public philosophy in the effective establishment of a federal union faces the formidable task of superseding the institutional history. Much more is required here than the shift in ideas. Full recovery of the 18th-century mind-set concerning the proclivity and prospects of politics and politicians to "do good" would not suffice to erase two centuries of experience, during which people came to seek out private profits or rents through manipulation of the political-governmental-bureaucratic structure, and, in the process, learned tools of a trade unheard of in earlier times. For well over a century, and throughout the world, private profits have been made at public (citizens') expense. We should hardly expect the rent-seekers to be deterred by any shift in the ideological currents.

As I have stated in a summary title for a different lecture, "socialism is dead, but Leviathan lives on." Or, if you choose, substitute the word "mercantilism" for "Leviathan" in the sentence. The attempts by well-organised interest or pressure groups to use political means to secure differential gains at the expense of the general polity-economy will not disappear in the post-socialist epoch, and, indeed, such attempts may prove even more successful in the absence of an articulated collectivist alternative. Public scepticism of politics and politicians has not been accompanied by a re-acquisition of faith in *laissez-faire,* in the efficacy of markets when left alone within a framework of law.

We seem to have come full circle to the setting confronted by Adam Smith in 1776, when he felt it necessary to demonstrate the fallacies in the argument that wealth is enhanced by particularised political intervention into the workings of markets. But, for citizens of Europe, there is a difference worthy of notice. For a large national economy, such as the United States, we are indeed facing the same task as that addressed by Adam Smith, as I have argued elsewhere.[6] It becomes imperative that the interest-driven political interferences with markets be constitutionally restricted. But Europe confronts a setting that will permit the rent-seeking pressures of modern democratic politics to be finessed, while, at the same time, ensuring that the damages inflicted by such pressures will be limited.

The "European difference" here lies, of course, in the juxtaposition of the historically familiar exercises of rent-seeking pressures *within* nation-states and the prospect for a constitution of federal union that will ensure *competition* among producers and consumers of goods and resources across the territory that encompasses the several nation-states. This setting makes possible the achievement of economic integration, and the promise of substantial wealth enhancement, without any necessity for direct political confrontation with those groups *inside* the separate national units that seek to remain inside the protection of mercantilist restriction. The independent efforts of interest groups, as they operate on and through the political processes within separate national economies, need not be explicitly prohibited by the constitution of the federal union. Nor need the responses of majority legislative coalitions to such efforts be expressly limited. So long as individuals and associations (firms) are protected by the constitution of the federal union in their liberties to purchase and to sell both producers' and consumers' goods freely throughout the territory of the union, particularised interferences with internal economic relationships within a single national unit will be policed with reasonable effectiveness by the forces of cross-national

6. J. M. Buchanan, "Constitutional Imperatives for the 1990s," in *Thinking about America: The United States in the 1990s,* A. Anderson and D. Bark, eds. (Stanford: Hoover Institution, 1988), 253–64.

competition. Politically orchestrated regulatory activity will tend to be restricted to that which increases overall efficiency, as this criterion may be defined by the preferences of citizens.

The "European difference" at this stage of history that I have emphasised here also remains important in that it facilitates a relatively painless transition for the institutionally relevant public bureaucracy. Existing agencies of nationally separate bureaucratic authority can be kept in place without nominal removal of their specific function to regulate specific sectors. There need be no overt shift of bureaucratic oversight authority from Bonn, London, Paris or Rome to Brussels. The separate national bureaucracies can continue to exist and to operate, but their genuine authority to exploit the citizenry will be forestalled, again by the competitive forces imposed by the constitutional guarantees of open markets across the federal union.

V. A Monetary Constitution for Effective European Union

The theme of this chapter, and especially of Section IV above, can be illustrated by reference to the monetary reforms necessary for effective economic integration. Clearly, such integration is not possible if central or reserve banks of the separate nation-states continue to exercise autonomous fiat-issue powers under legal structures akin to those in existence in 1990. This proposition holds regardless of the degree of political independence of the separate central banks. Monetary "integration" is a necessary element in a more comprehensive programme for effective European economic union. A change in the monetary "constitution" of each of the co-operating nation-states is required, as has already been widely acknowledged.

If the opportunity to achieve effective federal union is to be seized, however, attention must be paid to the particular design of the institutional reforms to be proposed, discussed and, ultimately, implemented. If the sort of institutional change suggested should be such as to facilitate the desired economic integration but, at the same time, it should fail to embody protection against undesirable consequences along other dimensions, generalised arguments in support of integration may be weakened, if not destroyed. If the fiat-issue autonomy of the separate central banks is simply replaced by fiat-issue autonomy of a monolithic European central bank, with no constitutionally credible guarantee against instability in the value of the fiat unit, the directional thrust of the argument for change may be reversed.

There are alternative institutional-constitutional monetary structures that would, ideally, facilitate genuine economic integration and, at the same time, contain credible protection against undesired fluctuations in the value of money. Political economists engage in long-continued debates over the relative effectiveness of commodity-based monetary standards, the constitutional rules that dictate rates of growth in base money, and constitutionally guaranteed targeted objectives to be generated by the monetary authorities of the separate nation-states.[7] For the most part, however, these debates involve the examination of the working properties of the idealised arrangements with little or no attention to the problems that arise in bringing about the transition between those arrangements in being and those that are to be achieved.

It is precisely at this point that the inquiry launched by Peter Bernholz, noted earlier, becomes relevant and prompts the question: Given the existence and history of quasi-autonomous, independent central banks of the separate nation-states in Europe, each of which possesses a monopoly of fiat issue within its national territory, does there exist one of the several proposed constitutional alternatives that dominates others when evaluated in terms of the minimisation of transitional problems? In the European setting of 1990, the answer to such a question seems clear, as Bernholz recognises.[8] The monetary arrangements for effective economic integration that must be constitutionally established are those that closely resemble the competing-currency scheme, advanced earlier by F. A. Hayek.[9]

The constitutional provisions required here are simple and straightforward, and they operate directly on the legal relationships among persons and

7. H. G. Brennan and J. M. Buchanan, *Monopoly in Money and Inflation,* Hobart Paper No. 88 (London: Institute of Economic Affairs, 1981).

8. P. Bernholz, "Institutional Requirements for Stable Money in an Integrated World Economy," paper for London Monetary Conference on Global Monetary Order (University of Basel, Switzerland, 1990, duplicated).

9. F. A. Hayek, *Denationalisation of Money,* Hobart Paper (Special) No. 70 (London: Institute of Economic Affairs, 1976, 1978).

only indirectly on the operation of the monetary authorities. Citizens of Europe, of each and all of the separate nation-states of the federal union, must be legally-constitutionally allowed to transact affairs, to make contracts enforceable in their own courts, in the monetary unit issued by the central bank of *any* of the nation-states of the union, including the discharge of all monetary obligations, and specifically the payment of taxes to any and all political authorities. If this right of each citizen is constitutionally protected, and explicitly so in a set of constitutional rules for Europe, there need be *no* accompanying directive to central banks included in the constitution. These banks, as they are separately organised in the nation-states, can continue to operate in nominal independence and autonomy, in accordance with policy criteria of their own choosing, and subject to whatever domestic pressures may arise in the separate states.

The potential competition among the central banks of the separate nation-states provides the disciplinary pressure that will offset the inflationary proclivity of fiat-issue authorities. Because individual citizens are constitutionally guaranteed the right to make enforceable contracts in any monetary unit of the union, an attempt by a single central bank, as a politicised agency, to levy an inflation tax on residents within the national territory would be doomed to failure. And predicting such results, no central bank will act to ensure that its own money issue falls into disuse.

Under this set of monetary arrangements, the bureaucracies of established central banks remain in place; no new bureaucracy of a "European" central bank need be organised. Citizens will, presumably, continue to use nationally issued fiat currencies, as well as nationally designated units of account, for the bulk of domestic economic transactions. Over some period of transition, cross-national transactions might tend to be made in the monetary unit of the nation-state with the best repute as a standard of value, as publicly perceived. In the 1990s, this unit might come to be the D-Mark or, if Switzerland is a member of the federal union, the Swiss franc. As citizens come to recognise the value of their right to contract in any unit, however, there need be no continuation of a single dominant unit for cross-national transactions.

Constitutional protection against collusion on the part of the separate central banks in the union would, of course, be necessary.

VI. European Federalism, German Unity and the Opening of Eastern Europe

To this point, the momentous events of 1989 have not entered into my discussion of Europe's constitutional opportunity, and, further, no change in the argument would have been dictated had 1989 simply not happened. But the revolutions in Eastern Europe *did* take place in 1989, and any treatment of a prospective European federal union must, at a minimum, attempt to assess the influence of these changes. I shall examine separately the effects of two related issues, as these may bear on prospects for Europe's seizure of its once-in-history opportunity. I shall, first, discuss briefly questions of German re-unification. I shall then discuss, more generally, the predicted effects of the opening of Eastern European economies to increased economic interaction with Western Europe and other parts of the world.

In a Europe historically described by the existence of autonomous, *fully sovereign* nation-states, whether or not these units are observed to co-operate in economic, environmental, political, social and military matters, the lesson of history is surely one that prompts concern about the potential imbalance that might be created by a straightforward merger of the two Germanies. Self-determination, as an extension of the liberal principle of voluntary agreement among the parties directly involved, is acceptable only to the extent that significant spillover effects on other parties are absent. But it is important to recognise that the potential harms that a unified Germany could impose on other Europeans emerge largely, if not totally, from the maintenance of the Hegelian mind-set that presumes nation-states to exert full and undivided sovereignty over their resident citizens.

The federalised alternative, in which sovereignty is genuinely shared, did not enter into the political consciousness in the socialist-collectivist century, a consciousness that accepted the necessity of a monolithic, centralised control over economic and social relationships. In the post-socialist mind-set that seems ready to emerge, in Europe as elsewhere, federal union for Europe becomes a real prospect. And with a genuine federal structure of governance, the bases for the fears of a dominant Germany are substantially reduced. If the constitution for Europe that establishes the federal union effectively ensures that any national unit, be it large or small, must remain open to the competitive forces that operate over all the inclusive territory of the union, why should, say, the citizen of Portugal be concerned much about the size of his nation-state relative to that of Germany?

As noted earlier, however, residual fears may remain that a large and unified Germany would ultimately seek secession from any European federalism established. The costs of secession due to the shrinkage in market size would be relatively small for a sufficiently large nation-state. Empirically, it is difficult to estimate how substantial such fears of future German secession may be among the European citizenry of the 1990s. If this barrier seems sufficient to prevent the establishment of European union, German political entrepreneurs should begin to consider the incorporation of East Germany as a separate member of the European federal union, without overt re-unification with West Germany.

Again, it should be recognised that the generalised German thrust or urge for re-unification stems, in part, from the collectivist mind-set imposed by the Hegelian mythology. In the public philosophy attuned to the realities of European federal union, the political dimension of the nation-state matters relatively little. If the nation-state, as organised, is to possess much less authority than that assumed by the collectivist-socialist model, there need be, on the one hand, less fear of dominance by large units, and, on the other, less demand for inclusion in the large units by those peoples historically associated territorially, culturally or linguistically.

The opening of Eastern Europe to increased market-like relationships with other parts of the world, and notably with Western Europe, enhances the prospect that a European federal union, as established, will itself remain more open to trade with citizens of non-member states than might otherwise have been the case. A closed European union, post-1992, which has been predicted by some anti-Federalists and some American critics, seems less likely to be realised, subsequent to the revolutionary events of 1989.

As noted earlier, there is a persuasive argument in support of constitutional guarantees for free trade both internally and externally, that is, both among the nation-states of the federal union and between the union and other countries of the world. The internal free trade area may be sufficiently large to capture most if not all of the scale advantages of an extended market. But freedom for external trade serves the equally important function of ensuring that internal political coalitions among majorities of the separate member nation-states will not successfully exploit minorities, and especially as concentrated in particular member-units. A federal union made up of Western European member-states that would have confronted a closed Eastern Europe, as seemed to be the prospect prior to 1989, might have succumbed to the protectionist temptations to discriminate against trade with America and the Far East. But, post-1989, with Eastern European prospects for trade in goods, migration of labour, and outlets for investment open, the internal political incentives should have shifted substantially in favour of leaving the European market open externally.

Citizens of Western Europe, when considering themselves as participants in the grand design for effective federal union, do not seem likely to support the formation of a closed trading area that would, itself, provide incentives for Eastern European economic and political isolation, and especially when there may exist prospects for including new members of the federal union drawn from the nation-states of Eastern Europe.

VII. Will an Effective European Federal Union Become a Reality?

In discussing Europe's constitutional opportunity, I have not carefully separated three different issues. To this point, the *mélange* has involved some consideration of the possibility of federal union, the inferred desirability of implementing such a union within appropriate constitutional guarantees and, finally, prediction that the citizens of Europe will, in the 1990s, seize their once-in-history opportunity. Controversy should arise primarily, if not exclusively, over the third of these elements of the discussion. There is, or should be, widespread agreement to the effect that European federal union is possible and that an appropriately designed constitution can contain guarantees sufficient to ensure that the gains from the integrated and extended market are secured while, at the same time, the liberties of all individuals of member-units are expanded. From this generalised agreement, the normative thrust in support of establishment of such union follows as a necessary consequence. In what follows in this section, I shall presuppose that the first two elements of the discussion are accepted. I shall limit further discussion to the third, that is, to *prediction*.

I have predicted that citizens of the several nation-states of Western Europe, acting through their existing political agents and processes, will take advantage of the constitutional opportunity that this moment in history offers to them. A European federal union will be established in the 1990s, with constitutional guarantees that will prevent the emergence of a monolithic "Europe," as a central political unit, that would take on control and regulatory functions characteristic of the socialist-collectivist régimes during the historical epoch that is ending. Existing national units will not be reduced to the status of provincial administrative districts or to subordinate positions resembling those occupied by the American states in the post-Lincoln United States.

Those who have predicted that, upon any movement toward federal union, the central state, "Europe," must assume critical dominance, and that Brussels, or the Brussels bureaucracy, will reduce national political agencies to submission are, I think, wrong. I base my contrary prediction on the particular convergence of ideas and events at the end of this century. As noted, the romanticised myth of the benevolent and omniscient state came to influence public perception of politics in application to the existence of the separately sovereign nation-states of modern Europe. The romantic myth has been substantially displaced in the public consciousness of the 1990s, and there are no longer philosophers around who promote its revival. Nowhere in the world, East or West, do we find, in the 1990s, the naïve faith in collectivist nostrums that characterised both intellectual and public attitudes for most of the 19th and 20th centuries.

A central European state that would come to share sovereignty with the separate national member-units in a federal union, could not, therefore, be expected to capture and to command loyalties even remotely akin to those exploited so tragically by the nation-states of the last two centuries. The central polity of Europe, in a federal structure, would be required to emerge, grow and survive in an attitudinal climate that embodies generalised scepticism about both the motives of political agents and the workings of political institutions, at all levels. An additional difficulty that would be faced by a central European state in seeking to take on powers reserved to member-polities in a constitutional federal union lies in the continued residues of sentiment defined by shared historical experience, by cultural, linguistic and ethnic homogeneity. Citizens of European federalism will, indeed, come to think of themselves as "Europeans," but they will scarcely stop thinking of themselves as British, French, German or Italian. Brussels, as the capital city of the federal union, would be expected to be more like Bern, in the Swiss confederation, than like Paris, in post-Napoleonic France.

My prediction may, of course, be falsified. If the proponents of federal union have not themselves fully escaped from residual socialist failures to understand the efficiency-generating forces of competition, both in markets for goods and among separately existing units in a federal system, they may advance nightmare versions of a regulatory "Brusselsisation" that would prove totally unacceptable to those who are reluctant to surrender any shares in national sovereignty. And the power of the incentives offered to prospective rent-seekers by any prospective establishment of a Europeanised bureaucracy should never be underestimated. Excessive Europe-wide regulations, controls, fiscal harmonisation, fiat-issue monopoly and so on would, of course, destroy much of the gain that economic integration might promise. In this case, the failure of the whole effort would be reflected in pressures from the separate national units to secede, if indeed the federal union itself should ever come to be established. Reversion to the *status quo* prior to the 1990s becomes the scenario of failure.

The task of designing, in detail, the *constitution* for an effective federal union for Europe is formidable, and this task has scarcely been commenced. But I emphasise again that the opportunity is in place; the time is ripe. Europe waits for its own James Madison who understands the constitutional economics of competition and who, at the same time, appreciates the nuances of persuasive argument, bargaining and compromise required to generate agreement among apparently divergent interests.

Europeans, generally, must be convinced that establishment of a constitutionally defined federal union is a positive-sum movement for all parties. Finally, to end this chapter where it started, Europeans generally, including the James Madison of the 1990s, must recognise the propitiousness of this moment in the world's history.

National Politics and
Competitive Federalism
Italy and the Constitution of Europe

In this chapter, I propose to examine, in a general and abstract sense, the constraints that are placed on the autonomy of a single political unit by its membership in an effective federal union or federalism that is described basically or primarily by an integrated and open economic nexus. Italy's membership in the emerging federalism of Europe becomes the obvious exemplar for my analysis here, even if detailed interpretations of the pre-Maastricht, Maastricht and post-Maastricht institutional prospects are not within my ken.

Italy's "constitutional interest" in the European federalism seems to me, as an external observer, to be unique. To summarize my conclusion at the outset, let me say that Europe and Europeanization offer to the Italian citizenry the necessary opportunity for the implementation of internal reforms without which Italian politics and politicians might continue the regime of fiscal profligacy well into the next century. Italian citizens-voters face a rare opportunity to put their fiscal house in order, as their political leaders are forced into fiscal responsibility, perhaps "kicking and screaming" on behalf of their special-interest constituencies, but moving nonetheless in the directions dictated by considerations of the general interest. In my view, far too much attention has been given, in the post-Maastricht discussions, to the need to constrain the powers of the potential federal authority of Brussels

From *Post-Socialist Political Economy: Selected Essays* (Cheltenham, U.K.: Edward Elgar, 1997), 243–53. Reprinted by permission of the publisher.

Material in this chapter was first presented in Catania, Sicily, in December 1994.

relative to the constraining influence on national politics and politicians that such federal authority might itself exert.

Supranational Economic Integration and Limits on National Sovereignty

Let me first define some terms, and, as economists always do, let me set up a model that will facilitate analysis and discussion. I want to examine the relationship between the range and extent of "the economy" or "the market" on the one hand and the range and extent of "the polity" on the other. My particular focus is on the problems that arise when the economic nexus is more extensive than the political nexus and not vice versa.

In one sense, of course, the economic nexus is world-wide; at least some markets are world markets in the true sense and would remain so almost regardless of political boundaries. And, in yet another sense, some economic relationships remain very localized; some markets are necessarily local. I want to cut through possible ambiguity here and stipulate that for my purposes, I shall presume that the size of the economic nexus is well defined by the limits within which economic or trading relationships *may* take place without politicized interferences. And the specific object for attention is the setting in which this economic nexus includes within its territorial dimensions several separately organized political communities, separate "nations," each of which has a history of national autonomy or independence.

The economy is characterized by freedom of trade in goods and services, by freedom of movement for persons and resources, including labour and capital, throughout the territorial limits. The necessary institutional structure is described as competitive, although, within limits, "public" as well as "private" ownership may be present. But there must be freedom of entry and exit into and out of all relevant productive and distributive processes. I shall leave aside analyses of possible economic interactions between persons or organizations inside this economy and persons and organizations beyond the defined limits. In other words, the trade that is external to the federalism is not under discussion here.

It is necessary to specify precisely how political authority (or "sovereignty") is divided as between the separate national political units within the federal union or federalism and the central political authority of the fed-

eralism itself (the "federal government"). I shall analyse that setting in which
the central authority is severely restricted; it is constitutionally empowered
only to enforce the guarantees for openness across the whole economy, to
ensure that trade and resource flows across national boundaries are not restricted or protected by actions of national political units. This central government authority is minimal, and the authority mirrors in effect the results
that would emerge if the separated national units should join in a genuine
free-trade zone, with some full enforceable guarantee against the violation of
terms by the autonomous units. Also, and importantly, this model becomes
descriptive of an integrated economy as driven by forces of technology coupled with a psychological shift in public attitudes away from nationalism *per
se* and towards supranational loyalties. It does not seem unrealistic to suggest
that the Europe of the late 1990s and early 2000s will be described by some
combination of these institutional forms.

In the setting stipulated, the separate national polities—the nation-states—
retain authority over all elements of potential policy except those that allow
overt interference with the free flow of goods, services and resources across
national borders, as within the federalism. I want to analyse the internal and
indirect constraints that membership in the integrated and open economy,
within the territory of the federalism, will impose on the political choices of
the member nation-states. For example, how will membership in an open
and integrated economy constrain national choices with respect to monetary
and fiscal policies? How will such membership affect national choices to provide genuinely public goods financed by general taxes? How will membership in the federal union with a supranational economy affect the ability of
national political units to implement transfer schemes through which some
citizens are taxed to finance payments to others?

The Protective State and the Productive State

These questions may be addressed by classifying political activities, the actions taken on behalf of the national unit, "the state," into several sets, as
these have been discussed in basic political philosophy. There is, first, that set
of activities that are necessary to define the rules of social interaction—activities that provide the framework for any economic and social relationships
between and among individuals and groups. This set includes the familiar

requirements for a legal order, those institutions that allow for the definition and enforcement of claims to valued endowments, both personal and non-personal. Private or separate property and the enforcement of contracts of exchange in rights to property—these are the recognized bases for social order, commonly recognized to be necessary elements in what I have called "the protective state," and which others have variously called "the night-watchman state" or "the minimal state."[1]

These most basic of all political functions are important with reference to the central questions examined here. In an integrated supranational economy, what would happen if the separate national units should differ widely among themselves in the performance of the protective-state role? Suppose, for example, that the legal-political authority in one national state does not protect persons and properties to the standards that are descriptive of the other nations in the federalism. Suppose that fraud, theft, brigandage, assault, plunder and other intrusions on persons, endowments, claims and contracts are more widespread in one polity than in others.

The economic results are easy to predict. Owners of productive resources will invest less in the national unit that fails, relatively, in its role of the protective state, at least less than they would otherwise invest. Rates of return would necessarily include a margin for losses that need not be included at all in more "orderly" units. Because of the relative shortfall in capital investment, competitively determined wage rates for comparable labour capacities will tend to be lower in the less orderly units. The differential in wage levels will, in turn, offer incentives for an outmigration of workers to other units in the free-trade zone. In the economic equilibrium across the whole territory of the integrated market, the less orderly unit pays for its political-legal failure by generating a lower-valued product than its basic resource potential would make possible.

But how will membership in the integrated economy of a supranational federalism affect this result, which would seem to emerge whether or not the national state in question enters in the inclusive economic nexus? Membership in the more inclusive market—one that extends across national political boundaries—will generate a more dramatic differential as among levels of

1. James M. Buchanan, *The Limits of Liberty: Between Anarchy and Leviathan* (Chicago: University of Chicago Press, 1975).

national product and, for this reason, will impose relatively higher costs on persons who remain in nonproductive roles in the less orderly unit. Owners of productive resources—labour and capital alike—can act to ensure against the exploitation inherent in the failure of the state to fulfill its protective function; they can do so by migrating to more orderly polities within the federalism. These owners need not remain among the continuing net losers under the failures of the protective state. Those citizens who do not, or cannot, take advantage of the possibilities offered by the widened economic nexus must lose out in the equilibrating process. They do so because they cannot secure benefits from the exploitation of those resource owners who can, and do, act on the opportunities offered by exit.

As this prospect comes to be recognized, the natural proclivity of governments might seem to point towards politically orchestrated interferences with the flow of resources beyond national boundaries, efforts that would, of course, violate the basic terms of federalized integration. And it is precisely to prevent such efforts that a strong, if limited, central federal authority is presumably established. Further, the prospect that such efforts may come to dominate the internal politics of nations undermines the argument to the effect that a supranational free-trade zone, without a central authority, may be a superior institutional form.

The analysis of the effects of possible differential performance in the role of the protective state by the separate national units in a supranational economy, as organized politically in a federal union or federalism, can be repeated, more or less without change, for the relative performance of nations in their roles as productive states. The classical Italian writers on the *scienze delle finanze,* and especially Antonio de Viti de Marco, stressed that the state can be productive as well as protective. Political units can provide services that are equivalent to inputs into the production of goods and services, and these inputs enhance the value productivity of complementary privately supplied inputs. In modern terminology, the governmental or political supply and financing of elements of economic infrastructure can, possibly, make the privately organized sector of the economy more rather than less efficient in producing final goods and services.

The ultimate test lies, of course, in the comparative results. And the primary, indeed, the central, effect of economic integration into a supranational nexus is the direct demonstration of the comparative political efficiencies of the separate political units—the separate member states. If a single nation-state, through the complex operation of its internal political institutions, succeeds in offering a mix of tax-financed public goods (infrastructure) that is economically more productive than its national counterparts (competitors), private investment will become marginally more productive in that unit, thereby providing an attractor for the inflow of capital and, ultimately, labour. By contrast, if a single nation-state essentially defaults in its productive-state role, through the tax-financing of resource-wasting, "public" projects that affect private productivity negatively, its citizens must lose out, relatively, in the competitive federalism, with the losses observable in net resource outflows to other units in the federalism.

The competition among the separate national units within the supranational federal arrangement that defines the inclusive territory for the economic nexus will, over time, tend to produce an observable "regularization" and "harmonization" of the economic activities geographically classified as located in the separate states. The relative productivities of publicly supplied infrastructure will tend towards some degree of equality. The national politics that fail to meet the competitive standards determined by the operation of competitive national politics in other units will be effectively forced to modify the mix of public-goods supply. But note in particular here that such regularization and harmonization *emerge* as a result of a potential and ongoing competitive process; these results do not, and cannot, emerge from dictates laid down in advance by the central authority, since this authority itself has no means of knowing what quality and quantity of infrastructure investment by the political units will prove, in the end, to be economically most efficient.

The Monetary-Fiscal Roles for the Nation-States in a Supranational Federalism

I shall not indulge in the taxonomic argument concerning whether or not the monetary-fiscal arrangements of a national state should be classified within the activities of the protective or the productive state. In any case, these monetary-fiscal arrangements warrant special consideration since it is the monetary-fiscal autonomy of the national units that may seem to be most directly affected by membership in a supranational federalism with an integrated economy. Recall that in my discussion here I do not stipulate any institutional centralization of monetary-fiscal authority. The separate nation-states, as separate polities, are at liberty to pursue internally chosen monetary-fiscal policies. I concentrate attention only on the indirect constraints imposed on such policy choices by the guarantee of openness of the market across the whole territory of the inclusive federalism.

We may presume that each of the separated nation-states would organize its monetary operation through the institution of a central bank that issues a national currency. The monetary unit of a national political unit is presumed to be freely exchangeable, at floating rates of exchange, against all other national monies in the federalism. (I shall not model the workings of fixed-rate schemes akin to the European EMS.) Internally politicized interferences with the movement of financial assets among the separate parts of the federalism are effectively prohibited by the central federal authority.

In this setting, if a single national central bank allows its own currency, and related instruments, to expand at rates that are higher, relative to internal demands, than comparable rates in competing units of the federalism, internal rates of inflation will exceed those observed elsewhere. Relatively higher inflation in a single nation-state will produce two predicted effects. There is empirical evidence to the effect that higher rates of inflation are accompanied by decreased predictability in the value of the monetary unit. This will increase the riskiness of investment and thereby reduce the flow of resources towards the inflating nation. Second, the indirect tax levied on all holders and users of assets defined in nominal money units will tend to reduce the net productivity of all resource investment, human and nonhuman, unless the tax proceeds are channelled into genuinely productive infrastructure spending. And although there is no necessary linkage here, it seems unlikely that government outlays financed by monetary expansion will be productive in economic value terms.

Monetary expansion by a national central bank is related directly to the budgetary stance of the government of the political unit. If internal political choices are made that generate rates of outlay in excess of projected revenues produced by explicitly legislated taxes, the budgetary deficit emerges more or less as a residual that must be financed, either by explicit issue of public debt or by money creation. As debt-financed deficits continue over a sequence of periods, and as the size (and consequent interest charges) of the national debt mounts, pressure increases for money creation by the central bank. Regardless of the organizational-institutional structure, the pronounced objective of maintaining some proximate stability in the value of the monetary unit becomes enormously more difficult as budget deficits increase and as these deficits come to describe permanent political reality.

These relationships between monetary and fiscal actions hold independent of the possible congruence or incongruence of the size of the polity and the size of the market nexus. But they clearly become more acute, and more readily apparent, in the setting that we are examining, where the separate national political units are smaller in territorial reach than the inclusive free-trade and resource-flow zone that is coincident in size with the supranational federal union. All government spending must be financed, one way or another, and any national government that spends nonproductively, relative to other units in the federalism, will reduce the rate of return on resource investment, with the resultant retardation in the relative rate of growth.[2] If the spending is financed, either by explicit public borrowing or by money creation, the differential between the rates of return between the "offending" nation-state and its political competitors in the federalism is further increased. The competitive pressures among the separate member units in an integrated economy tend to act strongly towards inducing both central bankers and governments to limit severely the relative disparities between their own and others' behaviour patterns in monetary-fiscal matters. (Waves of competitive inflation-financed deficit regimes cannot totally be ruled out, but the presence of even one national unit that adheres to "responsible patterns" of policy would make such situations unlikely to occur.)

Once again, however, the point to be emphasized is that these pressures towards regularization, towards relative conformity in policies as among the separated polities in the federalism, emerge from the competitive process itself. An empowered central federal authority is neither required nor desirable to secure the results. (In this context, some of the Maastricht Agreement's requirements about national debt and deficit limits reflect simple misunderstanding of the workings of the competitive process.)

---

2. I am, of course, assuming that the monetary framework operates to ensure macroeconomic sufficient stability. Hence, there are no Keynesian-like arguments for fiscal stimulus.

The Transfer State

To say that a government spends nonproductively is not equivalent to the charge that either the spending is frivolous or the decision to spend was not motivated by worthy purpose. "Nonproductive" in the context used here refers only to inefficacy in generating final product as evaluated in the marketplace and as measured in the national accounts. Nonproductive spending includes, therefore, all spending on transfers, whether these be directed towards the welfare support of those deemed deserving: the young, the old or the poor. And it also includes those transfers to members of constituencies that succeed in manipulating the political game to their advantages in securing transfer rents, for little or no legitimate purpose.

All political units engage in transfer spending of all varieties, and they finance this spending variously through some combination of taxation, debt and money creation. The issue of relevance to our discussion involves the relative importance of the transfer sector in the separate member units of the supranational federalism. If a single nation-state, among the competitive set of states, attempts to use the governmental budget to implement transfer levels that are significantly larger (as shares in national product) than other units, the net productivity of resource investment will be reduced, with the same consequences traced out earlier with reference to other politically generated differentials in resource returns. Regardless of the purpose of the transfer activity, whether in furtherance of genuine welfare or of self-seeking group interests, the combined revenue-raising–revenue-spending package must reduce the share of product value received by the owners of productive inputs, human and nonhuman. And if one of a set of economically interlinked polities gets out of line with its competition along this dimension, it will observe its relative productivity diminishing.

There is, however, a major distinction to be drawn between the effect of interunit competition with respect to transfer spending and the other activities that have been previously examined. Interunit competition within the integrated market nexus tends to force the separate political entities to fulfill their protective-state roles effectively, to provide economically productive infrastructure investment, to maintain monetary stability and to attain fiscal balance, all in a relative sense. Each of these results, as forced upon the competitive nation-states, is intrinsically desirable, provided only that the enhanced value of national product is deemed to be "good." What critic can suggest that the achievement of these objectives is not desired?

Transfer activities are not different in one respect. Competition will put pressure on the separate governments to generate an *economically efficient* set of fiscal transfers. By contrast with the other activities discussed, however, the economically efficient set of transfers may be *socially nonpreferred*. It seems quite possible that citizens in a particular nation-state may (and by some substantial consensus) prefer a level of transfer spending directed towards welfare recipients that is in excess of that level which might be forced on them in an operative supranational federalism. And this result may be more likely if differences in the income levels of the separate nation-states are large. The relatively "rich" nation-states may well choose levels of domestic transfer spending that are beyond the capabilities (and hence the preferences) of citizens in the relatively "poor" units. At the same time, citizens (especially those in the relatively rich units) may be reluctant to cede their autonomous authority over redistributive actions of government to the competitive pressures that membership in an economically integrated federalism implies. To this extent, there may be an argument for explicit harmonization of policies, perhaps to be coordinated through the auspices of the central federal authority—an argument that could scarcely be advanced with reference to the other activities of the separate states.

Even here, however, caution is in order. Transfer activities that describe what Anthony de Jasay has called the "churning state" can scarcely be justified as reflecting the preferences of citizens.[3] These transfers back and forth among and between the politically successful and unsuccessful organized interests cannot be socially preferred in any meaningful and well-understood sense to the economically efficient level of transfers that would be forced upon national politics in an effective competitive federalism. And how are genuine welfare transfers to be distinguished, politically, from the "churning" transfers? Once the grubby realities of national democratic politics are fully embodied in the sometimes idealized models of political redistribution, perhaps the sacrifice of political autonomy in this dimension does not appear large.

---

3. Anthony de Jasay, *The State* (Oxford: Basil Blackwell, 1985).

Italy and the Constitution of Europe

I have sketched out the elementary principles of the relationships between the political independence of the separate national governments and membership in an integrated economy that includes the territory of several such polities and which is politically organized as a competitive federalism with a limited central authority. I have not tried to use modern Europe as a descriptive or a normative example, but the parallels are clear. I now want to move to the second part of my title and to relate the argument specifically to Italy and to the Italian citizenry, while again emphasizing my illiteracy on matters of institutional history or current policy discourse.

There are many reasons why the citizens of a defined sovereign polity—a nation-state—might consider membership in a supranational federalism with a central authority that would enforce freedom of commerce over the whole territory. Since Adam Smith, we have known that the division of labour depends on the extent of the market and that resource productivity depends, in turn, on the division of labour. Citizens of all of the countries of Europe, whether these countries are large, medium or small in size, must expect to reap benefits from genuine economic integration, with the citizens of the relatively smaller units promised relatively greater differential gains. The geopolitical objective of securing protection by means of an included Germany may dominate the choices of many citizens who do not elevate economic interest to a dominant place.

My indirect emphasis has been on a basis for Italian membership in a federal Europe that is quite different from either the straightforward economic logic of a widened and more inclusive market or the geopolitical logic of an included rather than an excluded Germany. In my interpretation, a primary reason for securing membership in and promoting continued movement towards a genuinely integrated economy organized under a competitive federalism is that this institutional development offers a means of partial escape from the internal or domestic political exploitation suffered by ordinary citizens in the fully autonomous nation-states of nineteenth- and twentieth-century history. The ordinary citizen, of any member country, will, of course, secure benefits from the enlarged market area and may also sense greater security in an inclusive Europe. But this ordinary citizen may be affected much more by the constraints, or limits, that the Europeanization of the economy will place on the powers and authority of the politicians *within* his or her own country, to interfere with his or her life, both economic and otherwise. A competitive federalism can prove to be efficacious in limiting domestic political intrusiveness in ways that no formal constitution can approach. The exit option offered by the widened market is overwhelmingly more significant than the voice option offered by participation in democratic politics. And we should note here that the exit option need be exercised by only a few marginal resource owners in order to yield spillover benefits to all citizens.

I suggest that these relationships may apply with special force to the citizenry of Italy—a citizenry that has possibly been subjected to as much or more exploitation by its own political institutions and politicians than other member units of the emerging European federalism. Italians "need" the European federalism as an indirect constitutional means to force their own politicians to take the actions that are necessary for economic viability. And was it not, indeed, the prospect for Europeanization that in October 1992 forced the Italian government into taking measures that were deemed to be beyond the reach of prior governments?

In general terms, Maastricht was wrongly directed; the provisional agreement reflected far too much of the Delors-Brussels mind-set that concentrates on top-down harmonization and far too little understanding of the efficacy of genuine competition among separate units in a federalism. But, as Maastricht is reevaluated and possibly revised, there remains ample opportunity to move towards a Europe that will be in the interests of all citizens in all of the member states. The latent fear of Brussels' bureaucratic dominance tends to be overemphasized in many of the arguments that have been advanced against Maastricht, and especially by those in the United Kingdom who associate themselves with Mrs. Thatcher's position.

Personally, my own reading of the tea leaves tells me that the Italians, French, Germans and others have passed the psychological threshold. These peoples are Europeans in so many senses that I do not foresee a twenty-first-century Europe made up of autarkic nation-states as of old. Such a future is simply not in the cards. One way or the other, an integrated European economy is well on its way to becoming that which is. My advice and counsel to all Italians, as well as to all citizens in the other potential member countries, is to support, and enthusiastically, the Europeanization of their economies, while, at the same time, keeping a weather eye out for exploitation by all politics and all politicians, whether these be confined within national or supranational institutions. Competition remains, after all is said and done, the most effective element of any constitution that protects liberties.

On a Fiscal Constitution
for the European Union

James M. Buchanan and Dwight R. Lee

1. Introduction

As one of the authors has argued previously, Europe now faces a window of opportunity that may best be described as a "constitutional moment."[1] Only occasionally in the history of a country, or a continent, do circumstances motivate serious consideration of the fundamental rules under which political and economic decisions are made. The 1990s seem to offer such a moment for Europe; the rules defining the political economy both between and within the individual nation-states are being subject to major revision. The European countries are struggling with the trade-off between individual sovereignty-autonomy and subjection to central authority with the potential to insure the community-wide benefits that enforced economic integration can bring. Within the separate countries, political abuses and scandals have also emerged to prompt consideration of reforms aimed at protecting citizens from the excesses of their own national governments.

From *Journal des Economistes et des Etudes Humaines* 5 (June/September 1994): 219–32. Reprinted by permission of the publisher.

The authors wish to thank Robert Batterson of the Center for the Study of American Business at Washington University for his help on this paper.

1. See J. Buchanan, "La fase costituzionale degli anni novanta," *La Vie della Libertà: Il liberalismo come teoria e come politica negli anni novanta* (Rome: Fondazioni Luigi Einaudi, 1993), 25–44 (Italian translation of "The Constitutional Moment of the 1990s"), and J. Buchanan, "Europe's Constitutional Opportunity," in J. Buchanan, K. O. Pöhl, V. C. Price, and F. Vibert, *Europe's Constitutional Future* (London: Institute of Economic Affairs, 1990), 1–20.

The questions are: What is the appropriate trade-off? What are the preferred reforms? Constructive change must be informed by a realistic understanding of the workings of political processes, which includes an appreciation of the strong tendencies within these processes to subvert any reforms that impose genuine responsibility on the exercise of political power.

Ideally, constitutional reform embodies an element of self-enforcement that must continue to operate long after the public scrutiny that describes the constitutional moment has diminished.

In this context, we suggest a particular reform for the financing of the central governmental activities of the European Union. Important government functions must be performed centrally if the citizens of the European Union are to secure the advantages of economic integration, and these functions have to be adequately financed. But *how* the central government of the Union is financed may be more important than the level of financing. Depending on how the central authority in Brussels is financed, that authority can, on balance, be predicted either to enhance or to hamper the general prosperity of Europe. To enhance the general prosperity, the power granted to Brussels must be significant in degree but severely limited in scope, and it must be exercised in a way that both complements and constrains the power of the separate national governments. Our central suggestion is to *deny* the European Union the independent power to tax, which implies that all taxing authority should reside with the member nation-states. The central authority's revenue would be provided by the separate member countries, each of which would be required to transfer a uniform percent of tax revenue locally raised to the central fisc.

Before attempting to explain the advantages to be derived from our proposed revenue-sharing arrangement, it is useful to consider in more detail the potential benefits from a strong central authority in Europe as well as the dangers that must be avoided if those benefits are to be secured.

2. The Promises and the Perils

It is relatively easy to spell out theoretically the advantages that might be realized by the citizens of the individual countries of Europe from membership in a supranational competitive federalism. At their root, these advantages are found in the control of political power. Just as you can fight fire with fire, so it is possible for modern Europe to control potential abuse of political power with political power itself, if the rules defining the constitutional arrangements between the separate nation-states and an inclusive federal authority are properly designed and put in place.

The most obvious advantage from a central political authority in Europe would result from that authority's power to restrict barriers against the flow of resources and goods across national borders, that is, to enforce freedom of commerce over the entire territory. Since Adam Smith, we have known that the division of labor depends on the extent of the market and that resource productivity depends, in turn, on the division of labor. And since David Ricardo, we have known that no matter how productively resources are employed in one country, that country cannot have a comparative advantage in the production of all goods, and can benefit from trade with other countries. Citizens of all of the countries and regions of Europe, whether these countries are large, medium, or small in size, can expect to reap benefits from movements toward genuine economic integration, with the citizens of the smaller units promised relatively greater differential gains.

There is, however, also an indirect advantage from economic integration that, while almost totally overlooked, is every bit as important as the direct gains from greater trade among countries. Within the general rules of a Europe-wide economy, with freedom of entry and exit over the whole territory, enforced by a strong, but constitutionally limited, central authority, a competitive federalism offers a means of partial escape from the *internal* political exploitation suffered by ordinary citizens in any regime of fully autonomous nation-states, whether of the historical nineteenth and twentieth centuries or of any future. The ordinary citizen of any member country will, of course, secure benefits from the enlarged market area and may also sense greater security in an inclusive Europe. But this ordinary citizen may be affected much more by the constraints, or limits, that the Europeanization of the economy will place on the powers and authority of the politicians, *within* his or her own country or region, to interfere with his or her life, both economic and otherwise. A competitive federalism can prove to be efficacious in limiting domestic political intrusiveness in ways that no formal constitution can approach. The exit option offered by the widened market is overwhelmingly more important than the voice option offered by participation in democratic politics. And we should note here that the exit option need be exercised by only a few marginal resource owners in order to yield spillover benefits to all citizens.

Yet things are not so simple as a transfer of power to a supranational political unit for the purpose of guaranteeing that resources will flow across national borders unimpeded, with the subsequent constraints on the exploitative power of domestic national governments. This is an objective well worth pursuing. But it is also a promise that when pursued comes with genuine perils. Centralized government power is, in itself, a power that can be, and almost always has been, abused. Centralizing political authority in the European Union for the purpose of controlling the abuse of political power at national levels offers an opportunity for even greater abuse. An unavoidable reality is that, unless it is explicitly constrained either by formal constitutional limits or by the forces of institutionalized competition, political power always tends to be extended beyond the bounds that seem legitimate upon its conception. Hence, the establishment and enhancement of a European central political authority must be approached with great trepidation, until and unless ways may be found to guarantee against overextension. The fiscal structure that we propose here can do much to offer such guarantees.

3. The Pressure to Centralize

Political power has become increasingly centralized during the twentieth century, as has the size, intrusiveness, and abusiveness of government over the same period.[2] This is not a coincidence. The constant threat of government power is rooted in the fact that political processes allow organized interest groups to communicate their demands for government transfers and privileges more effectively than it allows members of the general public to communicate the costs of those demands. So, when considering an explanation for the centralization of political power, we have to examine how organized groups find their interests affected by such centralization. Organized interest groups, attempting to capture benefits by expanding government, favor increasing the authority of central, as opposed to local, government, and they do so for several reasons.[3]

2. For information on the growth of government centralization in European countries, see R. Vaubel, "The Political Economy of Centralization and the European Community," *Journal des Economistes et des Etudes Humaines*, no. 1 (1992): 11–48.

3. We shall concentrate most of our attention on the centralization of fiscal power even though we recognize that governments possess other powers as well. But the power of

Consider the advantage the concentration of political power offers an organized interest group that is concentrated geographically. More centralization increases the size of the exploitable population. The larger the population, the lower the per-capita cost of any transfer, the greater the rational ignorance and apathy of those paying the bill and, therefore, the less the political resistance. Even if members of an organized interest group are spread over a number of political jurisdictions, with centralization of control over its program having no effect on the number of those in the exploitable population, centralization can still increase the political effectiveness of the interest group. The cost per capita of the interest group's program remains the same after the centralization as before. But under centralization, the cost (saving) of expanding (reducing) the special-interest benefits to those in any one part of the jurisdiction is spread over a larger public which reduces both the political opposition to expanding those benefits and the political support for reducing them.[4] Also, an organized interest group realizes transaction cost advantages from centralization. It is easier to manipulate a few centrally located rent-seeking levers than to deal with a multitude of such levers located at different governmental levels and jurisdictions.

Entrenched politicians and bureaucrats within the individual countries might be expected to strongly oppose centralization. Why would they favor transferring power to the supranational government? But even those whose interests seem tied to the national governments may realize genuine advan-

---

the purse is a fundamental power and one that tends to be positively related to other government powers. As we shall argue, constitutional rules that impose effective constraints on the fiscal powers of government can also serve to restrain some of government's other powers as well. Also, it has been argued convincingly that it is not as easy as commonly thought for governments to circumvent limitations on its own spending by mandating spending by private organizations. See M. Flowers, "The Political Economy of Mandated Spending, *Cato Journal*, no. 2 (1992): 337–47.

4. One could argue that centralization, by creating one large interest group rather than several smaller ones, would reduce the interest group's effectiveness as the individual members' motivation to free ride on the effects of others will increase. This argument cannot be dismissed entirely. But it has to be recognized that there will probably be cooperative efforts between the local interest groups before centralization (indeed, the pressure for centralization will come in large part from such cooperative effort). Therefore, the free-rider problem faced by the "consolidated" interest group will not be likely to increase much, if any, since it was probably operating as a larger group even before the centralization.

tages in having more political power concentrated in an overarching central government. Transferring power from national governments to the central government is not necessarily a zero-sum situation for political operatives. The additional power the central government secures is not necessarily power that the other governments lose. Indeed, centralizing government may increase political overreach of all levels of government.

Consider the advantage for national government politicians when a supranational government assumes more fiscal control over the tax bases of individual countries. The larger the percentage of the total tax bill the central government imposes directly on taxpayers, the less will be the relative differences in tax burdens across different countries and, hence, the less relative advantage taxpayers can potentially realize from transferring physical and human capital in response to differences in country specific tax burdens. The political centralization may offset the tax competition between individual countries that would otherwise reduce the discretionary power of governments. This feature becomes especially important as technological developments make it easier to move, and coordinate the use of, capital throughout the world.[5]

In effect, transferring a power to tax to a supranational government, or increasing this power, is a way for separate national governments to form and enforce a tax cartel, and, thereby, collectively to extract more money from the citizenry. The additional revenue taken by the supranational government will more than offset any reduction in the revenue collected at the national level and can be partially reallocated back to the national governments through revenue-sharing arrangements with all government units securing more of the taxpayers' money.[6] Empirical evidence from both

5. In other words, centralizing the power to tax reduces the Tiebout effect, named after Charles Tiebout, who first formalized the implications of competition between political jurisdictions. See C. Tiebout, "A Pure Theory of Local Expenditures," *Journal of Political Economy* (1956): 416–24. For a discussion of how technological advances are intensifying the Tiebout effect, and forcing more competitive pressures on governments world-wide, see R. B. McKenzie and D. R. Lee, *Quicksilver Capital: How the Rapid Movement of Wealth Has Changed the World* (New York: Free Press, 1991).

6. Under a formal program of revenue sharing in the United States in the 1970s, the revenue-generating capacity of the individual states was enhanced by formulas for revenue allocation that favored those states that continued to raise as much revenue as pos-

the United States and Europe supports the view that centralizing taxing authority increases the tax burden at all levels of government.[7]

If government officials at the national level benefit from centralizing political power, then clearly officials in the supranational government will also benefit directly. Those who work for or expect to work for the central authority have vested interests in expanding agencies and departments. Obviously, the ability to obtain more tax revenue for the central government advances those interests. This is true even when, as indicated above, the central government shares much of its revenue with national governments. Through the control of tax revenues shared with the national governments, the central authority can entice national officials to provide services and demand programs that central authorities control and administer. By offering matching and categorical grants, the central government increases the demand from national authorities for centralized involvement in areas that should be the responsibility of national governments. When national politicians are able to provide, for constituents who can vote them out of office, projects paid for largely by the taxpayers in other countries, a constant demand for excessive and inefficient government spending (all of which enhance the power of central authorities) is assured.

The more centralized the taxing and spending power, the more the political process, responding to special-interest pressures, will reward national governments for pursuing projects worth less than they cost, and the less it will reward them for implementing projects cost-effectively. But regardless of the inefficiencies (or more accurately, because of them), organized groups will demand more and more spending on their programs and push for the centralization amplifying that demand.

---

sible through their own power to tax. See R. B. McKenzie and R. Staaf, "Revenue Sharing and Monopoly Government," *Public Choice* (1978): 93–97.

7. Economists Frye and McKenzie have found that local taxes in the United States increase in response to intergovernment grant programs that make federal revenue available to local government. See E. B. Frye and R. B. McKenzie, "Impact of Federal Aid on State and Local Taxes," working paper, Clemson University, 1983. Relatedly, empirical work by economists Martin and Schmidt show that when municipalities pool the growth of their tax bases, the effect is to expand the level of government expenditures. See D. T. Martin and J. R. Schmidt, "Expenditure Effects of Metropolitan Tax Base Sharing: A Public Choice Analysis," *Public Choice* (1983): 175–86. For similar evidence from Europe, see references in footnote 16 of Vaubel, op. cit.

4. Reverse Revenue Sharing

Given the arguments laid out above, arguments that must yield the prediction that the establishment of a supranational governmental authority may only enhance the overall politicization of economic life at all levels, the normative inference seems clear. The best hope for securing the advantages of genuinely productive economic integration among the European nation-states remains at the level of national politics, where economists' traditional support for free trade zones may occasionally carry the day.

We do not accept this pessimistic prospect, because it is based on a misunderstanding and a lack of appreciation of a genuinely competitive federalism, one that can be deliberately designed and implemented, and one that would be self-enforcing, once put in place. We propose a fiscal structure where the only power to tax resides within the political subunits of the central government, such as the separate nations in Europe or the separate states in the United States. The political subunits should, in turn, be required to "share" with the central government some fixed percentage (which should be uniform over all subunits) of the tax revenue they raise.[8] This fiscal arrangement is the obverse of the revenue-sharing arrangement tried in the United States during the 1970s, and which remains a reasonable characterization of the fiscal relationship between the states and U.S. federal government (where much of the tax revenue obtained by the federal government is returned to the individual states and municipalities in the form of localized grants, programs, and projects). Therefore, we refer to our recommended arrangement as "reverse revenue sharing."

While the reverse revenue-sharing proposal may appear to be a radical re-

---

8. If the revenue-sharing proportion were allowed to be different for different nations, considerable amounts of resources would be expended in rent-seeking attempts by each national government to have its proportion reduced. Such rent-seeking would, of course, be motivated by the desire to free ride on the contributions of others and would likely result in a level of contributions to the central government that is too low from the perspective of the contributing units of government. With the same revenue-sharing proportion imposed on all, and subject to change only by close to unanimous agreement by the member countries, the decision on that proportion is not distorted by free-rider temptations and is more likely to be consistent with generally beneficial outcomes.

form for the United States,[9] the situation for Europe is different. Indeed, the proposal amounts roughly to maintaining one central feature of the fiscal status quo. Currently the central government in Brussels has four sources of revenue: (1) a common duty imposed on industrial imports into the European Union, which is collected by the customs agents of the individual countries but transferred to Brussels; (2) a common duty imposed on agricultural imports into the European Union, and again collected by the individual countries; (3) an assessment of 1.4 percent of the base used by member countries for their value-added tax (VAT) on businesses; and (4) in response to the financial crisis of the mid-1980s, an agreement was reached in 1988 that if the European Union's budgetary requirements exceeded the revenue provided by the above three sources each member country would pay a uniform percentage of its GNP to Brussels.[10]

This fiscal arrangement differs in important ways from that of our reverse revenue-sharing proposal, but the third revenue source is, in its essentials, equivalent to the proposal we advance. The revenue sources (1), (2), and (4) listed above are inconsistent with the scheme that we are here suggesting. Maintaining the present level of decentralization will be no simple task in the face of pressures for explicit fiscal centralization that exist within the European Union, pressures that can be expected to intensify in the coming years. Jacques Delors said in 1988 that "in a decade 80 percent of economic and perhaps fiscal and social legislation will emanate from the [Union]."[11] A commonly heard argument is "that [Union] expenditure programmes will be growing rapidly in future years . . . since parliamentary control over such expenditures cannot be exercized by any individual national parliament, it properly falls to the European Parliament to exercize this function. Thus, the European Parliament should have the specific possibilities to determine the overall size of the budget and all categories of expenditures within the total.

9. The case for reverse revenue sharing in the United States is developed in D. R. Lee, "Reverse Revenue Sharing: A Return to Fiscal Federalism," *Cato Journal*, forthcoming.

10. In 1989 the assessment was imposed and came to 0.1 percent of the GNP of each country. For a more detailed discussion of this revenue source, as well as the others, see G. Peters, "Bureaucratic Politics and the Institutions of the European Community," in *Europolitics*, ed. A. M. Sbragia (Washington, D.C.: Brookings Institution, 1992), 75–122.

11. Quoted in Vaubel, op. cit., 11.

On the revenue side, it would determine the size of contributions under the [Union's] 'own resources,' the source of those contributions (for example, whether VAT or GNP related), as well as gain the power to raise new taxes and to tax and collect directly."[12]

In 1994, the Union sought authority to impose a carbon tax, in the name of environmental protection, which would raise significant amounts of revenue.

We can identify several advantages that a fiscal arrangement along the lines of reverse revenue sharing would produce in resisting the centralizing pressures within the European Union. Reverse revenue sharing can be an important constitutional means to insure the type of economic and political competition among European member countries that allows for a strong but limited central government, and motivates a rational allocation of authority between the central and national governments. By facilitating a truly competitive European federalism, reverse revenue sharing can help protect the citizens of the individual countries against the excesses of the central government, and also against those of their national governments.[13]

4.1. OPEN MARKETS

As noted, the primary purpose of the central government in the European Union is that of insuring economic openness among the separate countries. While free trade between any group of nations is a goal that, unfortunately, will probably never be realized fully, reverse revenue sharing would provide the government of the European Union with a clear motivation to use its

---

12. See F. Vibert, "The Powers of the European Parliament: The Westminster Deficit," in J. Buchanan, K. O. Pöhl, V. C. Price, and F. Vibert, *Europe's Constitutional Future* (London: Institute of Economic Affairs, 1990), 104–5. It should be emphasized that Vibert rejects this argument.

13. Referring to a supranational government as an "international power," F. A. Hayek has stated: "The obstacle to the creation of such an international power was very largely the idea that it need command all the practically unlimited powers that the modern state possesses. But with the division of power under the federal system this is by no means necessary.

"This division of power would inevitably act at the same time also as a limitation of the power of the whole as well as of the individual state." See F. A. Hayek, *The Road to Serfdom* (Chicago: University of Chicago Press, 1944), 233–34.

authority to allow and promote economic openness among its member nations. While the political leaders in a single country may, perhaps falsely, expect to use trade restrictions to enhance the economy of that country at the partial expense of other countries, such efforts would be less likely to emerge at the central level. A central government of the European Union would be well advised to oppose all trade restrictions among member countries since its ultimate tax base is maximized by a fully integrated economy.

A supranational government with the power to tax citizens directly would also have a motivation to promote openness. The example of the United States is relevant here, where the federal government has done a reasonable job enforcing the free mobility of resources among the individual states (as required by Article 1, Section 10, Number 2, of the U.S. Constitution). But a reverse revenue-sharing arrangement would intensify the central government's interest in maintaining the productivity of free trade among the various political subunits by making it impossible for the central government to increase its own political intrusiveness through the exercise of an independent power to tax citizens directly.

Even if the European Union maintains an open internal market, it is still possible for it to protect European industries against outside competition. While not our primary concern in this paper, the issue of "fortress Europe" is a serious one, and worthy of brief comment. Under reverse revenue sharing, strictly interpreted, Brussels would not have the authority to impose a tariff on products imported into the European Union (which it unfortunately has now—recall our discussion of revenue sources, items [1] and [2]). It could, of course, erect nontariff barriers, and individual countries could impose both tariff and nontariff barriers against products coming in from outside the Union. But even here, the incentives from reverse revenue sharing to maintain open markets internally can also reduce the incentives to restrict trade externally. At least some of the pressure to restrict external trade comes from the distortions and inefficiencies caused by restrictions on internal trade. Reduce those internal distortions within the European Union with a competitive internal market and you reduce the likelihood of a "fortress Europe." We do not want to understate the unrelenting political force of protectionist sentiments, or overstate the incentives created by reverse revenue sharing to counter those sentiments, but neither do we want to ignore the link between the internal distortions caused by centralized government authority and protectionism.[14] And that link adds to the case for reverse revenue sharing for the European Union.

4.2. CONTROLLING THE SPECIAL INTERESTS

Much of the misuse and abuse of government power flows from organized interest groups and the political influence they wield. By maintaining decentralization in the power to tax, reverse revenue sharing would prevent organized interest groups in the European Union from securing an even greater political advantage than they currently have over the general taxpayer in communicating their demands through the political process. By confining taxing power to national governments, reverse revenue sharing would prevent the cost of special-interest spending proposals from being spread over all taxpayers in the Union. Hence, it would be far more difficult for the Brussels authority to exploit the rational apathy and ignorance of the public.

Of course, even at the national level, small and organized special interests can communicate the benefits received from spending programs better than the taxpaying public can communicate the costs imposed by these programs. So when each dollar raised by a national government can be spent on constituent groups within that nation, there remains a strong tendency for government taxing and spending to be pushed beyond the point where the social benefits are equal to the social costs at the margin. But this tendency is substantially reduced by the working of the competitive federalism that the reverse revenue-sharing arrangement would more or less enforce. Since under the same scheme suggested, some proportion of any revenue raised by a country must be transferred to the central government in Brussels, the motivation of taxpayers in each nation to oppose tax increases is increased

14. For a cautiously optimistic assessment of the chances of avoiding a "fortress Europe" emphasizing the link between internal distortions and protectionism, see V. C. Price, "The Threat of 'Fortress Europe,' " in J. Buchanan, K. O. Pöhl, V. C. Price, and F. Vibert, *Europe's Constitutional Future* (London: Institute of Economic Affairs, 1990), 53–68. However, Murray Weidenbaum, the first chairman of the Council of Economic Advisers under President Reagan, has pointed out that the European Union has increased exterior barriers to trade. See M. Weidenbaum, "The U.S./EC Relationship: Friends and Competitors," Occasional Paper 130 (St. Louis: Center for the Study of American Business, Washington University, 1993).

relative to local interest groups' motivation to champion such increases. In theory, the reverse revenue-sharing arrangement can shift the dominant political influence over taxing and spending decisions from organized interest groups to taxpayers. In the extreme case, for example, where the national governments would have to transfer 100 percent of any revenue raised to the central government, there would be no motivation for organized interests in any nation to lobby for taxes on local constituents.

As a practical matter, the percentage of tax revenue transferred to Brussels to carry out its legitimate functions should probably remain small. Hence, such transfer would do relatively little to reduce special-interest influence at national levels. Reverse revenue sharing could, however, also be implemented within countries, with each country consisting of a central government without the power to tax, and subgovernments with the power to tax and the obligation to share some percentage of their tax revenue with the central government. Such an arrangement would reduce the influence of special interests within each country and, when tied in with reverse revenue sharing at the level of the European Union, enhance the advantages being discussed in this paper.

4.3. MEANINGFUL SUBSIDIARITY

The concept of subsidiarity is a much talked about ideal in Brussels and throughout the Union. Certainly the ideal of "not letting a higher level of government perform a task that can be performed as well or better by a lower level of government" is one worthy of support. Unfortunately, subsidiarity is more talked about than practiced. And the more centralized the fiscal authority in Europe, the less likely subsidiarity will ever be more than a nice platitude. The incentives established by the reverse revenue sharing would create strong incentives to convert the ideal of subsidiarity into a meaningful practice.

Once a central government assumes significant control over the tax base of a community of subgovernments, it will invariably take on functions that are either best left to the subunits of government, or not worth performing at any level of government. Any doubt regarding this proposition is dispelled by considering the experience of the United States. The U.S. federal government routinely funds local projects that should be financed out of state and local revenues, if at all. A recent list of local projects recommended for federal funding included an indoor baseball field for Huntsville, Alabama, at a cost to the federal government of $1.08 million; a baseball and soccer park for Jonesboro, Arkansas, at a cost to the federal government of $5.3 million; three bike paths for Modesto, California, at a cost to the federal government of $1.3 million; expansion of the civic center in San Leandro, California, at a cost to the federal government of $12.8 million; a project to resurface tennis courts in Evanston, Illinois, at a cost to the federal government of $28 thousand; a movie theater in Columbus, Ohio, at a cost to the federal government of $2.7 million; research for a bike path in Eugene, Oregon, at a cost to the federal government of $800 thousand; and three swimming pools in Midland, Texas, at a cost to the federal government of $1.0 million.[15] These particular projects were not funded, at least not when first proposed. But they are representative of countless local projects that have been, and continue to be, funded by the federal government in the United States.

The reason such projects are politically viable in a centralized fiscal setting, even when they cost far more than they are worth, is that subgovernment officials can secure local benefits with the costs spread over the inclusive group of central government taxpayers. And the demand from subgovernment officials for central government funding is welcome, and readily responded to, by the central authorities since it reinforces their power and justifies yet higher taxes.

The central government's motivation to finance projects that are best provided by lower levels of government would largely disappear under the incentives of reverse revenue sharing. Projects that create benefits primarily for the citizens of a national government will generally be approved and financed by national authorities if they are cost effective. If the supranational government financed such projects, it would be undermining its only source of revenue by relieving the nations of the need to raise the tax revenue needed to finance them. The political advantage for the central government

---

15. These projects come from a larger list published in an editorial in the *Wall Street Journal* ("Pork Carry-Out, April 5, 1993, A-16). The *Wall Street Journal* list comes from a list of over 4,000 public works projects that are contained in the National Conference of Mayors "Ready to Go" projects that former Housing and Urban Development Secretary Henry Cisneros said the Clinton administration would work from if a $16.2 billion "stimulus" bill passed.

would be in providing only those services that create community-wide benefits which would improve the general productivity of the collective economy,
but which no country would finance unilaterally. Each nation would no
doubt remain anxious for the central government to fund country-specific
projects. But attempts to obtain such funding would run up against not only
strong opposing incentives, but also a central government budget constraint
much less yielding to political demands than would be the case if the power
to tax were centralized.

It is hard to think of a fiscal arrangement for the European Union that
would do more to promote genuine subsidiarity than reverse revenue sharing. On the other hand, giving Brussels an independent power to tax would
initiate a process of centralization that would render subsidiarity little more
than a hollow hope.

4.4. TAX AND SERVICE COMPETITION

The best protection citizens have against the abuse of their national government and its special-interest clients comes from competition. One of the
most important advantages of reverse revenue sharing for the European
Union is that it would insure a significant degree of tax and service competition among the governments of the member nations.

Reverse revenue sharing would prevent the differences in the taxing decisions of the various states from being obscured by a heavy overlay of centrally imposed taxes. The nation that attempted to increase its taxes without
a commensurate increase in the value of services provided would find its tax
base being competed away by other states.[16]

One indication of the potential benefits to citizens of the European Union
from the tax and service competition their governments will face under a decentralized tax structure is given by some of the initiatives out of Brussels to
frustrate this competition. We have already mentioned the desire on the part

16. This tax competition generated by reverse revenue sharing is intensified by, and
complements, the more general increase in competition between countries, and their
governments, prompted by the policy of open economies within the Union. For general
discussion, see J. Buchanan, "National Politics and Competitive Federalism: Italy and the
Constitution of Europe," working paper, Center for Study of Public Choice, George Mason University, 1994.

of those whose interests are attached to central government of the European Union to secure the power to tax for Brussels. There has also been discussion in favor of "harmonizing" tax rates in the European Union.[17] The rhetoric for harmonization emphasizes the need to protect the social programs of member countries against free-riding temptations that could arise in the absence of harmonization. The reality behind tax harmonization is the desire to prevent tax competition between the nations. Giving Brussels the power to harmonize tax rates in the European Union would amount to creating a tax cartel among the European countries. Such centralized power over taxation would be good for European politicians and special interests for the very reasons it would be harmful to European citizens.

Government spending would increase, taxes would be higher, and the general public would end up paying more to government for less of real value.[18]

5. Conclusion

Fiscal economists tend, initially, to react negatively to the proposal for reverse revenue sharing in a federal structure. In part, this reaction is based on a generalized carry-over of a traditional interpretation of American historical experience. The Articles of Confederation, the compact among the early American states, is alleged to have failed precisely because there was no independent power to tax granted to the central government under these articles. The establishment of such an independent power to tax has been traditionally identified as the hallmark feature of the basic U.S. Constitution drafted in 1789, largely by James Madison.

We should emphasize, however, that under the Articles of Confederation the financial support of the central government depended upon the voluntary subventions of the separate states. There was no provision that stipu-

---

17. According to *The European*, "The new president [of the European Commission] will be confronted with demands from some member states to formulate a common taxation policy, and it is clear that increased harmonization in the fiscal area will move high on the EU's agenda." See *The European*, "Presidential Policies under the Microscope," May 6–12, 1994, 19.

18. Frank Vibert, the Deputy Director of the Institute of Economic Affairs, argues that the consequences of the European Parliament assuming more control over the Union's budget would be "ever-increasing spending at the [Union] level, a high-tax Europe and a loss of accountability to the taxpayer." See Vibert, op. cit., 106.

lated that the separate states transfer a fixed, and uniform, share of all tax revenues to the central authority. It is our contention that had such a reverse revenue-sharing arrangement been in place the Articles of Confederation would have been more successful, and the whole history might have been dramatically different.

Fiscal economists may react negatively, however, quite apart from historical reference, if they do not carefully analyze the incentive structure that would characterize the reverse revenue-sharing scheme. The scheme is logically equivalent to an orthodox public finance model of a tax on a privately purchased commodity with proceeds earmarked for outlay on a publicly financed good or service. Consider a tax on cigarettes, uniform over all purchases, with revenues earmarked for outlay in schools. In this setting, each dollar spent comprises two components, the post-tax price of the good along with the tax payment for the public good. Persons who evaluate the private good (cigarettes) highly, relative to the evaluation of the public good (schooling), will prefer a lower rate of tax than persons whose evaluations run in the counter-relationship. Agreement on a preferred uniform rate of tax remains impossible so long as relative evaluations differ. (A full Lindahl-like fiscal equilibrium is unattainable.) Nonetheless, there is no necessary barrier to the attainment of an "efficient" level of public goods outlay. In the setting of competitive federalism, no national unit would be able, through changing its own behavior unilaterally, to impose either costs or benefits on citizens of other units without, at the same time, incurring burdens for its own citizens.

In conclusion, it is useful to refer again to the constitutional moment of the 1990s that Europe is now experiencing. The basic institutions of the Europe of the next century are in the process of evolutionary emergence, constructive design, and practical implementation. Structures introduced today, almost regardless of consequent operating properties, will not be easy to dismantle. An initial grant of independent taxing authority to Brussels cannot be withdrawn at will. It is critically important that a fiscal structure be evaluated for its long-term impact on the development of the relationship between supranational and national political authority. Reverse revenue sharing, which does provide a source of revenue for the central government while, at the same time, keeping independent taxing-power at national levels, offers a means of securing and maintaining the development of a genuinely competitive federalism.

Secession and the
Limits of Taxation
Toward a Theory of Internal Exit

James M. Buchanan and Roger L. Faith

Since the publication of Charles Tiebout's now-classic paper, fiscal economists have made significant progress in analyzing external exit.[1] By "voting with their feet," individuals are able, in the limiting case, to ensure overall allocative efficiency in the supply of local public goods. Competitive governmental units are forced to supply these goods and services in preferred quantities and to "price" them, at least broadly, in line with relative-marginal evaluations. Elaborations of the analysis have largely involved departures from the limiting case assumptions through such elements as locational rents, the attenuation of ownership rights, interjurisdictional spillovers, absence of residual claimancy, nonhomogeneity in tastes, and nonconstant returns over membership sizes and public goods quantities.[2]

From *American Economic Review* 77 (December 1987): 1023–31. Reprinted by permission of the publisher.

We would like to thank referees for some helpful suggestions.

1. Charles Tiebout, "A Pure Theory of Local Expenditures," *Journal of Political Economy* 64 (October 1956): 416–24.

2. The paper by J. Vernon Henderson ("The Tiebout Model: Bring Back the Entrepreneurs," *Journal of Political Economy* 83 [April 1985]: 248–64) is the latest in a long series. See, especially, James Buchanan and Charles Goetz, "Efficiency Limits of Fiscal Mobility: An Assessment of the Tiebout Model," *Journal of Public Economics* 1 (April 1972): 25–43; F. Flatters, J. Vernon Henderson, and Peter Mieszkowski, "Public Goods, Efficiency, and Regional Fiscal Equalization," *Journal of Public Economics* 3 (May 1974): 99–112; and Eitan

By contrast with these developments in analysis, almost no attention has been given to *internal exit,* which takes the form of secession by a coalition of people from an existing political unit along with the establishment of a new political unit that will then provide public goods to those who defect from the original unit. The neglect of internal exit may be due, in part, to the implicit presupposition that secession is legally-constitutionally impermissible and, in part, to the unexamined assumption that secession is prohibitively costly due either to the locational interdependence among people in a polity or to the difficulties of forming coalitions among potential members of any seceding group. But if other margins of adjustment are costly or foreclosed, and if organizational difficulties are overcome, internal exit becomes a viable mode of response.

Since we do observe local governments that are clearly competitive and at least some competitiveness even among nations, the external-exit model both seems to be, and is, more "realistic" than its internal-exit counterpart. However, secession in various forms does occur. An example is incorporation in which a subset of citizens of an existing jurisdiction, say a county, set up their own policy, and provide and finance by themselves many of the public goods provided by the county. More dramatic examples of secession are threats and declarations of independence from existing national governments. If, in fact, successful secession is not often observed to occur in practice, the existence of pressures for internal exit may exert effects on the behavior of governments. That is to say, internal exit may be a "road not traveled," save under exceptional circumstances. The existence of such an alternative opportunity, along with its characteristic features, must, however, affect the attitudinal stance of people in their acquiescence in and/or criticism of political decisions beyond their individual control. For example, taxation beyond the limits defined by a plausibly estimated internal-exit option may erode the moral basis necessary for essentially voluntary tax compliance. Indirectly, a model of internal exit may be helpful in deriving testable implications relative to the growth of tax evasion-avoidance or, conversely, to the pressures for tax reform effort.

Berglas, "Distribution of Tastes and Skills and the Provision of Local Public Goods," *Journal of Public Economics* 6 (November 1976): 409–23.

This paper introduces such a model. We shall assume throughout that people possess legal-constitutional rights of secession, which may or may not prove costly to exercise. It is immediately evident that any such liberty imposes constraints on the potentially exploitative behavior of those in the dominating or ruling political coalition, which, for reasons that will be apparent, we call the *sharing coalition*. The ability of members of this coalition to extract fiscal surplus is potentially restricted in ways that are analogous to those present under the external-exit prospect.

A broad interpretation of the sharing coalition includes all groups that are successful in obtaining net transfers from the government. These groups, by actively participating in the political process, may be able to redistribute wealth from other unorganized or less effective groups in the polity. The people or groups remaining outside the sharing coalition might represent the politically ineffective, unrepresented, or rationally nonparticipating segment of the population. But such a group also presents a potential for secession—literally or figuratively—such as evading taxes or withholding moral support for the institutions of governance.

The government provides public goods here assumed to be inherently monopolistic. The minimal rate of tax, therefore, for a polity of any size, is the rate that generates just sufficient revenue to finance the production of the public goods. But the monopolist provider (an individual or a coalition) will also try, to the extent that is possible, to use the taxing power to transfer revenues to itself. We proceed under the highly stylized assumptions that taxes must be levied proportionately on incomes of *all* members of the polity, whether inside or outside the sharing coalition, that any available fiscal surplus must be shared *equally* among people who are members of the sharing coalition, and that no person outside the sharing coalition receive any fiscal transfers.[3] Given this stylized setting, the critical assumption that places limits on the amount of fiscal surplus is the liberty of secession. Individuals in any size group may secede and, without cost, form a new political unit. This unit, once it has seceded, must provide its own public goods.

---

3. In general terms, such asymmetry between the taxing and spending sides is historically descriptive of the constitutionally constrained U.S. fiscal structure. The uniformity clause severely restricts discrimination in taxation; no such limit is imposed on the spending or transfer side of budget.

The effectiveness of potential secession or conversely, the extent of possible surplus extraction depends on such parameters as the costs and publicness of the services that are collectively financed, the form of the production function in the market sector, the differentiation of people in economic characteristics, and the overall size of the polity's membership. The extent of possible surplus extraction is also affected by the threat of change in the *composition* of the sharing coalition in government, by either political competition or more violent means. Certainly, seeking change in the composition of the sharing coalition is a margin on which individual response may take place along with or in place of internal exit. In our analysis, we concentrate solely on the secession option.

We shall see how the tax rate, total transfers, the gain from entry into the sharing coalition, and the effect of entry on existing sharers change as the sharing coalition increases in size. We shall show that the optimal-sized coalition from a sharer's viewpoint is not the smallest possible coalition due to scale economies in the production of private and public goods. In fact, over a wide range of sizes of the sharing coalition, entry into the government may be encouraged. We shall also concentrate on the possible conflicts that arise between sharers and nonsharers regarding entry into the sharing coalition and entry into the original polity. How entry is achieved or prevented, how the composition of the sharing coalition is determined, and how nonsharers choose between secession and other modes of response such as external exit, voice, or revolution will not be addressed here.

1. The General Model

Government has a necessary function; it must provide "order," a nonexclusive, lumpy, and costly good. Without "order" there is no private product. The cost of providing the required amount of the public good to a community of K people is $f(K)$, where $f'(K) \geq 0$. Each person in a community of K has a private product, or income, of $g(K)$. We assume $Kg(K) > f(K)$. The original polity consists of N identical individuals, M of them belonging to the government, or sharing coalition. The remaining $S = N - M$ individuals form the set of potential seceders.

Total fiscal surplus, or transfers, T, is the difference between the tax revenue obtained by levying a nondiscriminatory tax rate, t, on private incomes, minus the total cost of the public good. Each member of the sharing coalition has a post-tax net income B equal to his post-tax private income $P = g(K)(1 - t)$ plus an equal share T/M of the fiscal surplus.[4] A non-sharer's post-tax net income is simply P.

An equilibrium tax rate is one which given M and N maximizes the post-tax net income of the sharers without inducing secession.

In a community of K people, the minimal, nonexploitative tax rate is t_0 $(K) = f(K)/Kg(K)$, which generates just enough revenue to finance the public good. Since the S nonsharers on their own in a new polity realize a post-tax income of $g(S)[1 - t_0(S)]$, the maximum tax rate a sharing coalition of size M in a polity of size N can levy without inducing secession is $t^*(M, N) = t_0(S) = f(S)/Sg(S)$.[5] Since B is an increasing function of t, the tax rate $t^*(M, N)$ is an equilibrium rate.

Substituting t^* into T, P, and B, we obtain

$$T = t^*Ng(N) - f(N) = \left[\frac{f(S)}{Sg(S)} - \frac{f(N)}{Ng(N)} \right] Ng(N), \qquad (1)$$

$$P = g(N)(1 - t^*) = g(N) - \frac{g(N)f(S)}{Sg(S)}, \qquad (2)$$

$$B = \frac{T}{M} + P = [t^*Ng(N) - f(N)]/M + g(N)(1 - t^*). \qquad (3)$$

If $f(S)/Sg(S) > f(N)/Ng(N)$ for all $S < N$, that is, if the ratio of total cost to total product is lower for a polity of size N than for any smaller-size polity, transfers are positive.

Differentiating (1) through (3) with respect to M yields

$$T_M = Ng(N)t^*_M, \qquad (4)$$

4. To avoid problems of indifference, we shall assume that nonsharers are given a tiny amount of the fiscal surplus, $T - f(N)$.

5. This tax rate assumes the seceders will employ the nonexploitative tax rate to finance the public good in the new polity. It might be argued that even in the new polity, the government will again behave in an exploitative manner. If so, it turns out that as long as each potential seceder sees himself having an equal probability M/S of belonging to the new sharing coalition, the maximal tax rate in the original polity will equal $f(S)/Sg(S)$. See James Buchanan and Roger Faith, "Secession and the Sharing of Surplus," working paper, Arizona State University, October 1986.

$$P_M = -g(N)t_M^*, \tag{5}$$

$$B_M = \frac{1}{M^2}[t_M^* SMg(N) - T]. \tag{6}$$

The sign of t_M^* is the same as the sign of T_M and opposite the sign of P_M. Thus, if the maximum tax rate increases with the size of the sharing coalition, transfers increase and the post-tax position of nonsharers decreases. Because T is positive, a necessary condition for $B_M > 0$ is $t_M^* > 0$. However, the positivity of t_M^* does not imply the positivity of B_M. The reason is that as M increases and transfers increase, the increased transfers are divided over a larger group, and the tax paid by each sharer also rises, canceling some of the gain from the increase in transfers.

Differentiating t^* with respect to M reveals that

$$t_M^* \gtreqless 0 \rightleftarrows \frac{Sg'(S) + g(S)}{g(S)} \gtreqless \frac{Sf'(S)}{f(S)}. \tag{7}$$

The maximum tax rate increases in M, if and only if the elasticity of total product $Sg(S)$ with respect to community size is greater than the size elasticity of the total public good cost $f(S)$. A larger sharing coalition means a smaller population, a lower total product and tax base, and a lower total cost of the public good in the secessionist polity. If the size elasticity of product is greater than the size elasticity of cost, the tax base falls more than cost as the new polity shrinks in size and the tax rate necessary to finance the public good increases.

Using t^* and t_M^* in (6), rearranging and multiplying by S, we find

$$B_M \gtreqless 0$$

$$\rightleftarrows \left[\frac{Sg'(S) + g(S)}{g(S)} - \frac{Sf'(S)}{f(S)}\right]$$

$$\gtreqless \frac{N}{M}\left[1 - \frac{f(N)}{f(S)}\frac{g(S)S}{g(N)N}\right]. \tag{8}$$

The first bracketed term is the difference between the size elasticities of private product and public good cost. By (7), this difference is positive if $t_M^* > 0$. If $f(S)/Sg(S) > f(N)/Ng(N)$ for all S, then the second bracketed term is also positive, and B_M may be positive or negative.

The difference in the conditions for positivity of t_M^* and B_M implies a potential conflict between existing and potential members of the sharing coalition. Nonsharers will seek entry into a sharing coalition of size M if the net gain G to the potential entrant is positive,

$$G = B(M) + B_M(M) - P(M) \tag{9}$$

$$\cong B_M + \frac{T}{M} > 0.$$

Using (4) and (6) in (9) shows that $G > 0$ if $t_M^* > 0$. The effect of entry on current sharers is B_M, which as just shown may be negative even if $t_M^* > 0$. If $B_M > 0$, entry into the sharing coalition will be encouraged by current sharers. If $B_M < 0$, current sharers will resist attempts by current nonsharers to join the sharing coalition. If entry beyond the point where $B_M = 0$ is precluded by barriers to entry not discussed here, those denied entry will not secede. Equilibrium implies unequal treatment of fiscal equals. If there are no barriers to entry and $t_M^* > 0$ for all $M < N$, then the size of the sharing coalition will be N, with an equilibrium tax rate $t^* = t_0(N) = f(N)/Ng(N)$. There is no exploitation.

It is clear from the discussion that the amount of fiscal exploitation and the tendency for the government to get larger depend on the behavior of the product and cost functions. Note, however, that if the cost of the public good does not increase less than proportionately with private production, there is no efficiency-based argument for collective or public provision of any good stemming from nonrivalry in usage. Only technological nonexclusiveness might then justify collective provision.

A. Some illustrative cases

Assume that the average cost over individuals, $f(K)/K$, falls in K, and average product $g(K)$ is constant and equal to $\bar{g}$.[6] Declining average cost is standard

---

6. If we assume that average public goods cost rises with polity size, in the absence of any locational rents, the polity would break apart into smaller polities to avoid the diseconomies of scale. This would occur independent of the taxing proclivity of the government. If average cost were U-shaped, then we expect the polity would again break into several smaller communities, perhaps until minimum average cost is reached. At that size,

in public goods theory which postulates the existence of some degree of non-rivalry in consumption, hence, increasing returns over group size, at least over some ranges. Constant average product may be interpreted as an absence of agglomeration economies.

Equations (1), (2), and (3) now become

$$T = N \left[\frac{f(S)}{S} - \frac{f(N)}{N} \right], \tag{10}$$

$$P = \bar{g} - \frac{f(S)}{S}, \tag{11}$$

$$B = \frac{T}{M} + P = \frac{f(S) - f(N)}{M} + \bar{g}. \tag{12}$$

Since $f(N)/N < f(S)/S$, then $T > 0$ and $B > P$. Any secessionist group faces a higher average cost of producing the public good. The sharing coalition, in essence, taxes the nonsharers for the benefit of living in a larger polity—the reduction in the average cost of the public good. Using (7) and (8) gives

$$t_M^* \gtreqqless 0 \rightleftarrows \frac{f(S)}{S} - f'(S) \gtreqqless 0, \tag{13}$$

$$B_M \gtreqqless 0 \rightleftarrows \frac{f(S)}{S} - f'(S) \tag{14}$$
$$\gtreqqless \frac{N}{M} \left[\frac{f(S)}{S} - \frac{f(N)}{N} \right].$$

Expression (13) says that the maximum tax rate increasing in M is equivalent to declining average cost. Expression (14) says that for entry to go unchallenged, average cost must not only decline with polity size, but do so at a sufficiently high rate.

If the government-provided good ("order" in our example) is a pure public good, then $f(K) = F$, and equations (10), (11), and (12) become

$$T = \frac{M}{N - M} F, \quad P = \bar{g} - \frac{F}{N - M}, \quad B = g.$$

---

any further size reductions would result in an increase in average cost and our model would apply.

The value of B is independent of coalition size; therefore entry is costless to the sharing coalition until $M = N - 1$. Because *total* cost of the public good is constant, the sharing coalition taxes away from the nonsharers the benefits of dividing cost over a larger group size.

Assume now that average public good cost is constant over polity size but that larger polities have greater per capita private product. If there are agglomeration economies, larger polities will generate proportionally more total product. If part of the original polity secedes, the secessionists face a lower average product (on the assumption that inter-polity trade does not emerge to capture gains of interdependence) and a higher tax rate.

The basic relationships, given $f(K)/K = \bar{f}$, are

$$T = \bar{f}N \frac{g(N) - g(S)}{g(S)}, \tag{15}$$

$$P = g(N) - \frac{\bar{f}g(N)}{g(S)}, \text{ and} \tag{16}$$

$$B = \frac{\bar{f}N}{M} \frac{g(N) - g(S)}{g(S)} + g(N) - \frac{\bar{f}g(N)}{g(S)}. \tag{17}$$

Since $g(N) \geq g(S)$, then $B \geq g(N)$ and $P \leq g(N)$. Members of the sharing coalition can improve their lot over and above the "free" consumption of the public good. Even though average public good cost does not change, the smaller private productive capacity of the seceding group relative to the original polity implies that the opportunity costs of leaving are higher than before. This difference is recognized and taken advantage of by the sharing coalition.

Expressions (7) and (8) become

$$t_M^* \gtreqless 0 \rightleftarrows \frac{Sg'(S)}{g(S)} \gtreqless 0, \tag{18}$$

$$B_M \gtreqless 0 \rightleftarrows [Sg'(S) + g(S)] - g(S) \gtreqless \frac{N}{M}[g(N) - g(S)] \frac{g(S)}{g(N)}. \tag{19}$$

Note that increasing average product is necessary but not sufficient for entry to not harm the existing sharing coalition.

B. PRICE-ELASTIC PUBLIC GOOD DEMAND

We have assumed that the government-produced good, order, is consumable in only one quantity. Either there is order or there is not. Alternatively, we can say that the demand for order is perfectly inelastic at the required quantity. Suppose, instead, that the government provides goods such as schools and roads, which exhibit nonzero price elasticity. The nonsharers can provide the public good at the tax rate $t_0 = f[Q^S(t_0)]/Sg(S)$, where $Q^S(t_0)$ is the quantity demanded by the nonsharers at the tax rate t_0. From our previous discussions we know that the equilibrium tax rate in the original polity t^* equals $t_0(S)$.

The quantity produced in the original polity, we assume, is determined by the sharing coalition and depends on the *effective,* post-transfer tax rate paid by the sharers defined as the equilibrium rate t^* minus the transfers per unit of income $T/Mg(N)$. Given $t^* = t_0$, the effective tax rate is

$$t_e = \frac{1}{M}\left(\frac{f[Q^M(t_e)]}{g(N)} - \frac{f[Q^S(t_0)]}{g(S)}\right), \tag{20}$$

where $Q^M(t_e)$ is the quantity demanded by the sharing coalition at the effective tax rate t_e.[7]

If cost is an increasing function of output, then $f[Q^S(t_0)]$ is less than $f[Q^M(t_e)]$, since t_0 is greater than t_e and $Q^S(t_0)$ is less than $Q^M(t_e)$. Thus, the more price elastic the demand for the public good (evaluated at Q^S), the lower the equilibrium tax rate and the more effectively the liberty of secession constrains the government's ability to transfer.

II. Two-Class Model

The analysis to this point has proceeded under the assumption that individuals are identical in terms of their income levels. The *identity* of those making up the sharing coalition does not emerge as a relevant consideration. We shall now relax this assumption.

---

7. This assumes no congestion effect. A combination of congestion and price effects may act to cancel or reinforce each other in determining the magnitude of the equilibrium tax rate in the N-sized polity (see Buchanan and Faith, "Secession and the Sharing of Surplus").

Assume a polity of size N consists of two internally homogeneous groups of individuals, high-income (H) and low-income (L), so that $N_H + N_L = N$. Total product in the polity is $N_H g_H + N_L g_L = W$. The equilibrium tax rate is

$$t^* = \frac{f(S)}{N_{HS} g_H + N_{LS} g_L} = \frac{f(S)}{W_S},\qquad (21)$$

where N_{ij} is the number of people of a particular income level in a particular group (for example, N_{LS} is the number of low-income people in the non-sharing group).

Our basic relationships, using (21), are

$$T = f(S)\frac{W}{W_S} - f(N),\qquad (22)$$

$$P_i = g_i\left[1 - \frac{f(S)}{W_S}\right],\ i = H, L;\text{ and}$$

$$B_i = \frac{1}{M}\left[\frac{f(S)W}{W_S} - f(N)\right] + g_i\left[1 - \frac{f(S)}{W_S}\right],\ i = H, L.\qquad (24)$$

Equation (21) implies that sharing groups with a greater proportion of low-income people are taxed more heavily than nonsharing groups with a greater fraction of high-income people. Now consider the difference between moving one high-income person from the nonsharing group to the sharing group, and moving one low-income person from the nonsharing to the sharing group. The differential effect on any original member of the sharing coalition with income g_i is

$$(g_H - g_L)\frac{f(S)}{W_s^2}\left(\frac{W}{M} - g_i\right),\qquad (25)$$

$$i = H, L.$$

For a low-income member of the sharing coalition, (25) is always positive; while for a high-income member, (25) is positive (negative) if $[(W/M) - g_H]$

is positive (negative).[8] That is, it typically benefits the members of the sharing coalition *more* to add a high-income person rather than a low-income person to the sharing coalition. Equation (25) implies that the greater the income difference between classes, $(g_H - g_L)$, the greater the incentive to bring high-income people into the sharing coalition.

This result has a powerful implication. It suggests that if the sharing coalition can control entry the government will tend to be dominated by people with relatively high income. Indeed, even if the original members of the government are low-income persons, they will prefer that a high-income person join the sharing group rather than another low-income person.

A. THE EFFECT OF POLITY SIZE AND IMMIGRATION

We now permit polity size to change through immigration. For ease in interpretation, we shall assume no congestion—$f(K) = F$, all K. Assuming new citizens enter the polity as nonsharers, the marginal effects on sharers' and nonsharers' net incomes are

$$\frac{\partial B_i}{\partial N_{js}} = \frac{F g_j}{W_s^2} \left(\frac{W_s - W}{M} + g_i \right),$$

$$i, j = L, H. \tag{26}$$

$$\frac{\partial P_i}{\partial N_{js}} = g_i g_j \frac{F}{W_s^2} > 0.$$

$$i, j = L, H. \tag{27}$$

8. Bringing a high-income person versus a low-income person into the sharing coalition generates differentially higher tax rates. Intuitively, it is possible that if a coalition has already attained sufficient size and if a member of the coalition is sufficiently rich relative to low-income individuals, the higher tax rate costs him more in taxes than he gains in increased transfers. The sufficient condition for this possibility, $g_H > W/M$, can be rewritten as $(g_H/g_L) > N_L/(N_{LM} - N_{HS})$. The greater the high-low–income ratio, the greater the likelihood that a high-income member of the sharing coalition will prefer a *low-income* rather than a *high-income* entrant.

Because $g_H \geq (W - W_S)/M$ and $g_L \leq (W - W_S)/M$, equation (26) is non-positive for low-income sharers and nonnegative for high-income sharers regardless of the income of the newcomer, j. Adding another person to the polity as an outsider cannot harm and may benefit high-income members of the sharing coalition and cannot benefit and may harm low-income members of the sharing coalition.[9] Equation (27), however, is always positive, indicating that current nonsharers do better if their group grows, since it lowers the equilibrium tax rate. Note also that $\partial P_j/\partial N_{LS} < \partial P_j/\partial N_{HS}$. Any nonsharer, regardless of income, prefers high- rather than low-income individuals to enter the polity. Thus, conflict over immigration policy—who, if anyone at all, shall be allowed to *enter the polity*—will arise when incomes differ in the original polity.

B. Income-elastic public good demand

In Section I, Part B, we discussed the effect of nonzero price elasticity for public goods on the model. In the two-class model, similar effects are produced if demand is income elastic. Specifically, we shall assume that the demand for the public good depends on average income in the polity, or $Q^K(\overline{W}_K)$; $\partial Q^K/\partial \overline{W}_K > 0$, where $\overline{W}_K = W_K/K$. Assuming no congestion or price effects, the equilibrium tax rate is $t^* = f[Q^S(\overline{W}_S)]/W_S$, and

$$
\begin{aligned}
B_i = \frac{1}{M} & \left(\frac{f[Q^S(\overline{W}_S)]W}{W_S} - f[Q^M(\overline{W}_M)] \right) \\
& + g_i \left(1 - \frac{f[Q^S(\overline{W}_S)]}{W_S} \right),
\end{aligned}
\qquad (28)
$$

$$
i = L, H,
$$

---

9. The entry of a new nonsharing person to the polity increases the aggregate tax base, but reduces the maximally exploitative tax rate. The low-income member of the sharing coalition secures some part of his transfer from high-income members of the coalition. Since the maximum tax rate falls, the within-coalition part of the transfer falls, hence, benefiting the high-income member and harming the low-income member of the sharing coalition.

$$P_i = g_i \left(1 - \frac{f[Q^S(\overline{W}_S)]}{W_S} \right) \tag{29}$$

$$i = L, H.^{10}$$

Assuming $\overline{W}_M > \overline{W}_S$, the nonsharing group imposes a stricter constraint on the sharing coalition than in the income-inelastic case, since nonsharers demand less of the public good and therefore face lower total costs of producing the public good. The greater the income elasticity, the greater the reduction in the equilibrium tax rate.

Other effects are generated also. First, the sharing coalition's incentive to favor rich over poor entrants into the coalition is reduced, since the higher the average income in the nonsharing group, the greater the nonsharers' demand for the public good. This means a higher equilibrium tax rate and greater transfers. Next, if average private product is subject to agglomeration economies, a positive income elasticity partially offsets the effects of lost economies of scale in the secessionist polity. Third, in an external-exit model, individuals of like income tend to group together because their public good demands are similar and group welfare is enhanced. In the internal-exit model, the potential for transfers may outweigh the efficiency gains from attaining unanimous agreement over the quantity of public goods. This suggests there are forces which keep polities of mixed income intact.

III. Implications and Extensions

We have subtitled this paper "*Toward* a Theory of Internal Exit," and we have stressed the restrictiveness of the assumptions within which our basic models have been presented.

Despite the restrictiveness of the models, to us the implications derived are both interesting and potentially relevant. First, in the absence of elements not considered here, the size of the governing coalition tends to increase. There is an asymmetry which ensures that over a range of sizes the costs of

---

10. The effects of nonzero price elasticity, income elasticity, and congestion can be combined to generate a more general set of relationships. See Buchanan and Faith, "Secession and the Sharing of Surplus," for details.

new entrants, to members of any initial ruling coalition, are less than the benefits to those who are successful in securing entry. As the size of the sharing coalition increases, absolute tax rates increase, the total revenue side of the budget increases, and the relative size of transfers in the budget increases. Appealing to the conditions for unchallenged entry, the government will grow where per capita public goods cost is declining relative to average private product. If we may characterize mature economies as ones in which average private product growth slows, as population grows, and the average cost of order increases, due, perhaps, to increased congestion, we may expect to find greater resistance to increasing the sharing coalition from those within the coalition. In young, vigorous economies, the opposite may be expected.

A second interesting result emerges when we allow for differences among the economic positions of those who might be members of the ruling coalition. The rich are favored over the poor as potential entrants into the sharing group, quite independent of the identity of those who might initially hold the power of governance. Outside the coalition, the rich can, under our assumptions, more readily set up seceding polities. Hence, the threat that they will do so must reduce the maximal tax that may be imposed. Further, once the rich are inside the sharing group, as both transfer recipients and as taxpayers generally, those within the group who are poor can gain. Once all of the rich are within the sharing coalition, the additional entry of members who are poor will tend to be opposed. Those who are poor remain outside the sharing coalition, and, because they remain poor, they cannot readily secede. They either remain subject to maximal fiscal exploitation or possibly resort to extreme measures such as revolution. This seems to be broadly descriptive of modern politics despite the extreme restrictiveness of our model. The transfer state of modern political reality is not the transfer state as idealized by the egalitarian philosophers.

Third, the model implies that expansion policy will be viewed differently by the sharers and nonsharers. An example is annexation. Whether one community votes to absorb another community depends, in part, on the fiscal effects of the absorbing new citizens on existing citizens, some of whom may be classified as net beneficiaries (sharers) and some as net tax contributors (nonsharers) of local public services.

Our model also applies to any organization which provides collective benefits to its members, with the authority to tax its members, and competing organizations are not cheaply available. Social clubs, religious groups, home-owner associations, and labor unions are potential examples.

Implicitly, Tiebout's model of local government behavior offered a positive theory of the limits of taxation by governmental units in competition, one with another. There has been no comparable effort to work out, either implicitly or explicitly, a positive theory of absolute limits to taxation in a polity where external exit is not available to members. Realistically, of course, secession is less likely to be observed than direct overturn of governments, whether through democratic or nondemocratic means. The secession models presented in this paper would seem to provide a useful beginning stage for the more complex analysis that would be required to examine how the prospects for removal from authority might exert limits on the taxing proclivity of government.

PART THREE

Liberty, Man, and the State

Man and the State

Among us there are some who are able to imagine a viable society without a state. These libertarian anarchists, or anarcho-capitalists, have made major contributions in demonstrating how many of the modern state's activities might be better carried out through the spontaneous processes of the market. And these arguments are exerting an effect now in the cross-national movements toward privatization. I do not want to underestimate the importance of the challenge that the libertarian anarchists have posed for all of us who defend state action.

Social order without a state is not readily imagined, or at least in any normatively preferred sense. We find it difficult to model the working properties of such a social arrangement, especially as we look at the behavior of persons in the world about us. We fall back on Thomas Hobbes to provide the description of what the genuinely stateless-lawless society might be like. The normative rejection of this model forces us to raise a whole set of issues that the libertarian anarchist need not concern himself with at all.

Of necessity, we must look at our relations with the state from several windows, to use the familiar Nietzschean metaphor. To consider two extremes, we can, with Herbert Spencer and the libertarians, consider the state as an adversary and convert my title into "Man versus the State." At the same time, however, we must also recognize that "man is the state" in the basic sense that it describes the set of institutions through which we organize ourselves

From *Socialism: Institutional, Philosophical and Economic Issues,* vol. 14, *International Studies in Economics and Econometrics,* ed. Svetozar Pejovich (Dordrecht, Boston, Lancaster: Kluwer Academic Publishing, 1987), 3–9. Reprinted by permission of the publisher, Kluwer Academic Publishers.

This chapter is based on his presidential address given at the Mont Pelerin Society meeting in St. Vincent, Italy, 1986.

politically and collectively for the achievement of purposes that simply cannot be otherwise secured at all efficiently.

Some understanding of the operation of the state is required before any discussion about the assignment of this or that function to the state or about policy options in the carrying out of this or that function. This very simple principle was simply overlooked by most economists until the middle of this century, and with tragic consequences.

Descriptively, we know that the state fits no single model, and that the two general models mentioned do not nearly exhaust the set of the possible. The state is not a monolithic entity empowered with a monopoly of coercion and equipped with a will of its own. It is not voluntaristic in the Wicksellian sense where all collective decisions reflect unanimous agreement among all persons in the polity. It is not the embodiment of the will of the possibly shifting median voter in majoritarian processes. It is not the instrument through which a ruling coalition, temporarily in office, enriches itself at the expense of others in the polity. It is not a freely floating bureaucracy constrained only by its inner organizational logic. It is not the mere agent for a ruling class or establishment.

There are elements of each of these models, and possibly others, in the state as it variously exists in different nations. How we choose to model the state depends on the purpose to be served, on the questions to be asked, and answered.

Rather than concentrate attention on what the state is, however, it may be best to examine the position of the individual in relation to the state. In this context it may be helpful to think of the state as an organization that possesses the peculiar feature of *compulsory* membership, thereby contrasting it with other organizations in which membership is *voluntary.* As with most models, this is a limiting case. We know that states vary widely in the "compulsoryness" of membership, and further that the costs of exit vary widely among persons. Nonetheless, the absence of a cost effective exit option does distinguish the state from almost all other organizations. For most purposes, the individual is a member of the organization that is the state, and a member he must remain.

What does it mean to say that the individual is a member of an organization? Membership implies adherence to the rules of the organization, whatever these may be, and, in application to the state, this approach calls attention immediately to the importance of the rules, the constitution of the polity. There are two dimensions of the rules that define the organization of the state, dimensions that can vary independently. One dimension involves the extent to which the individual is subject to the state's authority, or, conversely, the extent of his private sphere protected from state intervention. The second dimension of rules concerns the structure of the decision-making process through which the state's authority is exercised. In particular, this dimension defines the participation or nonparticipation of the individual in political choice.

In a totalitarian society, there are no rule-protected spheres within which the individual is guaranteed exercise of liberty. The individual is a slave to the state-as-master, quite independent of the ways in which state decisions are made and also of the benevolence or malevolence reflected in the patterns of state choices. The answer to the question posed by Robert Nozick is clear.[1] Even in the final stage where the individual is subject to the will of the majority he remains a slave.

In nontotalitarian societies, however, there remain rule-protected spheres within which the individual has liberty of choice and action. But it is worth emphasizing that in all areas of action within which the state may act, the individual is necessarily subject to the state's authority. The well-being of the individual, however this may be measured, *depends* on the state. The individual's position in the polity is fully analogous to that of the resource owner in an economic relationship embodying *rent*. The size as well as the magnitude of the rent finally assigned to the individual are beyond his own powers of control through choice. There is no *exit* option. This relationship is not affected, in its fundamental aspect, by the possible participation of the individual in collective-political decision processes, save in the limiting case where the operative voting rule is unanimity.

Recognition of the necessary vulnerability of the individual to state action does not imply that "voice" is an unimportant attribute of membership in the compulsory organization that is the state. Most persons may prefer a participatory democracy to government by an elite, even if both are bound by the constitutional-legal order to the same range of authority.

1. Robert Nozick, *Anarchy, State, and Utopia* (New York: Basic Books, 1974), 290–92.

My emphasis, however, is on the critical importance of the rules that limit the exercise of the state's authority, rules that are independent of the way collective choices are made within such rules. The participatory exercise of voice in an unrestricted parliamentary democracy may be valued, but limits on the range and extent of state action may be substantively of much more significance. Possible participation in the shaping of the polity's constitution, the set of rules that constrain the potential exercise of state authority, is categorically of greater import than any guarantee of voting franchise within a given constitutional structure.

In a very real sense, the set of rules that define the respective spheres for state and private action locates the individual along the freedom-slavery spectrum. Once these rules are settled, and independent of how they may have been derived, and/or how much or how little voice the individual is allowed to exercise in shaping state action, the individual remains a *subject* within the domain of the state's constituted authority. Within the authorized sphere of collective action, the individual remains dependent on the state. Dependence need not, of course, imply impoverishment; the individual may fare well or poorly under the dependence umbrella. But it is self-evident that recognition of dependency status invokes a behavioral pattern quite different from that which genuine independence affords.

My argument may seem fully consistent with that of the libertarian anarchists who see individuals as subjects of the state on the one hand and as adversaries of the state along the boundary lines of state power. I part company with the libertarian anarchists, however, as noted above, when I accept, with Hobbes, that individuals would, if given genuine constitutional choice, grant some authority to the state, even in the full recognition that such a grant of authority comes at the certain sacrifice of individual autonomy.

We should never be trapped in the delusion that the enhancement of the state's authority to "do good things for us collectively" involves no cost to us as free individuals. But recognizing that this cost exists is not the same as saying that it is a cost we shall never pay. The cost in liberty will, over some ranges of state action, be lower than the expected benefit from the exercise of state authority within the defined limits. We are able to satisfy our preferences, to achieve a higher level of utility, where some of our liberties have been sacrificed and where there does exist a well-defined but limited domain for the exercise of the coercive power of the state.

But we must recognize full well that within the limits of the authority so assigned to the state we are necessarily subjects, or, more dramatically, slaves, to the state, as master. The slave may, indeed, enjoy a higher standard of living than the free man, but he is a fool if he neglects for a moment the elementary fact that he remains a slave. In a very real sense, the constitutional contract that sets the limits of state authority over individuals is a slave contract, and we sell ourselves into slavery with each and every extension of the state's power.

Why is a slavery contract, as such, different from any other contract? Why do all of us (except possibly for a few extreme libertarians) think that the slavery contract is not normally an ethically legitimate embodiment of voluntary exchange? We reject such an "exchange" because it does not allow for a post-contract viable exit option; the person who finds himself in a slave relationship does not have effective alternatives. Membership in a state embodies this attribute of the slave contract to the extent that the state, as such, possesses the authority to direct the activities of the individual, including the authority to extract a share of the resource or product that is nominally under the individual's "private" possession. We are dependents, slaves, rent-recipients (these are equivalent terms for purposes of my argument here) to the extent that we are unable to escape the extractions demanded by the state. It took me two decades to shuck off the normative trappings of orthodox economics and to write in defense of tax loopholes.

Confusion arises here because there seems to be no identifiable master in the democratic polity. As an individual, a person may well acknowledge his dependence on the state, but he may also recognize that there seems to be no single person or group that can be identified as master. In the idealized model of majoritarian democracy, the individual's fate depends on a process, and, in the limit, no one person has more than minimal influence in determining the result. We are, in such a setting, all "slaves without masters."

We are, however, slaves-subjects only to the extent that the state is authorized to act, quite independent of the decision rules through which it operates. (Again, save in the limiting case of a unanimity rule.) We are free men within those spheres of our activity that are protected from state intrusion by effective constitutional order.

The monumental folly of the past two centuries has been the presumption that so long as the state operates in accordance with democratic procedures (free and periodic elections; open franchise; open entry for parties, candidates, and interests; majority or plurality voting rules) the individual does, indeed, have insurance against exploitation, quite apart from any viable exit option. Modern states have been allowed to invade increasing areas of "private space" under the pretense of democratic process. (In saying this, I do not want to imply that the legal form of state expansion is unimportant. States that broadly adhere to the rule of law are, of course, more protective of individual liberty than states which discriminate among persons arbitrarily, even with the same level of total activity.)

I hope that my argument here has shifted the emphasis somewhat. Failure or success has too often been measured in terms of the standard economists' criterion of efficiency, the ability to get goods and services produced and distributed, to add to the wealth of nations. This emphasis has, I think, been mistaken, at least in part. Markets may fail against the efficiency standard, even in some relative sense. But even in failure markets allow persons to retain exit options without which liberty cannot be secured. The state may succeed against the efficiency standard, even in some relative sense. But even in success, the state necessarily closes off (or narrowly restricts) the exit option for its members, implying necessarily that while liberty may be allowed, it cannot be guaranteed. In retrospect, it seems singularly unfortunate that Adam Smith chose to entitle his great work "The Wealth of Nations" rather than "The System of Natural Liberty."

Finally, let me express the main point of these remarks by reference to Hayek's notable *The Road to Serfdom*.[2] In my view, the thesis should not be that an initiation of state intrusion must lead, ultimately, to man's serfdom to the state. The thesis should be interpreted to suggest that *any intrusion* by the state insures man's serfdom, *within the limits defined by the intrusion*. Man is, and must remain, a slave to the state. But it is critically and vitally important to recognize that ten percent slavery is different from fifty percent.

---

2. F. A. Hayek, *The Road to Freedom* (Chicago: University of Chicago Press, 1944).

Criteria for a Free Society
Definition, Diagnosis, and Prescription

In this book, as well as in other works, I have examined basic issues of political, legal, and social philosophy from the perspective of a political economist. From this discussion should emerge an internally consistent position, although I do not claim that ambiguities are absent. It may be useful, in this final chapter, to bring apparent loose ends together and to try somewhat more explicitly than before to lay down criteria that must be met for a society to be legitimately classified as free. In the process I can assess the America of the late 1970's against these criteria and suggest conceptual requirements for meaningful prescription. I shall develop the following arguments:

1. Freedom is possible only under rules, under law.
2. The choice of rules, the constitution of society, must be categorically separated from the choices made within rules, private and public.
3. The choice of rules which define the structure of social order must be conceived as endogenous to and inclusive of all members of the community.
4. Pragmatic drift, along with inattention to structural change, may produce and, in my view, has produced, with consequent dangers to the maintenance of individual freedom, grossly inefficient results that may have been designed by no one, intended by no one, and, in some ultimate sense, desired by no one.

From *Freedom in Constitutional Contract: Perspectives of a Political Economist* (College Station: Texas A&M University Press, 1977), 287–99. Reprinted by permission of the publisher.

5. This diagnosis suggests that improvement is conceptually possible; general prescription for improvement may be made, but major difficulties arise in making specific prescriptions for change.

In shorthand, and with the required qualifications, these separate arguments may be summarized as (1) the rule of law, (2) constitutionalism, (3) contractarianism, (4) the social dilemma, and (5) prospects for constitutional revolution. These may be used as subheadings for the sections of this chapter.

The Rule of Law

There should be relatively little dispute about the proposition that individual freedom, in any meaningful sense, is possible only under law, along with the implied consequence that the rules, "the law," must be enforced by some collective entity, some state. Only the anarchists, of either the romantic or the libertarian variety, would question this proposition. Dispute may, of course, arise over the origins of law, of the rules, and I shall discuss the matter of origins briefly in the contractarian section below. But the alternative to a society with law is one without law, that is, anarchy. Therefore, in order to establish the validity of the proposition here, we need only to examine anarchy as the universal principle for organizing social life.

In some ultimate sense, anarchy must always represent a utopian ideal for anyone who places a high value on freedom of the individual. The idealized society is one peopled by beings who have somehow come to share a common set of definitions concerning the assignment of claims to scarce resources and who behave with mutual respect in regard to these universally acknowledged claims. In such a setting there could arise no conflicts among putative individual claims and no invasions or "boundary crossings" among claims. But we scarcely recognize the people in such a world. Human nature, as we observe it or even as we might imagine it, forces us to allow both for the emergence of conflicts among claimants and for violations of acknowledged claims. Reality requires that we reduce our sights, even when discussing first-best institutional arrangements, and discard anarchy as a self-sufficient organizing principle.

While we should never overlook the wide and varied range of human interactions that are essentially organized by principles of anarchy and that do not, for that reason, necessarily degenerate into chaos, for discussions of social philosophy generally my own procedure is to commence analysis from a model of Hobbesian anarchy in which nature is "red in tooth and claw," in which there is an acknowledged "warre" of each against all, and in which the life of solitary man is indeed "poor, nasty, brutish, and short." This model is helpful because it accentuates the possibility that the dilemma created in a world without law may be all-inclusive. Each and every person in the group may be in the worst possible position; agreement upon law, upon general rules for behavior, may, if adopted and enforced, be expected to improve the lot of everyone. From this it follows that unanimous agreement should be possible, agreement on any one from among alternative sets of rules or alternative sets of assignments among claims. This derivation of agreement does not require the introduction of some transcendent moral or ethical code or some imposition of the privately preferred values of a self-anointed person or group.

Agreement on a set of rules, on a legal arrangement, is not, however, in itself sufficient to remove the Hobbesian dilemma. Rules must be enforced; violations of agreed-on standards must be punished; this punishment must be anticipated. This enforcement-punishment role must be assigned to an agent on behalf of the whole community of persons. This agent or agency then becomes what I have called "the protective state."

Constitutionalism

The enforcement of an assigned set of claims, a set of defined rights of persons to do things, along with the appropriate punishment of those who violate these claims and rights must not be confused with the decision process in which these claims and rights are established. The latter may be called the constitutional stage of decision, the outcome of which is the whole set of legal-political arrangements, including the definitions of the rights of persons, groups, and the state. It is the constitution, in the broad meaning of the term, which establishes the limits or constraints within which the whole range of post-constitutional choices or decisions takes place, whether they be the decisions of private persons, those of the enforcing agent in the form of a state, or those of persons acting collectively through what I have called the productive state.

The constitution defines the rules of the game, and the choice of these rules is categorically distinct from the enforcement of these rules and must be conceived as such both by the players and by the referees or umpires. The agent who is appointed as referee does not himself participate in the choice of rules, at least in his role as referee, and in an abstract logical sense he makes no choices in carrying out his assigned task. He is ideally limited to finding fact. He asks the questions: What rules are in existence? Have these rules been violated? What punishment rules are to be applied? The enforcing agent or referee is *not* allowed to ask, and indeed it is wholly inappropriate for him to ask the questions: What would be a good set of rules? How might the existing rules be reformed to make for a better game? What criteria (justice, efficiency, and so on) should be employed to assess alternative rules?

I stress these very elementary points, and I do so in a game setting because it is precisely at this level that profound and ultimately dangerous confusion emerges about the role of the state in making constitutional law and in modifying the whole set of legal arrangements, including the assignment of individuals' rights and claims. In its most blatant form this confusion emerges in the form of legal positivism, which states that "the law" is what the state determines it to be and that individual rights are, and must be, defined by the state and, as a consequence, are necessarily dependent on the state. In this vision of reality the state itself, along with its various arms and agencies, is subject to no rules beyond its internal limits. Individuals are vulnerable to the whims and fancies of those persons who wield power on behalf of the state. There is no meaningful constitution in this construction.

It is, nonetheless, relatively easy to appreciate the tendency to slip into this mode of conceiving state activity. In the real world the existing set of rights and claims contains many areas where precise boundaries are unclear. Conflicts emerge among persons and groups over these disputed boundaries, and the arms and agencies of the enforcing agent, the protective state, are observed to be drawing clear lines of demarcation among claims where none seemed to exist before. In such actions the state is clearly "making the law." But its own conception of what it is doing and the conception of those affected by its actions are extremely important in the sense of establishing some normative limits on state power. As long as the fiction is maintained that the agency of the state is discovering those boundaries that may have been obscured or hidden and over which conflict has emerged, there is no tendency for the agency or its clients to invade the domain where "the law" is clearly established and understood or to claim powers to rewrite existing law independent of prior obscurities and potential conflict.

The confusion between the constitutional stage of decision, in which the choice of basic rules takes place, and private or public action taken postconstitutionally, or within the chosen set of rules, emerges in a more subtle and ultimately more pernicious form under what we may call legal normativism. In this form, as in the most general legal positivism, "the law" remains what the state determines it to be. But in this normative variant the state is to be guided in its determination by externally evoked criteria. Judges can "make law"; this is acknowledged. But they are supposed to do so on the basis of precepts for justice, efficiency, or like criteria. "The law," in this conception, is the instrument for social reform; its meaning as a set of rules within which the game is played out is lost in the process.

This conception of "the law" as the instrument for reform is now pervasive among American law schools and among members of the American judiciary. The essential meaning of the constitution has been perverted, and I am personally more pessimistic about a reversal of these particular ideas than I am about almost any other of the many shifts in attitude that seem to be required for the maintenance of a free social order. And here the particular features of the American constitutional structure and constitutional history are relevant and important. The judicial branch of the United States national government throughout much of our history did stay within its role as the enforcing agent for the rules, as defined in the initial constitutional document. Its powers of enforcement extended also to cover the boundary crossings made by the government itself, through its legislative and executive arms and agencies.

It is for this reason that the traditional and more familiar variant of what I have called legal normativism has never been so important in America as elsewhere. Even in the America of the late 1970's we find common reference to the inappropriateness and inability of either Congress or the president to modify "the law of the land," as defined by the judiciary. Within certain areas (although not in others, as I shall note below) the public political philosophy of America today embodies severe limits on the powers of legislative assemblies or elected executives to change the rules—to change the constitution itself. These limits are not, however, extended to apply to the judiciary. The public political philosophy in other Western democracies is, I think, quite different in this respect. And the more relevant confusion is presumably that between the making of law, in the basic constitutional sense, and the activity of elected representatives through parliamentary assemblies in legislating, a distinction which Hayek stresses, I think correctly.

At base, of course, the confusion is the same in the two cases. The American judiciary views law as an instrument to promote the "social good," as this good is defined by the judges, and it also allows, in its "majesty," the legislative bodies to promote the "social good" in those areas where the judiciary has chosen to remain aloof, and notably in so-called economic legislation. In matters of economic policy the effective American constitution is what Congress determines it to be; the judiciary adopts a hands-off attitude here. With the other Western democracies the range of legislative or parliamentary determination of the basic rules, of the effective constitution, is presumably wider, and that of the judiciary more limited than in the United States. But some variant of the confusion between the constitutional stage of choice, where law is made, and collective actions taken within "the law" will almost necessarily arise as long as the objectives of the state are seen as those of promoting "social good." To the extent that the institutions of law and government, along with the prevailing public attitudes toward these institutions, reflect this teleological conception of the state, constitutional order is necessarily undermined. In its most elemental meaning a constitution is a set of rules which constrain the activities of persons and agents in the pursuit of their own ends and objectives. To argue directly or by inference that the constitution in itself embodies or should embody a "social purpose" is to negate its very meaning.

Contractarianism

In the preceding discussion I have implicitly defined "constitutionalism" broadly, and in my interpretation the basic conception becomes equivalent to one that elevates to center stage criteria for process or procedure as opposed to criteria for end states.[1] That which is to be evaluated is the pro-

---

1. Robert Nozick's discussion of the differences between process and end-state criteria in *Anarchy, State, and Utopia* is to be recommended here.

cess through which the rules are made instead of the content of the rules, per se. That which emerges from an acceptable process is, by inference, acceptable, and indeed, acceptability has no independent meaning beyond this.

It is interesting to note that all of the major protagonists in the philosophical discourse of the 1970's are constitutionalists in the sense herein defined. Hayek, Nozick, and Rawls share with me an emphasis on the relevance of process criteria in evaluating the basic legal-constitutional framework. All of us are constitutionalists in the sense that we separate categorically the basic rules, "the law," from actions taken within these rules. Beyond this point of conceptual agreement, however, there arises a distinct divergence among us concerning how the rules should be conceived as being made and changed. Both Hayek and Nozick may be classified broadly as evolutionists in their positive explanations of how "the law" emerges. They go further, however, and make normative inferences to the effect that explicit efforts toward constructive reforms are not desired. Law emerges spontaneously, as if by an "invisible hand," as the result of the adjustments made by many persons to the localized choice situations they confront. The development of the English common law is the archetype or, more generally, the spontaneous order produced by the decentralized process of the competitive market.

By contrast and comparison with the evolutionists both John Rawls and I can, I think, be classified as contractarian. In this position we do not necessarily reject the evolutionary explanation of how the basic rules, in fact, emerge. But something akin to a contractarian position seems to be essential if we are to go beyond explanation, if we are to be able to evaluate existing elements of the constitutional order with any prospect of securing improvement. This is true quite independent of how the existing rules might, in fact, have been generated through history. There seems to be no basis for the presumption that whatever may have emerged that we may now observe is necessarily "efficient" or "just."

But how are criteria for "efficiency" or "justice" to be introduced without reference to end states? It is precisely at this point that the notion of agreement, of quasi-contract, becomes critical in the argument. That rule is acceptable which is itself defined by agreement among all participants in the game. We may, if desired, substitute *fair* for *acceptable* here, and if we want to go one step further semantically, we may replace *fair* with *just*. Or, perhaps more eloquently, we may follow John Rawls in defining justice as fairness. Note carefully that the attribute assigned to the rule in this way is derived from the agreement instead of any independent quality or property of the rule itself. (Of course, in choosing among rules upon which they might conceivably agree, persons will necessarily examine the predicted working properties of alternatives.) There is no notion of some intrinsic "goodness" involved in the argument at all.

This contractarian argument may be accepted in its idealized version. If there is observed agreement among all persons affected, a rule so chosen might be acknowledged to be acceptable. But we live in time; there exists a set of legal rules, a constitutional order, and persons in the here and now have not been observed to agree, and have not so agreed, on this order in whole or in part. There has been no explicit act of consent to the particular set of institutions in existence. The contractarian response to this situation is subject to much misinterpretation. The individual who finds himself as a participant in a social order defined by legal rules that he had no part in choosing must ask the question: Are these rules within the set of alternative possibilities that might have emerged from an agreement among all persons who are now participants in the game? To even begin to answer such a question, the individual cannot look merely at his own well-identified position in any time-dated end state. He must look at the pattern of positions and also at the changes in these positions over a sequence of rounds of play, over time. He must account for probabilistic elements in the results. Something like "the original position" behind the "veil of ignorance," made familar by Rawls, must be introduced to make evaluation possible.

Misunderstanding tends to arise in moving from this process of individual evaluation toward inferences for constitutional reform—for changes in the rules that are in existence. There has been some tendency to interpret the contractarian position as implying that conceptual consent or agreement offers a criterion for *imposing* constitutional change, independent of agreement on change itself. That is, the argument has been advanced that a judge (or a legislator), considering himself to be empowered to change the law, should, by contractarian logic, make his own Rawlsian assessment of an existing rule and act accordingly. This argument represents, however, a gross perversion of the contractarian position, properly understood. Once again the central importance of agreement must be stressed. Change in an existing rule, or changes in a set of rules, finds a contractarian justification only on agreement among all participants.

This necessary consequence of the contractarian position tends to generate the criticism that, so interpreted, the position amounts to little more than a dressed-up justification for the status quo, for whatever set of rules might exist, regardless of the historical origins of such rules. This criticism must be squarely faced. If existing rules are to be changed without agreement, some external criteria for change must be introduced. Beyond agreement there is simply no place for the contractarian to go.

We may, however, respond more positively to the status quo restrictiveness by pointing out that the prospects for achieving consensus on basic changes in rules are much wider than a simplistic application of the unanimity requirement might suggest. In the first place we must keep in mind that we are concentrating on genuine constitutional rules, which are known to be quasi-permanent and which, once changed, are predicted to remain stable over a whole sequence of time periods. To the extent that the modifications under consideration are treated as quasi-permanent by those who participate in the discussion and debates, the position of any one person is necessarily uncertain. An individual cannot know just what specific rule will benefit him under a particular set of future circumstances. He will, therefore, be forced under precepts of rationality to move toward an attitude akin to that described by Rawls.[2] In the second place, there may be more prospects for general agreement on a whole set of changes in the basic rules, in the whole constitutional order, than there would be on any one change taken singly. The packaging of several prospective changes allows for trade, for compromise, for compensation, for side payments. These are all instruments of agreement which allow the differing intensities of preference to be weighted by the individuals affected. A person may well agree to a modification of an existing rule that seems to impose limited damages to his own position in exchange for some reciprocal agreement by others for another change or set of changes that will greatly benefit him.

---

2. The uncertainty concerning the particularized application of the rules in future periods was the device used by Gordon Tullock and me in *The Calculus of Consent* to accomplish the conceptual agreement on efficient rules for making collective choices. This device serves the same purpose as Rawls's original position.

The Social Dilemma[3]

I have referred to the present situation in the United States as one of "constitutional anarchy." The effective constitution has been allowed to erode to the extent that the predictability that should be inherent in a legal structure is seriously threatened. In part this situation is the result of what might be called "pragmatic drift," the piecemeal adjustments made to situations as they are confronted without attention to the design of the structure as a whole, either in a backward-looking or a forward-looking direction. Indeed, my primary critique of those philosophers who hold up the evolutionary process as ideal is based on my reading of what this process has now produced. But the situation is also attributable to intellectual error of monumental proportions. The basic confusion noted above, in its several forms, has destroyed our understanding of "the constitution of freedom," an understanding that the American founding fathers did possess.

My central diagnostic hypothesis is that the status quo is not "efficient," that it does not qualify as "fair" or "just" even in the most limited application of the contractarian precepts. The legal-constitutional order (or disorder) that we now observe places us *all* in a dilemma that is akin to the one described in the Hobbesian jungle, where the privately rational behavior of each person produces a result which all persons find unsatisfactory. (This diagnosis explains my own interest in analysis of the means for escaping from this setting.) Continued drift will worsen the situation for all, or substantially all, participants. We shall, slowly but surely, be swallowed up by an insatiable Leviathan. The freedoms that we now possess will be continually eroded by an enveloping array of bureaucratic regulation.

This scenario which is unfolding around us, and in which we are unwilling and, for the most part, unwitting participants is *not* the working out of some grand design aimed at the destruction of a social order based on freedom of the individual. In making this statement I am explicitly rejecting the significance of any "march through the institutions" that may be present in Western democracies. Rejection of the significance of such a march is not, however, equivalent to denying the possible existence of such efforts which

---

3. In his book under this title Gordon Tullock discusses several applications of the more general dilemma that I examine briefly here.

may, of course, complement in some small way the more important underlying forces for change. But it would indeed be tragic if attention comes to be unduly concentrated on minuscule destructive conspiracies to the neglect of the obvious fact that what we see is explainable as the unintended consequence of individual actions, taken pragmatically, locally, and with no sense of overall design or purpose, either destructive or constructive. In a real sense my diagnosis turns those of the evolutionists, of Hayek, Oakeshott, and Nozick, on their heads; we can adequately explain what is happening to us by an "invisible-hand" logic. And who can, even by inference, label this as desirable or acceptable?

But precisely because we can employ such a logic to explain and to understand what we see, we are also able to identify a rational basis for improvement, which again can be consistently defined by agreement, allowing us to hold fast to contractarian precepts. If my diagnosis is correct, there should exist means of securing very general agreement, genuine consensus, on change. We are, on this diagnosis, all trapped in what we may properly call a "constitutional dilemma," in which the basic rules of the game have been eroded, forgotten, and allowed to wither away.

Prospects for Constitutional Revolution

The prescription that follows from my diagnosis is straightforward. Genuine constitutional revolution should be possible. All, or substantially all, persons and groups in the United States of 1978 should be able to reach agreement on a carefully designed and properly orchestrated set of legal-institutional arrangements which could then replace those that are in existence and in disarray. As we move beyond such general statements, however, major difficulties emerge. How is such a constitutional revolution to be organized? How are the rules of the game to be changed while the game continues to be played under the old rules?

I shall acknowledge my own inability to offer satisfactory answers to such questions as these. I have called for the adoption of a "constitutional attitude," by which I mean an appreciation and understanding of the difference between choosing basic rules and acting within those rules. But this does not get me far. Suppose, by some miracle of the educational process, the prevailing public philosophy should shift rapidly toward that which I would personally prefer. In this setting let us presume that each and every person would come to share the basic constitutional attitude suggested, and further, let us presume that each person independently arrives at a diagnosis roughly equivalent to that outlined above.

This imagined world of rational beings, all of whom recognize the dilemma confronted, would still face the problem of getting a constitutional revolution organized. The public-goods problem would necessarily emerge to make individual action toward promotion of such change unlikely. Why should a single person make the investment of time and effort required in evaluating alternative proposals for constitutional change, in discussing these alternatives with his fellows, and in arranging for some means of collective choice among alternatives?

It is easy to become extremely pessimistic about prospects for effective constitutional revolution when such questions are raised. But economists tend to overlook the interests of men that extend beyond the narrow confines of *Homo economicus.* Men who are excited by the grand design of the new constitutional order that is possible may, in fact, be willing to overcome the public-goods threshold noted above. That some men will do this may be admitted. But will these same persons be willing to design and to propose rules changes that are not aimed to further their own interests or those of their social group? More importantly, will these persons be willing to accept agreement among all participants as the test, even when they recognize that the large majority of their fellows have not undertaken, and will not undertake, the effort necessary to understand and to appreciate the alternatives offered to them?

I raise these questions rather than answer them. But lest this chapter, and this book, end on an overly pessimistic note, let me recall that in 1976 we celebrated two bicentennials. In addition to the American Declaration of Independence, 1776 was also marked by the publication of Adam Smith's *Wealth of Nations.* What did this book accomplish? I think that it does not exaggerate to say that a genuine constitutional revolution did take place in Great Britain during the half-century that followed. Is it too much to hope that after 1976 we are on the verge of a renewed faith in and an understanding of the strengths of a society in which men are free? Is the current mistrust of governmental solutions, surely an increasingly relevant part of the prevailing public philosophy in the West, the first step toward a genuine constitutional revolution that may take place without our recognizing explicitly what has happened?

The Individual as Participant
in Political Exchange

Introduction

An important element in James S. Coleman's scientific enterprise has been the derivation of collective organization and collective action from the rational choice behavior of individual decisionmakers. Therefore, it is not surprising that he was a contributor to *Public Choice* and an active participant in the Public Choice Society, when both the journal and the society were in their infancy.[1] In a very real sense, Coleman's has always been a "public choice" perspective, as this somewhat misnamed, and widely misunderstood, subdiscipline emerged into a viable research program.

On several occasions, I have suggested that a necessary component in the public choice perspective is a conception of politics as a complex exchange process in which individuals participate in some sense analogous to their participation in markets.[2] I have compared and contrasted this exchange model of politics with (1) the pure conflict model and (2) the truth-judgment model. My concern has been to demonstrate the relative superiority of the exchange model for both descriptive analyses of observed political reality and any normative justification of government as political agency. I have not di-

From *Social Theory and Social Policy: Essays in Honor of James S. Coleman*, ed. Aage B. Sørensen and Seymour Spilerman (Westport, Conn.: Praeger, 1993), 11–21. Reprinted by permission of Greenwood Publishing Group, Inc.

1. James S. Coleman, "The Marginal Utility of a Vote Commitment," *Public Choice* 5 (Fall 1968): 39–58.

2. James M. Buchanan, "The Public Choice Perspective," *Economia delle scelte publiche* 1 (January 1983): 7–15.

rected sufficient attention to explicating the several variants of the exchange model itself, which is the objective of this paper.

First, I shall set out the two distinct exchanges in which the individual may be presumed to participate in the role of a member of an organized polity. Then I shall describe in some detail the idealized operation of the voluntaristic exchange model, and extend its potential applicability by shifting attention to the constitutional stage of interaction. Next I shall examine the second model, that of coerced or unequal Hobbesian exchange between the monolithic sovereign and the individual citizen. Finally, I shall discuss the institutional marriage of the two exchange models in political regimes.

Exchange among Individuals and between the Individual and the Collectivity

In its most abstract formulation, political exchange takes place among all members of the set of individuals who share a common objective and who can secure this objective more effectively through joint action. This setting describes the familiar public goods model of interaction; individuals are conceived to be exchanging, one with another, shares in the costs of the joint undertaking. Note that in this formulation there is no state or government, as such. Politics is limited to the cooperative activity that is involved in the joint demand for the commonly desired good, which is, presumably, "purchased" directly from ordinary suppliers on a market.

The exchange involved here is complex because of the necessary inclusion of all participants in the demand enterprise. There is no possible factoring of the exchange into a single-buyer/single-seller relationship. And, because of the nonexclusive characteristic of the good, all participants must be brought simultaneously into the contract. Bargaining among participants takes place along two dimensions, that which measures the relative shares in the costs of the good that is to be purchased and that which measures the quantity to be purchased.

In its idealized limits, this is a model of purely voluntary exchange, analogous in important respects to exchange in private goods markets, with the significant exception being the extended number of participants. The relevant exchange takes place among demanders; the derivative exchange between demanders (as a collective group or as a corporate actor) and some single supplying agent is treated as an ordinary market relationship, with the good that is purchased being supplied at a competitive price.

As some public choice critics noted early, the political exchange model in orthodox public goods analysis is limited to the demand side of the fiscal process and leaves out of the account any organization of public goods supply. In real-world politics, governments exist, and they can scarcely be modeled as passive transmitters of the preferences of citizens, who have presumably completed the tradeoffs among themselves so as to arrive at some collective determination of cost shares and public goods quantity. As they are observed to function, governments extract tax payments from and supply goods and services to citizens; the transaction between each citizen, as taxpayer-beneficiary, and the government would seem amenable to analysis in terms of political exchange between government-as-supplier and individual-as-demander, much as with an ordinary exchange between a seller and a buyer in the marketplace.

Such an exchange is, however, quite different from either a market transaction in private goods or the idealized contractual agreement on cost shares in the pure public goods setting. A central characteristic of exchange is absent; the individual does not voluntarily participate in the fiscal exchange with government, at least in a sense that is analogous to ordinary market behavior. The individual does not retain the relatively low-cost exit option that is ever present in the market, nor does the individual retain the effective veto power that is present in the idealized Wicksellian contract for the demand of collectively purchased goods. In direct fiscal exchange, the government confronts the individual, as taxpayer, with a bill that must be paid, upon pain of penalty for failure. At the same time, the government supplies to the individual some flow of goods and services from which some benefits are enjoyed. But there is no individual behavioral adjustment available at relatively low cost, adjustment which can insure that at least at the margin benefits are subjectively measured to be equal to costs. If such adjustment to the exchange offered by the fisc were possible, the individual would, of course, accept the flow of services offered while at the same time withholding all payments. Voluntariness, in this sense, is impossible in this transaction between the government and the individual.

The presence or absence of this central feature of exchange does not modify the formal definition of the conditions that must be met to insure that the results of the overall or inclusive relationship between the individual and others in the political unit, including those who act as governmental agents, are analogous to those that emerge in market exchange. And it may be useful here to specify precisely the idealized fiscal process in its entirety, if for no other reason than to suggest the incentive incompatibilities that must arise at some critical spots where persons confront choice alternatives.

Consider, then, a setting where all members of a political community enter initially into a discussion-dialogue on the prospect for collective action directed toward buying a good that is to be made available for consumption-usage by all persons simultaneously. An agreement is signified when and as each person voluntarily accepts an obligation to contribute a specified sum toward the joint costs in exchange, with matching contributions specified for all other members of the group. The complex agreement describes the allocation of cost shares (tax prices) among persons as well as the quantity of the good that is to be purchased and subsequently made available.

Government then enters the calculus solely as an agent directed to implement the agreement that has been reached through the voluntary exchange among members. Acting as agent for the collectivity, government then confronts each citizen with a tax charge, the one that the member in question has agreed to pay, and then uses funds so collected to finance and to supply the collective-consumption good in precisely the quantity that had been earlier agreed to by all members.

Each individual attains an equilibrium at which the assigned tax price per unit of good is equal to his relative marginal evaluation of the good, defined in some numeraire. In this sense, each person is in a position that is allocatively analogous to that attained by his own individualized behavioral adjustment in the market for a partitionable private good. But despite this formal equivalence, the individual in the exchange with government-as-agent is not faced with an incentive-compatible structure that will be voluntarily sustained. The individual will find it rational to defect on the prior agreement, to become a free rider; the benefits of the nonexcludable public good will be available independent of the individual's own behavior. Hence, the government-as-agent must be assigned powers of coercion; persons must be forced to contribute shares in the financing of the collectively consumed good, even if they have agreed to the terms of the more inclusive exchange.

If, however, the government-as-agent is assigned powers of coercion over citizens in order to overcome the incentive incompatibility in citizens' behavior, another potential incentive incompatibility emerges as government is allowed to depart from its role as idealized agent. It will be useful to specify precisely the form that the coercive charges levied by government must take, if government should strictly remain in the role of idealized agent. The government could not, in this role, be empowered to tax in any orthodox meaning of the term; it could not impose a coercive charge against any measurable base such as income, expenditure, or use of particular goods. Each individual must be confronted with the tax price per unit of public good that he has agreed to pay in the inclusive contractual process. But since, by the nature of this charge, the individual cannot behaviorally adjust so as to modify his liability (per unit of public good), there is no direct negative feedback exerted on government when it departs from its idealized role, either by levying higher-than-agreed taxes or utilizing some share of funds collected to finance goods for agents' rather than citizens' benefits. Just as individual citizens have incentives to free ride in the absence of governmental coercion, government itself, through its agents, has incentives to depart from the terms of its own mandate by exploiting its coercive powers.

Constitutional Extension of the Model of Exchange among Individuals

The procedural requirements that any pure model of voluntary fiscal exchange must meet in order to accomplish the defined purpose are indeed extreme. Unanimous agreement among all members of the polity must be reached on each and every component item in the budget. Each outlay must be treated separately in the collective decision calculus. Further, government must be established and assigned powers of coercion to enforce the agreed-on contractual terms, but means must be found to restrict government to these limits. Recognizing the immense practical difficulties of approximating such requirements, it is all too easy to reject the voluntary exchange model out of hand, even as an ideal conceptualization of the relationship between the individual and the collectivity.

If, however, the exchange model is modified by shifting attention to the level of constitutional choice, essential elements may be retained while moving some considerable distance toward plausibly recognizable institutional features of real-world politics. Suppose that the separate individual members of the political community acknowledge that the costs of attempting to reach agreement on each and every item of proposed collective outlay will be prohibitive. Suppose further that they also recognize that any assignment of coercive powers to government must be accompanied by restrictions or limits on the arbitrary use of such powers. In this setting, agreement may be reached on a structure of collective decisionmaking that will facilitate collective action while at the same time keeping the exercise of coercion in check.[3] In place of idealized agreement on each and every proposal to inaugurate joint action, a periodically elected legislative body may be empowered to use majority voting rules to make spending and taxing decisions, provided that the degree of arbitrary discrimination in these decisions is limited by some appropriate criteria of generality. That is to say, legislative majorities may be authorized to impose taxes on all citizens, but only so long as taxes are levied on acceptable and well-defined criteria of generality. Supporters of legislative minorities cannot be singled out for discriminatory tax treatment, nor can supporters of majorities be discriminatorily favored. Analogous constitutional criteria of generality may be applied to the distribution of benefits from goods and services that government is authorized to finance with tax funds, although this fully symmetrical application is much less familiar in observed fiscal systems.

The provisions that establish the whole structure—involving the voting franchise, the periodicity of elections, the voting rule among the electorate, the size of the legislative body, the bases of representation, the voting rule within the legislature itself, the veto powers of the executive, the range and scope of fiscal and nonfiscal legislative powers, and so on—may be set out in a political constitution for the community. And agreement or potential agreement on the provisions in the constitution provides the ultimate legitimation for action taken within the terms of the structure that is described.

Note that this shift of idealized agreement to the constitutional level allows for very substantial departures from the procedural conditions described earlier as necessary to bring any fiscal exchange into close analogy to market exchange. The process through which constitutional agreement is

3. James M. Buchanan and Gordon Tullock, *The Calculus of Consent: Logical Foundations of Constitutional Democracy* (Ann Arbor: University of Michigan Press, 1962).

reached, conceptually, remains contractual, and remains in this sense political exchange, in which each individual trades off or exchanges his or her own interests with others. Each person or group accepts the potential constraints defined by the constitution in exchange for the acceptance of comparable constraints by others in the community. But, acting strictly within the constitutional limits that may have been accepted, a legislative majority may impose tax charges upon an individual to finance an outlay that the individual values much less than the private goods that might be purchased by the tax funds extracted. There need be little, if any, relationship here between the tax charges that are imposed coercively on an individual and the value that is placed by that individual on the flow of goods and services made available by the government. Almost every person in the polity will prefer a budgetary mix different from that which is provided, and, universally, each person will prefer a tax structure that involves lower charges against his or her own account. Further, there may exist substantial numbers of citizens who consider themselves to be net losers in the complex fiscal exchange process, which includes the whole taxing-spending package; they may value the total flow of benefits from public goods and services lower than the value of taxes extracted.

The limits on such fiscal exploitation rest in the constitutionally dictated electoral processes. A government acting through the constitutionally authorized legislative majority is subject to electoral replacement, in whole or in part, if its combined package of outlays and taxes gets too far beyond the limits dictated by the ultimate preferences of a majority of citizens. But such limits are so broad indeed that the conceptualization of the fiscal process in the exchange metaphor may be called into question.

There are two difficulties with the exchange or contractual model of politics that must be acknowledged, even at the level of abstract analytical discourse. The first invokes the familiar and long-standing criticism of any contract theory of the state. Individuals find themselves born into membership in an ongoing political structure, with a well-defined set of constitutional rules. They have never participated in any process from which general agreement on the set of constitutional rules might have emerged. In this situation, which is acknowledged to describe empirical reality, how can the individual's acquiescence in the constraints of politics be meaningfully discussed as an element of an exchange with others?

At this point, those who defend contractual or exchange models find it useful to introduce conceptual as opposed to actual agreement to retain some explanatory value. The exercise becomes one of potential legitimation of existing constitutional structures rather than one of historical explanation. Could the existing rules that define the overall operations of the polity have been agreed upon by all citizens if there could have been some imagined initial dialogue? At this point, the potential conflict among the separate interests of persons and groups is mitigated by resorting to constructions that introduce a veil of ignorance or uncertainty.

Even if this major criticism of the exchange or contract model of politics is somehow countered, there remains a second difficulty, related to the incentive incompatibility previously noted. In a large-number polity, individuals will have little or no incentive to become informed about relevant choice alternatives or even to participate actively in any discussion leading to ultimate agreement upon the general constitutional rules that define the constraints upon their private or public actions. That is to say, it remains fully rational and in their own interest for persons to remain disinterested in such processes, and this disinterest, in turn, offers potential political entrepreneurs the opportunity to exploit emotion-based prejudices as opposed to reasoned expressions of interests.[4]

Exchange between the Individual and the Sovereign

Recognition of the attenuated nature of any exchange model derived directly from the democratic-contractual setting, even as extended to the constitutional as opposed to the within-constitutional level of political action, prompts attention to the alternative conceptualization in which there is a two-party relationship between the citizen and the government (state or sovereign). This model can also be interpreted in exchange terms, although in a sense that sharply contrasts to that examined in the democratic setting previously discussed.

4. Geoffrey Brennan and James M. Buchanan, "Voter Choice: Evaluating Political Alternatives," *American Behavioral Scientist* 29 (November/December 1984): 185–201; James M. Buchanan and Viktor J. Vanberg, "A Theory of Leadership and Deference in Constitutional Construction," *Public Choice* 61 (April 1989): 15–27.

The setting for the second model presumes some prior existence, or the initial emergence of, a putative sovereign entity which confronts the individual (any and every individual) with the ultimate choice: Pay tribute in exchange for the protection and security of person and property offered, along with whatever other goods and services the sovereign chooses to make available. This fundamental Hobbesian challenge is nonvoluntary, in any other than a purely semantic sense, and it is equivalent to the highwayman's offer: Your money or your life. This sort of exchange takes familiar nonpolitical form in the various illegal protective rackets operated by organized crime syndicates.

Historically, this model of political exchange may well be more descriptive than any version of the democratic-contractual model, which involves citizens' agreement on the political rules under which they will live. Most states, or governments, emerge from conquest and coercion; rarely have constitutions emerged from general contractual process. In the noncontractual governance model, for the individual's relation to the state, the source of the legitimacy of coercion is quite different from that which characterizes the voluntary exchange and participatory model. In the basic Hobbesian contract between the individual and the sovereign, coercion by the latter is legitimate only to the extent that the value of the security (and other services) thereby guaranteed exceeds the value of the resources extracted from the individual. The government, as the sovereign agency, is armed with a monopoly on coercive force, and it makes no pretense of offering to the individual that bundle of goods and services that most closely corresponds to the latter's preferences, as in the response of producers and suppliers of goods in the marketplace.

The political exchange involved here is unequal in two respects, making it categorically different from exchange among persons in competitively organized markets for private partitionable goods. First, the sovereign is a monopolist, and thereby possesses power to set price on its own terms. Second, the sovereign also exercises monopoly control over the good or bundle of goods that the individual purchases. The government can supply the bundle of goods and services along with the price charged for this bundle in accordance with its own objectives, which may or may not include explicit concern for the satisfaction of individuals' preferences for public goods. To the extent that the government seeks to enhance the value base upon which it can levy claims, that is, so long as the sovereign acts as a residual claimant of economic value in the system, it will be motivated to tax and to spend in such fashion as to insure that measured economic growth will take place. An efficient sovereign, in this sense, may place greater emphasis on growth-enhancing public goods and on growth-promoting taxation than the preferences of citizens would dictate.

Whether or not the sovereign acts in this way depends, in part, on the effective time horizon that guides its action. Because of its monopoly, the sovereign can exploit the whole resource base of the political economy. But uncertainty about the length of its own tenure as sovereign may provide the motivation for an inefficient drawdown, or mining, of the value potential in the economy.

Institutional Marriage: The Sovereign within Electoral and Constitutional Constraints

The two models of political exchange that have been discussed embody categorically different relationships between the individual and political authority. In its idealized limiting case, there is no independently motivated sovereign in the first model. Such authority exists exclusively for the purpose of carrying out the expressed objectives of citizens, particularly the joint consumption of public goods. In the second model, by dramatic contrast, the political authority, as an independently existing person or association, finds its own expected utility enhanced by specializing in the supply of services which it monopolistically sells to the citizens as demanders-users.

Analytical models are, of course, constructed with the aim of imposing some sort of intellectual order on complex reality, and different models carry with them differing perspectives on the reality being observed. It is not at all surprising, therefore, that any empirical description of political institutions would, in most cases, identify features of each model. In a sense, it is necessary for individuals in most political settings to live with the tensions created by the conflicts imposed by the two exchange relationships. This result applies to individuals in their roles as citizens who, on the one hand, participate in electoral processes and constitutional dialogue, and, on the other hand, face the monolithic and coercive agency of government. But the result also applies to those persons who are political agents, who are constrained through electoral feedback mechanisms to satisfy the preferences of citizens, but who at the same time face opportunities to further their own agendas.

Differing political structures reflect differing weightings of the two models, as reflective of the relationships sensed by individuals. Concentrated authoritarian regimes may be almost totally described by the second model, in which the individual, as citizen, faces unequal exchange with the monopolistic sovereign which itself remains unconstrained by either electoral or constitutional feedback. Romania before 1989 offers the polar case. Regimes described as parliamentary and majoritarian move considerably along the spectrum toward the participatory-voluntaristic pole. But the individual-as-citizen remains subject to the dictates of the parliamentary majority, subject only to the prospect of removal through electoral processes. The market analogue to parliamentary majoritarianism is that of the monopolist franchisee, who holds a franchise subject to periodic renewal (e.g., cable TV). The constitutional democracy, along the lines of the United States, shifts somewhat further toward the voluntaristic model of political exchange while remaining some distance from the ideal. Legislative majorities are constrained by both electoral feedback and explicit constitutional restrictions, and majorities reflect some bargained vector of interests which may shift among separate policy issues. Majorities do not govern in the parliamentary sense, and because they do not, there is a somewhat greater sense of direct participation by citizens in the political process. At the same time, there is a loss of the possible consistency in ordering that comes with the replacement of the monolithic, if constrained, Hobbesian sovereign.

It is not within my purview to join the debates among political scientists concerning the relative strengths and weaknesses of parliamentary and nonparliamentary political regimes. But the thrust of my argument is clear. In any and all political regimes there is a sense in which the individual citizen qua individual feels locked into the unequal and bilateral exchange with the monopolistic sovereign, essentially the second of the models discussed above. To the extent that institutional-constitutional structures shift the weighting so that the individual senses governmental responsiveness to his or her expressed preferences, there must exist a greater acceptance of shared responsibility for political outcomes, no matter how such outcomes may be assessed externally.[5]

---

5. Robert Nozick's clever "Tale of the Slave" obscures the relevant distinction here. The individual who participates as one voter in a large-number electoral process may

Hence, the political exchange that matters in any normatively meaningful sense remains the first model discussed, even if the location of consent of agreement must be shifted almost exclusively to the constitutional level, and even if the individual fully acknowledges the strict irrationality of rational inquiry and discourse. In realpolitik, the Hobbesian sovereign always exists, but we tolerate its incursions if we know that we share in the construction of the constraints that limit its behavior.

Conclusion

By necessity, the individual in a democracy participates simultaneously in the two political exchanges isolated for discussion in this paper. There is the idealized exchange among equals deriving from universal suffrage, which may find expression in consensual support for the constitutional structure that constrains the activity of agents who act on behalf of the collective unit. In contrast is the exchange between unequals, which materializes in the continuing and unavoidable confrontation between the individual and the collective unit. Note that the first of these exchange relationships may remain below the individual's level of conscious evaluation; the second exchange is brought to the individual's attention by the necessity of paying taxes. The selfsame person who agrees, implicitly or explicitly, with fellow citizens in consensual support of the basic rules of political order may, in accordance with the dictates of rational interest, seek to subvert these rules as a player in the two-party game with the sovereign collective. The tensions created by the requirement that the individual act in these two roles provide the source of the fundamental political dilemma.

Finally, I have limited discussion in this paper to the two relationships of exchange in politics. It is obvious that the same duality exists in the structure of any large organization. The individual, as a participant in the collective,

---

be subject to the external dictates of the collective unit, and, objectively, his position need be no different from the slave subject to the dictates of the master. But the two situations may be dramatically different to the individual, and this difference may exert behavioral effects. See Robert Nozick, *Anarchy, State, and Utopia* (New York: Basic Books, 1974).

trades off interests with others to attempt to achieve shared objectives. At the same time, the individual, as subject to the constraints internal to the collective, bargains with the collective as a unit in attempts to further his or her particularized interests.

ACKNOWLEDGMENT

I am indebted to my colleague, Viktor Vanberg, for helpful comments.

Towards the Simple Economics
of Natural Liberty
An Exploratory Analysis

All systems of preference or of restraint, therefore, being thus completely taken away, the obvious and simple system of natural liberty *establishes itself of its own accord.* Every man, as long as he does not violate the laws of justice, is left perfectly free to pursue his own interest his own way, and to bring both his industry and capital into competition with those of any other man, or order of men. (Italics supplied.)

> —Adam Smith, *The Wealth of Nations,*
> Modern Library Edition, 651

I. Introduction

The "wealth of nations" is maximized when persons are "free to choose." This instrumental relationship between liberty or freedom and economic welfare emerges directly from the conventional theory of economic interaction. Liberty is valued as an attribute of the institutional arrangements that are necessary to generate maximal economic welfare rather than directly in its own right.

From *Kyklos* 40, fasc. 1 (January 1987): 3–20. Copyright 1987 by Blackwell Publishers Ltd. Reprinted by permission of Blackwell Publishers Ltd.

The author is indebted to Geoffrey Brennan, Hartmut Kliemt, Robert Tollison, and Viktor Vanberg for helpful comments on an earlier draft. A preliminary version of this paper was presented at the Brunner Seminar on Analysis and Ideology, Interlaken, Switzerland, in May 1986.

Given an initial imputation of endowments that is protected by the legal system, the idealized market structure operates to channel the self-interests of participants towards overall results that are efficient, thereby eliminating any need for corrective adjustment. Within this idealized structure, individuals exercise wide-ranging liberties; they choose what, how much, and to whom to buy and sell; for what and with whom to make contracts; where and how to live; upon what, how much, and for whom to work. These are the natural liberties about which Adam Smith wrote, but how do they come to be established? Specifically, how do individuals come to possess these liberties since they do not seem to be independently evaluated, at least in the sense that these liberties enter as "goods" in the utility functions of the market participants whose behavior is analyzed. It is as if these liberties somehow emerge as by-products within the process through which individuals maximize their welfare by seeking those goods and shunning those bads that are explicitly incorporated in their utility functions.

Political economists and philosophers have criticized the relegation of liberty to by-product status in orthodox economic theory, and they have questioned the elevation of allocative efficiency to its role as the unique criterion for evaluation of economic organization. These critics have defended the market economy for its political rather than its allocative properties, for its potential ability to minimize decision-making through and by collective institutions. But there has been no integration of these two quite separate strands of argument.

This paper is an attempt to accomplish such an integration. I propose to use the tools of elementary value theory to demonstrate that with only a slight shift of emphasis and interpretation the evaluation of liberty by those who participate in the market economy can readily be incorporated into the familiar analysis. Further, the simple exercise allows the "allocation of liberty" to be discussed in a manner analogous to the allocation of other valued goods. Not surprisingly, the evaluation of liberty is closely linked to the presence and magnitude of economic rents.

The analysis here differs from many treatments of liberty in that I make no attempt to define liberty at the outset of discussion.[1] A meaning or defi-

---

1. For example, F. A. Hayek commences his book with an attempt at definition (*The Constitution of Liberty* [Chicago: University of Chicago Press, 1960]). M. Jensen and

nition of liberty does emerge from the analysis, a fact which, in itself, provides support for the definition. However, by making analytical rather than definitional issues central to the discussion, I explicitly avoid entering the lists too early on either side of the "positive liberty versus negative liberty" debate.[2]

II. Individual Evaluation of Liberty

Individual liberty or freedom of choice is not normally introduced as a "good" in the standard theory of consumer's choice, which simply presupposes that the individual whose behavior and position are analyzed possesses effective freedom to choose among alternatives. It is, nonetheless, relatively easy to demonstrate that the idealized consumer does, indeed, place a value on liberty, and to measure this value in terms of goods that are explicitly introduced into the utility function.

Consider an individual, i, who is presumed to have well-defined preferences, and who is initially endowed with some quantity, Y, of a numeraire good, y. A second good, x, exists which may or may not be potentially available for purchase by i. If i has no liberty to purchase x, his consumption opportunity set commences at and remains at Y. If, however, i is offered the "liberty to purchase x at price p_x," there will be a maximum value that i will place on having such a liberty, a value that can be conceptually measured.[3] This value is, of course, the familiar consumer's surplus or consumer's rent that i might expect to secure from having available the liberty to purchase x freely at the offered price.

Consumer's rent may, of course, be measured over the whole integral of units purchased or it may be measured seriatim for each unit. How much

W. Meckling devote their whole paper to an extended attempt at definition (*Human Rights and the Meaning of Freedom* [Rochester: University of Rochester, February 1985, mimeographed]).

2. For recent surveys of some of the discussion, see Z. Pelczynski and J. Gray, eds., *Conceptions of Liberty in Political Philosophy* (London: Athlone Press, 1984), and T. P. Terrell, "Liberty: The Concept and Its Constitutional Context," *Notre Dame Journal of Law, Ethics, and Public Policy* 1 (1985): 545–94.

3. In a draft paper that is in some respects similar to this paper, U. Witt uses the term "transaction rights" to refer to what I here call "liberties" (*Entrepreneurs, Bureaucrats, and Transactions Rights* [Mannheim: University of Mannheim, 1986, mimeographed]).

will i give up, maximally, for the "liberty to purchase *one* unit of x at price p_x"? This evaluation is measured by the difference between the marginal rate of substitution and price, defined at the one-unit interval, or,

$$\frac{MU_x}{MU_y} - p_x. \tag{1}$$

Precisely the same construction can be carried out for each successive unit of x that might be purchased. Individual i will place some positive value on the "liberty to purchase an additional unit of x at whatever price is placed on that unit" so long as the full buyer's equilibrium is not attained.

The precise location of this equilibrium position (the familiar tangency solution) depends on the distribution of rent over the inframarginal range of purchase. At equilibrium, however, the individual's marginal rate of substitution is brought into equality with price. Hence, the value placed on the liberty to purchase the final unit of x becomes zero; there is no increment to rent resulting from a small change in the rate of purchase. If price is parametric to the individual purchaser, this condition of equilibrium implies that there will be no value placed on the liberty to purchase any identified unit of x. I shall return to this point in Section V below.

III. Sellers as Substitutes

Consider, now, the individual as potential purchaser who may be offered the liberty of purchase from sellers of substitute goods. Suppose that Y is a numeraire and that there is a set of x goods $(x_1, x_2, x_3, \ldots, x_n)$ each one of which is a substitute for any other in the preference function of the potential purchaser. In the limiting case, suppose that the separate x's are perfect substitutes; suppose that the x's are identical products offered by several selling firms in an industry.

In this setting, the individual will place a value on the "liberty to purchase from the set of x goods," but any value placed on the "liberty to purchase *one* of the x goods" will depend critically on the presence or absence of the liberty to purchase one or several of the other x goods. If the individual already has free access to the markets in which $x_2, x_3, \ldots, x_n$ are sold, he will place no value on the "liberty to purchase x_1." Since this good is, by definition, a perfect substitute for any one of the others in the set, all of which are readily available for purchase, there is no prospect of securing additional rent or surplus from access to the purchase of x_1. The single good from among the whole set of substitute goods becomes analogous here to the single unit of purchase in the full equilibrium discussed earlier. There is no rent on the marginal unit in equilibrium, and, in the case examined here, each good in the substitute-goods set becomes marginal. The individual values the liberty to purchase his preferred quantity of some one from among the x goods, but he places no value on the liberty of purchase of the last unit or on the liberty of purchase of any one of the set of substitutable goods.

Because no value is placed on the liberty to purchase any one of the goods from the set of perfect substitutes so long as others from the set are available, it seems to follow that the individual would be indifferent as to the size of the set. Consumer's rent is maximized by extending the rate of purchase to the preferred level for any of the x's. Why should the individual prefer a regime in which there are several x's from among which he may choose, or as in the example, several sellers of the identical product?

The more inclusive set will be preferred because the individual recognizes the value of the potential consumer's rent and, further, that this value is *not* assigned to him as a legally protected and enforceable right. Precisely because this value is a rent or surplus, it becomes an object for competition, as the rent-seeking literature emphasizes. The person who confronts a single good from among the set of close substitutes, or who faces the single seller of a good that might have otherwise been marketed by many sellers, is vulnerable to exploitation with respect to the anticipated rent, some or all of which may be extracted from him. A single seller can, for example, withhold from the buyer the liberty of free purchase through any one of many contractual devices. In the limiting case, through idealized quantity discounting or idealized all-or-none contracts, the single seller can extract the full amount of the potential surplus from the buyer.[4]

The consumer or purchaser recognizing this as a prospect, will prefer a regime in which there are several substitute sellers for every good as well as several goods that may be defined as substitutes for each effective region of the preference function. If required, the prospective purchaser will invest

---

4. J. M. Buchanan, "The Theory of Monopolistic Quantity Discounts," *Review of Economic Studies* 21 (1953): 199–208.

some resources to protect the value of the potential rent. Efficiency in rent-protecting investment dictates, however, that resources be committed only if necessary.

The purchaser possesses, however, the right to *grant liberty of access or sale* in the particular submarket that he or she, individually, represents. Just as the potential purchaser values the liberty of free purchase, the potential seller will value the liberty of sale. A market exchange reflects the reciprocal exercise of a *liberty to buy* and a *liberty to sell,* with the seller granting the former to the buyer and the buyer granting the latter to the seller.

The potential purchaser who seeks to protect prospective rents will have no interest in restricting liberties to sell in his own submarket. The purchaser will recognize that offering access to a large number of sellers provides an institutional means of ensuring against the extraction of potential surplus or rent. The vulnerability of rent is reduced as sellers of substitutes are allowed the liberties of making contract offers. It is clearly in the direct interest of any potential purchaser to allow many sellers to possess the liberties of selling their wares. And, further, note that the potential purchaser can make such liberties available without resource cost. Investment in rent protection is costless. Hence, such investment will be extended to the point where productivity, at the margin, is zero. For most purchasers, the limit is reached only when *all* potential sellers of closely substitutable goods are allowed the liberty of making offers of sales contracts. And since there is no way of knowing in advance just what goods may become effective substitutes, one for another, rational behavior on the part of prospective purchasers will extend liberty to all potential sellers, regardless of the descriptive attributes of the goods offered. In more conventional terms, it is in the interest of each person, as a potential purchaser, to allow freedom of entry on the part of all potential sellers.

IV. Buyers as Substitutes

We may readily apply the arguments developed in Sections II and III above to the other side of the market relationship. Consider, now, a single person in a role as the potential seller of good x, and who holds an initial endowment measured in the numeraire good y. This potential seller will place a positive value on the "liberty to sell units of x at price p_x." The value of this liberty to sell now becomes the producer's surplus or rent that is anticipated from being able to engage in the selling activity. Again, and just as with the analysis of the purchaser, the value of the liberty to sell can be measured unit by unit or over the integral, and, also, at equilibrium there is no increment to producer's rent to be gained from any small change.

The application of the basic construction to the single seller extends also to rent protection. The single seller will recognize that any producer's surplus or rent is a value not assigned to him as a legally guaranteed right. It will prove advantageous, therefore, to invest in rent protection to ensure receipt of this anticipated value. But each seller does have, within his legally protected domain, the authority to grant to buyers the liberties of purchase on proffered contractual terms. If this liberty of purchase is extended to only one buyer, such a buyer may, in the limit, extract from the single seller the full value of the anticipated producer's rent or surplus. The idealized monopsonistic quantity premium purchase offer or the idealized monopsonistic all-or-none purchase offer can prevent the seller from securing more than an infinitesimal share of the potential producer's surplus.

The individual, as potential seller, may, however, protect against such exploitation by extending liberties of purchase to many potential buyers, and, in the limit, to all persons who might emerge as buyers. There is no resource cost involved in extending such liberties of purchase. Hence, liberties of purchase will be made available to all persons, or, in more familiar terms, each person, as a potential seller, will allow freedom of entry to all buyers.

V. The Optimal Allocation of Liberty

As suggested, the analysis in Sections II, III, and IV involves only a shift of emphasis and interpretation in the presentation of the familiar tools of elementary value theory. Nonetheless, by explicitly introducing liberties as goods that are valued by individuals who participate in market exchanges, we can generate normative implications for efficiency in the allocation of these liberties that are fully analogous to those that are applied to the utilization of other goods (resources) that are valued.

In a competitive equilibrium, goods are placed in their most highly valued uses, and the imputation of values to goods exhausts the total valuation, appearing thereby to leave nothing over for imputation to liberty as a good.

This result is, however, precisely as it should be in the normative sense. Liberty should be allocated so that it is utilized as a free good; it is valued inframarginally by persons in their roles as both buyers and sellers. It is fully efficient that liberty be used up to the satiety limits because it can be supplied at zero cost by those persons who are in positions to make it available. Further, these suppliers of liberties of access to exchanges will find it advantageous to supply such a good in the required amounts. They will have no interest in withholding liberties from persons who might seek access from the *other* sides of the potential exchanges. Buyers will never have rationally based interests in restricting the liberties of sellers; sellers will never have rationally based interests in restricting the liberties of buyers.

VI. The Definition of Liberty

The whole of the analysis in Sections II, III, IV, and V presupposes that there exists a well-defined imputation of endowments among persons, an imputation or assignment that exists prior to the initiation of any market exchanges, and one that is legally protected. In this sense, a framework of "laws and institutions," or a "state," is presumed to exist prior to the emergence of market exchange institutions. The imputation of endowments and claims is often referred to as an assignment of rights, and critics may suggest that most of the problems associated with the concept of liberty in conventional discussions are simply bypassed in the presupposition that rights are assigned. If a person possesses a legally protected endowment, that which is possessed is often described in terms of the actions that possession thereby authorizes.

If a person, i, is assigned a legally protected endowment, a property right to human or non-human assets, then the "liberty" of person j (any other person) seems to be necessarily restricted. But who is person j in this context, whose "liberties" are restricted by the delineation of the boundaries of i's endowments? Without some presumptive definition of j's rights, how could we talk about his "liberties"? It appears meaningless to define liberty or freedom as applying to the range of actions open to a person unless there is some relation to a social setting. The whole analysis implies that any definition of liberty necessarily involves social content. In the Hobbesian jungle, when there are no legally protected private spheres, no delineation of "mine and thine," there is no liberty in any definitional sense appropriate for the analysis in this paper. There is no liberty because there is no starting point from which grants of liberty may be made. A person cannot secure "liberty of purchase" from a seller or "liberty of sale" from a buyer because there is no authority open to anyone to grant such liberties. In the genuine Hobbesian jungle, the person who wants a good in the nominal possession of another has no incentive to resort to voluntary cooperation.

Liberty, to be meaningful for the analysis here, must refer to actions open to an individual in a setting in which persons possess legally protected property rights, rights that may be exchanged in cooperative social processes. Liberty may be generally interpreted as an attribute of the basic relationship of exchange. An individual does not possess the "liberty of exchange" of a legally protected right or endowment until and unless such liberty be granted to him reciprocally by others who possess legally protected rights on their own account.

Consider two simple examples. Suppose, first, that I have an acknowledged and enforceable legal claim to the $100 that I hold. My liberties are measured by the number of alternative dispositions that I can make of the $100, liberties that are granted to me by those who may hold legally enforceable claims to other assets that I may possibly prefer to the $100. My liberty is minimized when I can find no potential seller who is willing to grant me liberty of purchase of an alternative right (asset, endowment, or claim). My set of liberties is maximized when all other owners of legally protected claims grant me liberty of purchase, subject only to the requirement of voluntary agreement on the terms of possible exchange. My liberties are restricted if *any* legal owner of any claim fails to offer me liberty of purchase. Such action reduces the size of the choice set that would otherwise represent the feasible options within my overall budget constraint. As the earlier analysis indicated, there will arise no such restrictions of my liberties to the extent that potential sellers of other claims seek rationally to protect their own potential rents.

As a second example consider a model in which I own myself, but in which I have no legal claim to any non-human asset. I control my own time, my potential labor power. My liberty is minimized if I can find no potential purchaser to whom I can voluntarily sell my labor, when no such purchaser offers me the liberty of entering into mutually agreed-on exchanges of my labor for other claims that such purchaser holds. My set of liberties is maximized when I am extended the liberty of entering into a labor contract with whomever I prefer from among the whole universe of possible purchasers. My liberties are restricted when there exists so much as a single prospective purchaser of my labor power who fails to grant me liberty of sale (freedom of entry) into the buying market that his custom represents. As the earlier analysis demonstrated, however, it will be in the rent-protecting interest of all prospective purchasers to extend to me such liberties.

The conclusions are the familiar ones already noted. So long as individual rights are well defined and legally protected, self-interested behavior on the part of all participants in social interaction will ensure not only that valued resources of the ordinary sort are allocated to their most highly valued uses but also that individual liberties, properly defined, will be maximized.[5] There is no required "allocation" of liberties to their most highly valued uses akin to that applicable to costly resources. Allocative choices involving liberties, as such, are not necessary because liberties are not scarce; the optimal or efficient allocation is one that provides liberties to all who value them and in sufficient quantities to sate all demands. Liberty, in the meaningful definition emergent from the analysis here, is indeed a free good.

VII. Equal Liberty

The implied definition of liberty that emerges from the analysis in this paper is clearly related to the conception of equal liberty that has been central in much of the philosophic discussion. If we commence with a well-defined and legally enforced imputation of endowments or rights, the social interaction that will take place between and among those who own the separate endowments will be characterized by an equality of liberties. Each owner, being defined by the dimensions of his endowments or rights, will be granted equal liberties with all others to engage in any and all voluntary exchange agreements with all others.

The whole analysis emerges from and applies most readily to the set of individual liberties that are usually classified to be "economic," those that describe purchase and sale, whether of final goods, intermediate goods, initial

5. J. Gray, *Hayek on Liberty* (Oxford: Blackwell, 1984), 67.

endowments, capital goods, or personal services. Extension of the analysis to the set of liberties often classified as "civil" by political and legal philosophers is logically straightforward, despite its dramatic difference from ordinary discussion.

Consider liberty of speech, a civil liberty that is normally included within the set of "equal liberties" that are normatively required in a free society. This example illustrates how the analysis of this paper can be extended to such liberties, but, also, it illustrates the sources of confusion that may arise when liberties and rights are defined ambiguously.

Suppose that in the initial imputation of rights each biological person is assigned ownership of his own vocal chords and his own ear drums; this is not an assignment of liberties, but rather an assignment of rights, which, in this illustration, are equal among all persons. The ownership of vocal chords carries with it no "liberty of being listened to" by anyone. This latter liberty is within the power of rights of the potential listener to grant or to withhold since only this person has rights over his ear drums. And it will be to the rent-protecting interests of the potential listener, who does place a value on the "liberty of listening" to allow all potential speakers access to his auditory nerves, provided only that they offer speech on agreed-on terms. It would, of course, be self-contradictory to apply equality to the "liberty of being listened to" since only one voice can be heard by one person at one time.

The speech example, as noted, illustrates how confusion arises when the distribution of legally protected rights is interpreted as a distribution of liberties. We simultaneously use the terms "rights to free speech" and "liberty of free speech," without recognizing that rights and liberties are separate and distinct. Liberties refer to the range of uses or exercises of the rights that are legally protected. And the equality of liberties that will emerge from the rational self-interest of those who possess rights does not, in any sense, rectify possible distributional differences among persons in the domain of protected rights. There may, of course, be powerful and convincing reasons for equality of protected rights among persons, and notably with reference to rights of control over aspects of biologically defined units. But these are rights, not liberties.

I shall not extend the applications of the analysis further to discuss other familiar non-economic liberties, although such applications could be developed analogously to the treatment of speech.

VIII. Constraints on Liberties

I have demonstrated that over the domain in which there exist well-defined and legally protected separate rights to all resources, capacities, or goods that may be valued, there will characteristically exist equal and maximally extensive liberties in the exercise of those rights among units ("persons") to whom the rights are assigned. If the analysis is accepted, there would seem to be no rationally based argument, relating either to individual action or to contractually agreed-on collective action, to be derived in support of any constraint on liberties. We observe, however, that constraints on the liberties to exercise rights are pervasive in modern social arrangements. Must we conclude that all such constraints are illegitimate by the implied criteria that emerge from the analysis in this paper?

Such an extreme and dramatic conclusion is indeed dictated over the domain described by the imputation or assignment of rights to persons or corporate bodies. The distributional partitioning is complete in this domain; hence, there could be no legally permissible externalities.[6] No holder or owner of a right, endowment, or claim could invade the domain of another without first securing consent or agreement, through some explicit or implicit exchange process. All valued or potentially valued assets, resources, and goods, both human and non-human, would be protected under a strict property rule. The dimension of that which is protected must, however, be emphasized. The ownership or control of an asset does not, in itself, embody any protection of the *value* of that asset. The value will depend both on the liberties of access to exchanges offered by owners of other possibly preferred assets and upon the terms of trade negotiated in contractual agreement processes.

In the domain characterized by complete and exhaustive partitioning of all valued resources, capacities, assets, and goods, there could arise no generalized contractual agreement upon any constraint on liberties of access to exchange. There will, of course, be universal desire on the part of owners and holders of rights to constrain the liberties of other owners and holders who are potential competitors in any exchange. The person who seeks to exchange money for a valued good, say for an automobile, would prefer that

---

6. Economic externalities would be eliminated through the exchange process, which includes small-number as well as large-number contracts.

the owner of the desired item restrict the liberties of all other potential buyers of the same item. The potential buyer seeks the producer's rent which may be gained by constraining the liberties of others who might make counteroffers to the seller. As the analysis above shows, however, the seller will rationally engage in rent protection by opening up entry to all who might make counteroffers. The motivations are fully symmetrical on both sides of any exchange. The potential seller of the automobile in the example will have a rent-seeking interest in limiting the liberties of competing sellers who might make alternative sales offers to potential buyers. But potential buyers will retain rent-protecting interests in keeping open the prospective entry of all sellers. In the setting postulated, there could never emerge general agreement among both potential buyers and potential sellers on any constraint on liberties.

Sellers (or buyers) of a well-defined good may, of course, find it advantageous to agree among themselves to restrict the liberties of sale offered to them by potential buyers (sellers). By contracting to "share the market," sellers (buyers) can, effectively, ensure extraction of buyers' (sellers') rents. Such liberty-constraining contracts may emerge voluntarily among actors who are on the same side of potential exchanges of rights, that is, among sellers or among buyers, rather than between actors on separate sides of exchanges. Such liberty-constraining contracts must be classified as "systems of restraint" that are "completely taken away" in order for the "simple system of natural liberty" to establish itself "of its own accord." In specific terms, such contracts cannot be made enforceable under the legal structure. The laws of contract must be limited to voluntary exchanges of rights; they cannot be extended to include "exchanges" of liberties, even if these are voluntary among direct parties to agreement. Sellers must be prevented from contracting away liberties of sale that buyers may offer, either in terms of market shares, territorial boundaries, or prices. The same prohibition must apply to buyers. An understanding of Smith's system of natural liberty provides the normative basis for the non-enforceability of contractual agreement among members of either selling or buying cartels.

The analysis here, as such, remains silent on possible grounds for restrictions on liberties of access to and use of valued resources that are not within the domain of partitioned rights. The liberties of access to "the common" that may emerge "naturally" need not be such that maximize the value of rents, and, as familiar analyses have demonstrated, the exercise of such liberties may dissipate fully any values emerging from the use of such resources. I shall not introduce further discussion here on the extent to which "the common" as historically observed might or might not constructively be shifted organizationally to the partitioned domain through a reassignment of rights. It seems best to limit the treatment in this paper to the partitioned domain of valued rights and to limit any conclusions concerning constraints on liberties to those involving access to rights within that domain.

IX. Liberties and the Distribution of Rights

I have suggested above that much of the confusion in the discussion of liberty stems from a failure to distinguish carefully between liberties and rights, the failure to distinguish the liberties to utilize or to exercise rights that are assigned and the distribution of these rights or endowments. The "positive liberty" to satisfy a want or desire has been advanced as a more meaningful notion than the "negative liberty" that is defined simply as the absence of coercion of one person by another.

The approach here allows a reconciliation of these differences, at least in part. The satisfaction of a want or desire requires *both* a right and a liberty. A person may be assigned a legally protected endowment that would enable a want to be satisfied, but he may be restricted in his liberty of using that endowment in a way that is necessary to accomplish this purpose.[7] There are two dimensions here, and conflation of the two can only confuse discussion. A person who, say, holds legal claim to a piece of land but who is also highly restricted in the set of potential buyers (leasers) clearly has less liberty than the person who holds legal claim over only his own labor power but who remains totally unrestricted as to the uses to which this power may be put.

Care must be taken not to define liberty exclusively in terms of the size of the choice set confronting the person who chooses.[8] The size of the choice

7. See G. Stigler, "Wealth, and Possibly Liberty," *Journal of Legal Studies* 7 (1978): 213–17. In several respects, Stigler's discussion comes closer to that of this paper than do other treatments.

8. For a related discussion on the relevance of the size of the choice set, see P. Jones and R. Sugden, "Evaluating Choice," *International Review of Law and Economics* 2 (1982):

set is a function of both the legally protected endowment and the liberties to use or exercise this endowment. The person who has legal claim to $100 has a larger endowment than the person who has claim to only $10. But the two persons may or may not have equal liberties of disposition. The familiar budget set of the first person is larger than that of the second only on the implicit presumption that both have the same liberties of disposition.

X. Liberties and Rents

The theory of natural liberty advanced in this paper is closely related to the theory of rents in conventional economics. The maximization of individual liberties is equivalent to the maximization of the combined values of consumers' and producers' surplus. And these maximizations occur simultaneously when individuals and organizations with well-defined and legally protected claims to resources are allowed to engage in non-restricted market exchanges in such claims or rights. To this point, I have not related the analysis to more specific elements in the theory of economic rent.

In the analysis itself, I have presumed that individuals, as consumers, do exhibit preferences as among separate bundles of goods, whether these "specializations" be natural or artificial. Similarly, I have presumed that individuals, as producers-sellers, also exhibit preferences as among separate placements for the resources or goods they offer, again without concern whether these "specializations" arise from natural or artificial bases. The analysis, as such, makes no distinction among varying degrees of specialization in either consumption or production. The theory of rent, by contrast, makes much of the specialization of resources to particular uses.

Consider pure Ricardian land which, by definition, is specialized for only one use, e.g., growing wheat. All of the return from this resource is economic rent and, as such, is totally dependent on the price that will be placed on this product by the interactions of the many demanders and other resource suppliers in the market. The person who owns the pure Ricardian unit of land has an incentive to allow all potential purchasers of the single product full

---

47–66, and D. Beavis and C. K. Rowley, "Evaluating Choice: A Note," *International Review of Law and Economics* 3 (1983): 79–84.

access to the making of offers for his output, but he does not, by definition, have the capability of opening up his potential sale to prospective purchasers of other products than wheat, e.g., oats, corn, barley, suburban development, etc. It is, therefore, meaningful to say that the owner of the unit of Ricardian land is more restricted in his "liberties to sell output" than are the owners of land that may be used for the production of alternative products. The restriction on liberties stems, in this instance, from the natural or physical attributes of the resource itself rather than from any imposed barriers. There is, for this reason, no required modification in the general conclusion noted above to the effect that the liberties of all owners, including the owner of Ricardian land, will be maximized by the workings of the competitive market order.

To say that the owner of the highly specialized resource is more restricted in his liberties to sell output implies that his prospective producer's surplus (all of his return in the case of pure Ricardian land) is more vulnerable to extraction by buyers. Upon recognition of this vulnerability, the owner of the specialized resource may be willing to invest more in rent protection than will the comparable owner of a non-specialized resource. Unless there are many prospective buyers for the single product, the owner of the specialized resource may go beyond the granting of liberties to all prospective buyers. He may seek to invest costly resources in attempts to guarantee the terms of trade between his output and other goods that he may purchase in exchange.[9] There is, of course, no means of discriminating between efforts to fix terms of trade for purposes of preventing producer's rent extraction and efforts to fix terms of trade for the purpose of extracting consumers' rent from buyers. The analysis does offer a provisional explanation, however, of the observed fact that attempts at fixing terms of trade seem pervasive in ag-

9. Another way of putting this point is to suggest that to the extent that the "exit" option is more costly the actor will have more incentive to invest in "voice," to use Hirschman's familiar terms here (see A. O. Hirschman, *Exit, Voice, and Loyalty* [Cambridge: Harvard University Press, 1970]). A. Alchian and S. Woodward have analyzed the possible relationships between the receipt of what they call "composite quasi-rents" by owners of resources and the structure of organizations (*Reflections on the Theory of the Firm* [Brunner Interlaken Conference on Analysis and Ideology, May 1986, mimeographed]).

riculture and industry which, organizationally, lends itself to a high degree of competitiveness.

Analogous reasoning to that applied above to producers and owners of specialized resources can be extended to the possessors of specialized consumer preferences. A person whose preferences exhibit low cross-elasticities of substitution among goods and baskets of goods will enjoy fewer liberties than the person whose preferences exhibit high cross-elasticities.

Qualifications of the generalized conclusions reached with reference to the relationships between liberties and rents are necessary when genuinely non-producible but partitionable resources are concentrated in ownership. Efforts at extracting potential buyers' rents may, in this setting, involve deliberate restrictions on buyers' liberties of purchase. However, buyers who find their liberties so limited are themselves motivated both to seek out liberties of purchase from sellers of substitute resources (goods) and possibly to invest in efforts designed to modify their own preferences so as to reduce the vulnerability of rents to such extraction. If no "original and indestructible" resource units exist, these qualifications disappear. Most of the discussion in this paper has been based on the implicit presupposition that, even if not totally absent, concentrated ownership of generally non-reproducible sources of value gives little cause for the concern of political economists.

XI. Conclusions

I have stressed that the analysis in this paper involves only a shift of emphasis and interpretation in the application of the basic tools of elementary value theory. I should claim, nonetheless, that by explicitly incorporating individuals' evaluation of liberties, insights may be gained into the logic of the emergence of the market order, as well as the tendency of that order to generate results meeting the required conditions for "efficiency" over the domain of fully partitioned rights.

I have made no exhaustive attempt, in this paper, to relate directly the definition or conception of liberty that emerges from the analysis to those that have been the subject of long-continuing debate among philosophers. Only in the brief discussion in Section IX did I suggest that my approach offers a means of reconciling the positive liberty–negative liberty distinction that has been central in this debate. I consider this paper to have been written by a political economist for political economists, not for philosophers. Whether or not my approach can withstand critical scrutiny from other schools of academic discourse, or indeed whether it warrants attention at all—these are questions of interest, import, and relevance that must be left for extended examination in other places and other times, and by other scholars.

Property as a Guarantor of Liberty

1. Introduction

Historically, linguistically and legally, "the common or commons" is common property. Several (many) persons (families) share in the usage of a potentially valued resource. Privatization involves the partitioning of this resource among separate users with a specific delineation of boundaries. Incentives for use are modified, and valued product will increase. This simple argument is as old as Aristotle, and it is an important element in the understanding of basic economics.

My thesis in this book is that this simple argument, that we may for convenience label Aristotelian, is categorically different from an alternative defence of private property that has been present, but which has not been nearly so well understood, either by economists or legal-political philosophers. This second argument does not put efficiency or productivity in resource usage in the exclusively dominating criterial role. Liberty, rather than efficiency, assumes critical importance, although these two objectives are complementary in most applications.

A person seeks to minimize the effects on his own well-being exercised by others, whether these effects be expressed directly or indirectly. Independence from the effects imposed by the behaviour of others is a desired end objective. Individuals want to be "free to choose" among alternatives, and they do not want their choice sets constrained by the actions of other persons, individually or collectively. We may think here of a spectrum ranging

From *The Shaftesbury Papers*, vol. 1 (Hants, England: Edward Elgar, 1993), 1–64. Reprinted by permission of the publisher.

from maximal interdependence on the one extreme to maximal independence on the other.

As a sharing participant in the common, the individual is maximally interdependent. The value of the share in the jointly produced "good" that is
secured depends on the behaviour of *all* members of the sharing group, and
this value is influenced by the behaviour of the individual only in proportionate relationship to the size of the group. A partitioning of the common
with a specific assignment for private and separated spheres of action reduces
the dependence of the individual on the behaviour of others, quite apart
from any incentive-induced motivation that might generate higher values of
product. The liberty of the individual is increased, if we define liberty to relate inversely to the dependence of the individual's well-being on others' behaviour.

Maximal independence is attained only if the individual exists in total isolation from the social nexus, characterized by an absence of even so much as
voluntary interaction through trade and exchange. Metaphorically, maximal
independence is represented by the self-sufficient family frontier homestead
that subsists totally on its own. Hence, the shared common and this self-
sufficient homestead stand at opposing ends of the imaginary spectrum introduced earlier.

The efficacy of private or several property, along both the productivity
and the liberty dimensions, warrants extended analysis and discussion. Introduction of the second of these dimensions opens up areas of inquiry involving comparative institutional analysis that tend to be overlooked by the
concentration on the efficiency dimension alone. The first step, however, is
the clarification of the standard or orthodox analysis in such a fashion that
will facilitate the ensuing comparative discussion. Chapter 2 takes this step,
and, in particular, examines the removal of the "tragedy of the common"
and the "leap from the Hobbesian jungle" in standard efficiency logic, but as
interpreted in a basic contractarian framework. The next step, in Chapter 3,
involves the introduction of the liberty dimension and describes a setting in
which independence is maximized. Chapter 4 modifies the economic assumptions in order to allow the derivation of a rational or logical basis for a
shift from independence to market interdependence. Chapter 5 examines the
effect of market dependence on the attitude and behaviour of individual par-

ticipants, along with the residual role played by property ownership, all of which is analytically illustrated in Chapter 6.

In Chapter 7, some dynamic features of specialization in exchange are analysed, with attendant feedbacks on the dependency status of participating parties. Chapter 8 elaborates a model of competitive process in which the existence of multiple market alternatives, along with free entry and exit, restores to the participant an independence of sorts, but an independence that is based on less secure foundations than that offered through property ownership. In Chapter 9, I suggest that this market independence, as idealized by economists, is not fully understood by individual actors, as is evidenced by apparently "inefficient" preferences for ownership arrangements. Chapter 10 models ownership, especially of consumer durables, in terms of the self-production of services and traces the effects of such ownership on individuals' market positions. In Chapter 11, private property in assets that yield money income rather than direct services is discussed, and again the effects of such ownership on market positions are examined. Chapter 12 isolates the role of private ownership of assets in facilitating the accumulation of value through time, and this discussion is followed, in Chapter 13, by specific treatment of the relationship between property ownership and inflation.

With Chapter 14, the book is shifted in its focus, and the effects of socialist organization on ownership, and through this, on liberty, are discussed. Chapter 15 is exclusively devoted to a summary of an early (1893) recognition of socialism's destruction of private ownership to be found in an encyclical by Pope Leo XIII. Chapter 16 discusses briefly the Marxian vision of capitalism as it relates to property and liberty; Chapter 17 includes some final speculations, and an endnote (Chapter 18) suggests the political-constitutional implications of the whole discussion.

2. The Hobbesian Jungle; the Tragic Common

A familiar starting point for analysis is the state of nature imagined by Thomas Hobbes, in which there is no acknowledgement of what is "mine and thine," no acceptance of boundaries among persons, no law, no conventions. In this imagined state, the life of any person is described to be "poore, solitary, nasty, brutish, and short." Hobbes used this description of the anarchistic jungle as the basis for his quite convincing argument to the effect that all persons would value security highly enough to surrender authority to an emergent sovereign who promises subsequent protection.[1]

No person would, however, voluntarily acknowledge a sovereign's enforcement authority if it is anticipated that, in the enforced civic order, that person's position will be worse, by his or her own reckoning, than the position attainable in the anarchistic jungle itself. The "natural equilibrium" of the Hobbesian jungle provides the distributive bench-mark from which the contract between the individual and the sovereign is negotiated. The existence of this back-up, fall-back or exit position places limits on the terms of the contract, as initially negotiated, and it also affects the enforceability of the contract in all subsequent periods of its operation.[2]

It is important to notice that in this construction the individual exists prior to, and hence independent of, the contract with the sovereign, even if such an existence is not pleasant by comparison with the ordered alternative that the sovereign offers. The difference between the measured well-being of the individual in the ordered structure guaranteed by the sovereign and the well-being expected in the anarchistic jungle reflects, in one sense, the "productivity" of the sovereign, and this difference can, for some purposes, be referred to as "social rent."

The Hobbesian construction is conjectural and ahistorical. It was not, and is not, intended to be descriptive of reality, past or present. Presumably, individuals have never existed outside the bonds of some collective unit, the extended family, the tribe or the nomadic band. We owe to Hobbes the reductionist explanatory step of imagining the autonomous individual, whose behaviour we might analyse by criteria for rational choice. Such a step serves to facilitate discussion without undermining in any serious way the implications of the analysis.

1. T. Hobbes, *Leviathan* (1651; New York: Collier, 1962).

2. The argument here has been developed at length in earlier writings. For my own argument, see J. M. Buchanan, *The Limits of Liberty* (Chicago: University of Chicago Press, 1975). For other contributions, see W. Bush, "Individual Welfare in Anarchy," in *Explorations in the Theory of Anarchy,* ed. G. Tullock, The Public Choice Society Book and Monograph Series (Blacksburg, Va.: University Publications, 1972), 5–18; G. Tullock, ed., *Explorations in the Theory of Anarchy,* The Public Choice Society Book and Monograph Series (Blacksburg, Va.: University Publications, 1972); and G. Tullock, *The Social Dilemma: The Economics of War and Revolution,* The Public Choice Society Book and Monograph Series (Blacksburg, Va.: University Publications, 1974).

To modern social scientists, a starting point that is even more familiar than the Hobbesian jungle is the tragic commons, with which I commenced Chapter 1. The formal structure of interaction among participants is, of course, identical in these two settings. This structure is best summarized as the classic prisoners' dilemma (PD), where participants who adhere to strategies that are individually dominant generate outcomes that are less favourable to all parties than those that might be produced by alternative strategy combinations. I want to suggest, however, that, despite this structural identity, the two stylized models of social interaction carry with them differing implications for an understanding of the role played by private or several property, as an institution.

Consider, now, the stylized tragedy of the commons. There is a potential value-generating resource that is used in common by all participants, each one of whom is led, by utility maximizing considerations, to extend individualized usage of the resource beyond that level that would be optimally agreed upon as that participant's proportionate share in an idealized setting for collectively determined utilization. The resource is over-used when private choice is combined with common access; each participant's behaviour, at the relevant margin of use, imposes external diseconomies on the well-being of others in the sharing group; all participants can be made better off, as signalled by their own agreement under some collectively chosen constraints on private choice.

In this stylized example, one implied means of internalization of the relevant externalities is the partitioning of the shared resource among the separate users, the replacement of common usage by private and separated property in specifically assigned parcels. This step involves a removal of all commonality or jointness in utilization of the resource in the apparent direction of independent private usage. In the post-privatization setting, again as stylized, the individual no longer has a utility maximizing incentive to overextend resource use; in the modified setting of private ownership, the individual is led by utility maximizing considerations to use the resource (property) "optimally" or "efficiently," since any departure from efficiency results in opportunity costs that are imposed directly and exclusively on the person who makes the decision on usage.

The overall difference in the value of product generated under private ownership and that which is generated under common usage of the resource may be defined as the "social rent" that emerges from the institutionalization of the regime of private property. In a formal sense, this "rent" is equivalent to that emergent from the contract with the sovereign in the Hobbesian exemplar. This rent measures the productivity of the institution of private property in the one case and the productivity of the institution of the sovereign in the other.

But something seems to be quasi-contradictory in the juxtaposition of the two familiar models here. The privatization of the commons suggests that productive reform lies in the direction of increasing individual independence (reducing interdependence), whereas agreement among individuals in the contract with the emergent Hobbesian sovereign suggests that productive reform lies in the direction of increasing individual interdependence through membership in the commonly shared institution of the sovereign. The apparent divergence here stems from the differing emphases in the two models. The metaphor of the tragic commons draws attention to the *assignment* of separated rights of exclusion, separated private spheres, to individuals. This metaphor tends to cause neglect of the problem of *enforcement* of the separated rights, once assigned. By comparison, the metaphor of the anarchistic jungle draws initial attention to the need for some enforcement and protection of the separable claims made by individuals, claims that are presumed established in some prior "natural equilibrium." The assignment problem, as such, is conceptually outside the contract with the sovereign, except in application to the rent that emerges from the effective enforcement of claims.

The distinctions between the two models are important in both their explanatory and their normative potentials. The Hobbesian model offers more explanatory power in deriving a theory of legitimacy for a coercive political-legal order from some ultimate agreement among individuals who participate in that order. At the same time, this model also suggests that the sovereign political authority is constrained in its assignment of rights by the set of prior claims advanced by individuals. By comparison, the commons model is less comprehensive in its explanatory power. The defence of private property derived in this model is almost exclusively based on efficiency criteria, and there is no direct reference to problems of enforcement. It is perhaps not surprising that this model seems more congenial to modern welfare economists who have been quite willing to presume that the political authority acts benevolently.

The commons model remains vague on the definition of separated individual claims to shares in the commons, and hence on the basis that might be employed by the collectivity in making any initial partitioning. By implication, the model suggests that the assignment of shares, as such, is somewhat arbitrary, and subject to the unconstrained choice of the collective unit. That is to say, the mind-set encouraged by this model seems to allow readily for the often met claim that the state "defines property rights." A more complete analysis of the possible contractual means of emerging from the commons tragedy would, of course, necessarily confront some of these issues. But the very absence of such elements tends to locate the tragic commons metaphor in non-contractarian rather than in contractarian efforts to derive a fundamental logic of private property rights.

3. The Partitioned Commons; the Rule of Law and Boundary Crossings

In Chapter 1, I suggested that a central theme of this book is that the classic Aristotelian defence of private property offers only one part of a two-dimensional normative explanation, and that the relationship between private property and liberty must be added to the relationship between private property and productivity. Chapter 2 presented, in highly summarized fashion, the familiar metaphorical settings that facilitate an understanding of the logic of property, a feeling of how and why private property may emerge from the rational choices of individuals. In this Chapter, I want to extend this discussion and to introduce specifically the relationship between property and independence or liberty.

As the earlier analysis suggests, all individuals who share in the usage of the non-partitioned commons or who find themselves in the anarchistic jungle, will find it in their own interests to enter into some sort of agreement under which the commons will be partitioned or privatized, with each participant thereby securing some assignment of a share with well-defined limits or boundaries. I want to concentrate attention on the agreement here among the separate participants themselves and to neglect, for now, the possible simultaneous agreement between and among individuals and an emergent sovereign. In other words, I want to work within the setting for a Lockean rather than a Hobbesian contract. The initial agreement establishes the boundaries among the separated properties, whether defined in terms of person or thing. For convenience, and without loss of logical structure, the initial agreement might be thought of as assigning to each individual property in his or her own person and also some designated area of physical space. The initial agreement establishes the law of property and defines violations of this law to occur when boundaries are crossed.

I want to assume further that in this first post-partition model there are no advantages to specialization in production. Within his or her own boundaries, each person (or family) finds it possible to use his or her own personal capacities to produce all "goods" that are demanded, and to do so as efficiently as if specialization and exchange should be introduced. The model then becomes one of self-sufficient homesteads, each one of which operates in total independence of the social nexus, and protected from encroachment on its territory, including its persons, by the established legal structure.

As constructed, this setting is one in which the individual (or family unit) enjoys maximal independence and, at the same time, maximal efficiency in resource or capacity use. By the prior partitioning of the commons, each decision-making unit now faces incentives that make utility maximization compatible with optimal resource usage, inclusively defined. And, by the presumed productivity of the autarkic organization of the economy, there is none of the interdependence that is introduced by specialization, trade and exchange. The individual's well-being, in his or her own reckoning, depends not at all on the behaviour of others. The "goods" that are available for consumption or final use are related in quantity and quality only to the "bads" that the individual is willing to take on in securing them. Quite literally, each person does his or her own thing with no impact on others in the community.

Indeed, there is no community, as such, other than the membership described by adherence to the law of property, as laid down in the initial agreement. There are only two sharp distinctions to be made in this stylized setting: first, that among individuals as delineated in the law of property, and, second, that between those who are participants in the legal structure that defines the separate properties and those who might be outsiders or foreigners.

I propose to neglect, for now, discussion of the relations between insiders, those who are within the legal structure, and outsiders. For simplicity, assume that there are no outsiders; everyone is a participant in the initial agreement that defines the separated property rights and is thereby subject to the law of property that emerges. The problem of enforcement cannot, however, be neglected if the analysis is to have any claim to logical coherence. Boundary crossings must be expected to occur, even when property is clearly defined, because at least some persons will seek to attain differential advantage through cross-boundary resource use in the absence of an enforcing authority. At the same time that the initial contract is implemented, some provision must be made for policing boundary crossings, to identify and to punish persons who violate the defined property rights of others.

So long as the task of law enforcement cannot be turned over to some non-human technology, elements of the Hobbesian setting necessarily present themselves. Enforcement of the law of property requires an enforcing authority; some person or persons, whether chosen from inside or outside the initial set of contractors, must be assigned the specialized task of enforcing the boundaries. The presumption of absence of specialization is not sustainable to this extent. And, if the enforcer is granted powers to identify, define and punish lawbreakers, how is this power itself to be contained within desired limits? Who guards the guardians?

The functionalist may respond by pointing to the evolution of the rule of law in some Western societies over some historical epochs. If persons who are assigned powers of enforcement are, themselves, subjected to the same law that they are required to enforce on others, severe limits are placed on their abuses of authority. The complex institutions that involve separation of powers, multiple sovereigns, overlapping jurisdictions, an independent judiciary and a jury system all find their logical justification in responses to the question posed. Under an effectively operating rule of law, the individual is protected against the arbitrary exercise of political-legal authority. And, in the stylized setting of economic autarky assumed in this initial model, the independence or liberty of the individual need not be seriously impaired by the necessary presence of the enforcement structure. In this rarified setting, the "state" exists solely to carry out its protective role and is, literally, a watchman, night or day. Note that, in this extreme model, there is no need for any role as enforcer of separate contracts among persons, since these contracts are not made.

The stylized model considered in this chapter warrants further discussion.

As noted, it is not really appropriate to refer to "an economy" beyond the level of the individual or family unit, since, by construction, each and every such unit is fully self-sufficient and does not enter into exchange with other units. In terms of our earlier classification, the individual or family unit is maximally independent of other like units in society. The choice set confronting the unit is not affected, in any way, by the choice behaviour of other producing units with which it is associated only through adherence to the law of property. Such independence breaks down only as and if the law of property is violated, either as a result of some failure of the sovereign to police boundary crossings effectively or as a result of the sovereign's own behaviour in crossing boundaries beyond its limits of authority.

I have discussed, elsewhere, problems constraining the sovereign.[3] Here, I want to call attention to features of the stylized model that may be important in shaping attitudes towards the institution of property. How is it possible even *to imagine* a fully self-sufficient economy of the individual or family? Some hypothetical construction of how such an economy would work is required here, a construction that, in its turn, must introduce some imagined classification and definition of the choice problem faced by any such unit. Attention is drawn to the biological necessities: food, shelter, clothing. And we tend to assume that these "goods," which are universally desired, do not "grow on trees"; that is, they are not simply available in quantities sufficient to sate all demands. In other words, we presume that scarcity describes the choice setting; the individual or family unit is presumed to be unable to survive without making some internal trade-off between "bads" and "goods." Our whole imagination is shaped for us by the condition of man in some post-Edenic state, man who is forced to labour in order to get that which makes his very existence possible.

It may, of course, be suggested that this universal condition of scarcity is, quite simply, a fact, and that little or no imagination is needed to generalize the condition into individualized settings. I submit, nonetheless, that such imagination may amount to a mental feat of some measure where the relationship between labour and access to items of consumption becomes increasingly attenuated.

I want, however, to go beyond the scarcity implications, as stylized to apply

3. Buchanan, *The Limits of Liberty.*

to the economy of the self-sufficient unit, and to flesh out an imaginary description of such a unit's operation. Almost universally here, we would think in terms of an agricultural metaphor, a setting where persons in the self-sufficient unit work *on the land* to produce the goods that are necessary for survival. In economists' terms, the model of self-sufficient homesteads becomes a labour-land, two-factor model of production. Goods are extracted from the land through labour aided and abetted by the forces of nature. This metaphor suggests that *locational fixity* is a characteristic of the self-sufficient autarkic producing-consuming unit. This characteristic has been important in shaping attitudes on the law of property, as I shall note in subsequent discussion.

It should, however, be pointed out that the agricultural metaphor need not be introduced at all. Nature itself may offer abundance, provided only that the individual unit forego the pleasures of idleness and work to exploit that which nature offers. Think of the early American Indians in the Plains when buffalo were superabundant. Self-sufficiency did not imply locational fixity, and land, as a resource, was not scarce.

4. Alienability through Contract: The Emergence of Market Interdependence

Assume that the initial setting is one described by the existence of many self-sufficient homesteads, defined locationally, with private property in person and in land, as protected and enforced by an effective legal structure. I want now to drop the assumption that self-sufficient production is ideally efficient. Assume that specialization is productive; more output can be produced if inputs are specialized. The range of increasing returns is not exploited by the requirements of the single economic unit. Further, assume that this relationship is recognized by all persons.

In this situation, the maximal independence that self-sufficiency makes possible is achieved only at an opportunity cost. To remain isolated in economic autarky, an individual or family unit must forego the "larger" bundle of goods that might be secured through specialization in production followed by exchange. Autarky involves a utility loss that may be measured in economic value sacrificed. Reciprocally, however, the individual or family unit must also recognize that the larger value promised as a result of specialization and exchange itself involves a utility loss measured in the sacrifice of independence.

If advantages of specialization exist, rational utility maximization will suggest that these advantages would be exploited, to *some* degree. Adam Smith called attention to man's natural propensity to truck and to barter as an explanation of the origins of exchange. But modern economists would not see any need to adduce special propensities, and they would locate the emergence of specialization and exchange in the rational calculus of economic actors. The norms for utility maximization cannot, however, define how much specialization will take place, since independence is also presumed to be a positively valued argument in individuals' utility functions. The precepts of rational choice dictate only that the corner solution represented by economic autarky does not describe behaviour under the conditions postulated. But the individual or family economic unit may enter into the production-exchange nexus over a whole spectrum of economic interdependence, ranging from minimal commitment to maximal.

Analytically, it is useful to proceed in stages. For expository simplicity, let us here assume that the self-sufficient unit allocates its working time among N separate activities, defined in terms of end-items of final consumption, such as growing *grain*, gathering *fuel*, killing *game*, tanning *hides*, building *huts*, etc. For additional ease in exposition, assume that an equal share in working time is devoted to each of these separate activities. Recognizing that there are increasing returns in production, after some talk, members of the separate economic units in a territory, all of whom are within the protection of the law of property, take the initial steps towards market interdependence. A single unit chooses to exploit the returns to scale in, say, one of its activities. It generates a surplus, over and beyond its previously consumed amounts, in one of the N goods. Let us say that unit F_1 chooses to specialize minimally in X_1, by devoting $2/N$, or double, the amount of working time to X_1. By so doing, it produces three units, whereas in the autarkic arrangement only one unit was produced. In this stage of minimal specialization, the economic unit may well continue to produce for its own consumption all of the N goods; the extra time devoted to producing X_1 may be drawn from time spent on all other goods.

The surplus of the one good that exploitation of the returns to scale has generated will be taken to "the market," in the expectation that other economic units will, reciprocally, bring forth surplus supplies of other goods, thereby facilitating mutually advantageous trades. The favourably expected results are that each individual or family unit can achieve a higher standard of consumption, as measured in more of each and every good, with no more work, than that standard achieved under self-sufficiency.

My purpose here is not that of describing the conjectural history of emerging markets. I leave the medieval fairs and market days to the historians. I want to examine the effects on property rights that are introduced by even minimal entry into the exchange nexus. I shall presume that the legal structure is extended to the enforcement of voluntary contracts between persons and to the effective prevention of fraud in trading.

To the extent that an economic unit specializes in the expectation that a surplus beyond own-use can be traded for other goods desired, the unit is necessarily subjected to the "blind forces of the market" or to the results of choices made by others over whom no direct control may be exercised. As contrasted with its situation under autarky, in which the isolated unit depends only on its own choices along with the forces of the natural order, there is now a necessary dependence on the behaviour of other economic units. And this behaviour of others is *not* subject to control by the sovereign through laws of property and contract.

Note that, in this setting, entry into the specialization-exchange nexus remains voluntary; the individual or family unit enters "the market" only in pursuit of the expected higher value of end-items that is promised. The autonomous self-sufficient existence is presumed to exist as a back-up prospect, with own-production of all goods. In a sense, therefore, while entry into the nexus increases the dependence on others, there is no loss of liberty, especially if liberty is defined strictly in negative terms as the absence of coercion by others. The prospect of entering the exchange economy seems, in this setting, to represent an expansion of the choice set.

The positions in the expanded part of the choice set are, however, expectational only, and they are necessarily uncertain. The individual cannot, upon choosing to enter the market nexus, select from among a parametrically defined menu, as he or she presumably can do within the confines of the internal "economy" under self-sufficiency. The individual or family cannot unilaterally choose the terms upon which trade of surpluses will take place, and, because of this, cannot choose under certainty the ultimate value enhancement that specialization will make possible.

As the discussion makes clear, the locationally fixed unit that can, if necessary, exist and survive under autarky has nothing to lose and much prospect for gain from limited entry into specialized production and exchange. This model remains, I suspect, the basis of the economists' imagination, and it leads directly to the emphasis on gains-from-trade and mutuality of advantage. The model is perhaps also central to the emphasis on land in attitudes towards the institution of property. If, as we depart from this model, self-sufficiency ceases to be a viable alternative for the individual or family unit, the relationship between property and liberty must be examined in different terms.

5. Market Dependence, Exploitation and Justice in Exchange

As noted in Chapter 4, the person who enters into the nexus of exchange of surplus goods made possible by the advantages of specialization does so voluntarily with the aim of increasing command over whatever bundle of end-items may be desired, even in the full recognition that some sacrifice or loss of independence is involved. That is to say, entry into exchange necessarily produces *dependence* on the behaviour of other persons. Even if there is no coercion, the individual's well-being is subject to change as the result of others' behaviour. And this behaviour will be considered to be variable by the individual who is affected. Hence, others' behaviour will be at least within the domain of criticism, if not of control and manipulation. The individual is "interested in" the behaviour of others, as such behaviour impacts on his own utility via the market relationship, and in a manner that is different from, say, interest in the ultimate forces of nature, such as weather. This attitude of the single exchange participant carries through even in the setting where no identifiable "other" person is recognized to exert market power. But the simple fact that any seller must exchange with a single buyer, and vice versa, tends to cause participants to impute market power to others even when such power may be minuscule or absent.

It is not surprising, therefore, that the terms of exchange have been classified as just or unjust almost from the emergence of analysis, and with the implication that some participants, even in wholly voluntary exchanges, may be exploited by others. The very relation of dependence seems to create the potential for exploitation, defined vaguely as some unequal or unbalanced sharing of the gains that exchange makes possible.

Consider, again, the initial shift from self-sufficient economic autarky into exchange interdependence. The farmer produces, say, a surplus of eggs in the expectation that this surplus may be exchanged for, say, potatoes, the own production of which has been reduced by the concentration of resources on eggs. The terms of exchange depend on the number of others in the relevant market who produce surpluses of both eggs and potatoes, along with the relative sizes of these surpluses. If, perchance, the farmer should discover that there are many traders with surpluses of eggs and only one with a surplus of potatoes, the terms of trade will be highly unfavourable. He will surely consider himself to be unjustly treated, or exploited, by the monopolist.

Before entering into market exchange, the individual may, of course, recognize the vulnerability such entry involves and forego some of the advantages promised by specialization by preserving opportunities for exit from market dependency. In our example, the farmer's property holding, in his own labour and in land, allows him to place limits on the potential exploitation that might be generated by unfavourable terms of trade. If all of the resources under his control should be devoted to egg production, the farmer might, in the market circumstances noted, find that he is worse off in market dependency than he would have been by remaining wholly self-sufficient. To forestall such a worst case outcome, the farmer may dedicate a share of his resources to producing potatoes on his own, or some appropriate substitute. In order to take such steps, however, the individual must retain private control over the disposition of productive resources. He must be "at liberty" to use both labour and land resources in whatever ways he deems fit. Private-property ownership allows for specialization and for trade, hence for capture of some share in efficiency gains, but equally important, private property allows for some protection and insulation against the market's "blind forces," regardless of their ultimate sources.

This second role of private property, which I emphasize in this book, is often neglected, perhaps especially by economists, with their concentration on efficiency, but also by participants in developed market economies where exit options of the sort that occur in the illustration do not exist for other than a few participants. It is important to recognize, however, that the development of market networks (including futures markets) along with the accompanying legal-institutional structure, and also associated with the development of an understanding of this structure, allows the individual participant to secure, in the limiting case, the full advantages of specialization while at the same time enjoying the equivalent of costless exit options. This near magical result is, of course, generated by the existence and operation of a fully competitive economy, that is definitionally described by viable entry and exit into all value-producing activities, in a market nexus of sufficient size to ensure that there can be many economic units on both the buying and selling side of any market. In the limiting case, as described in the economists' models, each person, as a price-taking buyer and/or seller, confronts an "objective" set of choice options that allows behaviour "as if" the interdependence does not exist.

6. Analytical Illustration

The argument sketched out in Chapter 5 may be clarified by an analytical illustration, one that economists may skip over if desired.

Consider, once again, an idealized fully self-subsistent family farming unit, with only two goods of scarcity value, eggs and potatoes. Assume that these goods occupy roughly equal significance in the family budget, or, technically, as arguments in the utility function. Assume, further, that each of these goods may be produced under increasing returns to units of input, in this case, units of labour measured in hours, and also that the two goods are fully symmetrical in the sense that the production functions are the same. In isolated existence, the economic unit faces a production possibility frontier depicted by the curvilinear PP in Figure 6.1, if we assume that the supply of inputs is fixed. Since, by assumption, both potatoes and eggs are defined as goods, and of roughly equal significance, the unit maximizes its utility at E, producing and consuming equal quantities of the two goods. Despite the presence of increasing returns, the unit can do no better than the equilibrium position shown at E.

Note that, in achieving the utility level shown at E, the family is dependent

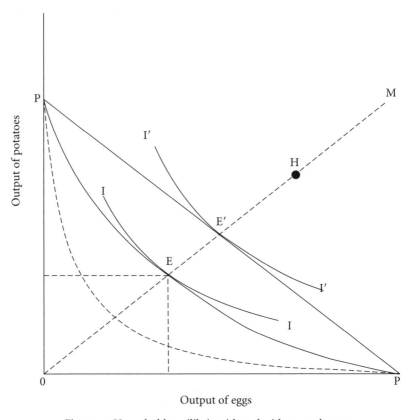

Figure 6.1. Household equilibria with and without exchange

exclusively on its own choices, along with natural forces that operate as constraints. The activity of other persons remains totally irrelevant; there is no economic interdependence present.

We may now change the illustration by introducing a second economic unit, a second farm family, which we shall assume to be, in all respects, identical to the first. This second unit faces precisely the same production function and has precisely the same utility function as the first family. In this setting, there are evident gains to be secured from specialization and exchange. Assume that each of the two units now fully specializes in one of the two goods; one family allocates its total input to the production of potatoes and the other allocates its total input to the production of eggs, with each family devoting the same quantity of inputs to economic production.

Under such conditions, total production in the economy is now depicted in M in Figure 6.1, rather than H, which measures the total product in the economy when the two units produce in isolation and without trade. If the economic units specialize and trade, at an exchange rate of unity (as normalized), each unit can achieve the utility level depicted at E', clearly higher than that achieved at E.

My emphasis here is on the part of this exercise in elementary economics that economists usually neglect. Each economic unit that specializes and trades does, indeed, secure utility gains by comparison with its position under autarky, but in the process it becomes vulnerable to the behaviour of others beyond its own control. Under autarky, the single unit in the illustration faces the curvilinear possibility frontier, PP, from which it may, presumably, choose its preferred position by selecting, simultaneously, its rate of production-consumption of the two goods. Under specialization and exchange, the single unit does not face the linear exchange possibility frontier, PP, in the comparable sense of being able to choose simultaneously the final quantities of the two goods. Having specialized in production of, say, eggs, the family has within its own control only the quantity of this good; it depends for its final utility attainment on the behaviour of the other family that specializes in the production of potatoes.

When there are only two economic units, as introduced in the illustration to this point, each unit will, of course, find itself in a position of a bilateral monopolist, with its final utility attainment being dependent on its relative bargaining skills. In this bargaining "game," the autarkic production possibility frontier defines the limits of vulnerability for the single economic unit; if the other unit is superior in its bargaining skills, the remaining unit may, at worst, resort to autarky, and attain E. In the illustration here, the private property in land and labour, which allows the single family to produce both goods for its own consumption, guarantees the attainment of a utility level not lower than that depicted at E.

The indeterminacy in the solution of the two-person bilateral monopoly game is reduced as the economy, the production-exchange network, increases in size. As each economic unit that specializes in the production of a single good faces the exchange nexus that contains more than a single producer of each other good, its vulnerability to market exploitation decreases. And, as noted earlier, when the network of exchange expands to ensure that there are large numbers of buyers and sellers in all markets, the individual unit may act as if it does indeed face an objective exchange possibility frontier, the linear PP in Figure 6.1.

Beyond the textbook exercises, however, the objectivity of this setting may be questioned. Consider the single person, the seller of eggs, who has within his or her own control only the supply of eggs to be placed on the market. The anticipated price, indicated by the slope of the linear PP in Figure 6.1, depends on there being enough demanders of eggs to sustain this market price for the expected supply, and on there being just enough but not too many other suppliers to make up this expected supply. At best, the price upon which supply adjustments are made by the single seller must be expectational, with its final realization being critically dependent on the aggregate behaviour of many other participants on both sides of the market for the good in question. And, as we know from the historical experiences in those markets where the textbook models of competition have been most nearly matched, the shifts in prices over relatively short periods of time can be dramatic. Any participant who specializes, whether as a buyer-user or as a demander-supplier-producer, remains vulnerable to the behaviour of many others, behaviour which is, to the individual participant, indeed "blind."

7. Learning by Doing—Forgetting by Not Doing

In the highly abstracted and simplified illustration discussed in Chapter 6, the vulnerability of the participant in the production-exchange nexus is limited by the availability of the extra-market exit option, as represented by the possible autarkic existence. And the availability of this option does depend critically on the presence of individualized or private property rights that allow voluntary withdrawal from the exchange relationship, either wholly or partially.

The differential attained in the utility level under specialization-exchange and that level that is possible in autarkic isolation, measures the opportunity cost of independence, or, conversely, the benefits of market interdependence. It will be useful to examine briefly some of the factors that may affect the size of this differential. As presented in Chapter 6, the gains from specialization and exchange arise exclusively from increasing returns. I have not introduced the gains that differential factor endowments, including individual skills, capacities and talents, may make possible. The increasing returns emerge because inputs become more adept as rates of output increase, and this relationship may well be accentuated as we move beyond a static to a dynamic model. As production is organized with specialized inputs, participants supplying those inputs learn by doing, and the rate at which inputs are transformed into outputs increases as learning takes place over time.

Economists have recognized that learning by doing is an important element in explanatory models of economic growth. But, to my knowledge, they have not fully incorporated the converse relationship into their analytical models. Participants who specialize in particular activities learn by doing; they become increasingly productive in the activities in which they have chosen to specialize. But they also *forget by not doing;* they become less and less productive in those activities from which they have withdrawn inputs in order to specialize. We may depict this effect in the geometry of the figure used in Chapter 6, Figure 6.1, by indicating that as the economic units specialize over a sequence of periods, learning by doing and its necessary complement, forgetting by not doing, the extra-market production possibility frontier shifts inward, as shown by the dotted curvilinear line PP. The individual economic unit becomes increasingly dependent upon, and hence vulnerable to, market forces that are beyond its own control. The differential in utility level attainable under specialization and that attainable in autarky increases over time; the extra-market exit option becomes increasingly costly to exercise.

The limits to this dynamic sequence are reached, of course, when the single specialized economic unit has totally forgotten how to, or becomes incompetent to, produce goods other than those for which it is specialized. In our family farm example, suppose that the family unit that specializes in eggs gradually loses all knowledge and capacities that are required to produce potatoes. In this limit, the extra-market exit option takes on a different form. In terms of the geometry of Figure 6.1, the non-market production possibility frontier would now be traced out by the horizontal and vertical axes inside of the Ps on the abscissa and ordinate. Autarkic existence would require continued specialization in one of the two goods, which would be available only for own or internal consumption. The attainable utility level would be that which could be reached at one of the production corners. And this level of utility may not be sufficient to ensure survival and subsistence, especially if the specialization of inputs is on the production of a good that is not sufficiently basic to be counted as a general consumable. The economic unit becomes, in this case, totally dependent on the market's ability to purchase that upon which it specialized, and the only input that can be supplied at all.

8. Private Property, Market Competition and Freedom of Entry and Exit

The limiting case described for the simple analytical illustration in the previous chapters would seem to be applicable for almost all participants in the complex modern economy, where specialization has long been extended to the point where very few, if indeed any at all, families could subsist in extra-market, isolated autarky. Each and every participant, or participating unit, in the modern economy must depend on the behaviour of other persons and units in the system, as organized through markets or otherwise, both to supply the necessary end-items for consumption usage and to demand or purchase the goods and/or services supplied by that single participant or unit.

If extra-market autonomy is not feasible, what protection against potential exploitation is provided by legally guaranteed property rights? Consider, now, the setting in which each participant holds a property right in his or her own person. (We may disregard, for now, private rights in non-human assets.) There are no slaves, and each person remains at liberty to supply those goods or services available to whomever he or she chooses and upon mutually agreed terms. Absent the autarkic exit option, however, what is the value of this property right?

If there is only one prospective buyer-demander, that is, if a person confronts a monopsonist, the property right to person may, indeed, be of relatively little value. The individual must, somehow, secure access to necessary end-items of consumption in order to subsist, and the monopsonist buyer of the services that can be supplied may extract these on terms that are highly unfavourable to the person who supplies them. But the individual participant need not be put in the position of confronting only a single prospective buyer if the market is organized competitively and is large enough to ensure the presence of multiple buyers and sellers in the markets for all goods and services. In this latter case, the value of the property right in one's own person, as expressed in the liberty to choose among alternative buyers, is measured by the full amount of the goods (purchasing power) received in exchange.

(Consider, by contrast with the competitive market setting, that of a socialist regime, where the collectivity owns all means of production. In this situation, each individual who supplies productive services confronts only the single purchaser, the collectivity, and any liberty to choose among alternative purchasers, even if nominally within the individual's possession, becomes almost valueless.)

It is relatively easy to define a market environment in which each participant is confronted with multiple alternatives (buyers-sellers), hence ensuring that the property right to person has maximal value, as this right might be potentially exercised. It is, however, more difficult to describe the institutional rules that encourage the emergence of the competitive environment that is so attractive when defined. Suppose, for example, that all persons in an economy are granted liberty to utilize their personal capacities as they see fit; they are free to choose among any options that appear before them. What is there to ensure that there will be multiple opportunities among which choices are possible?

In order to ensure the emergence and maintenance of a competitive market environment in this sense, individuals must also be allowed the liberty to enter into association, one with another, for the purpose of organizing production units, business firms, which can implement exchanges with persons and other firms. That is to say, individuals must not only be allowed the liberty, as sellers-suppliers, of marketing their own services freely; they must also be allowed the liberty of becoming "traders" in the grander sense of organizing units that produce and supply goods and services that will ultimately exchange for those services supplied by persons in their individualized capacities.

The economic position of the supplier of productive services is protected by the potential exercise of two complementing sets of property rights. The individual's right to his own person allows him to choose among alternative purchasers of his or her services. It also allows *any* participant to attempt to become a purchaser. Together, these rights operate so as to guarantee severe limits on potential exploitation of the individual through unfavourable terms of trade. The individual supplier retains the right to *exit* from the exchange relationship with any purchaser, and any other individual retains the right to *enter* into an exchange with the individual who sells productive services.

The supplementary condition that is necessary for a competitive market environment, beyond those of free exit and entry, is that the effective size of the exchange nexus be sufficiently large so as to make viable the simultaneous existence of multiple buyers and sellers in each market. This condition may be met, at least in large part, by rules that keep all markets *open* to all potential traders, whether as suppliers or demanders, both those who may be members of the polity and foreigners. Even in markets that may be relatively small, as defined geographically and by membership in a political unit, openness will fix limits on potential abuses of market power by buyers and/or sellers of goods and services that can, either directly or indirectly, be moved across space.

I have suggested that in the complex modern economy few, if any, participants can subsist in autarky. An extension of the analytical illustration introduced earlier may have been taken to imply that all participants tend to become narrowly specialized to the production of a single good or service. Such an implication does not, of course, follow, and the disappearance of the autarkic exit option may occur without any such narrow specialization. The individual participant may remain wholly dependent on some market purchase of his or her services, but, at the same time, need not be specialized narrowly to the production of any particular product. This potential substitutability in production serves to make the requirements of effectively competitive markets less restrictive than the earlier discussion might have made them seem. The right to exit from the exchange with any single purchaser allows the participant-supplier to shift among as well as within occupational, industrial and locational categories. Recognition of the enhanced value of the right to exit when the set of options is expanded may cause participants, when considering investing in the human capital required for becoming specialized, to maintain some preferred level of potential flexibility in their productive service capacities.

In the discussion of the minimal requirements of a competitive structure to ensure that liberty in one's own person has significant economic value, I have concentrated on the input or the supply side of the individual's market participation. The individual enters exchange in order to sell his or her productive capacities for money, with which he or she expects to be able to purchase end-items of consumption. Protection against exploitation through manipulation of the terms of trade is provided by the liberty to choose among alternative purchasers, and the competitive process that acts to ensure that alternative purchasers are available at relatively low costs of search and shift.

In some formal sense, the requirements for competition on the demand or output side of an individual's market participation are fully symmetrical with those on the supply side. As a prospective buyer of final end-items, or outputs, the individual is vulnerable to terms-of-trade manipulation unless he or she has the liberty of choosing among alternative sellers along with the availability of such alternatives. But the potential for exploitation on this side of the market is given less attention, properly so, because specialization in consumption rarely extends to the limits of specialization in production. Even if the individual retains the capacity to offer productive services suitable for any of several occupational or industrial categories, once a choice is made, he or she normally supplies inputs to only one purchaser at a time. Rarely do we find persons who work part-time as a carpenter, part-time as a plumber and part-time as a professor of economics. On the demand side, however, such a pattern of consumption is standard behaviour. The individual spends his or her income on a whole set of goods and services, and several goods are consumed or used simultaneously and in mutually complementary ways. The individual is necessarily less dependent on the market structure of supply for any one of the several goods and services in his consumption bundle than he or she is on the market structure of demand for whatever productive services he or she supplies in order to earn income.

This difference in the individual participant's potential vulnerability on the two sides of the market process does not imply that maintenance of an effectively competitive structure is unimportant in markets for consumption goods. The implication is only that the individual's freedom to choose among alternative sellers of goods and services is, in itself, somewhat more efficacious on the demand side, because of the greater substitutability of end-items in the individual's consumption pattern. By inference, the institutional or structural requirements needed to ensure the effectiveness of this freedom to choose become somewhat less critical than the supply side. To introduce a homely example, to the academician, monopsony control over all institutions of higher education and research is more damaging than monopoly control over all the suppliers of bread. It is easier to shift from bread to beans, than it is to shift from being a professor to being a plumber.

9. Professional and Private Images of Markets

Once an understanding of the logical structure of a competitive market economy is fully attained, its aesthetic attractiveness may emerge to render any evaluative judgement suspect. The idealization of the market, that interaction setting in which persons remain maximally interdependent yet where no person exerts arbitrary power over another, becomes a strong normative influence on the way that we interpret that which we can observe directly. And this romanticized interpretation may conflict with other images. The effect is to create an intellectual empty space between the professional economists' model of competitive order and the order that may be indirectly inferred from individuals' behaviour towards private property.

As emphasized in earlier sections of this book, private property protects the liberties of persons by providing viable exit from, or avoidance of entry into, potentially exploitative economic relationships. So long as the individual remains "free to choose" among alternatives and so long as there exist multiple alternatives from which choice may be exercised, there need be little or no concern about the descriptively observed dependence of the individual on the behaviour of many other persons through the market exchange nexus. In this romanticized vision of the competitive market economy, at least at a first analytical cut, there would seem to be no argument in support of private property, other than ownership of self, aside from the familiar incentive-efficiency evocation. In other words, the supplementary argument from liberty seems absent in the idealized model of competitive structure.

The theory of the operation of this model tells us that the ownership of non-human assets is simply an alternative to leasing the services of such assets, and that any choice as between these institutional alternatives should rationally be made on the basis of strict cost comparisons. Markets work so as to ensure that these alternatives remain roughly equal in value. Politicized intrusions into markets may, of course, bias the choice alternatives here (e.g., relative tax treatment), but in the competitive market, as idealized, there is no clear case to be made out for widely dispersed individual ownership of non-human assets, over and beyond the dispersal necessary to ensure the effective working of the competitive process itself. For example, so long as there exists effective competition among suppliers of rental housing units, there is no liberty-based argument for individual family ownership. The same result holds, or carries over, in application to individual ownership of means of transportation such as motor cars and even to the wider set of consumer durables of all varieties.

There seems, however, to be a disparity between the economists' model of competitive markets and the reality of markets as their workings might be inferred from the behaviour of individual participants. Persons do not behave as if markets offer effective alternatives for choice in many situations, and dependence on market-determined terms of trade is treated as a "bad" in individual utility functions, as we have previously noted. Even in the absence of politicized intrusions that may bias the choice alternatives, individuals place ownership arrangements in a preferred position relative to lease or rental arrangements for many goods and services. Individuals (families) prefer to own their own houses; they prefer to own their own motor cars, as private property, no matter how competitive are the markets for lease-rental arrangements. I suggest, further, that many individuals will prefer ownership to leasing, even if there should exist quite substantial cost or efficiency differences that favour the second of these alternatives. That is, even if the same quality motor car might be leased at, say, $100 per month less than the full monthly cost of owning a motor car, most persons may continue to prefer ownership. The efficiency gains from increased market interdependence are not sufficient to offset the utility loss incurred with reduced independence. As we observe them to behave, therefore, individuals place a positive value on the liberty of the withdrawal from the market nexus that private ownership makes possible, and this evaluation will persist regardless of the degree of competition in particular markets.

10. Private Ownership as Own (Self-)Production

One way of interpreting private ownership of non-human assets is to suggest that this institution allows persons to produce the services yielded by those assets for themselves, akin to our earlier example of the egg and potato farmers. The family that owns its residence *produces* its own housing services through time, it does not need to engage in any ongoing contractual or market exchange with suppliers. The individual who owns his own motor car produces transport services day by day as these are needed.

Private ownership allows the individual to move out of the network of exchange-market interdependence and towards the valued position of self-sufficiency. Self-production directly reduces the need that the individual might have to enter the market as a demander-buyer for particular goods and services. And, in this sense, the self-production made possible by ownership of assets is not different, in kind, from the self-production that takes place from applying inputs outside the market structure (e.g., vegetables from a garden). To the extent that ownership is extended to include a larger range of assets (housing, motor cars, furniture, appliances, livestock, fruit trees, etc.) self-production of the goods and services yielded by these assets also reduces the dependence of the individual on the operation of the market for that which is sold in exchange for generalized purchasing power (money income).

This point deserves more detailed discussion. Consider the elementary wheel-of-income diagram shown in Figure 10.1. The individual at A, whom we shall call A, enters the market for inputs (labour services) as a seller-

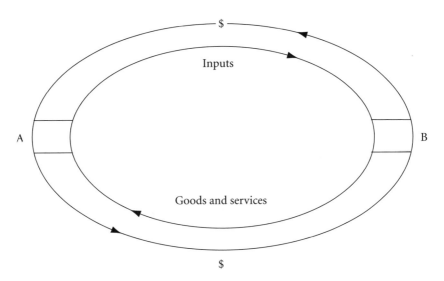

Figure 10.1. The wheel of income

supplier. At the same time, A enters the market for outputs (goods and services) as a demander-buyer. In a fully interdependent market economy, the individual is dependent on the behaviour of others in the establishment of the terms of trade in both input and output markets. This structure of interaction was discussed earlier.

As and if the individual at A finds it possible to withdraw from the market nexus through self-production, the *size* of the required return flow on the demander-buyer side of the wheel of income is reduced. (Ownership of a house eliminates monthly rental payments.) And, as and if the individual (family) requires less income flow to purchase the goods and services dictated by preferences, the need to secure generalized purchasing power (money income) on the supplier-seller side of the wheel is correspondingly reduced.

The self-production made possible by the ownership of property may be more important in reducing this dependence of the individual as a seller of inputs than as a buyer of outputs, for reasons related to, but somewhat different from, those discussed earlier. Individuals may consider themselves more vulnerable on the supplier side of the wheel, both because of the relatively greater specialization involved, and because of the relatively higher transactions costs incurred in shifting among alternative buyers, costs that may include locational adjustments. Consider the position of the person who becomes unemployed as a result of market forces. If this person owns a house, car, furniture and appliances, the vulnerability to the market shock is very substantially mitigated. Self-production of the services yielded by these assets facilitates subsistence on much more acceptable terms than would be the case in the absence of property holdings.

Economists should, I think, recognize that the institution of private property presents a paradox in the sense that it exists as a publicly acknowledged counter to the presumed superior "efficiency" of market interdependence. In its idealized operation, the market should be able to offer more services for the same outlay, or the same services with less outlay, than that ratio experienced under the self-production arrangements of private property. An ideal housing market could supply persons with the identical housing services at less cost due to the economies of scale in production. (Why should every suburban household own its own lawn mower?)

The vulnerability of the individual in the market relationship is not incorporated in the standard analytical exercises which implicitly presume that the models work ideally. But the freedom from the shocks that the market may deliver must be entered as a positively valued argument in a meaningful utility function. In the more inclusive formulation that would allow for this change in utility functions, the self-production that the ownership of property makes possible becomes "efficient" relative to that of the market, at least within some limits.

11. Private Property in Assets That Yield Money Income

The efficacy of private ownership in insulating individuals from market shocks discussed to this point applies only to those assets that yield goods and services directly, in kind, to the owner. References were made to housing and consumer durables in particular. The implications do not extend to private ownership of assets that yield money income to the owner rather than direct services. Note that the distinction here is not equivalent to that between real assets and financial assets, since some real assets also yield money income rather than income in kind. Almost by definition, of course, financial assets yield money income rather than direct services.

The owner of a financial asset, say, a bond, produces nothing directly that is comparable to the housing services produced by home ownership. Clearly, the ownership of a claim to money income does not represent a withdrawal from the market nexus to the same extent as ownership of an asset yielding income in kind. The owner of the bond must still pay his monthly rent for housing, must meet the lease payments on his or her car and finance the TV rentals when due. Ownership of a claim to money income exerts no influence on the position of the individual as a demander-buyer of final end-items of consumption or use. The potential vulnerability to market shocks through terms of trade for purchased goods is not affected. On the supplier-seller side of the income wheel, however, any claim to money income attributable to the ownership of an asset must act to reduce the necessity of selling current inputs in order to finance consumption goods. The person who gets $100 per month in interest on a bond or money-market account needs $100 less in current earnings from the sale of labour services to finance spending on consumption goods. One way of putting the point here is to say that the owner of an asset produces income that facilitates the purchase of a higher-valued bundle of end-items from the market, or the sale of a smaller bundle of inputs to the market. But the income must, in either case, be processed through the market. By contrast, the owner of an asset, yielding services directly in kind, is relieved of any market throughput, and necessary transformation of value through the exchange nexus.

A further distinction must be made between those privately owned assets that yield services which are then sold by the owner for money and those assets that yield a direct money return without intermediate sale. In both cases, ownership produces a money income flow that decreases dependence on the sale of current inputs to the market. But there are differing vulnerabilities to forces beyond the control of the owner. In the first case, where a real asset yields services that must then be sold in order to secure money income, the owner remains vulnerable to the vicissitudes of the market for similar earning assets. In the second case, where the ownership claim yields a money return directly, the vulnerability is to shifts in the terms of trade between money and goods generally. This vulnerability is maximal when private property takes the form of money, as such, or in claims that guarantee returns stated in nominal monetary units. I shall defer explicit discussion of the relationship between private property in money or money claims until Chapter 13.

12. Private Property and Time: Accumulation through Ownership

To this point, I have neglected any discussion of the role of private property, regardless of the form that ownership takes, in facilitating individual adjustments *over time* from those patterns of income flows, both in receipts and outlays, that the market generates to those patterns that might be preferred whether from life-cycle or intergenerational motives. In other words, the analysis has been limited to the role of ownership in satisfying essentially the precautionary motives, which would be absent under the workings of idealized markets. Implicitly, the analysis has presented the argument for private ownership in a model where all participants in an economy live forever and remain fixed in their capacities to supply inputs and demand outputs over time. If time is introduced meaningfully into the model, it becomes evident that preferred temporal adjustment to income and outlay flows within individual life spans or between generations requires some institution that allows partitionable claims to values that are realizable in later time periods. Full ownership of personal capacities will allow partial satisfaction of this requirement through the accumulation of human capital, but ownership of non-human assets, in whatever form, is a necessary supplement.

My concern here is not with the relationship between private ownership of property and rates of capital accumulation and, hence, rates of aggregate economic growth in a nation. This argument is akin to that derived from the standard efficiency norm. I do not, of course, question either the validity or the importance of property institutions in generating either economic efficiency or growth, both of which may be widely accepted objectives. But my purpose in this book is limited to an attempted justification of private ownership as a means of protecting the liberties of persons, quite independent of efficiency or growth considerations.

As suggested earlier, private property, whether or not the asset yields an income through time, allows the owner temporally to withdraw from the market nexus. The person who has income from an owned asset, or an asset that is itself valued, may, if he or she so chooses, either increase current period outlays on final goods or reduce current period sale-supply of inputs to the market. In either case, ownership of valued assets allows for an increase in the individual's choice set. And note that the owner has available an exit option that carries value, whether or not this option is exercised. The owner of the valued asset remains "free to choose" over a wider range of options, so long as the asset value itself is not eroded. As Samuel Johnson suggested indirectly, the person is most at liberty when he or she owns valued assets that are *not* dissipated.[4]

The role of private ownership of property in facilitating preferred temporal adjustment in flows of income and outlay is not directly related to the efficacy of the operation of competitive market forces, as is the case with the precautionary motivations previously discussed. Even if the competitive process is such as to present the individual with multiple alternatives in each and every market at all points in time, partitionable claims to value, or property, will be needed to allow adjustment to the inexorable forces of "life in real time." The

---

4. J. Boswell, *The Journal of a Tour to the Hebrides with Samuel Johnson* (London: Everyman's Edition, 1946).

individual who may express little or no concern about exposure to the "blind forces of the market," who holds fast to the classical liberal's faith in competitive process, will continue to require private ownership of valued assets.

There are implications for the preferred form of property to be derived from the differing motivations for acquisition and holding assets. For the person who does place full trust in competitive market process, and whose sole or primary motivation is to be able to make intertemporal adjustments in income and outgo, the preferred form of asset should be that which is most readily transformable into other holdings of value, which is, of course, money itself. If we can ignore the precautionary motivation, even with reference to shifts in the terms of trade between money and goods, money or claims to money must be the preferred form of accumulation. The person who finds no advantage in the self-production of services in kind from property and who seeks some store of value asset exclusively for the purpose of intertemporal adjustment will opt for the purchase of financial claims with any funds released from current spending.

13. Private Property in Money: Inflation and the Confiscation of Value

The relationship between inflation and the liberty-based defence of private property requires further examination. As noted, the individual who remains unconcerned about vulnerability to particular market shocks will find property ownership necessary to allow for temporal adjustment in income and outlay flows, but, ideally, would choose to hold property in generalized purchasing power, in money or claims to money. Such an idealized setting, however, requires more than the effective operation of the competitive process in every market for goods and services. The setting must also ensure that there are no shocks in the terms of trade between money and goods against which some protection is deemed to be desirable. And this condition is not one that can be met by the working of markets in real-world settings.

It is possible to construct an analytical model in which money takes the form of a commodity or commodity bundle, in which case the workings of the competitive market might be expected to ensure reasonable stability in the money-goods terms of trade. In economies as we observe them, however, money is not a commodity produced and sold through markets; it is, instead, a creation of the state, or political unit, and its supply bears little or no relationship to its production cost. For an individual who seeks to hold property in money or money claims, therefore, the protection sought is that against the potential exploitation through the state, or collective agency, rather than against the workings of the market, as such.

The sources of a possible precautionary motive for seeking protection against potential confiscations of expected values are psychologically different in the two settings examined. The person who seeks protection against the "blind forces of the market" need not fear the machinations of identified or even identifiable persons or groups of persons. The protection sought here is against the aggregate reaction behaviour of large numbers of sellers and buyers, as such behaviour produces emergent results in the pattern of input and output prices in markets. This sort of protection, as sought, is inversely related to what might be called "trust" in the market process, a "trust" that depends for its rational origins only on some broad presumption that persons tend to seek their own economic advantage. By dramatic contrast, the person who seeks protection against shocks to the money-goods terms of trade must be concerned, not with the behaviour of many suppliers-demanders in market settings, but with the particular behaviour of agents who can be identified as acting for the political unit. By the law of large numbers, the aggregate behaviour of many persons in markets is more predictable, other things equal, than the behaviour of particular persons in their roles as monetary agents for the state.

Relatively few persons will be unaware of the potential for exploitation by the state through its authority to manipulate the terms of trade between money and goods to its own economic advantage. Some lessons from history are learned. Persons who seek only to acquire property to adjust income and outlay flows through time will modify their behaviour in efforts to forestall such potential exploitation. The exercise of the precautionary motive here will reflect preferences for real assets as opposed to financial assets. Real assets will be demanded neither for their potential self-production of services nor for their measured rates of return, but, instead, for their capital-value accretion as the money-goods terms of trade shift against money. The absence of confidence in the politicized agency that directly influences the money-goods exchange rate represents a restriction on the domain of private property as evaluated in terms of the potential protection of the liberties of persons.

This property-expanding role of monetary credibility is not normally considered in discussions of monetary arrangements. Here, as elsewhere, economists tend to stress the efficiency-enhancing characteristics of predictability in the value of the monetary unit. Such characteristics are, of course, critically important; contractual arrangements of all varieties are vastly simplified in a regime where predictability in the value of a numeraire exists and is expected to exist. Over and beyond this familiar normative argument for an effective monetary constitution, however, economists (and others) should also recognize that individuals, in their personal-private role, and wholly divorced from any contractual interactions, are made more *independent,* in the sense emphasized in these chapters, under a regime of predictability in the money-goods exchange rate than under a regime where such predictability is absent. By being able to hold stores of value in money, or claims to money, the individual secures generalized protection against particular market fluctuations, on either the input or the output side.

The implications are straightforward. A regime that includes legal protection for private-property holdings is severely limited in its efficacy if predictability in the money-goods exchange rate is absent. And a regime that seeks to privatize ownership of ordinary assets must accompany any privatization steps by the implementation of a monetary constitution that will introduce such predictability, and make it credible. So long as the political authority retains the effective power (and is understood to do so) to confiscate property-holdings that are denominated in monetary units of account, the legal structure that allows persons to own and control assets remains crippled; the potential efficacy of the institution of private property itself remains only half-way exploited.

14. Socialism, Private Property and Liberty

Concentration on the liberty-extending elements of private-property ownership offers perhaps a more comprehensive appreciation of the necessary restrictions on liberty that socialism, as an organizational structure, must entail. Socialism, by its classical definition, has as its central feature the displacement of private ownership by collective or state ownership. And, as the domain of activity brought within the organizational umbrella of socialism expands, the domain of private ownership diminishes, *pari passu.* The domain of socialist organization is never total in the sense that persons are pro-hibited from the ownership of any and all valued assets, including the values in their own capacities. Even the most totalitarian regimes allow for *de facto* private ownership of some valued assets, even if these be restricted to pre-cious metals and trinkets.

But consider the position of the individual in a socialist regime in which all productive assets are owned and controlled by the collective authority, in-cluding those that could be represented in the individual's own human cap-ital. The individual is *assigned* to a specific occupational, locational role as a supplier of inputs and is *assigned,* in turn, a designated share or quota in the final outputs that the system generates, outputs that are, themselves, selected by the collective authority.

In this setting, the participant in the inclusive socialist enterprise is maxi-mally dependent upon, and hence vulnerable to, the decisions of others, and there is no systemic guarantor against exploitation akin to that offered in a competitive market structure. The individual confronts, simultaneously, a mo-nopsony "purchaser" of services and a monopoly "seller" of goods that are re-quired for subsistence. There is no exit option available, in either the input "market" or the output "market." And, holding no value-producing assets pri-vately, the individual has no recourse to self-production, even in any limited sense.

Even if (and contrary to both analytical and empirical evidence) the so-cialist regime could be "efficient" in some questionably meaningful sense, the argument for independence or liberty in the individual's utility function would not be allowed expression. Most participants, even in the idealized and imaginary socialist paradise, would prefer, if necessary, some sacrifice in productive potential in exchange for some protection against exploitation by collectivized authority. In reality, of course, no such trade-off between do-mains exists. Instead, both logical analysis and historical record suggest that "the economy" becomes less rather than more "productive" as the domain of collectivization is extended. Only as the boundaries of collective control are reduced, and as private ownership of valued assets increases, do we ex-pect increases in overall economic productivity. But, also, and importantly for the emphasis in this book, persons place positive value on the limited in-dependence that any such shift to private ownership embodies, value over and beyond any increase in efficiency-productivity.

From the temporal perspective of the early 1990s, it is perhaps too easy to understand what seem to be the flaws in the socialist model of political-economic reality. Conversely, it is difficult for those of us who have observed socialism's collapse, both in idea and in application, to understand the dominance of the socialist-collectivist vision in good minds for more than a century, both in the positive analysis of institutional working properties and in the accompanying normative comparative evaluation. F. A. Hayek is surely correct in suggesting that much scholarship will go into attempts to determine why and how "the fatal conceit" that was socialism could have commanded and maintained the intellectual heights for so long.[5]

My suggestion here is that one source of the fatal conceit or delusion stems from the undue concentration of economists on the efficiency-productivity elements of social organization to the neglect of the liberty dimension. If efficiency is taken, even if implicitly, to be the end objective of relevance, a series of related *scientific* errors could have generated the historical record of the socialist century. In retrospect, we may interpret this record as a falsification of the hypothesis that collective ownership and control of the means of production generate product value equal to or even superior to that generated under private ownership arrangements. At least until the 1950s and 1960s, this hypothesis seemed to remain unfalsified. But consider, by way of contrast, the parallel hypothesis that might have been, but was not, made central in comparative institutional-organizational analysis, the hypothesis that incorporates the liberty dimension. Even as an initial hypothesis, no one could have seriously advanced the proposition that collective ownership and control involves an extension in the liberties of individual participants. The restrictions on liberty that necessarily characterize any socialist organization, large or small, comprehensive or piecemeal, were more or less acknowledged by all observers from the onset of the experiments.

15. *Rerum Novarum*

As we review the discussion over the course of the socialist century, we note that the issues were not exclusively joined along the efficiency-productivity

---

5. F. A. Hayek, *The Fatal Conceit: The Errors of Socialism* (Chicago: University of Chicago Press, 1988).

dimension. The effects on individual liberty that a shift from a regime of private to collective ownership involves became the basis for an independent and important critique of socialism, and a critique that did not reflect either an understanding of the efficiency argument or even an appreciation of the competitive market process. I refer to the papal encyclical of Leo XIII that was issued in 1893 and widely known by its Latin title, *Rerum Novarum*.[6]

Extended citation from the early sections of this encyclical seems warranted:

> . . . the *Socialists*, working on the poor man's envy of the rich, endeavor to destroy private property, and maintain that individual possessions should become the common property of all, to be administered by the State or by municipal bodies. They hold that, by thus transferring property from private persons to the community, the present evil state of things will be set to rights, because each citizen will then have his equal share of whatever there is to enjoy. But their proposals are so clearly futile for all practical purposes, that if they were carried out the working man himself would be among the first to suffer. Moreover they are emphatically unjust, because they rob the lawful possessor, bring the State into a sphere that is not its own, and cause complete confusion in the community.

> *Private Ownership*
> It is surely undeniable that, when a man engages in remunerative labour, the very reason and motive of his work is to obtain property, and to hold it as his own private possession. If one man hires out to another his strength or his energy, he does this for the purpose of receiving in return what is necessary for food and living; he thereby expressly proposes to acquire a full and real right, not only to the remuneration, but also to the disposal of that remuneration as he pleases. Thus, if he lives sparingly, saves money, and invests his savings, for greater security, in land, the land in such a case is only his wages in another form; and, consequently, a working man's little estate thus purchased should be as completely at his own disposal as the wages he receives for his labour. But it is precisely in

---

6. Pope Leo XIII, *The Condition of Labor in Five Great Encyclicals* (*Rerum Novarum*), ed. G. C. Treacy (New York: The Paulist Press, 1939), 1–36. This encyclical was first called to my attention by Michael Novak, American Enterprise Institute.

this power of disposal that ownership consists, whether the property be land or movable goods. The *Socialists,* therefore, in endeavoring to transfer the possessions of individuals to the community, strike at the interests of every wage earner, for they deprive him of the liberty of disposing of his wages, and thus of all hope and possibility of increasing his stock and of bettering his condition in life. (pp. 2–3)

. . . it must be within his (man's) right to have things not merely for temporary and momentary use, as other living beings have them, but in stable and permanent possession; he must have not only things that perish in the using, but also those that, though used, remain for use in the future. (p. 3)

. . .

And to say that God has given the earth to the use and enjoyment of the universal human race is not to deny that there can be private property. For God has granted the earth to mankind in general; not in the sense that all without distinction can deal with it as they please, but rather that no part of it has been assigned to any one in particular, and that the limits of private possession have been left to be fixed by man's own industry and the laws of individual peoples. (p. 4)

. . . We are told that it is right for private persons to have the use of the soil and the fruits of their land, but that it is unjust for anyone to possess as owner either the land on which he has built or the estate which he has cultivated. But those who assert this do not perceive that they are robbing man of what his own labour has produced, for the soil which is tilled and cultivated with toil and skill utterly changes its condition; it was wild before, it is now fruitful; it was barren, now it brings forth in abundance. That which has thus altered and improved it becomes so truly a part of itself as to be in a great measure indistinguishable, inseparable from it. Is it just that the fruit of man's sweat and labour should be enjoyed by another?

These statements from *Rerum Novarum* may be interpreted, I think naively, as simple assertions to the effect that persons have natural rights to own separable properties, rights that are independent of any assessment of the relative productivity or efficiency of private and state ownership arrangements. A more careful reading suggests that the author(s) of these passages understood the intimate relationship between individual rights of property ownership and liberty. The empirical proposition is that individuals desire ownership of property in order to secure and to maintain the liberty over the disposal of resources, without which liberty there could be no hope of bettering the conditions of life.

Note that the hope of betterment is individualized. The individual may, if secure in a regime that allows the acquisition of property, along with the maintenance and increase in value through time, *on his own account*, better his condition, and quite independent of any complementing collective action, beyond that required for the necessary functioning of the legal order. Note that there is no consideration at all given to the prospect that the betterment of the working man's condition may be achieved through collective or community ownership. Implicitly, *Rerum Novarum's* defence of private property embodies a recognition of the value persons place on the independence that only a private ownership regime can offer.

16. The Marxian Proletariat and Malthusian Prophecy

The passages from *Rerum Novarum* in Chapter 15 make it clear that the right to own property is the means through which workers can better their own condition. Implicit in the whole discussion there is the denial of classical economists' cost-of-production theory of wages. In order for the acquisition of property to be a meaningful objective for workers, wages must be more than sufficient to ensure survival at a mere subsistence level that allows only for the reproduction of labour. In the Marxian extension of classical economics, workers remain unable to achieve the minimal liberty that property ownership makes possible; workers remain trapped within the industrial proletariat, subject to the inexorable operation of the capitalist production process that necessarily directs all of the economic surplus to the capitalist owners of the non-labour means of production. Workers are maximally vulnerable to the "blind forces of the market" which ensure their exploitation independent of any failure or breakdown of the market process itself. In this Marxian model of industrial capitalism, workers cannot acquire the property that could offer even a partial exit option from the economic nexus, and any ability to choose among alternative buyers for their labour services offers no in-market analogue since the exploitation is in no sense imputable to particular employers.

The Marxian failure to escape the intellectual strait-jacket imposed by the classical theory of distribution reflected itself in a blindness to the potential equilibrating activity of entrepreneurs who emerge to seek profit from any differential between the productive value of labour and the level of wages. An understanding of the competitive market process would have suggested that even if the Malthusian prophecy concerning rates of population increase holds, workers would, in all periods prior to the ultimate, and quite dismal, stationary state, find property acquisition possible. Nonetheless, the Malthusian devil would operate over time to reduce the viability of the liberty offered to workers through property ownership. Workers would increasingly find themselves squeezed towards subsistence level of existence.

The whole classical Marxian model of economic development reflects a failure to recognize the potential for innovation, for enhanced resource productivity, for expansion in income growth, that might act to keep any Malthusian forces in abeyance. It remains the case, however, that population growth did occur during early stages of industrial expansion, and that the early patterns of capitalist production did generate large urban concentrations which made separable individual units of real property impracticable for many participants in the inclusive production process. In relation to the analysis of this book, we may say that the guarantee of liberty afforded through property ownership was necessarily weakened, thereby making the viability of effective market competition more important in some relative sense. This conclusion holds even if the empirical record seems to have falsified the Malthusian prophecy, without which the whole classical Marxist model loses meaning.

In his last book, Hayek stressed the relationship between the productive efficiency of a market economy and the size of the population that can be sustained.[7] And he suggested that any revolutionary shift away from market institutions would, ultimately, ensure that population size be adjusted downwards. What Hayek fails to sense, however, is the relationship between the increasing market interdependence with its related increases in numbers of participants and the increasing difficulty that participants face in acquiring and holding property that might serve its traditional liberty-enhancing purpose. The modern urban man enjoys the fulsomeness of the highly inter-

7. Hayek, *The Fatal Conceit.*

dependent order of markets; but this person, at the same time, becomes increasingly dependent on the behaviour of others beyond any range of personal influence or control.

To an extent, this development is countered by the shift towards a post-industrial economic order, towards a service economy, which, as accompanied by the communication-information technological revolution, makes spatial concentration less necessary for the generation of economic value. The modern social problems do not lie in the Marxian proletariat, whose participants are property-less and subject to capitalist exploitation. The modern social problems, those that arise in the welfare-transfer state, are quite different, and, indeed, become almost the reverse of those sketched out by Marx. The modern urban underclass is not forced to levels of subsistence because wage levels are forced to the costs of reproduction of labour. The modern underclass does not produce value at all; transfer payments rather than wages become the source of living. And productive participants of economies are not likely to acquiesce in payments that enable non-producing recipients to accumulate property that will, to an extent, free them from dependency status. The urban underclass in the welfare-transfer state participates in the economy only as a consumer. The members of this class become the exploiters rather than the exploited; they secure *negative* surpluses; they use up value that they have no part in producing.

17. Final Speculations

Karl Marx understood neither the statics nor the dynamics of the capitalist economic order that he so persuasively criticized. Failing such understanding, Marx thought it necessary to replace the market order with some collectivist alternative that he understood even less. Nonetheless, we may interpret Marx as being acutely sensitive to the loss of liberty experienced by persons who shift into market-exchange relationships and away from the idyll of self-sufficient private, family or small community independence. In this sensibility, Marx joined one strand of classical political philosophy, Thomas Jefferson and the southern agrarians of this century, all of whom questioned the viability of a free society in the absence of peasant proprietorship, broadly defined.

We know, in 1992, that private ownership of property is necessary for efficiency in the production of economic value. We also know that extensive specialization is required in order for the scale economies of production to be realized. Individuals must concentrate their input capacities despite the knowledge that, in so doing, they increase their dependence on others beyond their own influence and control, either directly or indirectly. Even in complex modern economies, however, specialization need not be total. And through private ownership, persons may be able substantially to reduce their dependence on markets. Ownership of durables, including housing, allows space for own-production of a flow of services, hence alleviating any need for market purchase. In addition, private ownership of income-yielding assets allows adjustment of consumption-use patterns through time. These aspects of private ownership in modern Western economies remain significant, even if they are often overlooked. Only in the contrast with the pre-1989 socialist regimes do these liberty-enhancing qualities of property ownership come into full focus.

Nonetheless, even the complex web of interdependence that describes the modern economies of the United States, Japan and Western Europe seems far removed in its dimension of independence from the regime of yeoman farmers in Jefferson's idealized republic. Can measures be suggested that would maintain or even increase the value productivity that extended specialization makes possible and, at the same time, capture or recapture some of those attributes of independent existence that are universally valued in themselves?

The importance of monetary stabilization can scarcely be over-emphasized in this respect. Through its arbitrary authority to modify the exchange rate between money and goods, the nation-state, even in Western developed economies, reduces dramatically the potential protection that the citizen may secure through legally guaranteed holdings of property. The prospects for confiscation of value through monetary inflation reduce the intrinsic advantages of holding claims denominated in many and create a distortion in favour of real assets. An effective monetary constitution (which exists nowhere in the world) that would guarantee stability in the value of the monetary unit would, indeed, work miracles, whether measured against criteria of liberty or efficiency.

Monetary stability would also work to ensure that the macroeconomy function so as to prevent massive institutional failures akin to those experienced during the 1930s. Unemployment arising from macroeconomic sources would be largely eliminated, thereby reducing the dependency status of all market participants.

A second major dimension that warrants notice here, even if the direction of effect is obvious, is that which measures the overall size of the politicized sector of economic life. To the extent that the individual is coercively subjected to taxes which, in turn, finance governmental programmes that presumably return assigned shares in benefits, there is no available exit option. The argument from liberty, as advanced in this book, suggests that, even if the overall size of the politicized sector of the economy should be set precisely at some efficiency-enhancing optimum, the utility value of independence itself would dictate some reduction in public sector size.

As discussed earlier, the availability of alternative buyers and sellers in both input and output markets becomes more important as the economic unit shifts increasingly from the self-production afforded by property ownership towards dependence on market exchange. Competition in the market-place protects the individual from undue exploitation even when property-holdings are limited. But institutional structures can be adjusted so as to facilitate individuals' ability to exercise choices. Mobility among market options can be encouraged along many dimensions.

In a more general sense, the individual values private ownership that allows for a definition of a "private sphere" of activity, even in the most interdependent of settings. Even the person who provides highly specialized input services, and who depends for income on markets for such services, can remain at liberty in the choices that are made on buying sides of markets. There are exit options available in the modern competitive economy that are much more extensive than those faced by the yeoman farmer of Mr Jefferson's dreams. But the critically important linkage between market competition and individual liberty may not yet be fully sensed by those who continue to express preferences for asset ownership even when terms of trade seem unfavourable. Market forces may not be trusted for several reasons, including the lack of understanding of how these forces work. But, also, markets may be recognized to be vulnerable to interferences by politicians. *Laissez-faire*, as a policy stance, may be trusted more than its opposite. And individuals who feel too dependent on markets may seek greater protection for their residual liberties through structures of property ownership. But with modern jurisprudence on the legitimacy of governmental takings of privately owned assets, such security may be impossible to achieve.

The intricacies of the relationships between individual liberty and private property, analytically, empirically, historically and legally are surely deserving of critical attention. I do not claim to have done more than to scratch the surface of a research programme that remains largely undeveloped.

18. Endnote

The editor has strongly urged me to include explicit discussion of the implications of the above analysis for political organization and particularly for democratic institutions. The central argument is that private or several property serves as a guarantor of liberty, quite independent of how political or collective decisions are made. The direct implication is, of course, that effective constitutional limits must be present, limits that will effectively constrain overt political intrusions into rights of property, as legally defined, and into voluntary contractual arrangements involving transfer of property. If individual liberty is to be protected, such constitutional limits must be in place prior to and separate from any exercise of democratic governance.

An understanding of priorities in this respect should, of course, offer the basis for an extension of constitutional constraints on majoritarian legislative processes in modern polities and notably with reference to potential monetary and fiscal exploitation, quite apart from the more obvious "takings" activity that must everywhere be condemned.

The omnipresent confusion that has corrupted Western attitudes and that threatens to close off the opportunities now presented to emerging post-socialist societies involves the failure to recognize that "constitutional" must be placed in front of the word "democracy" if the political equality of individuals is to be translated with any meaningful measure of freedom and autonomy. The tyranny of the majority is no less real than any other, and, indeed, it may be more dangerous because it feeds on the idealistic illusion that participation is all that matters.

PART FOUR

The Constitution of Markets

On the Structure of an Economy
A Re-emphasis of Some Classical Foundations

Abstract: Economic choices are made by many buyers and sellers as they participate in many markets for many goods and services. "The Economy" is best described by the structure (the rules) within which these market choices take place. Efforts to reform the pattern of results observed in an economy should be directed exclusively at this structure; attempts to modify directly the outcomes or results of market process within structures are based on fundamental misunderstanding.

The sovereign is completely discharged from a duty, in the attempting to perform which he must always be exposed to innumerable delusions, and for the proper performance of which no human wisdom or knowledge could ever be sufficient; the duty of superintending the industry of private people, and of directing it towards the employments most suitable to the interest of the society.

—Adam Smith, *The Wealth of Nations,* Book IV, Ch. ix, 51, p. 687. Oxford University Press Edition, 1976.

To those of us who share the view expressed so well by Adam Smith in my frontispiece citation, there is both "good news" and "bad news" in the global

From *Business Economics* 24 (January 1989): 6–12. Reprinted by permission.

James M. Buchanan is indebted to his colleague Viktor Vanberg for helpful comments on an earlier draft. This paper was presented at the 30th Annual Meeting of the National Association of Business Economists, September 25–28, Pittsburgh, Pa.

political economy of 1988. The "good news" is reflected in the developing recognition that centrally planned economies everywhere remain glaringly inefficient, a recognition that has been accompanied by efforts to make major changes in internal incentive structures. More extensively, throughout the developed and the developing world of nations, the rhetoric of privatization in the 1980s has, occasionally, been translated into reality.

The "bad news" emerges from the United States, where in a single week in early May 1988 two separate stories in the media caught my attention. The first was a report that the Greenspan Federal Reserve Board had returned full circle to the once-abandoned effort at monetary fine tuning. The second was a report that councils well placed in the Democratic Party are increasingly disposed to promote specific and directed governmental intervention into industrial operation. These two stories came on top of the protectionist-mercantilist absurdities abroad in the land, absurdities that seemed excessive, even by presidential election years standards.

These items, along with the formal title of this, The Adam Smith Lecture, prompt me to devote my attention exclusively to a restatement and re-emphasis of what I think was Adam Smith's own normative attitude on the structure of a national economy, and, by inference, on his attitude toward political-governmental directions for economic policy. Let me say at the outset, however, that I am not an exegetist, and that my concern is really not what Adam Smith may have said or failed to say. My concern is, instead, with articulating what I think would be a consistent position, for Adam Smith, in the context of the United States political economy in the late 1980s. And you will not, of course, be surprised that I shall exploit yet another opportunity to present my own perspective on political economy generally.

I propose, therefore, to defend the categorical distinction to be made between the structure of an economy and the operation of that economy within such structure. I shall argue that the appropriate domain for political economy, for politically directed reform as well as for discussion and analysis of that reform, is exclusively limited to structure. Efforts directed toward effectuating modifications of results that emerge only from complex interdependencies within structure are misguided, as are all canons of putative advice advanced by pundits who fail to understand the necessary distinction. My argument may be properly interpreted as a restatement of the positive case for *laissez-faire* that Adam Smith might have made had he used this term.

Above all else, Adam Smith was a man of prudence, who would never have countenanced those fools of right or left whose caricatures through the decades have reduced a potentially meaningful slogan to polemical absurdity.

I shall proceed as follows. In the next section, I shall offer a precautionary tale about the dangers of terms that seem semantically and didactically useful but that may have the effect of making enlightened understanding more difficult to achieve. Functionalism, the familiar scourge of explanatory analysis in the other social sciences, also works its spell among economists. The third section is devoted to a necessarily foreshortened discussion of the order of an economy, as it operates within its own constraining structure. The next section examines elements of structure and analyzes relationships between structure and operations within structure. In the following section, I argue that elements of structure offer the only appropriate targets for reform. In the final section, I demonstrate how confusion in understanding the distinction between structure and operation-within-structure, between rules of the game and play within the rules, between process and end states, produces misdirected, and ultimately self-defeating, ventures in economic policy. The lecture falls clearly within "constitutional political economy," although, by comparison with some of my other papers, discussion here is concentrated on the structure of the economy rather than on the structure of the polity. In other words, the analysis examines the impact of politics on the economy, both in its positive and normative variants. The analysis does not, at least directly, introduce constitutional politics.

The "Functions" of an Economy

Any economist who was exposed directly to the teachings of Frank Knight at the University of Chicago or indirectly through access to one of the many elementary textbooks that incorporated elements of Knight's introductory monograph, "The Economic Organization,"[1] is familiar with the listing of the "functions" of an economic order. As initially presented by Knight, these are:

1. establishment of a scale of values;
2. organizing production;

---

1. Frank H. Knight, "The Economic Organization" (Chicago: University of Chicago, 1933, mimeographed).

3. distributing final product;
4. making provision for growth;
5. adjusting demand to supply over periods of transition.

This listing is indeed useful, both semantically and didactically. It allows the student to focus on distinguishable categories of the economic interaction process, while continuing to recognize that the process, as it operates, carries out or performs the five functions simultaneously.

I want to suggest, however, that this Knightian introduction to our central subject matter may be misleading because it may be interpreted to imply that "the economy," "the economic organization," or "the economic order," accomplishes the listed functions, whether efficaciously or not, in some purposefully directed sense. If the economy, as such, has an acknowledged function or functions such as the establishment of a value scale, does it not seem to follow that the economy, modelled perhaps as a corporate actor, or perhaps through its politically organized agents, acts in furtherance of the stipulated and functionally defined objective? Should we really be surprised when the state, in its perceived role as helmsman of the national economy, takes upon itself those tasks presumably assigned to it by the economists who purport to understand their own domain of scientific competence?

To interpret the listing in this way is, of course, a mark of misunderstanding and confusion, both of Knight's own purpose in setting it out, and of the whole interaction process that defines the central subject matter of our discipline. Indeed we look to Adam Smith for one of the first explanations of how the economy does "perform" the listed functions without such functions, as such, being within the consciously pursued purposes of anyone, whether the individual participant as buyer or seller in a market or the political agent for such a participant. It becomes functionalist fallacy to impute purpose to "the economy" from the observation that the listed functions are, somehow, carried out. The argument from result to conscious design has been, since the eighteenth century, the argument that the economist must counter. And it is but small exaggeration to say that the core of our discipline embodies the understanding that the observed results of economic process emerge without conscious design while at the same time they describe an order that is amenable to scientific analysis.

The Order of an Economy

I apologize for re-emphasizing basic principles of economics that may seem both to insult your intelligence and to be remote from practical relevance. I submit, however, that these principles are ignored, forgotten, or deliberately violated in too much of what passes for learned wisdom in our profession. I submit that many modern economists do not know what they are talking about, or, more charitably, that they talk about a realm of discourse beyond that constrained by the origins and history of their scientific discipline.

Adam Smith laid out the boundaries. We take as our assigned task to understand and to explain how an economy generates patterns of order that incorporate achievement of our objectives without requiring either benevolence on the part of economic actors or explicit direction by political agents. The principle of spontaneous coordination of the market is *the* principle of our discipline. Perhaps the most widely cited statement in *The Wealth of Nations* is that which suggests that we get our supper's meat not from the benevolence of the butcher but from his regard to his own self-interest.[2]

The butcher has a private pecuniary interest in having inventories of meat that will meet the demands of buyers. The qualities of desirability and availability take precedence over those qualities that may seem aesthetically superior by the butcher's own standards for the simple reason that the butcher seeks a larger relative share in the overall surplus generated by the nexus of trade and exchange among specialized participants. As we add the baker, the candlestick maker, and all of the other producing specializations in the modern complex economy, we explain the emergence of the set of goods and services that we observe, along with quality and locational characteristics. The butcher, in trying to meet the demands of his buyers, who bring to the market their autonomous demands, along with all other potential and actual producers-suppliers and demanders, establishes the scale or standards of valuation, the first of the listed functions that we discussed earlier. This scale or standard emerges from the whole interaction process; it does not directly enter into the self-interest calculus of any participant. The butcher acts on the basis of strictly localized information concerning the demands of his cli-

---

2. Adam Smith, *The Wealth of Nations* (Oxford: Oxford University Press, 1976).

entele; the relative evaluation of beefsteak does not emerge as if from a poll of public opinion; it emerges from the set of interdependent choices made by sellers and buyers, each of whom responds directly to the incentives that he or she faces in a localized market setting.

The complex order of a market economy emerges from a large set of interlinked game-like cooperative interactions between individual sellers and buyers, each of whom maximizes his or her utility in the localized setting of choice. No "player" in any of these game-like interactions chooses on the basis of an ordinal ranking of "social states" that describe the possible economy-wide inclusive imputation of goods and services, post-exchange. A "social choice" among "social states" (allocations, distributions, value scales) is, therefore, conceptually as well as practicably impossible, so long as any person is allowed to adjust behavior independently in the localized choice setting that is confronted.[3]

Order within Structure

I have re-emphasized the familiar proposition that so long as individual buyers and sellers retain liberties to choose among the alternatives offered for sale and purchase in the separate markets there can be no economy-wide "choice" of the particularized results of the economic interaction process, as these results might be described in terms of allocations, distributions, or evaluations. This conclusion holds independent of how any such attempted choice may be organized, whether under the auspices of an authoritarian regime or a democratically elected government. The results emerge from the whole set of interdependent choices made by individuals as these choices are constrained by the *structure* of the economy. In its inclusive definition, this structure must incorporate the resource and tech-

---

3. This point was central to my early criticism of Arrow's extension of his impossibility theorem to apply to the results of market process. Only in writing this lecture did I realize that although stated quite differently and developed from a differing perspective, Amartya Sen's demonstration of the paradox of the Paretian liberal comes ultimately to the same conclusion. (James M. Buchanan, "Social Choice, Democracy, and Free Markets," *Journal of Political Economy* 62 [April 1954]: 114–23; Kenneth Arrow, *Social Choice and Individual Values* [New York: Wiley, 1951]; A. K. Sen, "The Impossibility of a Paretian Liberal," *Journal of Political Economy* 78 [January–February 1970]: 152–57.)

nology limits that describe the natural environment. These more or less immutable limits are not among my principal concerns here. My emphasis is placed instead on those elements of structure that are subject to purposeful modification and change.

The terminology of game theory is helpful. The structure of an economy describes what we may call the "rules" for the whole complex set of interdependent game-like interactions between and among many players, each of whom acts in pursuit of privately selected purpose. This interpretation of structure as a set of rules directly suggests that as an individual chooses and acts within the structure, as he or she plays in the inclusively defined game, there is, and can be, no conscious or explicit consideration given to the possible choice among alternative sets of rules. For purposes of rational choice behavior in the economic process, the individual must accept the structure of the economy (the rules) as fixed, as a relatively absolute absolute that is not subject to his or her own privately orchestrated change. For example, the pre-exchange endowments that are within the recognized entitlements of any person are defined by and in the structure of the economy; such a person cannot, separately and independently, modify these endowments.

A distinction must be made between the individual's influence on the overall results of economy-wide interaction (on allocation, distribution, and evaluation) and the influence on the structure. As noted earlier, the results of economic interaction, within a structure, emerge from the localized private choices made by all participants. Each individual choice must, therefore, affect the aggregate result, even if no person, as chooser, has any conscious sense of his or her own influence on this result.

Again a game analogy will be useful. A player chooses among strategies available under the rules that define the game; any player's choice will affect the solution that emerges from the choices of all the players, but no player "chooses" the solution, as such. By contrast, the rules or structure does not emerge from the within-rules choices made by participants; the structure remains necessarily independent of these direct in-structure or within-rules choices.[4]

---

4. The categorical distinction made here would be modified somewhat if we treat elements of structure as products of an evolutionary process. In this case, choice behavior within a structure might itself modify the development of structure over a sufficiently

The pattern of outcomes or results of the economic interaction process (allocations, distributions, evaluations) depends *both* upon the individual-ized choices made in the whole set of interlinked exchanges and upon the structure of the economy. I have argued that there can be no effective choice among alternative aggregate results, whether the attempt is made in-dividually or collectively. Only the pattern of results is subject to delibera-tive change and patterns can be changed only through effective changes in structure, i.e., in the set of rules that constrain the exercise of individual choices to be made within the rules. I have noted also that the individual can exercise no influence on the structure of the economy as he chooses sepa-rately and independently among the options that he confronts. From this it becomes evident that any choice among alternative sets of rules must be, and can only be, collective. The structure of an economy, the set of constraints that limit the choice options of individuals, that define the feasibility spaces, is *public* in the classic sense. This structure is both nonpartitionable and non-excludable. Any change in structure must, therefore, impact on all actors in the process, quite independent of how and by whom the collective action is motivated and carried out.

Constitutional Political Economy

The analysis of the working properties of alternative structures of an econ-omy, alternative sets of rules and institutions that serve to constrain the choice behavior of participants within that economy, defines the domain for constitutional political economy in its positive aspects. Until recently, neoclassical economists tended to neglect the necessary interdependence be-tween structure and potentially observable patterns of outcomes of the eco-nomic process. This neglect has been largely corrected by the emergence of the set of interrelated research programs summarized under the rubric "the new political economy": law and economics, property rights economics, the new institutional economics, public choice. In each of these research pro-

---

long period of adjustment. For my purposes, however, the categorical distinction made here serves a didactic function. By separating, both conceptually and analytically, the choices made within rules and the choices made among sets of rules, the appropriate do-main of normative political economy may be much more clearly set forth.

grams, the focus of analysis is the impact of differing structures of incentives on the choice behavior of economic actors and, through this impact, on the pattern of aggregative results in an economy.

The positive exercise must precede any normative judgment on structure, on any part thereof, whether directed at the *status quo* or at any proposed alternative. The only legitimate normative exercise involves institutional-structural comparison. Demonstration of "failure" against some idealized standard (efficiency, justice, liberty) that is not anchored in structural feasibility is irrelevant.

How are alternative structures to be arrayed in the normative exercise? What are the standards for ranking? Answers to these questions call for treatises, but I can be cryptic here, especially because I have written at near-disquisition length elsewhere.[5]

There are two, quite separate, responses to these questions that must be countered and shown to be untenable. The first is that which proceeds from the presumption that there is a unique, and agreed-on, objective, or objective function, for an economy that allows the working properties of alternative structures to be readily assessed. This direction of response, which continues to dominate the thinking of economists, reflects a carryover from idealism in political philosophy. Politics, inclusively defined, is conceived as the search for the "true," the "good," and the "beautiful," some ideal state of bliss waiting "out there" to be discovered or revealed.

As Adam Smith recognized so clearly, however, there is no agreed-on objective for the participants in an economic nexus, each one of whom seeks only to pursue his or her own privately defined aims (which may or may not reflect narrowly defined economic interest). Absent such agreement, there is simply no external standard by which alternative structures can be evaluated.

A second response commences from this very fact of individual differences. Each person, as participant in the political-economic nexus, can, presumably, array alternatives of structure as "better" or "worse" in terms of his

5. James M. Buchanan and Gordon Tullock, *The Calculus of Consent* (Ann Arbor: University of Michigan Press, 1962); James M. Buchanan, *The Limits of Liberty* (Chicago: University of Chicago Press, 1975), *Freedom in Constitutional Contract* (College Station: Texas A&M University Press, 1978), *Liberty, Market and State* (New York: New York University Press, 1986), *Economics: Between Predictive Science and Moral Philosophy* (College Station: Texas A&M University Press, 1988).

own subjectively defined interest. From these observed differences among persons, the inference is then drawn that no normative judgment that transcends individual evaluation is possible. Hence, if we differ on the ranking of structural alternatives, we fight; that is, the setting is one of pure conflict, out of which a single structure will emerge that satisfies the winners and coerces the losers.

I suggested above that neither of these responses to the basic normative questions is acceptable. We must reject the presumed existence of an ideal standard, and we must also reject the nihilism implied by the absence of agreement. And at this point it is, I think, important to recognize, and to acknowledge quite explicitly, that in some fundamental sense many of us, as citizens, behave as if the structure of the economic-political order embodies legitimacy, which implies voluntary acquiescence in the coercion of the state without attribution of either omniscience or benevolence to political agents. That is to say, we live with each other neither as nihilists nor idealists. In an empirical, practical sense, we reconcile the absence of an ideal agreed-on standard of evaluation and the implied conflict among individual objectives.

In a more formal exercise, we achieve this constitutionalist stance by the introduction of some means of dampening the potential for disagreement among individuals. Such means is provided in the use of something like a veil of ignorance and/or uncertainty, either conceptually or practicably, in the evaluation of alternative structures or constitutional rules. This device is, of course, familiar, from the works of John Rawls, John Harsanyi, Buchanan and Tullock, and others.[6]

The task of normative evaluation of alternative structures for an economy to be carried out after the positive exercise of comparison is assigned to individuals who are ignorant or highly uncertain about how the alternatives for structural choice will impact on their own identifiable interest. Such individuals will be led to agree, in their own interest, on structural features that ex-

---

6. John Rawls, *A Theory of Justice* (Cambridge: Harvard University Press, 1971); John Harsanyi, "Cardinal Welfare, Individualistic Ethics, and Interpersonal Comparisons of Utility," *Journal of Political Economy* 63 (August 1955): 309–21; Buchanan and Tullock, *The Calculus of Consent.*

hibit many of the characteristics of the classical liberal social order.[7] And the empirically observed acquiescence in the operation of many of the rules that define the existing structure suggests that for many participants there is implied agreement, even without the carrying through of the formal veil-of-ignorance evaluative exercise.

This contractarian-constitutionalist derivation of the elements of structure for an economy allows us to flesh out, in modern terms, much of Adam Smith's message that was left implicit in his own work. The construction here allows us to derive a regime of "laws and institutions" that offer protection to person and property on a nondiscriminatory basis, that enforce voluntary contracts among persons nondiscriminatorily, that protect the natural liberties of persons to enter into voluntary exchanges, that prohibit restriction on entry into trades, that prohibit agreement on restrictive terms of trade. This listing, which could be extended and elaborated, contains elements of the structure that has come down to us in classical liberalism. Adam Smith was straightforward in suggesting that within this broadly defined structure of an economy there was no legitimate basis for directed interference by political agents.

The listing of constituent elements of structure that might be derived from the contractarian normative exercise can be extended to include, importantly, the political-legal guarantee of predictability in the value of the monetary standard or unit of account in the economy. Historically observed political orders have rarely, if ever, provided this guarantee. (And, indeed, I suspect that this failure in structure offers the basis for much of the discussion at this conference and others of your association.)

The contractarian construction remains necessarily incomplete at critical elements of economic structure. While laws and institutions that protect the liberties of persons to enter and consummate voluntary exchanges command legitimacy directly, what are the limits suggested when voluntary exchanges affect other parties outside the exchange itself? The whole domain of externality, inclusively defined, does not find structural resolution directly in the initial normative exercise. As modern research has indicated, however,

---

7. For more extended discussion, see my paper "The Contractarian Logic of Classical Liberalism" (draft paper prepared for conference, Social Philosophy and Policy Center, Bowling Green University, 1988).

structural change that moves toward incentive-compatible imputation of rights may eliminate much of the contractarian ambiguity.

The Purposeless Economy

As my subtitle indicates, this lecture re-emphasizes the classical foundations of political economy, and especially as these are reflected in the encompassing vision of Adam Smith. Even Smith, however, is subject to criticism in his selection of the title of his treatise. By calling attention to the *wealth* of nations, Smith may be interpreted as setting up a single-valued criterion by which the functioning of an economy might be measured. As I have noted, a much-preferred title would have been "The Simple System of Natural Liberty," because what Smith demonstrated was that there is no need for us to conceptualize a single overriding or even an agreed-on purpose, aim, or objective for an economy, or for those political agents who may presume to take on the charge of furthering such purpose.

Properly understood, the economy has neither purpose, function, or intent. The economy is defined by a structure, a set of rules and institutions, that constrain the choices of many persons in an interlinked chain of game-like interactions, one with another. For any individual, there are, of course, "better" and "worse" economies, but these evaluative terms translate directly into references to sets of rules or structures. Within any given structure, *laissez faire* becomes the indicated policy stance, and this principle holds quite independent of the normative content of structure itself.

In one sense, there is absolutely nothing new or novel in what I have said in this lecture. But in yet another sense, the implications are revolutionary. The shift of emphasis to structure as the exclusive and only appropriate object for reform, along with implied principle of *laissez faire* applied to operation within structure, relegates to absurdity all proposals for reform supported on arguments from "national purpose," as well as all claims that the economy functions more satisfactorily if it is explicitly guided by presumably omniscient and benevolent political agents.

There are two separate, but related, aspects of the normative argument that I advance. The very definition of the economy as a structure, a set of constraining rules within which individuals seek to achieve their separately determined purposes, makes teleological direction of policy normatively self-contradictory. But alternative structures may be compared, and evaluated, in terms of their abilities to facilitate the accomplishment of the separately determined individual objectives. Because only individuals themselves can know what goals they seek, any direct delegation of authority to choose among structures reduces the information content of the constitutional choice process. The implied policy stance involves *laissez faire* within constitutional structure and consensus in the ultimate choice of structure itself.

No claim is made here that adherence to the normative precepts outlined will resolve all issues. Even within the constitutionalist-contractarian paradigm, differences among individuals may arise both in scientific interpretation-explanation-prediction and in a choice of ultimate moral norms. As noted earlier, many features of the classical liberal position would be predicted to emerge from the contractarian procedural test. But the precise boundaries of the constitutionally chosen structural limits on individual voluntary association, as well as the constitutionally derived definitions of the protected spheres of individuals themselves, cannot be drawn from sources other than as revealed by those who count as members of the body politic.

Let us by all means continue to strive for, and to support, efforts to analyze the structure of the economy, and to seek consensus on means to make this structure more capable of allowing us, as individual participants, to further those separately defined objectives that we seek. Let us, however, guard against allowing intellectual confusion about what an economy is to offer, legitimatizing cover for the efforts of some persons and groups to impose their own purposes on others. Beware of those who pronounce on the economy's purpose.

Market Failure and Political Failure

I. Introduction

On several occasions, I have summarized the theoretical welfare economics of the mid-century decades as "theories of market failure" and the public choice economics of the post-middle decades as counterpart "theories of political failure." This statement captures the central thrusts of the two research programs, but, nonetheless, the statement is confusing because it suggests that both positive analyses of institutional operation and criteria for operational failure are comparable over the two applications.

The criterion for success, and hence, failure, applied to the operation of a market order by the practitioners of theoretical welfare economics is widely recognized to be efficiency in the utilization of economic resources. But both the meaning and the normative appropriateness of the efficiency criterion can be questioned. If "efficiency" is attained only through the working of the market process how can it be set up as an independent criterion with which to evaluate the workings of the process itself? Even if this basic question is somehow finessed, justificatory arguments must be advanced in defense of the efficiency norm.

In extension to politics and political process, can something akin to allocative efficiency be invoked at all? Or is a totally different success criterion appropriate here? If so, how is it to be defined? And, once defined, how can

From *Individual Liberty and Democratic Decision-Making: The Ethics, Economics, and Politics of Democracy,* ed. Peter Koslowski (Tübingen: J. C. B. Mohr [Paul Siebeck], 1987), 41–52. Reprinted by permission of the publisher.

I am indebted to my colleagues Robert Tollison, Gordon Tullock, and, especially, Viktor Vanberg for helpful comments on an earlier draft.

the two potential institutional "failures" be assessed on some comparable bases until and unless the evaluative norms are themselves reduced to a common scalar?

The paper is organized as follows. In Section II, I briefly examine some of the basic issues that arise in assessing market or political failure. The heart of the paper is contained in Section III, in which an attempt is made to assess the prospects for political correctives for a single particular example of market failure, utilizing the standard efficiency criterion. Section IV is very short, but it introduces a discussion of changes in the basic structure of rules, in the constitution, that seem to be suggested if any prospect for attaining the efficiency gains promised upon diagnosis of either market or political failure is to be realized. Section V is also brief; it introduces the alternative of setting up some distributional ideal to evaluate the performance of market and political structures. The discussion in both Sections IV and V is severely restricted in this paper, since adequate treatment of either of these two areas of inquiry would require full-length treatment quite apart from the main thrust of the argument here.

II. Ideal Points and Feasibility Sets

Even if we remain within the confines of political economy, when we examine either market or political failure (or success) we must confront issues that have been centerpieces of philosophical argument for many centuries. Can an ideal be defined independent of that which can be observed? And if this question is answered affirmatively can an ideal state that lies admittedly beyond the limits of the set of feasibly attainable states serve as a standard of evaluation for an observed state?

These questions may be examined with specific reference to the identification of market failures stemming from theoretical welfare economics. Consider efficiency in the utilization of an economy's resources—can idealized efficiency be defined in other than conceptually formal terms? We can, of course, state specifically the necessary conditions that must be met in order to satisfy the ideal. Resources are placed in their most highly valued uses when units of each homogeneous resource yield identically valued returns in all uses to which they are put. Values are equalized on all margins of adjustment; marginal rates of substitution in final use are equalized with marginal rates of transformation in production.

But what is homogeneity among units of any resource? Do we define homogeneity by an observed equalization of market prices? If we do, how can any observed differences in prices be employed as a criterion for an absence of allocative efficiency? Until and unless the economist presupposes independent knowledge about preference functions and production functions, he cannot define idealized efficiency. And, if this epistemological limit to analysis is acknowledged, how can any market be judged to fail? Quite apart from this epistemological barrier to the very definition of efficiency, there remains the necessary dependence of the value-maximizing allocation of resources on the premarket distribution of endowments among persons. Acceptance of efficiency as a norm for success or failure carries with it implied normative support for (or at least acquiescence in) the initial distribution of endowments, or else it requires that corrective steps embody distributional objectives over and beyond those defined by the efficiency norm itself.

For purposes of discussion here, I shall assume, with the theoretical welfare economists, that the required information about preference and production functions may be presupposed, and that the premarket distribution of endowments be accepted as the basis from which value-enhancing changes are to be evaluated. Idealized efficiency can then be defined independent of any observation of market adjustment processes, and it would seem proper that this norm be used as a success indicator. Even within these limits, however, is it appropriate to use this idealized efficiency norm as a means of evaluating that which is observed? If the norm is so employed, market "failure" may be readily identified. Almost all observed market arrangements generate results that fall short of achieving the ideal. The reasons are familiar. Such an assessment of failure does not, however, carry any implication for ultimate institutional or policy change until and unless a pattern of results from an alternative set of arrangements demonstrated to be feasible can be shown to exist. If the attainment of the idealized efficiency norm is shown to require technological-institutional and/or behavioral characteristics that cannot be incorporated within the feasibility set, how much help is provided by resort to the norm as a criterion of success or failure?

III. Political Correctives for Market Failure: The Case of External Diseconomies

The theoretical welfare economists of mid-century did not raise this question because they assumed, implicitly, that the political alternative to the unimpeded operation of the market itself operated ideally. That is to say, it was simply presumed that "failures" in market arrangements could be ideally corrected by politically directed adjustments in the rules guiding market participants.

The prospect that any feasible political corrective for market failure might also fail when compared against the ideal standard of efficiency was not examined. Some positive theory of the workings of observed political process is required before this essential step in a comparative institutional analysis can be taken. The theory of public choice has, in a sense, made such an analysis possible. It remains nonetheless surprising that public choice economists have not concentrated more attention on the identification and analyses of political failures for purposes of making more specific comparisons with familiar market failure propositions.[1]

I propose to introduce a single highly stylized, simplified, and familiar model of market failure. There exists a small, but fully competitive industry that produces a final good, x, which trades at price, p_x, in full equilibrium. No resources are specific to this industry, and there are no rents received by owners of resource inputs, even short-run quasi-rents. Consumers secure some rents from the availability of this product on the market at the competitive price. The production of x, however, generates spillover or external damages on many persons. The producing firms do not take these external

---

1. I raised the issue in an early paper, but there my primary concern was with the presence of externalities in the political decision process generally and not with attempted political correctives for specific market failures. See my "Politics, Policy, and the Pigovian Margins," *Economica*, 29 (February 1962), 17–28.

In a second early paper, Gordon Tullock and I analyzed comparative market and political failure under reciprocal external economies. The analysis was, however, largely concentrated on a world-of-equals model, and we did not examine the politics of distribution that accompany attempts to correct for market failures. See James M. Buchanan and Gordon Tullock: "Public and Private Interaction under Reciprocal Externality," in Margolis, Julius (ed.): *The Public Economy of Urban Communities*, Washington (Resources for the Future), 1965, 52–73.

diseconomies into account in their decisions. Hence, relative to the idealized efficiency norm, there are too many resources devoted to the production of *x*. In traditional Pigovian language, marginal private costs faced by the firms are less than marginal "social costs."

The question then is: Will politicization of this external diseconomy insure correction? For purposes of simplicity in exposition, I shall initially assume that the control instrument is a per unit tax or subsidy on the industry's output. The constitution is altered to allow such a tax or subsidy to be imposed by the workings of a political decision rule.

I shall assume that all persons in the economy and polity have full information as to the incidence and effects of the tax, and, also, that all persons vote or otherwise act politically to further their own measured economic interest. In the market failure setting postulated, under these restricted assumptions, politicization of the externality will insure that the efficiency norm is satisfied only under an extremely narrow set of circumstances. If *all* persons in the polity are damaged by the external diseconomy, and are also *equally* damaged; if *all* persons are also consumers-buyers of the industry's product, and also purchase *equal* quantities; if the revenues from the tax are shared *equally* among *all* persons, and without pass-through loss, then politicization will insure full correction for the market failure, regardless of the political decision rule. In this setting, it will be in each and every person's interest to impose the idealized Pigovian tax. Market price will rise precisely by the amount of the tax; production will fall; some resources will shift to other uses. Revenues from the tax will be shared equally by all persons. Each person will gain an amount measured by the size of the familiar welfare triangle.[2]

Once we move beyond the world-of-equals restrictions on the model, politicization will *not* operate to correct for the efficiency loss imposed by the nonpoliticized operation of the market. Distributional effects must enter the calculus of individuals, and their interests must include these effects as well as the potential gains and losses in efficiency, as usually measured. And *dis-*

---

2. The result depends on the presumption that the unit tax will modify behavior in purchasing the good, but that the return of tax revenues in the form of transfers will *not* influence behavior, despite the direct relationship between the size of an individual's transfer payment and his rate of purchase. In other words, only the tax exerts a substitution effect.

tributional effects necessarily introduce potential conflicts of interests among persons. Hence, the predicted results of the operation of any political decision rule will depend both on the rule itself and on the relative sizes of those persons in the sets that secure distributional gains and losses under the imposition of a tax on the industry's product, along with the disposition of revenues.

The political economists might be prompted to inquire into prospects for working out some structure of compensations such that even in the setting that violates the highly restricted equality assumptions general agreement might be reached on the idealized solution dictated by the efficiency norm.

Suppose that all relevant members of the polity can be classified into three sets: (1) buyers of the industry's product, (2) sufferers of the external damage generated by production, (3) persons totally unaffected by the industry, neither buyers nor sufferers of damage. We know that if the external diseconomy is Pareto relevant the members of (2) should be able to compensate fully the members of (1) for the losses incurred in the price change consequent on the reduction of industry output.[3] Note, however, that this compensation will require payment over and above the return of all revenues collected under the efficiency-inducing unit tax rate to members of (1). Such a return of revenues will still leave purchasers with net losses measured by the familiar welfare triangle. The restriction to the single control instrument must be dropped if general agreement on the Pareto-superior shift to the idealized efficiency solution is to be attained.

Note, further, and more importantly, however, that even if political implementation is limited to the "exchange" between members of (2) and (1), and if some payments above and beyond return of tax revenues are arranged, the structure of compensations (return of revenues plus subsidies) must include individualized adjustments among persons in (1) to allow for variations in the quantities of the good purchased and in the elasticities of demand over the relevant range of price change. These purchase-related differentials in transfer payments would be required to insure that income effects be neutral for all members of (1), quite apart from the arbitrary assumption that there is no substitution effect of the transfer payments, despite the required direct rela-

---

3. Through our simplifying assumption about the absence of producers' rents, the incidence of the tax falls exclusively on buyers.

tionship between the sizes of the payments and the individual rates of purchase. If substitution effects are extended to purchase-related transfers, so that all members of (1) fully reckon that any excess outlay generated by the higher price will be returned as a transfer, then the whole attempt to "correct" behavior via the imposition of the unit tax will fail from the outset.

In order to insure that the levy of the tax modifies behavior, as well as for more general political reasons, the revenues from the tax would likely be returned to persons on some broad-based sharing scheme, even if the transfers could be limited to members of a single class, such as members of (1). But, once any such departure from the idealized scheme is introduced, however, distributional interests of persons are introduced that might be directionally counter to any efficiency-inducing "exchange" through the political process.

Even such partial political intervention as represented by the return of revenues generally to members of (1) would seem, however, to be highly improbable. Persons in (3), those who are totally unaffected by the external diseconomy, would almost necessarily be included in the political choice process, directly or indirectly, and they will have interests that are exclusively distributional. Suppose that the political economist proposes the levy of an efficiency-inducing unit tax on the industry's output, with revenues returned to buyers of the product, with the differentiation as required, along with some supplemental payments to cover the losses measured by the welfare triangles. In other words, assume that the "exchange" between members of (1) and (2) meets all of the requirements for agreement, as that the political implementation of this "exchange" promises to generate the idealized efficiency solution. But persons in (3) may not acquiesce in the observed payment of cash transfers to members of (1). Persons in (3) will insist on sharing in the funds made available from the apparently newly discovered revenue source. To the extent that members of (3) are brought into the revenue-sharing group, members of (1) will oppose the whole scheme, again on strictly distributional grounds. No longer would they be fully income-compensated for the change in price of the good consequent on the change in industry output. And members of (2), those who suffer the external diseconomy, can scarcely be expected to "bribe" all members of (3) sufficiently to insure the viability of the efficiency-inducing rate of tax. Politically, the efficiency-inducing tax seems a nonstarter.

We can extend the analysis and try to make some very general predictions about politicization of the externality in the example. We retain the three-set classification of persons, and we now introduce the assumption that the political choice process works as if it were a simple majority voting rule. For purposes of simplicity in exposition assume initially that the three sets are of equal size, and that a person holds membership in only one set. We can array the policy options or alternatives as follows:

1. T_0 leave competitive result alone; levy zero rate of tax.
2. T_e impose efficiency-inducing rate of tax; return all revenues to members of (1), buyers of product, in individualized shares appropriately adjusted.
3. T_m impose revenue-maximizing rate of tax; distribute revenues equally among all members of politically dominant coalition.
4. T_p impose prohibitive rate of tax.

We can now examine the ordinal ranking of these alternatives by the members of the three sets. There are two possible arrays, depending on the relationship of T_e and T_m. In the first array below, I assume that the efficiency-inducing rate of tax falls below the revenue-maximizing rate of tax; in the second array, this relationship is reversed. The rankings follow (Table 2.1).

Table 2.1. Rankings of alternatives about political correctives for market failure by three sets of persons

Set (1) Buyers	Set (2) Sufferers	Set (3) Unaffected
(I: $T_e < T_m$)		
T_0	T_p	T_m
T_e	T_m	T_e
T_m	T_e	T_0, T_p
T_p	T_0	
(II: $T_e > T_m$)		
T_0	T_p	T_m
T_m	T_e	T_e
T_e	T_m	T_0, T_p
T_p	T_0	

It is evident from examination of these arrays that under the assumption that the sets are equi-sized, T_m is the stable majority choice. The preferences are single-peaked. There is a two-group majority coalition favoring T_m over either of the other alternatives.

This result is relatively insensitive to changes in the distribution of revenues from the tax that is levied and to the amount of pass-through wastage in the fiscal process. The ranking for members of (3) will remain as indicated if there is any positive net transfer to them. And note that members of this set are the median preference holders; the interests of those persons in sets (1) and (2) are strictly opposed in either of the two rankings. Members of (1), the buyers, will have the ordinal rankings indicated if there is any drainage of revenues from their hands, and, in addition, if they do not secure the required supplementary payments over the simple return of all revenues. Sufferers (2) will always prefer the prohibitive tax, except in those cases where they might, as major sharers in revenues, prefer the revenue-maximizing tax.

The T_m result is also relatively insensitive to changes in the relative sizes of the three groups. So long as neither (1) nor (2) is sufficiently large, on its own, to enforce a majority choice, the members of (3) are in control, even if their size is small. If either (1) or (2) is sufficiently large to impose a majority choice, then T_0 or T_p will emerge. Note that in no case will T_e emerge from the operation of the voting rule. The efficiency-inducing rate of tax is dominated by one of the other three alternatives under any and all variations in the relative sizes of the three sets.

If the efficiency-inducing rate of tax falls below the revenue-maximizing rate (I in the arrays above), then politicization of the externality will generate an allocative result that involves final industry output below that which is Pareto efficient. Whereas the uncorrected market result involves industry overproduction, the politicized result involves underproduction relative to the standard efficiency norm. If the efficiency-inducing rate of tax lies above the revenue-maximizing rate (II in the arrays above), politicization will involve industry output that remains above that which the efficiency criterion would indicate to be ideal but below the output in the uncorrected market. In this case, politicization is at least directionally corrective.

The failure of politicization to correct for the externality seems clear in the single example examined in detail here. But does the divergence between the predicted political solutions and those that might satisfy the efficiency criterion depend on the "institutional structure of externality"?[4] The existence of *any* surplus, whether producers' or consumers', that results from the market generation of an activity that exerts large-number externalities, negative or positive, will insure that distributional aspects enter directly in any political control process. Participants in the political decision process seek to maximize their own utilities, given the instruments available to them. They may only be secondarily interested in their shares in the efficiency gains that idealized market correction might promise.[5] Models other than the single one analyzed in some detail above might, of course, be introduced to demonstrate the generality of the results.

But the overall conclusion remains the negative one that politicization of market failure will be highly unlikely to secure the objective of moving the economy toward satisfaction of the idealized efficiency norm so long as the political process itself embodies the expressions of differential interests by citizens.

IV. Can the Potential Efficiency Gains Be Captured?

As the discussion has indicated, there will remain unexploited efficiency gains in the operation of the market and/or the political process. In both cases, we can imagine or dream of idealized allocative changes that could prove advantageous to all parties in the economy or polity. And, as the simple analytics of the Pareto classification shows, there must exist means of moving from what is to an optimal solution in such a way that no person is harmed by the change. But the accomplishment of any such change may require a complex and sophisticated structure of highly personalized tax and subsidy schedules, compensations, side payments, and transition rules that are beyond the capacity of either market or political structures as we know

---

4. In an early paper entitled "The Institutional Structure of Externality," I examined several models in terms of the sources for market failure in each case. I did not, however, follow up and examine the same models for possible implications under political control. See "The Institutional Structure of Externality," *Public Choice,* 14 (Spring 1973), 69–82.

5. For a general recognition of this point, see Marilyn Flowers and Patricia Danzon: "Separation of the Redistributive and Allocative Functions of Government: A Public Choice Perspective," *Journal of Public Economics,* 24 (August 1984), 373–80.

them. It may not be institutionally feasible to capture more than some fraction of the efficiency losses that market and political failure seem to impose upon us.

The very existence of such gains should insure, however, that there will remain a role for the political economist who might be able to advance proposals that will embody mutuality of gain.[6] If he reckons on the predicted operating properties of both ordinary markets and ordinary politics, the political economist will presumably be led to consider reform at the level of basic institutional-constitutional rules, where the distributional aspects can be mitigated if not totally eliminated from consideration. Why should anyone, as a potential participant in political process, be interested in abstract efficiency? As the analysis has suggested, the participant will, in particular cases, place primary emphasis on distributive shares. If, however, general rules are considered, rules that are to be applied to a large number of separate cases of potential political control, the participant does have an interest in an efficient structure. Since he cannot know how, distributionally, he will be affected on any one from the whole set of issues that may emerge for political decision, the individual will be led from consideration of his own interest to promote efficiency in the predicted working properties of the inclusive institutional structure.[7]

If the inclusively defined set of institutional constraints is treated as exogenous, and hence not subject to change, there is a sense in which any observed allocation is efficient. To the extent that participants maximize their utilities, given the constraints within which they act, there remain no efficiency gains to be exploited. Reference to potential efficiency gains must, therefore, imply a belief that some constraints are subject to change.[8]

---

6. In a very early paper, I defined the role for the political economist to be that of seeking out possible proposals for change that would command consent. See my "Positive Economics, Welfare Economics, and Political Economy," *Journal of Law and Economics*, 2 (October 1959), 124–38.

7. The logical foundations of this bridge between efficiency and individual self-interest were presented in James M. Buchanan and Gordon Tullock: *The Calculus of Consent*, Ann Arbor (University of Michigan Press), 1962.

8. For further discussion, see my "Rights, Efficiency, and Exchange: The Irrelevance of Transactions Cost," in *Ansprüche, Eigentum und Verfügungsrechte*, Berlin (Duncker and Humblot), 1984, 9–24. Reprinted in my *Liberty, Market and State: Political Economy in the 1980s*, Brighton, England (Wheatsheaf Books), 1986; New York (New York University Press), 1986, 92–107.

V. The Efficiency Norm and Distributive Standards

To this point, the discussion has been exclusively contained within an acceptance of the efficiency norm as the basis for evaluating institutional performance. The epistemological claims of the theoretical welfare economists have been presupposed, even though these claims appear to me to be open to serious challenge at a more sophisticated level of philosophical inquiry. For most neoclassical economists trained in the post–welfare economics era, there is nothing unusual or unacceptable in using the efficiency norm for evaluating the performance of the market process. These same economists might, however, question the use of the same norm to evaluate politics. Why should politics be expected to generate efficiency in resource use? As noted, however, unless the same scalar is employed, how can relative "failure" or "success" be judged at all?

Some distributional norm or standard is perhaps the most likely alternative to efficiency. By comparison here, however, there seems to be little or no agreement in a precise definition of a distributive ideal. If such an ideal could be defined, then the operation of the market might be compared with that of political process. Once again, both processes would surely be judged to fail to achieve the norm.

In application to the achievement of any distributive norm, however, care must be taken to define the distributive potential of the two separate institutions. The market operates, and, in so doing, it generates a particular distribution of the surplus that emerges from social cooperation in the usage of the premarket resource endowments held under legally defined ownership of separate persons. The market cannot, and does not, act directly on the distribution of the endowments of persons. By contrast and comparison, politics may make little or no distinction between the distribution of the surplus emergent from social cooperation and the distribution of initial endowments among persons. There is no constraint on the operation of ordinary politics that is at all akin to that imposed by the legal structure on the operation of the market. When, therefore, the market is compared unfavorably with politics from the criterion of some distributive ideal, the relatively open-ended potential for political redistribution is seldom noted.

Even when such comparisons are made properly, however, the discussion is often concentrated on the prospects of idealized attainment of the distributive ideal rather than on any realistic analysis of the distributional changes that might be implemented in the workings of democratic politics. As is the case with efficiency, persons are not likely to express interests in abstract distributional ideals for the society in general when they participate in political decisions. They are likely, instead, to seek to further their own well-defined interests. Whether or not political process will, indeed, be able to "improve" on market-determined distributive results remains an open issue that social scientists have been surprisingly reluctant to analyze seriously.[9] Until and unless politics, as it works, and not as it might ideally be imagined to work, can be demonstrated to generate better distributive results than the market, "better" in terms of some reasonably acceptable standard, advisers should be reluctant to encourage distributional politics.

This paper does not deliver the assessment of analytical developments in the context of the experience of the quarter century, the assessment that was my assigned subject. The analysis has been aimed at raising more questions than it attempts to answer, and the paper's message is perhaps best interpreted as a sketch for a research program that seems hardly to have been commenced. By inference, the argument might be taken as a criticism of the naiveté of both the market-failure welfare economists and the market-works–politics-fails stance of many modern public choice and new neoclassical economists. By comparison with idealized standards, both markets and politics fail. Recognition of this simple point is a mark of "scientific" progress. Such recognition directs attention to comparative institutional analysis and to the structure of the set of constraints within which either market or political behavior takes place. The domain of "constitutional economics" beckons; let us get on with it.

9. For a preliminary attempt to analyze transfer or redistributive political process in positive terms, see Chapter 8 in Geoffrey Brennan and James Buchanan: *The Reason of Rules,* Cambridge (Cambridge University Press), 1985. Further work on this topic is in planning stages. For a related argument that concludes that the market process may be the only distributional system that avoids conflict, see Dan Usher: *The Economic Prerequisites to Democracy,* Oxford (Basil Blackwell), 1981.

The Market as a Creative Process

James M. Buchanan and Viktor J. Vanberg

Had Pyrrhus not fallen by a beldam's hand in Argos or Julius Cae-
sar not been knifed to death? They are not to be thought away.
Time has branded them and fettered they are lodged in the room
of the infinite possibilities they have ousted. But can those have
been possible, seeing that they never were? Or, was that only possible which came to pass?

—James Joyce[1]

1. Introduction

Contributions in modern theoretical physics and chemistry on the behavior
of nonlinear systems, exemplified by Ilya Prigogine's work on the thermodynamics of open systems,[2] attract growing attention in economics.[3] Our

From *Economics and Philosophy* 7 (October 1991): 167–86. Reprinted by permission of
Cambridge University Press.

An earlier version of this paper was presented at a Liberty Fund Conference, "An In-
quiry into Liberty and Self-Organizing Systems," April 26–29, 1990, Rio Rico, Arizona.
We received helpful comments on previous drafts from Hartmut Kliemt, Karen Vaughn,
Jack Wiseman, and an anonymous referee.

1. James Joyce, *Ulysses* (London: Bodley Head, 1960), 30.

2. Ilya Prigogine and Isabelle Stengers, *Order Out of Chaos: Man's New Dialogue with
Nature* (Toronto: Bantam Books, 1984).

3. Philip W. Anderson, Kenneth J. Arrow, and David Pines, eds., *The Economy as an
Evolving Complex System* (New York: Addison-Wesley, 1988); W. Brian Arthur, "Positive
Feedbacks in the Economy," *Scientific American* 262 (1990): 92–99; William Baumol and
Stephen Benhabib, "Chaos: Significance, Mechanism, and Economic Applications," *Jour-*

purpose here is to relate the new orientation in the natural sciences to a particular nonorthodox strand of thought within economics. All that is needed for this purpose is some appreciation of the general thrust of the enterprise, which involves a shift of perspective from the determinism of conventional physics (which presumably inspired the neoclassical research program in economics) to the nonteleological open-endedness, creative, and nondetermined nature of evolutionary processes.

Prigogine and Stengers refer to this shift in perspective as "a reconceptualization of the physical sciences," as a move "from deterministic, reversible processes to stochastic and irreversible ones."[4] The emphasis is shifted from equilibrium to nonequilibrium as a "source of spontaneous self-organization," to self-organizing processes in open systems far from thermodynamic equilibrium.[5] A characteristic feature of such systems is the presence of nonlinearities that can amplify "small causes" into "large effects." At critical points (referred to as "bifurcations"), very small events can have significant macroeffects, in the sense that they "decide" which particular path—among a number of equally possible paths—the system will take, a fact that introduces a stochastic element and renders self-organizing processes in far-from-equilibrium conditions inherently undetermined.[6] Such processes exhibit a mixture of necessity and chance that, as Prigogine and Stengers note, produces a unique and irreversible "'history' path along which the system evolves."[7]

What is suggested here is a generalized perspective that brings into focus creativity and open-endedness in the evolution of nonequilibrium systems, a perspective that has as its *leitmotiv* "that the future is not given,"[8] but is

nal of Economic Issues 3 (1989): 77–106; Philip Mirowski, "From Mandelbrot to Chaos in Economic Theory," *Southern Economic Journal* 57 (1990): 289–307; Michael J. Radzicki, "Institutional Dynamics, Deterministic Chaos, and Self-Organizing Systems," *Journal of Economic Issues* 24 (1990): 57–102.

4. Prigogine and Stengers, *Order Out of Chaos,* 177.

5. Ilya Prigogine, "New Perspectives on Complexity," in *The Science and Praxis of Complexity,* by S. Aida et al., 107–18 (Tokyo: The United Nations University, 1985), 108.

6. "Whenever we reach a bifurcation point, deterministic description breaks down. The type of fluctuation present in the system will lead to the choice of the branch it will follow. Crossing a bifurcation point is a stochastic process, such as the tossing of a coin" (Prigogine and Stengers, *Order Out of Chaos,* 177).

7. Ibid., 169ff.

8. Ilya Prigogine, "Science, Civilization and Democracy," *Futures* 18 (1986): 493–507, 493.

created in an unfolding evolutionary process.[9] Authors like P. M. Allen and J. S. Wicken speak of a *new evolutionary synthesis*,[10] a "unified view of the world which bridges the gap between the physical and the human sciences."[11] In his discussion on the relevance of the "new evolutionary synthesis" for economic theory, Allen stresses the concern with *microscopic diversity* as the critical feature. The "cloudy, confused complexity of the real world"[12] is the essential subject of an evolutionary approach—in contrast to a perspective that looks for types and classes, and that views microscopic diversity and variation as negligible aberrations, to be averaged out through classification and aggregation.[13] Variability and individual diversity at the microscopic level drive evolutionary processes; they are the crucial ingredient to the "creativity" of these processes, of their potential to generate novelty. As Allen puts it: "The fluctuations, mutations and apparently random movements which are naturally present in real complex systems constitute a sort of 'imaginative' and creative force which will explore around whatever exists at

9. "[W]e come to a world which is open, in which the past is present and cumulative, in which the present is there but the future is not. . . . The future does not exist yet, the future is in construction, a construction which is going on in all existing activities" (Prigogine, "New Perspectives," 117).

10. Peter M. Allen, "Evolution, Innovation and Economics," in *Technical Change and Economic Theory*, ed. G. Dosi, C. Freeman, R. Nelson, G. Silverberg, and L. Soete, 95–119 (London: Pinter Publishers, 1988), 99; Jeffrey S. Wicken, *Evolution, Thermodynamics, and Information: Extending the Darwinian Paradigm* (Oxford: Oxford University Press, 1987), 3.

11. Allen, "Evolution, Innovation," 118.

12. Ibid., 99.

13. The critical importance of individual diversity and variation from an evolutionary perspective is similarly stressed by biologist E. Mayr, who uses in this context the term "population thinking": "Population thinkers stress the uniqueness of everything in the organic world. What is important for them is the individual, not the type. . . . There is no 'typical' individual, and mean values are abstractions. . . . The differences between biological individuals are real, while the mean values which we may calculate in the comparison of groups of individuals (species, for example) are man-made inferences" (Ernst Mayr, "The Growth of Biological Thought: Diversity, Evolution and Inheritance [Cambridge: Harvard University Press, 1982], 46ff.). Mayr contrasts "population thinking" with "essentialist thinking": "Adoption of population thinking is intimately tied up with a rejection of essentialist thinking. Variation is irrelevant and therefore uninteresting to the essentialist. Varying characters are 'mere accidents,' in the language of essentialism" (Ibid., 487).

present."[14] Allen sees here the critical difference between an evolutionary perspective and one that centers around the notion of predetermined equilibrium states, the difference between the new self-organization paradigm and a "Newtonian paradigm" in which any "representation of 'creative processes' was entirely absent."[15]

As noted, our purpose is, first, to identify a body of criticism of orthodox equilibrium theory in economics that seems to correspond closely with the developments noted in the natural sciences, and, second, to elaborate on the implications of this (the *radical subjectivist*) criticism in some detail and, particularly, in its relation to its near neighbor, the entrepreneurial conceptualization of Israel Kirzner.

2. Subjectivism, the Growth of Knowledge, and Indeterminedness

P. M. Allen's article is but one example of the growing number of comments on the apparent relevance of the *new evolutionary synthesis* for a reorientation of economic theory. The reasons that limit the applicability of equilibrium models, even in the traditional realm of physics and chemistry, apply *a fortiori* to the domain of economics. The equilibrium concept is associated

14. Allen, "Evolution, Innovation," 108.

15. Ibid., 97. As P. Allen points out, one has to realize "that there is a critical difference between asking whether a system *obeys* the laws of physics, . . . or whether its behavior can be predicted from a knowledge of those laws" (Peter M. Allen, "Towards a New Science of Complex Systems," in *The Science and Praxis of Complexity,* by S. Aida et al., 268–97 [Tokyo: The United Nations University, 1985], 268ff.). For nonlinear systems, Allen argues, the first can be the case without the second being possible, due to the mixture of deterministic and stochastic aspects of nonlinear systems (Ibid., 270). Allen's argument parallels K. R. Popper's remark in *The Open Universe:* "[C]ausality has to be distinguished from determinism, and our world of uniqueness is—unlike Kant's noumenal world—in space and, even more important, in time; for I find it crucially important to distinguish between the determined *past* and the open *future*" (Karl R. Popper, *The Open Universe: An Argument for Indeterminism* [Totowa, N.J.: Rowan and Littlefield, 1982], 48). In reference to Prigogine's work, Popper argues in the same treatise: "We must not . . . blind us to the fact that the universe that harbours life is creative in the best sense: creative in the sense in which the great poets, the great artists, the great musicians have been creative, as well as the great mathematicians, the great scientists, and the great inventors" (Ibid., 174).

with a world view that treats the future as implied in the present. In principle, future states could be predicted based on sufficient knowledge of the present; that is, if it were not for *de facto* limits on our knowledge of an immensely complex reality. By contrast, a core insight of the new paradigm is that nature is creative, that novelty and genuinely unpredictable outcomes are generated as the evolutionary process unfolds over time. The creativity argument has all the more force where concern is with social processes that are driven by human choice and inventiveness.[16]

One criticism of economic orthodoxy that has been advanced from a strict *subjectivist* position (a criticism that has, to our knowledge, been developed independent of the literature discussed above) has, in some respects, a strikingly similar thrust.[17] It should be said at the outset that there is no clearly delineated body of thought that would fall under the rubric of *subjectivism*. The term has been adopted by, and used as a label for, a number of perspectives in economics that agree in their broad criticism of the neoclassical general equilibrium framework, but that are by no means theoretically homogeneous. With this proviso stated, we want to concentrate the discussion here on what is often referred to as "radical subjectivism," a position associated primarily with the name of G. L. S. Shackle[18] as well as with the work of such other authors as L. M. Lachmann, J. Wiseman, and S. C. Littlechild. In section 3, we shall take a closer look at the modern Austrian version of subjectivism, represented by I. Kirzner's work on entrepreneurship, and

16. "Clearly, a social system is by definition a nonlinear one, as interactions between the members of the society may have a catalytic effect. At each moment fluctuations are generated, which may be damped or amplified by society. An excellent example of a huge amplification . . . is the acquisition of knowledge. . . . Instead of seeing human systems in terms of 'equilibrium' or as a 'mechanism,' we see a creative world of imperfect information and shifting values, in which different futures can be envisaged" (Prigogine, "Science, Civilization," 503).

17. This similarity has been explicitly noted by Ulrich Fehl ("Spontaneous Order and the Subjectivity of Expectations: A Contribution to the Lachmann-O'Driscoll Problem," in *Subjectivism, Intelligibility, and Economic Understanding*, ed. I. M. Kirzner (New York: New York University Press, 1986), 72–86; see also Ulrich Witt, "Coordination of Individual Economic Activities as an Evolving Process of Self-Organization," *Economie Appliquée* 37 (1985): 569–95.

18. G. L. S. Shackle, *Imagination and the Nature of Choice* (Edinburgh: Edinburgh University Press, 1979).

we shall discuss the differences that Kirzner sees between his own position and "radical subjectivism."[19]

At the core of Shackle's attack on the "neoclassical citadel,"[20] and central to the radical subjectivist view in general, is the issue of what we can claim to know about the future in our efforts to understand the world of human affairs. The basic objection to neoclassical general equilibrium theory is that it embodies assumptions about the knowability of the future that are entirely unfounded, not only in their most extreme variant, the assumption of perfect knowledge, but also in their softer varieties, such as assumptions about rational expectations or Bayesian adaptive rationality. For radical subjectivism there is simply no way around the fundamental fact that whatever happens in the social realm is dependent on human choices, choices that—if they are *choices*—could be different, and could, if they were different, have different effects.[21] There can, therefore, be no "given" future, independent of the choices that will be made. Instead, there are innumerable potential futures of which only one will emerge as the choice-process unfolds. As Shackle puts it, "the content of time-to-come is not merely unknown but nonexistent, and the notion of foreknowledge of human affairs is vacuous."[22] Or in J. Wiseman's terms: "The essence of the radical subjectivist position is that the future is not simply 'unknown,' but is 'nonexistent' or 'indeterminate' at the point of decision."[23]

19. There are other versions of "economic subjectivism" that can be distinguished from both its "radical" and Austrian variety, in particular, the "opportunity costs approach" that has been systematically stated by one of the present authors (James M. Buchanan, *Cost and Choice: An Inquiry in Economic Theory* [Chicago: Markham Publishing Company, 1969]; "L. S. E. Cost Theory in Retrospect," in *Economics: Between Predictive Science and Moral Philosophy*, by James M. Buchanan, 141–51 [College Station: Texas A&M University Press, 1987]). This version, as well as others that could be identified, will, however, not be discussed as such in the present article.

20. Ludwig M. Lachmann, "From Mises to Shackle: An Essay on Austrian Economics and the Kaleidic Society," *Journal of Economic Literature* 14 (1976): 54–62.

21. "The response to this question of 'choice,' which makes modelling and predicting difficult, can be of two kinds. Either we can suppose that choice is an illusion and that the mechanical analogy is in fact legitimate, or we must find some new scientific paradigm in which 'choice' really exists" (Allen, "Towards a New Science," 269).

22. G. L. S. Shackle, "The Bounds of Unknowledge," in *Beyond Positive Economics*, ed. J. Wiseman, 28–37 (London: Macmillan, 1983), 33.

23. Jack Wiseman, *Cost, Choice, and Political Economy* (Aldershot: Edward Elgar, 1989), 230. Littlechild stresses that same point when he summarizes the "radical subjectivist"

The recognition that in human social affairs the future is undetermined but "created" in the process of choice, does not imply that the future is "beyond *conjecture*,"[24] nor does it ignore that individuals have *expectations* about the future on which they base their action. The subjectivist's understanding of the nature and role of such expectations is, however, critically different from their interpretation in a neoclassical framework. To the subjectivist, expectations may be more or less reasonable (in the sense of being more or less defendable in the light of past experience), but they can, ultimately, not be more than conjectures about an undetermined and, therefore, unknowable future. To the neoclassical economist, by contrast, expectations are about a future that is, in principle, *knowable*, even if its knowability may be limited by imperfections of the "expecters." Ignorance of the future is essentially seen as a source of inefficiency, as a problem that can, in principle, be remedied by learning.[25] By contrast, from a subjectivist position, such ignorance is simply "an inescapable characteristic of the human condition."[26] And "the possibility of learning does not imply that through learning the future will become knowable, but only that experience will change behavior."[27]

Arguing on the same theme, Shackle suggests that every person choosing among different courses of action can be seen "to be making history, on

---

view as implying that the "as-yet-undetermined actions of other agents" make for "the essential open-endedness of creativity" (Stephen C. Littlechild, "Three Types of Market Process," in *Economics as a Process: Essays in the New Institutional Economics*, ed. Richard N. Langlois, 27–39 [Cambridge: Cambridge University Press, 1986], 31) in human affairs, that "the future is not so much unknown as it is nonexistent or indetermined at the time of decision" (Ibid., 29).

24. Jack Wiseman, "Principles of Political Economy: An Outline Proposal, Illustrated by Application to Fiscal Federalism," *Constitutional Political Economy* 1 (1990): 101–27, 104.

25. "Mainstream economics deals with unknowability by assuming it away. In the simple model, this is done by assuming perfect knowledge of the future. . . . The more sophisticated models assume knowledge of the possible number of future states of the world. . . . They assume that *someone* has a knowledge of the future that no one can possibly have" (Ibid., 103). See also Wiseman, *Cost, Choice,* 159.

26. Wiseman, *Cost, Choice,* 225.

27. Ibid., 143. "*The future* has not yet happened. About it, men can have only *opinions,* related to past experience (learning). Since men can (must) choose how to act, their chosen acts, together with the evolution of the physical world, are continuously creating the emerging future. If this is so (as it must be), then the future cannot be known 'now' (that is, in the continuous present)" (Ibid., 268).

however small a scale, in some sense other than mere passive obedience to the play of all-pervasive causes."[28] Every choice can be seen as the beginning of a sequel that "will be partly the work of many people's choices-to-come whose character . . . the chooser of present action cannot know."[29] Our "unknowledge" of the future is, from this perspective, not "a deficiency, a falling-short, a failure of search and study." Rather, it reflects a fundamental fact of human existence, "the imaginative and originative source and nature of the choosables, and the endless proliferant creation of hypothetical sequels of choosable action." It reflects, in other words, "*the plurality of rival possibles.*"[30]

The emphasis on choice as an *originating* force, the notion of the *creativeness* of the human mind, and the outlook on history as an *open-ended,* evolving process, are intimately interconnected aspects of the same general theme that marks the critical difference between the subjectivist perspective and its neoclassical counterpart. It marks the difference between the *nonteleological* outlook on the human social realm that informs the subjectivist notion of an open-ended, creative-choice process, and the *teleological* thrust that underlies, if only implicitly, the neoclassical notion of an equilibrium solution that is "preordained by patterns of mineral resources, geography, population, consumer tastes and technological possibilities."[31] To Shackle and other radical

28. Shackle, "Bounds of Unknowledge," 28.

29. Ibid., 288ff. As a summary of Shackle's position, Littlechild states, "Choice . . . represents an origin, a beginning. . . . [I]t does have a sequel. It makes a difference to what comes after. This sequel cannot be foreknown, because subsequent events will depend partly upon other such choices yet to be made" (Stephen Littlechild, "Comment: Radical Subjectivism or Radical Subversion," in *Time, Uncertainty and Disequilibrium: Exploration of Austrian Themes,* ed. M. Rizzo, 32–49 [Lexington, Mass.: Lexington Books, 1979], 33.).

30. Shackle, "Bounds of Unknowledge," 33, 36, 37. "[I]f we had *all the data there are or could be* about the *present,* we might still not be able to infer what the sequel of any action now chosen would be. . . . If history, past and to come, is all one book already written at the beginning of time, what is choice? . . . But if choice is fertile, effective, truly *inceptive,* then there can be no foreknowledge. History-to-come, in that case, is not only unknown but *not yet existent*" (G. L. S. Shackle, "Comments," in *Subjectivist Economics: The New Austrian School,* by A. H. Shand, 59–67 [Oxford: The Pica Press, 1981], 60).

31. Arthur, "Positive Feedbacks," 99. We use the term "teleological" here in a more general sense than that of an explanation in terms of intended ends or purposeful design. We classify as "teleological" all theoretical perspectives that explain processes in terms of

subjectivists, the whole general equilibrium concept is questionable when applied to a constantly changing social world that has no predeterminable telos, whether in the pompous sense of a Marxian philosophy of history or in the more pedestrian sense of a conceptually definable equilibrium toward which the process of socioeconomic change could be predicted to gravitate. In a world in which creative human choice is a constant source of an "unknowable future," the notion of a "social equilibrium" is, in J. Wiseman's words, a "pseudo-concept," one that can "have only the most tenuous general meaning."[32]

Another way of stating the subjectivist objection against the neoclassical equilibrium concept is by saying that the latter does not provide for an adequate account of "real," historical time. It does not take seriously the fact that, as L. M. Lachmann puts it, "*Time* and *Knowledge* belong together," that "time cannot pass without modifying knowledge."[33] The common argument that "simplifying assumptions" allow general equilibrium models to ignore the complexities of the "time and knowledge" problem is rejected by Wiseman as unconvincing. The simplifying assumptions about human knowledge are, he argues, "not legitimate simplifications but a gross perversion of the nature of the decision-problem faced by people living in the real world,"[34]

---

some predeterminable end point toward which they are supposed to move, rather than in terms of explicitly specified forces and principles that actually "drive" them. It is in this sense that we classify as "teleological" an equilibrium theory that describes economic processes in terms of "where they are going," namely, their end-point equilibria, but does not provide an explicit explanatory account of the dynamics of these processes themselves.

32. Wiseman, *Cost, Choice,* 214, 265. "[F]or G. L. S. Shackle, the relevance of the whole concept (of general equilibrium) is in question. Every act of choice embodies the chooser's creative imagination of the future. The market therefore follows a 'kaleidic' process, with moments of order interspersed with disintegration into a new pattern. The economy is changing and developing, but in no sense does it have a single goal" (Stephen C. Littlechild, "Subjectivism and Method in Economics," in *Beyond Positive Economics,* ed. J. Wiseman, 38–49 [London: Macmillan, 1983], 48f.).

33. Ludwig M. Lachmann, "Professor Shackle on the Economic Significance of Time," in *Capital, Expectations, and the Market Process,* by L. M. Lachmann, 81–93 (Kansas City, Mo.: Sheed Andrews and McMeel, 1977), 85, 93. "The impossibility of prediction in economics follows from the fact that economic change is linked to change in knowledge, and future knowledge cannot be gained before its time. Knowledge is generated by spontaneous acts of the mind" (Ibid., 90).

34. Wiseman, *Cost, Choice,* 140.

a defect that cannot be remedied by sophisticated refinements of the models that are based on such assumptions.[35]

The contrast is between two critically different perspectives by which efforts to understand the world can be guided: (1) a *teleological* perspective, and (2) a *nonteleological* perspective. We argue that it is its uncompromising nonteleological character that marks the critical difference between the understanding of the market process suggested by the subjectivist perspective and various standard conceptions of the market that, if only in a very subliminal fashion, have a teleological undertone. And, as an aside, we want to submit that this "residual teleology" constitutes somewhat of a hidden common link between standard economic teaching on the self-organizing nature of markets and the blatant teleology of the socialist planning mentality.

3. Kirzner's Theory of Entrepreneurship

Israel Kirzner's work, with its explicit emphasis on the entrepreneurial role in economic interaction, is of particular interest in the present context because of Kirzner's claim that his own "alertness" theory of entrepreneurship keeps a balanced middle ground between "two extreme views," the neoclassical equilibrium view on the one side and Shackle's subjectivism on the other, or, in our terms, between a teleological and a nonteleological concept of the market process.[36] As we shall argue, however, in spite of his emphasis on innovative entrepreneurial dynamics and in spite of his verbal recognition of the *creative* and *open-ended* nature of the market process, Kirzner's approach fails to escape the subliminal teleology of the equilibrium framework.[37]

35. "But if what is assumed away is the essence of the problem, then greater complexity will generate not greater insights but more sophisticated confusion" (Ibid., 227).

36. Israel M. Kirzner, *Discovery and the Capitalist Process* (Chicago: University of Chicago Press, 1985), 7ff. "I claim, indeed, that the 'alertness' view of entrepreneurship enables us to have the best of both worlds: we *can* incorporate entrepreneurship into the analysis without surrendering the heart of microeconomic theory" (Ibid., 11). Stated differently, Kirzner claims to avoid the neoclassical orthodoxy's failure to account for "the creative entrepreneur" (Ibid., 13), without falling "into the seductive trap offered by the opposite extreme" (Ibid.), that is, by the radical subjectivist position.

37. G. P. O'Driscoll's and M. J. Rizzo's exposition of a modern Austrian-subjectivist economics is, in a similar way, characterized by a tension between the acceptance of basic

There is, as Littlechild has pointed out in some detail, a disharmonious mixture in Kirzner's work, between a basic affinity to, and remaining disagreements with, the radical subjectivist position.[38] Kirzner explicitly recognizes the creative dynamics of the market process, and indeed, makes this the central theme of his work. He criticizes the neoclassical position for assigning "*no* role . . . to the creative entrepreneur"; he talks of the role of entrepreneurship "in an open-ended, uncertain world," a world in which we "find scope for the unpredictable, the creative, the imaginative expression of the human mind"; and he talks of new products, new qualities of products, new methods of production, and new forms of organization that are endlessly generated in the course of the entrepreneurial process.[39] Yet, such emphasis on creativity, imagination, and novelty is combined with a theoretical perspective that located the essence of entrepreneurship in "the discovery of error," and the scope for entrepreneurship "in the possibility of discovering error," a combination that can hardly be called harmonious.[40]

Discovery of error means, in the context of Kirzner's theory, such things as the discovery of "erroneously low valuation" of resources, the "alertness to hitherto unperceived opportunities," or the noticing of "situations overlooked until now because of error," phrases that all invite the same questions: If the essence of entrepreneurial discovery is to "provide protection" or "rescue" from "earlier" or "past error," what is then the benchmark or *reference-base* against which the failure to do something can be judged to be an "error"? And how does the notion of *creativity* square with such definition of entrepreneurial activity? Are creativity and imagination the same as discovery of errors?[41]

---

tenets of radical subjectivism and the attempt to maintain "an appropriately revised idea of equilibrium" (Gerald P. O'Driscoll and Mario J. Rizzo, *The Economics of Time and Ignorance* [New York: Basil Blackwell, 1985], 79).

38. Littlechild, "Comment."

39. Kirzner, *Discovery and the Capitalist Process*, 13, 52, 58. "In the course of this entrepreneurial process, new products may be introduced, new qualities of existing products may be developed, new methods of production may be ventured, new forms of industrial organization, financing, marketing, or tackling risk may be developed. All the ceaseless churning and agitation of the market is to be understood as the consequence of the never-ending discovery process of which the market consists" (Ibid., 30ff.).

40. Ibid., 50, 51.

41. Ibid., 50, 52, 53.

There is, in our view, a fundamental inconsistency in Kirzner's attempt to integrate the innovativeness of entrepreneurial activity into an equilibrium framework—by modeling it as *discovery* of "erroneously overlooked opportunities."[42] The critical step in Kirzner's argument, the step that is intended to establish a "middle ground" between a teleological and a nonteleological understanding of the market process, is his extension of the notion of a divergence between "different parts of the market" from a *cross-sectional* to an *intertemporal* interpretation.[43] According to the cross-sectional interpretation, the entrepreneur acts essentially as *arbitrageur:* By taking advantage of hitherto unnoticed divergences between different parts in a present market, he helps to bring about greater consistency. According to the intertemporal interpretation, the entrepreneur takes advantage of yet unnoticed divergences between *today's* market and *tomorrow's* market, thus helping "to coordinate markets also across time."[44]

Whatever may be said about the knowability of divergencies in the cross-sectional interpretation, it should be obvious that the notion of *intertemporal* divergences between markets at different points in time is inherently problematic. If, as we must assume, divergences between today's and tomorrow's

42. "I postulate a continuous discovery process—an entrepreneurial discovery process—that in the absence of external changes in underlying conditions, fuels a tendency toward equilibrium" (Ibid., 12).

43. Ibid., 62. "What market entrepreneurship accomplishes is a tendency for transactions in different parts of the market (including the market at different dates) to become coordinated" (Ibid., 64).

44. Ibid., 61ff. Kirzner's crucial argument, in this context, is worth quoting at some length: "When we introduce the passage of time, the dimensions along which mutual ignorance may develop are multiplied. Market participants in one part of today's market may not only be imperfectly aware of the transactions available in another part of the market; they also may be imperfectly aware of the transactions that will be available in next year's market. Absence of consistency between different parts of today's market is seen as a special case of a more general notion of inconsistency that includes also inconsistency between today's transactions and those to be transacted next year. . . . It is still the case, as noted, that the entrepreneurial function is that of bringing about a tendency for transactions in different parts of the market (conceived broadly now as including transactions entered into at different times) to be made in greater mutual consistency. But whereas in the case of entrepreneurship in the single-period market (that is, the case of the entrepreneur as arbitrageur) entrepreneurial alertness meant alertness to present facts, in the case of multiperiod entrepreneurship alertness must mean alertness to the future" (Ibid., 62ff.).

markets are typically associated with differences between today's and tomorrow's *knowledge*, what does it mean to say that entrepreneurial alertness corrects the "failure to realize" divergences between *present* and *future* markets? What sense does it make to describe today's failure to possess tomorrow's knowledge as *error?*[45] If, to use Lachmann's phrase, "*Time* and *Knowledge* belong together," a comparison between present and future markets cannot possibly be made in a sense that would make such terminology meaningful. The kind of comparison that can be made, at least conceptually, across contemporaneous markets cannot be made along the "intertemporal dimension."[46] Time is not simply another "dimension," comparable to the spatial. Different parts of a present market exist, they are *present*, and differences in their characteristics can be discovered. Future parts of a market simply do not exist; they are, by definition, not present. There are, at any point in time, many *potential* futures imaginable, based on more or less informed reflections. Yet, which future will come into existence will depend on choices that are yet to be made. Of course, human beings aim to be "prepared for the future," and they act on their expectations of what lies ahead. The subjectivist argument on the unknowability of the future is certainly not meant as a recommendation to merchants not to anticipate the coming of winter in their storekeeping. Yet, if, and to the extent that, human choices and their complex interactions shape the emerging future, the latter can be a matter of speculation, but not of foreknowledge.

The supposition that the future is foreknowable clearly seems implied when, in talking about the problem of intertemporal entrepreneurial alertness, Kirzner speaks of pictures of the future that may or may not "correspond to the truth as it will be realized," of man's efforts to overcome uncertainty "by more accurate prescience," of "past failure to pierce correctly the fog of uncertainty," and so forth. It is far from obvious how such insinuation of a preknowable future can be consistent with a genuine appreciation of the creativity of the human mind. Indeed, when arriving at this issue, Kirzner simply retreats to the *ex cathedra* claim that his approach does en-

45. A well-known classical statement of the argument that we simply cannot anticipate future knowledge and, therefore, cannot predict future human choices that will be affected by such future knowledge, can be found in Karl R. Popper's Preface to his *The Poverty of Historicism* (Boston: The Beacon Press, 1957).

46. Kirzner, *Discovery and the Capitalist Process*, 62.

compass the two notions, without actually showing *how* this can be done. He emphasizes that intertemporal entrepreneurial alertness "does not consist merely in 'seeing' the unfolding of the tapestry of the future in the sense of seeing a preordained flow of events." Indeed, he insists that such alertness must "embrace the awareness of the ways in which the human agent can . . . in fact *create* the future."[47] Yet, as if the compatibility of the two arguments were obvious, he also insists that the function of market entrepreneurship in the multiperiod context is nonetheless still that of "discovery of errors" in the sense explained above.[48] And he leaves undiscussed the issue of what one entrepreneur's creativity means for the truthfulness of another entrepreneur's picture of the future.[49]

If, as Kirzner's construction seems to suggest, today's failure to possess tomorrow's knowledge qualifies as *error* from which entrepreneurial alertness is to provide rescue, one could conclude that the ultimate benchmark or reference base for such judgment is an imagined world in which everything that humans may ever imagine, think, or know will be revealed.[50] Judged against

---

47. Ibid., 55, 58, 53, 56.

48. Ibid., 56. The same kind of tension between Kirzner's chosen theoretical framework and his attempt to incorporate the notion of entrepreneurial inventiveness in the creation of new products and new ways of doing things is also visible in his more recent discussion on the subject (Israel M. Kirzner, *Discovery, Capitalism, Distributive Justice* [New York: Basil Blackwell, 1989], 84ff.). In her review of this book, K. Vaughn comments on Kirzner's attempts to account for the creative aspects of entrepreneurship while retaining his earlier language: "It has become obvious to this reviewer that the old language no longer fits his new theoretical insights" (Karen I. Vaughn, "Profits, Alertness and Imagination," review of I. M. Kirzner's *Discovery, Capitalism, Distributive Justice, Journal des Economistes et des Etudes Humaines* 1 [1990]: 183–88, 185).

49. Kirzner indirectly refers to this issue without, however, discussing it: "In particular the futurity that entrepreneurship must confront introduces the possibility that the entrepreneur may, by his own creative actions, in fact *construct* the future as *he* wishes it to be. In the single-period case alertness can at best discover hitherto overlooked current facts. In the multiperiod case entrepreneurial alertness must include the entrepreneur's perception of the way in which creative and imaginative action may vitally shape the kind of transactions that will be entered into in future market periods" (*Discovery and the Capitalist Process*, 63ff.).

50. And, by implication, one could argue that the "equilibrium" toward which intertemporal coordination—as it is promoted by entrepreneurial discovery of error—tends to gravitate can only be some final state of universal enlightenment, at the end of all times. Support for such, admittedly exaggerated, interpretation may be seen in statements such

such a benchmark, every act, however imaginative and creative, can be seen as a discovery of something that was already waiting to be found. And failure to discover may be discussed in terms of error and overlooked opportunities. It seems questionable, however, whether the mental construct of such an imagined world is a helpful analytical guide when applied to the study of socioeconomic change.

What might be misleadingly suggestive here is the analogy to the scientific discovery process. To the extent that science is concerned with an objective reality "out there," our conjectural knowledge of this reality can be expected to grow over time, through a process of discovery. Although we cannot know at present what we will know in the future, any future increase in knowledge can, in some sense, be viewed as a finding of something that could, in principle, be currently discovered. There is something knowable out there, to be discovered sooner or later. Any such account of the discovery process in science is itself seriously challenged by the new conceptions advanced by Prigogine and others, because of its neglect of real time. But, even if, for the purpose of our discussion here, we should leave this issue aside, the analogous challenge advanced by the radical subjectivists to neoclassical equilibrium economics applies with full force to the concept of the market as a discovery process. Entrepreneurial activity, in particular, is not to be modelled as discovery of that which is "out there." Such activity, by contrast, *creates* a reality that will be different subsequent to differing choices. Hence, the reality of the future must be shaped by choices yet to be made, and this reality has no existence independent of these choices. With regard to a "yet to be created" reality, it is surely confusing to consider its emergence in terms of the discovery of "overlooked opportunities."[51]

---

as this: "My view, therefore, sees initial market ignorance indeed as an inescapable feature of the human condition in a world of change, but also as subject to continual erosion. . . . (Entrepreneurs) discover where existing decisions were in fact mistaken. Here lies the source for any equilibrating tendencies that markets display" (Ibid., 13).

51. The discussion here, and elsewhere in this article, is related, at least indirectly, to a criticism of Michael Polanyi advanced by one of us in two related articles (James M. Buchanan, "Politics and Science," in *Freedom in Constitutional Contract,* by James M. Buchanan, 64–77 [College Station: Texas A&M University Press, 1977]; "The Potential for Tyranny in Politics as Science," in *Liberty, Market and State,* by James M. Buchanan, 40–54 [New York: New York University Press, 1986]). Polanyi conceptualized the scientific process as exploration or discovery, and he argued persuasively that decentralized orga-

4. Conceptions and Misconceptions of the Market

The essential characteristic of the radical subjectivist position that marks its critical departure from a neoclassical framework is, at the same time, the feature that it shares with the new evolutionary synthesis discussed at the beginning of this article: Its conception of "a world in which time plays a vital role," of history as an open-ended evolving process, and of a future that is not predetermined, merely waiting to be revealed, but that is "continuously *originated* by the pattern and sequence of human choice."[52] Such a conception has clear implications for the theory of the market that sets it apart from various theoretical constructs that have been used to explain or to illustrate the adaptive nature of the market process. If the emphasis on the creativity of human choice is taken seriously, it is not only the standard neoclassical equilibrium notion that seems questionable, but also less orthodox conceptions of the market process, including Kirzner's more subliminally teleological perspective on markets and entrepreneurship. By stating this we certainly do not want to suggest that "radical subjectivism" exists as a well-specified theoretical paradigm ready for adoption—it clearly is not. What we want to suggest, however, is that the creativity of human choice poses a problem that any effective socioeconomic theory cannot evade.

The critical shift in perspective may be further illustrated by reference to three separate understandings of the spontaneous order of the market that have been advanced by scholars who have been generally supportive of market organization of the economy, no one of whom would ever have referred to the market as an "analogue computer" for the "computation of equilibrium prices."

1. One of us (Buchanan) learned basic price theory at the University of Chicago in the 1940s, when all students, undergraduate and graduate, were

---

nization of the scientific enterprise would insure more rapid advance in "solving" the "jigsaw puzzle." From this conceptualization of the scientific process, Polanyi supported, by analogy, the spontaneous ordering properties of decentralized market processes.

Buchanan's criticism suggested that, even if the discovery-exploration metaphor remains applicable to the enterprise of the physical sciences, such a metaphor is misleading when applied and extended to economic or political interaction among freely choosing individuals.

52. Littlechild, "Comment," 38.

required to master the Syllabus written by Henry Simons.[53] This Syllabus contained three well-known rent problems that were designed to provide an understanding of how a competitive economy allocates scarce resources among uses. And, as a test of the efficacy of competitive adjustment, one task given to the students was that of comparing the total product of the economy in competitive equilibrium with that which might be achieved under allocation by a benevolent and omniscient planner.

2. In a deservedly famous article, "The Logic of Liberty," Michael Polanyi introduced the metaphor of a sack of potatoes that need only to be shaken to insure minimization of volume to demonstrate how localized, decentralized adjustment, akin to that which is characteristic of market organization, works better than centralized adjustment.[54]

3. In a monograph-length essay devoted to an explication of the spontaneous order of the market, Norman Barry stated that the results of a market "appear to be a product of some omniscient, designing mind."[55]

In each of these illustrative examples, there is revealed, at least by inference, an understanding of the spontaneous ordering properties of a market process that is sharply different from the understanding held by the radical subjectivists. In each example, the efficacy of market adjustment is measured *teleologically* in terms of the relative achievement of some predefined goal or objective. In Simons' problems, the objective is, simply, economic product, which is wheat in his one-good economy. In Polanyi's case, the objective is explicitly stated to be minimization of volume. In Barry's essay, the argument is more sophisticated, but any conceptualization of an omniscient, designing mind must imply some well-defined objective that exists independently from the separate participants' own *creative* choices.

If the efficacy of market organization is, as insinuated in the above ex-

---

53. "The Simons' Syllabus" was circulated only in mimeographed form. Gordon Tullock, himself a student of Simons in the 1940s, edited and published a somewhat incomplete version in 1983 (Gordon Tullock, ed., *The Simons' Syllabus*, by Henry Calvert Simons [Blacksburg: Virginia Polytechnic Institute and State University, 1983]).

54. This article was the title essay in the volume *The Logic of Liberty* (Michael Polanyi [Chicago: University of Chicago Press, 1951]).

55. Norman Barry, "The Tradition of Spontaneous Order," *The Literature of Liberty* 5 (1982): 7–58. For a commentary on Barry's essay, see James M. Buchanan, "Order Defined in the Process of Its Emergence," *The Literature of Liberty* 5 (1982): 5.

amples, evaluated teleologically, in terms of its capacity to approach an independently (that is, independent of the choice process itself) determinable state, then there remains only an ambiguous discourse over comparative performance as between such an organization and centralized economic planning. Even if Simons, Polanyi, and Barry, along with others, may have succeeded in demonstrating that decentralized arrangements are superior in achieving some objectively identifiable goal, their conceptualization of the market process forces them into a line of comparative defense that a radical subjectivist understanding of the market would have rendered unnecessary from the outset. If the market is genuinely perceived as an open-ended, non-determined evolutionary process in which the essential driving force is human choice, any insinuation, however subtle, of a "telos" toward which the process can be predicted to move must be inherently misleading. There is, in our view, no systematically sustainable middle ground between a teleological and a nonteleological perspective. And all conceptualizations of the market process that suppose, whether explicitly or implicitly, a "something" toward which the process is moving are, by this very fact, *teleological,* whether the "something" is specified as an equilibrium or otherwise. This applies to the notion of a mechanical equilibrium as implied in the standard textbook models of intersecting demand and supply curves, as well as to the thermo-dynamic equilibrium concept that is implied where the market process is interpreted in terms of exhaustion of potential gains from trade. And it also applies to images of the market that are intended to capture the constant change in the equilibrium-telos, such as K. Boulding's image of the "dog chasing a cat."[56]

It should be noted that to question the appropriateness of teleological conceptions of the market is not the same as denying the apparent fact that the human participants in the "catallaxy," the game of the market, reasonably *adapt* to the circumstances that they confront and to changes that they expect to occur. The predictive potential of microeconomic theory lies in the uniformity of such adaptive response among persons. But such adaptive behavior does not imply that the overall process is moving toward some determined goal, whether conceived as a predetermined equilibrium or as a "moving cat." The game described by the market may be misunder-

56. Littlechild, "Three Types," 32.

stood if interpreted in a teleological mind-set. The market economy, *as an aggregation,* neither maximizes nor minimizes anything. It simply allows participants to pursue that which they value, subject to the preferences and endowments of others, and within the constraints of general "rules of the game" that allow, and provide incentives for, individuals to try out new ways of doing things. There simply is no "external," independently defined objective against which the results of market processes can be evaluated.

We may illustrate the nonteleological perspective on market interaction by dropping the familiar presupposition that potential traders initially possess quantities of well-defined marketable goods. Assume that no goods exist, and that persons are described by certain talents, capacities, and skills that enable them to produce consumable goods from nature. Assume that the rules of the game allow persons to claim enforceable rights to the shares in natural endowments and to their own capacities and skills. In this model, trade will take place when persons recognize that their well-being can be enhanced by producing *and* exchanging rather than producing for their own consumption only. But the chain of choices is extended, and, also, there is an added requirement that any participant exercise *imagination* in choosing to specialize in production with the ultimate purpose of achieving an increase in well-being through exchange.

Think of the choice calculus of a person in this setting. What can I produce that will prove of exchange value to others? Response to this question allows the participant not only to select among a preexisting set of goods, but, also and importantly, to *create* new goods that are expected to be of potential exchangeable value. Once the creative-inventive-imaginative element in choice is introduced into the game here, then any idealized omniscience on the part of a planner who might attempt to duplicate the market result would become patently absurd. Individuals would use their own imagination, their own assessment of the potential evaluations of others, in producing goods wholly divorced from their own consumption, goods that are anticipated to yield values when put on the market, values that, as income to the producers, can be used to purchase goods from others in the nexus. This seeking to satisfy others through producing marketable value as an indirect means of producing value for themselves—this characteristic behavioral element in a market order was central to Adam Smith's insight. And it is this feature that allows us to compare the performance of market organization with alternative social arrangements, even in the absence of an independently existing scalar. Markets tend to satisfy the preferences of persons, regardless of what their preferences might be, and even when we acknowledge that preferences emerge only within the process of choice itself.

The market conceived as a "game without goods" also suggests the tenuousness of the whole notion of equilibrium, defined as the exhaustion of gains from trade, which looms so important in the alternative teleological perspective. In the production and exchange of preexisting and well-defined goods, it is relatively easy to think of the game as having a definitive and final outcome once the goods have been so allocated that no participant seeks out further trades. Goods are, by definition, then allocated to their highest valued uses. But the usefulness of this equilibrium notion becomes less clear when we assume that there is no definite set of goods to be allocated. Conceptually, it remains possible to "freeze" the imaginative elements in individual choice at some point and allow the production-exchange process to work itself out to an equilibrium, where no further gains from trade, *and from imagination of new trading prospects,* are possible. The artificiality of such an equilibrium construction is apparent, however, since there seems nothing in the mind that is even remotely analogous to the cessation of exchange. There is no determinate limit to the potential of market value to be created as the process of human interaction proceeds.

What has made, and continues to make, the equilibrium concept attractive even to economists who, like Kirzner, are explicitly critical of the neoclassical orthodoxy is, it seems, its perceived capacity to readily capture the coordinative properties of markets, and the suspicion that the radical subjectivist critique may leave one incapable of systematically accounting for the orderliness of markets. Even if such suspicion may have been invited by some of the radical subjectivists, the emerging *new evolutionary synthesis* suggests a theoretical perspective that allows the subjectivist emphasis on the creativity of human choice, with all its implications, to be taken seriously, while, at the same time, it offers nonteleological explanations for the adaptiveness and coordinative properties that markets exhibit.

5. Conclusion

We have suggested that a perceptual vision of the market as a *creative process* offers more insight and understanding than the alternative visions that elicit interpretations of the market as a *discovery process*,[57] or, more familiarly, as an *allocative process*. In either of the latter alternatives, there is a telos imposed by the scientist's own perception, a telos that is nonexistent in the first stance. And removal of the teleological inference from the way of looking at economic interaction carries with it significant implications for any diagnosis of failure or success, diagnosis that is necessarily preliminary to any normative usage of scientific analysis.

We may illustrate the differing implications in application to the observed failure of the centrally planned economies of Eastern Europe and elsewhere. The neoclassical economist, trapped in the allocationist perception, tends to locate the source of failure in the distorted incentive structure that causes persons to be confronted with choice alternatives that do not reflect authentically derived evaluations. Resources do not flow to their most highly valued uses because persons who make decisions about resource use do not find it privately in their own interest to shift allocation in such fashion as to accomplish this conceptually definable, and desirable, result.

Some of the modern Austrian economists, and notably Kirzner, add an important element to the neoclassical critique. They suggest that, even if the incentive problems could, somehow, be ignored or assumed corrected, there would still remain the epistemological or knowledge problem. Only a decentralized market structure of economic interaction can exploit fully the knowledge of localized circumstances required to allow a definition of the ultimate valuation that is placed on resource use. Only the market can allow persons the effective liberty to discover the particular localized eccentricities that give form to value. This extension of the neoclassical emphasis on incentive structures is important and relevant to any overall assessment of the central planning model for an economy.

We suggest, however, that the critique, even as extended, falls short of capturing an essential element in any comparative assessment of the market and

57. Although the thrust of his work clearly supports the vision of the market as a creative process, Hayek's illuminating discussion "Competition as a Discovery Procedure" is not entirely free of the ambiguities that the concept of *discovery* tends to invoke when applied to the market process. Potentially misleading are, in this regard, his comparison between the discovery processes in science and in the market and some of his comments on the problem of measuring market performance (Friedrich A. Hayek, "Competition as a Discovery Procedure," in *New Studies in Philosophy, Politics, Economics, and the History of Ideas,* by F. A. Hayek, 179–90 [Chicago: University of Chicago Press, 1978], 181, 185ff.).

the planning alternatives. The teleological feature remains to be exorcised. In the neoclassical setting, even as extended by Kirzner, an *omniscient* and *benevolent* monolithic planner could secure the ideally defined result. Omniscience would, of course, insure access to any and all knowledge; benevolence could be such as to match the objective function precisely with whatever it is that individuals desire. But even the planner so idealized cannot create that which is not there and will not be there save through the exercise of the creative choices of individuals, who themselves have no idea in advance concerning the ideas that their own imaginations will yield.

The fundamental misunderstandings of the theory of the market economy that provided the analytical-intellectual foundations for socialism as a principle for socioeconomic organization are exposed by any one of the three interpretations contrasted here. The market as an allocative process, responding to the structure of incentives that confront choice-makers; the market as a discovery process, utilizing localized information; or the market as a creative process that exploits man's imaginative potential—socialism cannot, organizationally, be made equivalent to any one of these idealized perceptions. But, the "fatal conceit" that was socialism, to use Hayek's descriptive term here, would have surely faced more difficulty in achieving dominance as an idea if the creative spontaneity of the market process had been more fully appreciated.

Cultural Evolution and Institutional Reform

I. Introduction

In his widely and justly acclaimed treatise *Knowledge and Decisions* (1980),[1] Thomas Sowell explicitly acknowledges his indebtedness to F. A. Hayek, and the book may be interpreted as variations on and applications of Hayekian themes. Sowell's primary stress is on the diffusion of localized knowledge among all participants in social interaction and upon the possible benefits achievable by an appropriate matching of the informational and institutional structures. The mismatch between the hierarchically organized decision-making institutions that presume and require a centralization of knowledge that simply does not exist is an identifiable and reformable source of inefficiency.

The Hayekian emphasis on the diffusion of knowledge or information is corollary to a second major Hayekian theme, one that has eighteenth-century origins, a theme that stresses the spontaneous coordination of the results that emerge from the operation of decentralized institutional structures (the market). This theme is of course encapsulated in the principle of the invisible hand, perhaps the major intellectual discovery in the whole his-

From *Liberty, Market and State: Political Economy in the 1980s* (Brighton, England: Wheatsheaf Books, 1986), 75–86. Copyright 1986 by James M. Buchanan. First published in Great Britain in 1986 by Wheatsheaf Books Ltd, Brighton, Sussex. Reprinted by permission of Pearson Education Limited.

This chapter was initially presented as a paper in a Liberty Fund Conference in Savannah, Georgia, in March 1982.

1. Thomas Sowell, *Knowledge and Decisions* (New York: Basic Books, 1980).

tory of economics, and upon which the normative precept of *laissez-faire* was constructed and defended.

The coordination emerges as an unintended consequence of human actions that are motivated by divergent localized purposes. An understanding of the principle of such coordination enables the economist to shed the vulgar prejudice towards "constructed" or "planned" integration and to suggest that *laissez-faire* maximizes not only liberty but also the wealth of the nation. This principle of spontaneous order, "the logic of liberty," to introduce Michael Polanyi's felicitous designation, becomes the Lakatosian hard core for the economist, around which and from which his research programme emerges.

I endorse fully both of the Hayek-Sowell central themes noted, and I yield to no one in my admiration for Hayek's insightful contributions and for Sowell's imaginative applications. However, there is a third theme that has become increasingly important in Hayek's recent writings, and which is not wholly absent from Sowell's treatise, that does give me concern. This theme involves the extension of the principle of spontaneous order, in its *normative* implications, to the emergence of institutional structure itself. As applied to the market economy, that which emerges is defined by its very emergence to be that which is efficient. And this result implies, in its turn, a policy precept of non-intervention, properly so. There is no need to evaluate (indeed there is no possibility of evaluating) the efficiency of observed outcomes independent of the process; there exists no external criterion that allows efficiency to be defined in objectively measurable dimensions. If this logic is extended to the structure of institutions (including laws) that have emerged in some historical evolutionary process, the implication seems clear that that set which we observe necessarily embodies institutional or structural "efficiency." From this it follows, as before, that a policy of non-intervention in the process of emergence is dictated. There is no room left for the political economist, or for anyone else who seeks to reform social structures, to *change* laws and rules, with an aim of securing increased efficiency in the large. Any attempt to design, construct, and change institutions must, within this logical setting strictly interpreted, introduce inefficiency. Any "constructively rational" interferences with the "natural" processes of history are therefore to be studiously avoided. The message seems clear: relax before the slow sweep of history. Shades of the Hegelian mysteries!

In some parts of his recent writings Hayek has come close to the counsel of despair sketched out above.[2] In yet other parts of his work, however, Hayek himself seems clearly to be a "constructive rationalist," or a "rational constructivist," since he does not shy away at all from advancing specific proposals for institutional-constitutional reform. Two examples are provided in his widely discussed proposal for the denationalization of money issue[3] and in his proposal for changes in the division of functions as between two separate elected assemblies.[4]

My aim in this chapter is to reconcile the Hayek critique of constructive rationalism with his advocacy of institutional reform. In an earlier paper I criticized Hayek's extension of the principle of emergent and spontaneous order to institutional and legal structures.[5] In that paper I presented the Hayek stance as being internally contradictory; I made no attempt to remove or resolve the contradiction. My effort at reconciliation in this chapter is prompted specifically by an initial and highly stimulating paper by Professor Viktor Vanberg, who sought not only to reconcile the contradiction within Hayek's own work but also to reconcile Hayek's approach with my own, which Vanberg called that of the "contractarian constitutionalist."[6] The ideas that I present in this chapter are fully consistent with Vanberg's argument, and in a sense reflect little more than my own variations, as initially developed in a prefatory note designed to accompany the ultimate publication of his paper in monograph form.

2. See especially *Rules and Order,* Vol. 1 of *Law, Legislation and Liberty* (Chicago: University of Chicago Press, 1973).

3. See F. A. Hayek, *Denationalization of Money,* Hobart Paper 70 (London: Institute of Economic Affairs, 1976).

4. See *The Political Order of a Free People,* Vol. 3, *Law, Legislation and Liberty* (Chicago: University of Chicago Press, 1979).

5. See James M. Buchanan, "Law and the Invisible Hand," in Buchanan, *Freedom in Constitutional Contract* (College Station: Texas A&M University Press, 1977), 25–39.

6. Viktor Vanberg, "Libertarian Evolutionism, Constructivist Rationalism, and Contractarian Constitutionalism—The Issue of Constitutional Reform," presented at Liberty Fund Conference on Economic and Philosophical Foundations of Capitalism, Freiburg, Germany, February 1981. A revised version of this paper is published as a Walter Eucken Institute monograph, *Liberaler Evolutionismus oder Vertragstheoretischer Konstitutionalismus?* (Tübingen: J. C. B. Mohr, 1981).

II. Market Order and Natural Selection

Economists who understand and appreciate the spontaneous order generated by a competitive market process are aesthetically attracted to the theory of natural selection expounded by their colleagues in biology. There are evident similarities between the selection process that takes place as a market functions to reward the efficient and to drive out the inefficient and biological evolution that accomplishes what seem to be comparable results. Observed survival becomes the test for efficiency in either case.

The differences may be more important than the similarities, however, and these differences tend to be too readily overlooked by economists. The selection process of the market is guided by self-seeking actions of persons who explicitly try to improve their own positions, by entrepreneurs who quite deliberately do things differently than they are being done on the basis of a vision of potential reality that might be but is not. Some entrepreneurs succeed; others fail. But it becomes difficult, if not impossible, to model a market interaction process analogously to natural selection. In an economy without entrepreneurs, how could measurable change occur? Biological man, if dependent on mutational shifts, would be foredoomed to remain at or near the level of animal subsistence if, indeed, he could survive at all. Is there any evidence that man, considered solely as a reacting rather than as a choosing animal, could survive in the evolutionary chain?

Having long since moved beyond the level of animal subsistence, man is dependent on his entrepreneurial talents, his wit, his intelligence, and his explicitly directed adaptability to changing circumstances. At some stage of human history, some man "invented" rules for interacting with his fellows, and then convinced (by force or by persuasion) these fellows to abide by these rules. Some of these rules (institutions, conventions, mores) survived; others did not. The critical question for my purposes here concerns the equation between survival and efficiency, as applied to institutions themselves.

The level of existence for man in civil society remains much above that level that would characterize minimum survival as a species. Hence, there exists a very large "cushion" between where we are and where we might be pushed to before species survival might be threatened. If we take our whole complex structure of social institutions (rules) as a unit, therefore, the mere fact of survival tells us nothing at all concerning whether or not this structure, as a whole, is efficient by comparison with alternative structures. We might be able to do much, much better as well as much, much worse than we do by living within the particular institutional structure that we have inherited.

The fact is that we do not have the opportunity to try out alternative institutional structures; there is no close analogue to the selection process in a many-product, many-service competitive economy. In the latter, selection proceeds by the substitutability of "better" for "worse" in a setting where persons face alternatives that may be simultaneously observed and valued. In an institutional context, by contrast, persons face one structure at a time; alternatives may only be imagined, not "tasted"; alternative rules describe that which might be rather than that which is.

To the extent that differing institutional structures exist simultaneously in different communities (nations), something more akin to market selection may be present. Individuals do observe across community limits, and countries do build walls to prevent the competitive selection process from working its way. But even those who adhere most strongly to an evolutionist perspective with regard to institutions would not place much reliance on international migrations to ensure efficiency in institutional form.

They seem, instead, to rely on some sort of piecemeal, pragmatic adjustment process that generates gradual improvement in institutional structure through time without attention being paid by anyone to the overall design or pattern of coordination or discoordination. Emphasis is placed on the unintended consequences of limited-vision actions, with an implicit faith that these consequences will be benign. It is as if the many entrepreneurial choices, in the small, act always to push the institutional frontier towards efficiency, in the small *and* in the large. The analogy with the developments of English common law joins with that of the market economy.

There are, of course, logical reasons for accepting the notion that imaginative persons will seek always to improve the rules under which they operate, given the limited informational perspective that they must necessarily adopt. Institutions that embody major inefficiency presumably do not exist, when inefficiency is strictly measured by the presence of potential for improvements in the small. The critical question concerns the possible coincidence of this efficiency in the small and efficiency in the large, or rather as applied to the order of the whole institutional structure. Is it not possible that those very changes that may well reflect movement towards local optima can shift the whole system away from rather than towards some global optima? If this possibility is admitted, what rules out the legitimacy of extending entrepreneurial effort to effect changes in the large, to act as "rational constructivists," and to discuss alternative grand designs for the whole set of rules that exist?

At this point it is useful specifically to recall the central logic behind the conclusion that the market process generates coordinated results that are, indeed, likely to be more "efficient" than any alternative organizational structure for delivering ordinary goods and services. The market accomplishes this "miracle" because self-seeking individuals, who are presumably made secure in their persons and properties by the legal framework, carry out exchanges largely if not exclusively in *separation* or *isolation* from spill-over effects on other individuals who are not directly parties to the exchanges in question. In somewhat different and perhaps more familiar terms, the results of efficiency-seeking in the small, guarantee efficiency in the large because Pareto-relevant *externalities* are either absent or insignificant. The institutions of property and contract are presumed to be such that third-party or neighbourhood effects are minimized.

But we cannot simply extend such logic backwards, so to speak, and presume that, for the organization of "institutional exchanges" any such separability exists. Almost by definition, an institution or rule constrains the behaviour of many parties in a relevant interaction. In a very real sense, "publicness" necessarily enters which, in turn, ensures that "exchanges" must be complex in the sense of including all affected parties if they are to meet any efficiency test analogous to the market. This publicness of institutions suggests that any correspondence between efficiency in the small and efficiency in the large vanishes. Entrepreneurial efforts applied at the institutional margins, in the small, may represent efficiency gains, in the small, but there is no implication that these, taken separately, enhance efficiency in the large since, by definition, all parties affected are not brought into the agreed "exchanges" that are made.

Hayek seems to raise his objections against any attempts to look and suggest improvement in the whole structure of institutions, referring to such activity as dangerous "rational constructivism." At the same time, however, Hayek proposes basic changes in the institutional-constitutional structure of the social order. He remains quite unwilling to adopt a *laissez-faire* stance towards institutions, the stance that would seem to be dictated by his critique of rational constructivism.

III. Hayek on Cultural Evolution

Hayek is a sophisticated rather than a naïve evolutionist. He does not fall into the absurdity that models the evolution of social institutions on strict biological foundations. He recognizes explicitly that biologically the whole epoch of recorded history is well below the minimal time required for any effective adaptation of the human species to environmental changes. Hayek is a cultural, not a biological, evolutionist. Within historically comprehended time, the ages of civil man, patterns of behaviour have emerged, have adapted to changing environmental circumstances. "Human nature" has been modified within the more inclusive biological limits of animal man. Cultural evolution has produced or generated abstract rules for behaviour that are not instinctual but which we live by without understanding. These rules explicitly counter the instinctual proclivities that man carries always with him, but they do so in ways that we cannot appreciate and understand at the personal level germane to individual choices.

Hayek's strictures against the rational constructivists are directed at those putative scholar-reformers who would ignore the boundaries established by these culturally evolved abstract rules for behaviour, who would, quite literally, seek to make "new men," who would overturn the eighteenth-century discovery of the essential uniformities of human nature upon which any understanding of, and hence prospect for reform of, social interaction must rest.

IV. Rules for Human Behaviour: Institutions within Which Behaviour Described by Such Rules for Behaviour Can Take Place

The central, indeed the only, point of emphasis in this chapter lies in my suggestion that we distinguish categorically between culturally evolved rules for behaviour, which we do not understand and which cannot be explicitly ("constructively") modified, which act as ever-present constraints on our ability to act, and the set of institutions within which we may act, always within these rules for behaviour. The culturally evolved rules for behaviour clearly impose constraints on this set of institutions, but they need not define a unique and specific institutional structure.[7] There are many possible structures within which men may behave, and these structures (sets of institutions) may be normatively evaluated one against the other. The discussion of institutional structures that are inconsistent with the nature of man as he exists is properly subjected to Hayek's contempt. Such discussion charitably interpreted may seem little more than romanticizing about unrealizable Utopias. But, when taken seriously, the romantic delusions wreak havoc on constructive dialogue.

As among those alternative sets of institutions that do not place unduly severe demands on man's behaviour in accordance with the culturally evolved rules, there are clearly "better" and "worse" adjectives and adverbs to be assigned, given sound analysis along with defensible evaluative standards. Hayek's proposals for constitutional-institutional reform can be interpreted as suggestions that existing institutions are indeed "worse" than that set which he proposes in their turn. His effort in presenting these reform proposals can be interpreted as rational constructivism in the sense that he is examining the whole complex network of interaction in recognition of the inherent publicness embodied in rules-institutions. In advancing these proposals for change, Hayek is *not* directly relying on the processes of institutional selection in any analogue to natural selection to generate efficiency in the large. He is not expressing confidence that entrepreneurial efforts by limited-vision participants exerted on the margins of institutional change will ensure movement towards the ideal society. In this respect, Hayek's position seems to be quite different from that expressed by other economists who do indeed reflect some such confidence.[8]

7. On this point, see below, section VI.

8. The work of Demsetz immediately comes to mind, with his early and much-cited reference to the emergence of private property rights among the Labrador Indians. See Harold Demsetz, "Toward a Theory of Property Rights," *American Economic Review,* 57 (May 1964), 347–59; see also S. Pejovich, "Towards an Economic Theory of the Creation and Speculation of Property Rights," *Review of Social Economy,* 30 (Sept. 1972), 309–25. More recently, Andrew Schotter has attempted to model a formal theory of institutional emergence, using game theory constructions; see Andrew Schotter, *An Economic Theory of Social Institutions* (Cambridge: Cambridge University Press, 1981).

Hayek's advocacy of institutional-constitutional reform is not to be classified as the work of a rational constructivist, however, if by this term we refer to the modelling of interaction structures that neglect or ignore the culturally evolved rules for human behaviour that constrain the set of institutional alternatives while not, at the same time, generating uniqueness in results. Hayek is rationally constructivist, within the limits of a human nature as culturally evolved, a stance that allows his position to be made both internally consistent and also consistent with that taken by those of us who, as contractarians, may be classified somewhat more readily as constructivists. This reconciliation is along the lines suggested by Vanberg in the paper noted above.

V. The Underground Economy: An Example

It will be useful to bring this overly abstruse discussion down to earth through resort to a simple and familiar example. In almost all Western countries, increasing concern was expressed about the growth of the underground or non-taxed sector of the economy in the 1970s, stimulated by very high marginal rates of tax, especially as non-indexed in an inflationary setting. As persons locally adjust to high rates, new institutions emerge that are designed to facilitate further adjustments; new loopholes are located by tax entrepreneurs and taxpayers move to exploit these as they are discovered.

The persons who act as tax entrepreneurs, along with the persons who respond by taking advantages of the loopholes, are acting to improve their own positions. Such an expansion of the underground or non-taxed sector of the economy reflects a shift towards increased efficiency in the small; those who are directly involved in the new institutions of adjustment shift towards a local optimum, given the tax structure as it exists. Continued expansion of the underground sector might ultimately lead to a shift in the tax structure itself. Interestingly enough, however, this ultimate reform would in this case be produced because efficiency in the large is reduced rather than increased by entrepreneurial efforts to increase profits in the small.

The point here seems worth some elaboration in detail. Consider a setting in which an individual earns a pre-tax return of $10 on an asset, and faces a 50 per cent marginal tax rate. The government collects $5; the taxpayer retains $5. A loophole is now discovered which allows income from the capital that the asset represents to escape tax. The new tax-exempt investment yields a gross return of $6, all of which is now retained by the taxpayer. There is a net loss of value of $4 in the economy, despite the gain to the taxpayer. In an overall or global sense, the economy is less efficient than it was before the discovery of the loophole.[9]

As more and more taxpayers learn of the new tax-exempt options, the economy becomes less and less efficient until, at some point, it may seem evident to all concerned, including governmental decision-makers, that structural changes in the tax code are required. Institutional reform may then emerge that will tend to enhance efficiency in the large, to shift the economy towards some sort of global optimum.

In a sense, of course, such institutional reform can be interpreted as being produced by the responses of persons to the increasing "badness" of the situations that they confront. But there are dramatic differences between this path of institutional change and the selection process that characterizes the competitive market economy. In the latter—that is, in the market—entrepreneurial effort that is successful displaces values by *higher* values. That is to say, a successful entrepreneur makes a profit on his venture; he increases localized efficiency. He may also create bankruptcy (losses in capital values) on the part of his competitors. But the gains in value to the entrepreneur, along with the owners of scarce inputs and consumers generally, will more than offset the losses incurred by those persons who are damaged. The efficiency of the economy as a whole, in the large, is increased, not decreased, as a result of each and every successful entrepreneurial venture.

As the tax-adjustment example shows clearly, however, comparable entrepreneurial effort decreases overall efficiency, or at least may do so. Ultimate institutional reform that may reverse this localized drift towards inefficiency in the large is postulated only because of some faith that a developing generalized recognition of the need for more basic structural change will emerge. Here there is no direct correspondence between the decentralized, localized responses to the limited-information settings in which persons separately

---

9. The illustration is, of course, oversimplified and the conclusion depends on the satisfaction of some conditions. If the $5 collected by the government should be *totally* wasted, the discovery of the loophole would then increase rather than decrease efficiency. If, however, as much as $1 is spent productively, even on pure transfers, the conclusion holds.

find themselves and the efficiency-enhancing results on the economy considered as an integrated whole.

A second dramatic difference between the process of efficiency-enhancing institutional adjustment traced out in the example and the selection process in the market lies in the implied necessity for decision-makers, at some point in the sequence, to consider structural-constitutional change, to shift their attention to changes in the rules that affect all persons in the community, *to look beyond the localized, individualized settings, and to do so explicitly.*

The world in which all persons act only as tax entrepreneurs and taxpayers responding to the potential advantages offered in a specified tax code could never achieve basic changes in the code itself. *Constitutions, as such, cannot emerge in a process of simultaneous coordination* analogous to that which allows us to classify the market as efficient or which characterizes natural selection. Criticisms of efforts aimed at genuine constitutional change that are based on mistaken notions about the superior efficacy of some sort of "natural selection" or "natural emergence" of institutions that meet overall efficiency criteria are simply misguided.

VI. Constitutional Reform and Human Nature

The critique advanced by the example is aimed less at Hayek and Sowell than at those economists who do, indeed, counsel a position of relaxation before the slow history of institutional evolution. As noted earlier in this chapter, Hayek does not stand still before the observed drift of institutional change, which he sees as going in the wrong direction. He explicitly advocates constitutional reform while at the same time he continues to castigate those who adopt the rational constructivist stance. As noted earlier, reconciliation is possible between these apparently contradictory attitudes if we limit the range of institutional reform proposals to those which are consistent with man's own behavioural capacities, as these are shaped in part by the culturally evolved rules that he does not understand. We may accept, with Hayek, that such behavioural rules probably do emerge slowly in a process that is in many respects analogous to natural selection.

The question to be addressed in this section is one that was answered by assertion and not analyzed in section IV above, and it concerns the size of the allowable set of institutional-constitutional reform proposals. How confining are the culturally evolved rules for behaviour that we find ourselves to be saddled with, for better or for worse? If "human nature" is, indeed, a "relatively absolute absolute," for purposes of analyzing institutional-constitutional alternatives, does not this imply, also, that there is a relatively narrow, and perhaps even unique, set of such alternatives that will meet "efficiency" criteria?

To this point I have been able to avoid defining "efficiency" in the overall sense of application to an economy or a polity. It is no longer possible to do this since the answers to the questions posed immediately above depend critically on the definition that is adopted. If "efficiency" is defined in terms of an objectively measurable and objectively identifiable value indicator, there would be a *unique* set of institutions for economic-political interaction that would maximize the indicator, given the relatively absolute absolute rule for behaviour that describes the reaction-responses of individuals to their circumstances. In such a setting, the suggested distinction between the restrictions imposed by "human nature" and those that might be imposed by institutional constraints loses most, if not all, of its usefulness. Hayek could have, in this sort of setting, reserved his criticism for those who might seek other objectives than maximization of the relevant value indicator (which need not of course be limited to simple economic value as ordinarily measured). There would have been little or no reason to talk about those constructivists who disregard the limits of man as he exists.

The distinction here takes on more usefulness, however, when the existence of such a value indicator that objectively measures efficiency of the economy-polity is categorically rejected. The alternative definition for efficiency relies in no way on the existence of such a measure. Instead, "efficiency" is defined as "that which tends to emerge from the voluntary agreement among persons in the relevant group." This definition becomes the only one possible unless it is presumed that the subjective evaluation of individuals is objectively known to external observers or that the evaluations relevant to efficiency are to be divorced from individual evaluations altogether. Once we define efficiency by voluntary agreement, however, we must allow for the non-uniqueness of the set of rules and institutions that may satisfy "efficiency criteria." Since that which is efficient is that which emerges from agreement, and not vice versa, we cannot restrict or limit the range of agreement to a unique outcome.

This point is so simple that it is often overlooked. Consider two traders, each initially endowed with a stock of a single "good," one with apples, the other with oranges. There is no *unique* result of the trading process that can be objectively identified as such. A whole set of outcomes will satisfy the efficiency criterion. In orthodox economic theory, the outcome can be shown to approach uniqueness in the limit as the numbers of traders on both sides of the exchange approach infinity. But for purposes of the analysis of "exchange agreements" on institutional changes, this general-equilibrium emphasis on uniqueness tends to be seriously misleading. As noted earlier, "publicness" is necessarily embodied in institutions. Hence, if efficiency criteria are to incorporate individual evaluations, all individuals must be brought into the relevant "exchange," and agreement among all these must be the only meaningful conceptual test.

Hayek's criticism of the rational constructivist can be interpreted in this light as an appeal to restrict proposals for institutional-constitutional changes to those that are possible, given the limits of human nature as it exists. To participate in the ongoing dialogue-discussion of constitutional alternatives and to advance proposals that fail to recognize man for what he is, this participation becomes equivalent to proposing that we transcend ordinary laws of logic or science. The difference lies in the immediacy of feedback in the latter cases, a feedback that may only occur after disastrous social experimentation in the former. The fools are not nearly so readily exposed, and it remains always possible that agreement will be reached (at least among a relevant decision-making group) on the introduction of social changes that would require some being other than ordinary man in order to generate the outcomes that are promised.

Tragedy of major proportions has, of course, been the result of such experiments throughout history. But political man especially remains the romantic fool, as Frank Knight emphasized, and we need the essential wisdom of the scholars like Hayek and Sowell to warn us against our own romanticism. But on balance it would surely have been more accurate for Hayek to have warned us all against the "romantic constructivist," since, properly interpreted, a "rational constructivist" stance must be taken if institutional reform, even within the relatively narrowed Hayekian limits, is to be seriously examined.

PART FIVE

Economists, Efficiency, and the Law

Good Economics—Bad Law

One of the most interesting developments in American higher education over the past decade has been the emerging recognition by lawyers that an understanding of elementary economic principles is a vital component in their professional equipment. This recognition has prompted the current quest by law schools for economists close enough to the institutional world to offer practical assistance. The Law School of the University of Chicago occupies a unique place in this development. Its heritage of resident economists—Henry Simons, Aaron Director, Ronald Coase (along with their economics department colleagues, notably George Stigler and Gary Becker)—has begun to pay dividends, and Chicago-trained lawyer-economists—Gordon Tullock, Henry Manne, Richard Posner—have been in the forefront of the law-economics intersection. Posner's *Economic Analysis of Law*[1] is the latest and most comprehensive attempt to marry these two sometimes contrary approaches to social interaction.

In assessing Posner's book, I have conducted the following mental experiment. I assume that Posner's book is widely adopted as textual material in first-year law school courses. (This is the author's purpose, and "textbook-ishness" sometimes detracts from the argument.) I assume, further, that the students are well motivated, diligent, and intelligent, and that they permanently retain the elementary economic principles that Posner teaches.[2] What

From *Virginia Law Review* 60 (Spring 1974): 483–92. Reprinted by permission of the publisher.

The author is indebted to Winston Bush, Gordon Tullock, and Richard Wagner for helpful suggestions.

1. Richard Posner, *Economic Analysis of Law* (1972), hereinafter cited as Posner.

2. Empirical studies concerning post-university retention of economic principles suggest that this is, indeed, a heroic assumption. These studies have suggested that exposure

will be the effects on those lawyers who later find themselves in positions of decision-making power, as judges, as legislators, as administrators, as legal scholars and educators who will themselves write other books and train still other lawyers?

The results of my mental experiment may be summarized briefly. Considered on a case-by-case basis, legal decisions would indeed be improved if those charged with authority should be made cognizant of economic principles. By accepted *pragmatic* criteria, the intrusion of economics into law gets, and deserves, high marks. Good economics, Chicago-style, which is what Posner teaches, is better than no economics or the bad economics picked up all too readily from the charlatans and the journalists on the fringes of the academy.

But the application of good economics (or bad) takes place within a legal setting. If this setting is considered invariant, pragmatic criteria are, of course, controlling. If, however, broader *philosophical* criteria are introduced, the law, itself, must be evaluated, and good economics applied within a bad or misguided conception of legal process need not promote the structural, procedural changes that may be urgently required. It is in this respect that Posner's work fails my test. The jurisprudential setting or framework within which his whole economic analysis of law is placed does not seem to have been critically examined.

I shall try to defend this "good economics–bad law" theme in the two sections that follow. In so doing, I am, of course, rewriting all the rules of the reviewing game. As a professionally trained economist, who shares a Chicago heritage (pre-empirical), these rules would dictate primary critical attention on the economic analysis, per se, with acquiescence on the embodied conception of legal process, presumably on the grounds that the latter is best left for the lawyers to criticize. But law is far too important to be left to the lawyers, especially since lawyers come increasingly to man the corridors of Leviathan.

---

to basic economics has little, if any, discernible effect on attitudes toward important economic issues only a few years after the learning experience. Perhaps it is plausible to suggest that budding young lawyers would be more professionally motivated. And, in addition, the elementary economics that they would learn from Posner would be superior in content to that taught in the average university course in the subject.

I

Posner's procedure is to apply hard-nosed, and often quite sophisticated, price theory to a long series of topics, all of which fall within the legal lexicon. Chapters are devoted to property, contracts, crimes and torts, monopoly, antitrust, labor, public utilities, price controls, corporations, capital markets, income distribution, taxes, poverty, federalism, and racial discrimination, along with less specifically "economic" subject matter. Posner's overriding purpose is to demonstrate that economic principles can offer guidelines for the legal resolution of conflicting claims, for the enactment of new legislation, and for the interpretation of existing statutes. Why does economics offer such valuable assistance here, aside from the trivial acknowledgment that more information is always better than less? At this point care must be taken to distinguish between positive economic analysis and the advancement of the efficiency norm that is often associated with this analysis. The latter, which involves an explicit value judgment, need not accompany the former. Posner does not fully appreciate this potential separability, and the efficiency criterion is too enthusiastically endorsed. Indeed, he is forced to justify abrogation of this criterion only by resort to an indirect reinstatement. For ordinary crimes, theft and rape for example, he is somewhat reluctantly willing to allow unconditional legal deterrence on the grounds that freely negotiated exchanges could emerge voluntarily in such cases if, in fact, the value to the "seller" falls below that value to the "buyer." That is to say, if the benefits secured by the potential rapist exceed the losses suffered by the potential victim, mutual gains from exchange should exist, and such trades should take place. Posner is trapped into this argument, which to me approaches absurdity, because of his insistence on the relatively unlimited applicability of the maximum value or efficiency criterion. The very bringing of criminal charges indicates a departure from maximum value, and, for this reason, suggests the necessity of some replacement of the maximum value criterion for legal resolution.

Despite the questionable normative status assigned to maximum value or efficiency, Posner's results can be interpreted in such a way as to make them more generally acceptable. Maximum value need not be adopted as the end objective. It may, instead, be assessed as an instrument to be used in attaining other objectives. It may be shown to be consistent with precepts of social order, with observable legality, precepts that are more in keeping with law's functional role. Posner recognizes this more general conception when he states:

> If the law fails to allocate responsibilities between the parties in such a way as to maximize value, the parties will, by an additional and not costless transaction, nullify the legal allocation.[3]

In somewhat broader and less emphatic terms, this can be interpreted as a lawyer's statement of the most basic of all economic principles: When mutual gains are present, parties will be motivated to initiate trades with a view to capturing the potentially realizable surplus value. Attempts to shut off or to forestall trade when mutuality of gain exists encourage costly evasions. The very legality of society itself may be seriously eroded if those who make collective decisions fail to understand this elementary consequence of the economists' teaching.

An example lies close at hand, one to which Posner's analysis and approach could be readily applied. Faced with a disruption in the normal channels of fuels supply, and especially in the face of a rapidly increasing demand for energy, many American politicians in late 1973 (most of whom are lawyers) commenced to talk seriously about the prospects of imposing mandatory controls over the allocation of supplies and about the subsequent necessity for rationing heating oil and gasoline among potential demanders. The chaos that any full-scale attempt to introduce such "solutions" must create could be understood and predicted by the decision-maker trained on Posner's book who retained his critical faculties. In predicting the stress put on social order by a regime of controlled prices and rationed allocations, this lawyer (be he judge, legislator, bureaucrat, or presidential adviser) need not place an overriding value on economic efficiency per se. But his elementary understanding of positive economic analysis would cause him to recognize more fully the genuine social costs of any such policy.

With such knowledge, the decision-maker should be motivated to search for and to support institutional alternatives which generate less social tension, less evasion of postulated standards of conduct, more general adher-

---

3. Posner, 99.

ence to legal norms. Law and legislation that are thoroughly informed by good economics will be based on an understanding of the market's function in maintaining social order, which is *not* primarily that of insuring efficiency, or maximizing value, as measured in market-determined prices. (The efficiency norm may, of course, assume secondary importance in its own right.) The market economy's socio-political function is that of *minimizing* the necessity of resorting to internal ethical constraints on human behavior and/or external legal-governmental-political restrictions. To the extent that men are allowed freely to trade, conceived in the broadest possible sense of this term, there is little need for the preacher or the administrative authority. In the example noted, if market pricing is allowed, and encouraged, to ration limited fuel supplies among potential users, the success of exhortations to voluntary behavior aimed at meeting "social needs" need not be of critical importance. Nor, when such exhortations fail, need they be replaced by overt legal restrictions on behavior, restrictions which will invite evasion, and which will serve to penalize the law-abiding and the nonclever law violators while benefiting those who are successful in accomplishing mutually gainful "trades" despite the artificial institutional barriers.

The distributional consequences of pure market pricing in the face of unanticipated reductions in normal supplies of a vital commodity may be deemed undesirable; the efficiency guaranteed by market pricing need not be the only criterion for policy. Good economics will, however, offer guidelines even to the lawyer-legislator who places distributional equity very high on his personal value scale. He may opt in favor of legislation that would introduce what is essentially a double currency in the allocation of limited supplies; individuals might be assigned specific ration points (although the criteria for determining the allocation must be largely arbitrary). So long as these ration points may themselves be freely traded, and market prices for them established, major social disruption may be avoided. Efficiency in allocation will be insured simultaneously with the attainment of any distributive result that may be desired by the decision-makers.

I have discussed the fuels allocation problem both for its current policy relevance and for an illustration of how good economics might greatly facilitate the making of public decisions, independent of the choice of ultimate social objectives. Posner's book would provide the lawyer-*cum*-politician with the basic economic analysis required here, although his attempt to be inclusive in his array of applications tends to distract attention away from the central principle that is embodied almost universally. This is not to suggest that Posner's book will fully substitute for more rigorous and careful economics texts, and that the lawyer who is trained on this book need not seek out the advice and counsel of the professionally trained economist. Posner does make errors, most of which are relatively minor and not worth noting here. In addition, his discussion of specific topics is sometimes unsophisticated (e.g., taxation). There is one ambiguity that warrants correction. Posner appears to confuse the productivity of resources in securing and maintaining monopoly positions, resources devoted to "monopolizing," with the productivity of resources in producing outputs in industries that are monopolized. The social productivity of the first of these investments is clearly negative; the social productivity of the second is higher than that of comparable resources in competitive industries.

A more important limitation is that imposed by the strict Chicago economics that Posner espouses. At the outset of his book[4] he dismisses modern welfare economics, which he calls "'Pareto optimality' and the like," as vocabulary and jargon, something to be carefully distinguished from "positive economic analysis." But it is precisely the problems posed in modern welfare economics that force the economist to come to grips with the basic issues in political and legal philosophy. As the discussion in Part II will suggest, a failure to appreciate these issues is the major criticism to be levied against the book as a whole, something which might well have been avoided by a willingness to move beyond the provincialism of post-Knightian Chicago economics into the sometimes murky waters of "Pareto optimality and the like."

II

There is a normative theory of law in Posner's book, over and beyond the series of economic applications. Posner's interpretation of legal history suggests that the common law, as it has developed, has been at least indirectly guided by the efficiency criterion of orthodox economists, a criterion which assumes special significance in Posner's scale of values, as I have pre-

4. Ibid., x.

viously noted. By implication, therefore, judge-made common law is superior to legislation, the decisions that emerge from the activities of politicians. This theory bears an apparent resemblance to that advanced by the late Bruno Leoni,[5] whom Posner does not cite. Leoni argued persuasively for the superiority of "law" over "legislation," developing in the process the interesting analogy between the structure of law, the legal order, that emerges from the separate decision-making of independent judges (governed by precedent, but without the uniformity imposed by any "supreme" court) and the spontaneous economic order that emerges from the separate decision-making of independent demanders and suppliers, each of whom acts on the basis of the limited information set that he confronts. The result, in both cases, is an order willed by no single decision-maker.

Leoni's distinction between law and legislation is not, however, that which is suggested in Posner's work. Leoni's categorization grew out of a profound philosophically based conservatism grounded on a sharp functional differentiation. The object of the never-ending search by independently acting and loosely coordinated judges is to find "the law," to locate and to redefine the structure of individual rights, not *ab initio*, but in existing social-institutional arrangements. The working of "law," as an activity, is not guided by nor should it be guided by explicit criteria for "social improvement." Law, in this vision, is a stabilizing institution providing the necessary framework within which individuals can plan their own affairs predictably and with minimal external interferences. To Leoni, legislation is functionally different in that its very purpose must be one of securing or implementing explicit social or collective objectives. This is the process through which politically organized groups of persons supply "public goods" to themselves.

One need not share Leoni's basic distrust of politicians and ordinary political processes to appreciate the relevance of the categorical distinction that he made. Nonetheless, an absence of this appreciation mars Posner's work, with the consequence that the implied theory of law becomes quite different from that of Leoni, which I have summarized briefly. In his array of economic applications, Posner appears to offer potential advice and counsel to future judges and legislators alike. But lawyers finding themselves in the role

5. Bruno Leoni, *Freedom and the Law* (1961).

of jurists should act differently from lawyers-*cum*-legislators. The divergent choice settings suggest that criteria for "good" decisions would be identical only by accident.

For the legislator, the solid economics which Posner teaches can be of great assistance. Regardless of social objectives, the "public goods" that he conceives himself to be promoting or producing through new or amended legislation, knowledge of the economic effects of alternative proposals will be helpful in constructing potentially workable schemes for change.

For the jurist, there should be relatively little comparable value of the economics input, save in the pragmatic sense noted earlier and elaborated below. Faced with the necessity of resolving a conflict among parties over the appropriate delineation of rights, should the judge invoke the efficiency criterion of the economist, either directly or in an instrumental sense? If he is to invoke *any* extra-legal criteria, a case might be made out for the economic, as I have tried to do in Part I of this paper. But is it not "bad law" to suggest that the judge be guided in his decision-making by criteria other than those offered in the existing institutional setting that he confronts? Precedent, custom, tradition, expected ways of doing things, predicted patterns of behavior—these intra-legal criteria provide ample searching ground for the imaginative jurist even in hard cases, criteria that are wholly consistent with the functional role of the jurist.

An example may be helpful. Monopoly is a recognized source of inefficiency in an economy, with relatively few offsetting social virtues. Informed by this knowledge, it becomes appropriate for the legislator to consider, and possibly to support, antimonopoly statutes. If he is successful in the complex set of political negotiations that characterizes representative legislative assemblies, such statutes may finally be enacted into law. And the law so enacted that emerges from a legislature composed of economically sophisticated lawyer-politicians will be "better" than that which emerges from a legislature that is peopled by unsophisticated lawyer-politicians. Suppose now, however, that no antimonopoly statute exists and that none has ever existed. A disgruntled consumer-purchaser brings suit against a producing-selling firm that is alleged to have attained a monopoly position, an allegation that is factually supportable, although no overt predatory action vis-à-vis other firms, existing or potential, is in evidence. Should the judge, informed by economic principle, effectively change the basic law so as to promote efficiency? Posner would apparently have the judge outlaw monopoly in such a situation[6] on the grounds that the transactions costs barrier would inhibit the effective organization of potential purchasers who could, if organized, strike a bargain with the monopoly firm. The existence of major transactions costs thresholds may be acknowledged in such cases, however, without the justification of explicit judicial intrusion into the legislative process. The situation calls for legislative action, the role designed for and fulfilled by politicians who putatively represent the interests of all parties in the community, potential consumers and producers alike.[7] It seems self-evident to me that the judge should not change the basic law because, in such behavior, he would be explicitly abandoning his role of jurist for that of legislator. He would be "making law," and regardless of the criteria which guide his decisions, his action is unbounded by the complex pull and haul of representation among separate interests, the very center of democratic process. In saying that the jurist should enforce existing law rather than enact new legislation, I am, of course, aware of the absence of any firm dividing line between these in any empirical or descriptive sense. I also recognize that the hierarchical structure of the American court system promotes rather than retards judicial intrusion into legislative process. My emphasis is on the desirability of keeping the two conceptually distinct, despite the practical difficulties that may be confronted.

Unfortunately, Posner's failure to make the vital distinction between the different functional roles that lawyers often occupy is not something uniquely attributable to him. Relatively few scholars in our law schools and our universities, and still fewer persons among working politicians and jurists, seem to understand the basic structure of *constitutional* democracy. This structure involves a conceptual separation between (1) the constitution, which defines the rights of persons and groups to do things and defines the rules under which collective decisions are to be made, (2) the institutions of "the law," which adjudicate the conflicting claims made within this set of rights and rules, and (3) the collective decision-making process of the ordi-

---

6. See Posner, 20–30.

7. For an elaboration of my position in the context of Coase-like examples, see Buchanan, "The Institutional Structure of Externality," *Public Choice* 14 (1973): 69.

nary legislative variety, which presumably promotes "public good," but again within the rules laid down in the constitution.[8] The contractual processes which ideally characterize (1) and (3), both of which may be interpreted as "legislation," despite the differing elements of structure, should, as a matter of course, satisfy the criterion of efficiency or maximum value appropriately defined. The problem arises when the jurist, abandoning his role in (2), attempts to intervene in either the first or third process, either in constitution-making or in producing "public goods."

Recognition of this gives me pause in what could be an otherwise unqualified endorsement of the developing interface between law and economics. If lawyers, and law schools, seek to introduce more economic theory into their training in order to become more informed potential legislators and advisors to legislators, my support remains unqualified and enthusiastic. If, however, they seek to become and to train potential jurists who are instructed to have no qualms about legislating for us all, the pragmatic improvements that result might forestall rather than hasten the changes in jurisprudential attitudes that are essential for a return to operative constitutional democracy. My mental experiment leads me to think about the potential excesses of a "Posner court" in the 1980s and 1990s, guided by its extra-legal criterion of "maximum value." Would such a court be comparable to the Warren Court in the generation of social unrest and disorder? Neither "maximum value" nor "social justice" is acceptable as a criterion for judicial decision because both are derived extra-legally; that is, independent of the effective constitutional rules in being, rules that may be modified only at a different and higher stage of social decision-making. The opportunity costs of introducing more sophisticated economics into legal training may be measured in the lost opportunities for attaining a better appreciation of fundamental constitutional precepts. On balance, "good political and legal philosophy" would surely hold its own against "good economics," if indeed this could be the choice

---

8. This distinction is elaborated in J. Buchanan and G. Tullock, *The Calculus of Consent: Logical Foundations of Constitutional Democracy* (1962). In a forthcoming book, I examine more specifically the necessity of role separation between those who act for the "Protective State," the jurists, and those who act on behalf of the "Productive State," the legislators. See J. Buchanan, *The Limits of Liberty: Between Anarchy and Leviathan* (1974) (to be published).

of alternatives. Unfortunately, given that the mind-set in modern academia probably precludes the teaching of "good legal philosophy" anywhere, the "good economics," which tenuously holds on even if in isolation from mainstream ideology, should dominate the alternatives in any practical curriculum decision.

Comment

I like this paper. Public choice, or the economic approach to politics, has long needed an analysis of the judicial branch of the governmental structure, and the Landes-Posner paper represents a good start in that direction.[1]

I share with the authors a rejection of the notion that the judiciary's role is one of representing the underrepresented groups in the political process. I join in their criticism of the romantic view that the members of the judiciary are the unique guardians of some mystical "public interest," something that is wholly ignored by other branches of government. Closely related to this, and perhaps even more relevant, I share with Landes and Posner the view that ethical norms should not be determining factors in judicial decisions.

From this common vantage point, it follows that I should be broadly sympathetic with the theory of the judicial branch developed by Landes and Posner. But there remain some differences, or rather difficulties with the paper as it now stands.

I am not willing to go all the way with an interest-group model for legislation and to label all enactments as special-interest benefits "purchased" by successful coalitions, achieved at net costs to losing coalitions. There is no doubt but that much of political activity can be explained by such a model. But I should not want to attribute this characteristic to all legislation. I am sure that this is not the intent of Landes and Posner, but this impression might well be gained from a hurried reading of their paper. Some legislation, some of the activity of legislative bodies, is surely aimed at the supply of

From *Journal of Law and Economics* 18 (December 1975): 903–5. Reprinted by permission of the publisher.

1. William M. Landes and Richard A. Posner, "The Independent Judiciary in an Interest-Group Perspective," *Journal of Law and Economics* 18 (1975): 875.

genuinely "public goods," by which I mean the collective provision and financing of goods and services jointly to all members of the community, and in such fashion that all or substantially all secure net gains. To acknowledge this need not modify the Landes-Posner role for an independent judiciary since, even when genuinely public goods are provided which benefit all groups, there may be major distributional differences in alternative financing schemes.

But there is a more basic problem. In my own conception (which I acknowledge to be an abstraction that must be forced on a possibly different empirical reality), the "rules" are fixed. The rules of the game, embodied in the effective "constitution" (whether codified or not) qualify as "relatively absolute absolutes" in the sense discussed by Frank Knight and Henry Simons. Ideally, these rules should be changed explicitly by constitutional amendment, and neither by ordinary legislatures nor by courts. Ideally, legislatures simply carry out productive activity that is allowed under the rules, under the law, activity that involves the provision of those goods and services that can best be provided and/or financed jointly. Ideally, courts interpret and enforce the rules, both for private parties and for legislative and executive branches of government.

I share fully with Landes and Posner the view that it is inappropriate for courts to change the rules, regardless of ethical content. But Landes and Posner seem to imply that ordinary legislation does involve basic rules changes. This is where I may differ most sharply with them. Ordinary legislatures, characterized often by the struggle among competing interest-group coalitions within some ultimate majority rule constraints, should not be empowered to modify the basic law of the polity any more than should the courts or the executive.

In fact, of course, administrative-executive agencies, courts, and ordinary legislatures do modify the rules, the basic law of the land. The effective constitution is changed by all branches, and we could scarcely expect anything different. But the normative abstractions that we impose on the actual workings of an imperfect political world are important themselves in placing limits on action. My own view is, therefore, somewhat more favorable to an independent judiciary than that of Landes and Posner. I want an independent judiciary to enforce the rules that exist, however these might have emerged. I want this judiciary to restrict the actions of legislative bodies and administrative agencies that try to modify these rules when they are not legitimately empowered to do so. This role for the judiciary extends further than the Landes-Posner one of forcing legislative and executive branches to keep past commitments. I want the courts to start once again to take a hard look at the constitutionality of legislative and executive actions, but in terms of the existing rules of the game, and not in terms of the judges' own social or ethical ideals. The tragedy of Earl Warren's court lay not in its activism but in its avowal of a role for the judiciary that is wholly inconsistent with the structure of constitutional democracy.

Many of my statements are explicitly normative. And this points to a matter of concern that arises with respect to the Landes-Posner paper, to some of my own work, and to much other work in the area covered in this conference. How do we separate normative and positive elements of analysis? In the Landes-Posner paper, how much of their analysis can be interpreted as explaining the political structure that we observe and how much can be interpreted as normative argument for that structure which might exist?

In a strictly positivist framework, the analysis does yield implications that may be tested, and it is possible that over a sequence of rejected hypotheses the basic paradigm might be modified. Many actions of the courts, and especially of the last quarter century, are not consistent with the role for the judiciary in the Landes-Posner model. But as and if we observe judges increasingly trying to promote their own private versions of "public good" should we modify our paradigm? Descriptively, scientifically, we must do so. But we may still hold fast to a normative description of the judicial role, to a paradigm that is consistent with "democratic values" in a more inclusive sense. The demonstration of this consistency is, itself, a part of positive analysis. But it is also normative argument, and, as such, valuable in the ongoing discussion of public philosophy. Through such analyses as that of Landes and Posner, we may explain why the public and the elected politicians should want a politically independent and ethically neutral judiciary, but we must also allow for the possibility that the judiciary which we observe has strayed beyond rationally desired limits.

I have found it useful to think of the basic rules, of the law, as public capital.[2] This economic dimension makes us think about the quasi-permanent

---

2. See James M. Buchanan, *The Limits of Liberty: Between Anarchy and Leviathan* (1975).

nature of law, about a whole sequence of periods in which income is yielded, about the necessity for maintaining the stock in order to maintain the income yield, about the dangers of allowing the stock to depreciate or to erode. The Landes-Posner role for the judiciary can be readily discussed within this metaphor. But the modern political science or Warren Court model of a judiciary which they criticize cannot, by any stretch of the imagination, be made consistent with a "public capital" conception of law.

Economists may be easily convinced. But this is not the problem. The Warren Court attitude informs far too many of our legal scholars, our lawyers, and our judges. We must, I fear, experience still further erosion in the public capital stock that our basic law represents before the reeducation process (which may only now be in its beginning stages) can have an appreciable effect.

Politics, Property, and the Law

An Alternative Interpretation
of *Miller et al. v. Schoene*

Warren Samuels has used the fascinating case of *Miller et al. v. Schoene*[1] as a vehicle for presenting his conception of the interrelationships between politico-legal and economic processes.[2] I share with Samuels the methodological conviction that only by moving beyond the narrowly conceived limits of economic theory and into the examination of the political, legal, and social constraints within which economic actions are bounded can we hope to unravel much of the confusion that currently describes the discussion of concrete policy issues. I differ profoundly with Samuels, however, on the theory of politics, property, and law that his interpretation implies. The arguments in *Miller et al. v. Schoene* may be examined from a different conception of the functional role of judicial process, of legislation in democracy, and of the appropriate means through which tolerable efficiency can be attained in a regime of economic interdependency.

Classificatory labels are subject to oversimplification, but for purposes of casual identification, my approach is that of the political economist who in-

From *Journal of Law and Economics* 15 (October 1972): 439–52. Reprinted by permission of the publisher.

I am indebted to Professors Roland N. McKean, W. Craig Stubblebine, and Gordon Tullock for helpful comments on an earlier draft.

1. 276 U.S. 272 (1928).

2. Warren J. Samuels, "Interrelations Between Legal and Economic Processes," *Journal of Law and Economics* 14 (1971): 435. For a more comprehensive statement of Samuels' methodological position, see his *Welfare Economics, Power, and Property* (Michigan State University, 1971, mimeographed).

terprets Paretian criteria in essentially Wicksellian terms and who can be described, somewhat more broadly, as falling within what has been called the "Virginia school."[3] By contrast, Samuels' approach is more consistent with post-Pigovian welfare economics, and notably with reliance on "social welfare functions" to provide guidance to the governmental authorities, treated as independent from the citizenry.

I

The following excerpts from Samuels' paper summarize the facts:

> *Miller et al. v. Schoene* is a case which involves red cedar and apple trees and their respective owners; and cedar rust, a plant disease whose first phase is spent while the fungus resides upon its host, the chiefly ornamental red cedar tree, which is not harmed by the cedar rust. The fungus does have a severely adverse effect upon the apple tree during a second phase, attacking its leaves and fruit. The legislature of the state of Virginia in 1914 passed a statute which empowered the state entomologist to investigate and, if necessary, condemn and destroy without compensation certain red cedar trees within a two-mile radius of an apple orchard.[4] *Miller et al.*, plaintiffs in error in the instant case, unsuccessfully brought suit in state courts, and sued to reverse the decision of the Supreme Court of Appeals in Virginia. The arguments for the plaintiffs in error were basically simple and direct, as well as of profound heuristic value. Their main contention was that the legislature was, unconstitutionally in their view, attempting to take or destroy their property to the advantage of the apple orchard owners.[5]

In Samuels' interpretation, the Virginia legislature and, ultimately, the Supreme Court "had to make a judgment as to which owner would be visited with injury and which protected."[6]

The legislature chose to favor the apple growers and to penalize the owners of the red cedar groves. The courts upheld the legislature in this action.

---

3. See Mancur Olson and Christopher Clague, "Dissent in Economics," *Social Research* 38 (Winter, 1971): 753.

4. Samuels, "Interrelations," 436.

5. Ibid., 436–37.

6. Ibid., 438–39.

According to Samuels, the result was an "effective new law of property."[7] An unforeseen and unpredicted natural event, the emergence of red cedar rust, necessitated State intervention and State decision, one way or the other. When previously existing rights to property are challenged by any party, the State, acting through its legislative-cum-judicial arms and agencies, must, willy-nilly, make a choice among conflicting claimants. Presumably, the State will be guided in its deliberations and in its decision by the relative pressure of divergent economic interests responsibly exerted. Samuels places his trust in the emergence of the measurably superior benefit even without the necessity of compensation. This approach offers a significant role for the cost-benefit analyst who may, presumably, measure relative monetary values independent of distributional consequences, and whose results will be, or should be, used by the legislator-cum-judge in his attempt at reaching a "correct" decision.

II

My quarrel with Samuels is more fundamental, however, than that which is inherent in reconciling outcomes of a collective decision-making process with those that might be classified as "efficient" by some idealized economic observer. Samuels appeals too readily to state decision-making which, in its very nature, forestalls the exchange or market-like pressures toward internalizing the interdependencies that may arise as exogenous elements to modify the overall social environment. There is, of course, no guarantee that the State will select that alternative which maximizes the values of the social product, and, even when this concern is dropped, there is nothing in the Samuels model which allows for the mutuality of gains that is part-and-parcel of an economic approach to social interaction.

The owners of adjoining plots of land coexisted peaceably before the onset of red cedar rust, a natural event that was not foreseen. There was no explicit economic interdependence between persons growing apple trees and those growing red cedar trees, and, with reference to this subset of the population, the system was on the Pareto efficiency frontier. That is to say, before the fungus, there existed no potential trades or agreements among the apple growers

7. Ibid.

and the cedar growers that remained unexploited. A natural event then occurred. The new fungus, which did not damage the cedar trees on which it
grew, did threaten severe damage to the apple trees. Between the owners of
apple orchards and the owners of red cedar lands a new interdependence
emerged. Potential gains-from-trade should have existed that would have allowed this interdependence to be eliminated. Before such "trade" could be
undertaken, however, individual participants would have had to be certain
as to their property rights. Presumably, in the case at hand, the structure of
rights in existence did not allow the apple grower to destroy diseased cedar
trees on neighboring lands. The set of "previously existing rights" allowed
the red cedar owners to grow diseased trees safe from molestation by damaged apple growers. This was acknowledged by all parties.[8]

This description of the historical setting should not, however, imply that
there was here, or ever is, a unique means of delineating property rights. It
could have been that the rights of cedar growers extended only to the nurture
of undiseased trees, and/or, conversely, the rights of apple growers could
have been defined in terms of the nurture of healthy trees, which might have
included the right to eliminate all neighborhood interferences. The principle
to be emphasized, however, is that *some* structure, *any* structure, of well-
defined rights is a necessary starting point for the potential "trades" that are
required to remove the newly emergent interdependence. When an unpredicted environmental change occurs, the structure of rights may, of course,
contain ambiguities and possibly alternative definitions. In such case, it becomes an appropriate and necessary task for the courts to lay down the precise limits of allowable actions by the parties in question. In this behavior,
however, the courts are "locating the limits" that exist in "the law"; they are
not, and they must not be seen to be, defining *new* limits or changing pre-
existing ones. The courts clarify ambiguities; they lend precision; they draw

8. One caveat must be introduced at this point. The evidence for the acknowledged
acceptance of previously existing rights lies in the absence of legal claims made by single
apple growers against cedar landowners. If the conditions outlined in Part III, below,
should have been present, however, no single apple grower might have been willing to
make the investment required to initiate legal action, which, had it been taken, might have
resulted in a modified definition of existing rights. For purposes of the more general purposes of my discussion in this paper, it seems best to assume that such a modified definition would not have been forthcoming.

black and white lines in gray areas. Once they have done so, the ground is laid for the emergence of those agreements which can serve to internalize the interdependence. If there should have been some confusion over the rights of the apple growers and the cedar growers under the "previously-existing law," the courts, but *not* the legislative arm of the Commonwealth of Virginia, should have been called upon for resolution. No dispute arose at this level, however; all parties were agreed on the precise structure of rights inherent in "the law" as it stood.

The model can be clarified if we think initially of the interaction between a single apple grower and a single cedar landowner. Once cedar rust was recognized to exist, it was to the apparent advantage of the orchard owner to initiate possible action to purchase or to lease the adjacent cedar land, to purchase the standing cedar, or to compensate the cedar grower for cutting his trees. A region of potential mutual gain existed, and bargains might have been struck which would have moved the solution toward the efficiency surface, possibly forestalled only by recalcitrant bargaining strategy on the part of one or both of the parties. In the trading process, of course, both parties would have secured gains over and above those secured in the post-fungus disequilibrium. Mutual agreement should have signaled mutual gain.

Consider the contrast between this procedure and that which is implicit in Samuels' discussion. Here the apple grower appealed directly to the State, and the State decided just which one of the two claims was to be favored. The issue became strictly one of *either/or*. The informational requirements for decision immediately arise. How could the damage to the apple crop be estimated as against the damage to the value of cedar trees from premature cutting? In this instance, the "expert," the Virginia entomologist, was called upon to make a determination. This tends to prejudice the general argument in Samuels' favor. In most economic interdependencies, there are no "experts," and there are likely to be major errors in any cost-benefit estimates. More importantly, even if the testimony of expert witnesses be introduced, who can claim that the collective decision-makers will, or should, follow their advice?

Note that, when the parties are allowed freely to bargain and to reach mutually satisfactory agreements, the apple grower's *own* assessment of probable damage to his crop becomes the measure of his own maximum payment to secure the elimination of the danger. On the other side, the cedar grower's *own* estimate of the value of his standing trees over and above their value as cut trees becomes the basis for his possible willingness to accept or to reject preferred compensations. The equity or inequity of compensation is irrelevant; what is relevant is the necessary place of compensation in the trading process between the two parties. Only when transfers are actually made can relative values be measured by those whose interests are directly involved.

If the number of apple orchard owners in every fungus area was small, there should have been no action taken by the collectivity so long as the previously existing structure of rights was well defined. The efficient solution could have been depended on to emerge from the interaction between the parties in each interdependence. In the tradition of classical political economy, the forces of self-interest could have been relied on to generate an outcome that would tend to maximize the value of social product. There is no means of determining whether this would have resulted in a cutting of the red cedar groves or the continued infestation of apple trees by cedar rust.[9]

III

If, however, the numbers on the apple grower side of the interactions in question should have been large, or beyond critical "small-number" limits, the familiar free-rider obstructions to voluntarily negotiated solutions might have arisen. In this situation, there might have remained a functional role for collective action. The legislative arm of the collectivity might have intervened, and it is possible for us to interpret the actual events of *Miller et al. v. Schoene* in this, quite different framework.

If, for example, there should have been *n* apple orchard owners involved in an interdependence with a single red cedar landowner, there might have been no voluntary agreement reached, despite the possibly relatively superior value of an undiseased apple yield. It might not have been to the economic advantage of any single grower to initiate agreements with the cedar landowner, or to make unilateral payments to this landowner in exchange for usage of the land. There would have been no means, in this case, through

9. In this small-number setting, the same result should have been predicted to emerge, regardless of the existent structure of rights. On this, see R. H. Coase, "The Problem of Social Cost," *Journal of Law and Economics* 3 (1960): 1.

which the single orchardman could have *excluded* his fellows from the enjoy-ment of the disease reduction that his own action might procure from the cedar landowner. Reduction in cedar rust would have been, in this situation, a purely "public good," in the modern usage of this term, to the community of apple growers involved in the particular interaction. Resort to collective or joint action might have been dictated.[10] The possible reason lies in the dual interdependencies that this setting involved; one, that between each apple grower and the cedarman or men, and, two, that among the separate apple growers themselves. The first of these interdependencies could have been re-moved by freely negotiated trades in the absence of the second. The presence of the second or public-goods interdependence, however, might well have prohibited the negotiation of a solution to the former.[11]

The failure of negotiated settlements to emerge, however, would have been consistent with continuing inefficiency only under a particular as-sumption about the land ownership pattern among apple growers. Only if this pattern was invariant would the public-goods dilemma have inhibited negotiated internalization. That is to say, if in each interaction there should have been a number of apple growers sufficient to have created a potential

10. Individual adjustment equilibria may be inefficient in all cases where there are large numbers of apple growers in a single interaction, regardless of the structure of prop-erty rights. A change in the distribution of rights will, however, change the direction of the allocative bias. To show this, assume that the cedar landowner had no right to grow diseased trees, and that destruction of such trees was enforceable on petition to the courts. In this instance, petition by any single apple grower would have been sufficient to initiate action. Each apple grower would, therefore, have been placed in a highly favorable stra-tegic bargaining position vis-à-vis the cedar landowner. The cedars would probably have been destroyed under these legal arrangements even if their premature cutting involved damages considerably in excess of that to the apple crops. For an extended general dis-cussion related also to the content of note 11, below, see James M. Buchanan, *The Insti-tutional Structure of Externality* (Virginia Polytechnic Institute & State University Re-search Paper 808231-1-6, Jan., 1971).

11. It is also useful to note that the existence of large numbers on the other side of the interaction need not have been obstructive in the reaching of voluntarily negotiated set-tlements. Consider a model in which there was only a single orchardman, affected ad-versely by the cedar rust on land owned by n separate cedar growers. So long as the amount of apple damage was related continuously to the amount of cedar rust, that is, so long as there was not a discrete all-or-none solution indicated, the single orchardman could have worked out agreements with the separate cedar growers separately and unilat-erally. There would have been no interdependencies among the cedar tree growers.

public-goods barrier to negotiated voluntary settlements, some assumptions must be made to the effect that this number was unchangeable within certain limits. If such a restriction is not imposed on the model, mutual gains-from-trade would have existed among the separate orchardmen, and individual owners of apple-land parcels would have had incentives to merge land holdings into units sufficiently large to remove or to reduce substantially the free-rider motivation that might otherwise have inhibited direct negotiation of agreements with the owner or owners of cedar lands. The interdependencies would have been, in a nonrestricted model, removed or internalized in a two-stage process of trading agreement. In the first, the many separate land parcels devoted to apples that were simultaneously affected by the cedar rust from a plot of trees would have been consolidated or merged into a single ownership entity. In the second, this entity would have negotiated an agreement with the cedar landowner or owners concerning the elimination of the diseased trees.

This model is fully applicable, however, only when transactions costs are negligible. "Transactions costs" offers a generalized rubric within which many of the barriers to negotiated settlements may be placed. The point is that the interaction among the separate apple growers generated by the cedar rust might have been only one, albeit a new, dimension that had economic content. There might have been many other variables that were relevant for land consolidation. If, for example, apples should have been a significant but not the exclusive source of external income for a large number of family-sized farms simultaneously affected by the cedar rust from a nearby plot of cedar trees, the opportunity costs of land-parcel consolidation directed at this interdependence alone might well have exceeded the benefits, while, at the same time, the damage to the apple crop exceeded the differential value of standing over cut cedar trees.

IV

The analysis suggests that there might have been an efficiency basis for resort to collective or state action in the apple-cedar interaction under discussion here, but that this basis required the presence of certain narrowly defined conditions. If there were large numbers of apple growers involved in each interaction, and if transactions costs were such that voluntary agreement on land consolidation could not have been predicted to emerge, the community of all apple growers might have called on the State to resolve the alleged dilemma in which they found themselves.[12] Interestingly enough, the Virginia Cedar Rust Act required the petition of *at least ten* freeholders before the State entomologist was empowered to act. This suggests that the large-number condition might have been recognized to be necessary for State action by the framers of the legislation. Samuels' discussion, however, nowhere suggests that these conditions are necessary for collective intervention to be justified.

It will be useful to examine the appropriate form of collective action, however, on the assumption that these required justifications were, indeed, present. The State might have responded to the issue by granting to appropriate-sized apple-growers' cooperatives some powers of coercion over members. Normally, however, we should have expected the legislative arm of the State to consider more direct action. The State may be conceived, therefore, as offering to supply a public good, one that will be made available to all members of the large community if it is made available to any one member. The standard and familiar requirements for efficiency in the provision of such a good or service can be readily defined. Total benefits must exceed total costs, and the summed marginal evaluations over all members of the community affected must be equated with the marginal cost of provision.

The question then becomes one of implementing this set of efficiency norms through the political process. If the conditions for justifying collective interference are held to be present, how can collective action be organized so as to insure that the net result involves a shift toward rather than away from society's efficiency surface? It is here that Knut Wicksell offers guiding principles.[13]

We may first consider the collective decision in question as an isolated independent event. Since there is no way of assessing the intensities of individual interests except through the revealed choice behavior of individ-

---

12. In so doing, those who request State intervention are advancing a personal judgment or hypothesis concerning the inefficiency of the existing state of affairs. They cannot, of course, determine unilaterally whether or not the alleged inefficiency is, in fact, real.

13. See Knut Wicksell, "A New Principle of Just Taxation," in *Classics in the Theory of Public Finance*, ed. Richard A. Musgrave and Alan T. Peacock (1958), 72.

uals themselves, a group-decision rule of unanimity was suggested by Wicksell. If so much as one person in the community is harmed, there is no insurance that the damage he suffers may not outweigh the benefits or gains to all other persons in the group. The rule of unanimity is the Wicksellian equivalent of a Pareto move, and the impossibility of securing unanimous consent for any change becomes the Wicksellian criterion for classifying an attained position as Pareto optimal. The ideal-type collective decision process is, therefore, an effective unanimity rule with all members of the community participating in the choice.

Cost considerations dictate departures from this ideal in several respects. Representation of individual or subgroup interests through the instrument of legislative bodies are accepted as a necessary practicable substitute for the fully participatory town-meeting type institutional structure. Again in some quasi-ideal limits, the members of the legislative assembly or assemblies represent, and hence act in the interests of, all citizens. The first stage in the practical implementation of the Wicksell scheme is, therefore, the application of an effective rule of unanimity in an appropriately selected legislative assembly.

With particular reference to the historical Virginia decision under discussion, we should note that collective action via the legislative body did offer an institutional means for internalizing the possible public-goods interdependence among the apple growers and for implementing the possible "trades" with the cedarmen. The legislative process is the instrument for reconciling the separate interests, for effecting some compromise and agreed-on solution. The legislative process, interpreted in this light, is functionally quite distinct from the judicial process. There is no role for the judiciary in the decision relating to the supply and financing of a public good. A categorical distinction must be made here, one that Samuels' treatment tends to blur over if not to disregard entirely.

Strict adherence to a rule of unanimity in a legislative body is not practicable. Wicksell himself recognized that the opportunities for strategic bargaining were too great here, and that these opportunities worked to make decision-making costs excessive. Such considerations aside, however, it will be useful to examine the type of legislative action that might have been expected to emerge under the operation of a unanimity rule in the Virginia legislature in 1914. In order to do this, simply assume that members of the legislative assembly did, in fact, genuinely represent all interests, and notably those of both the apple growers and the cedarmen, and, further, that each legislator voted strictly in terms of the estimated interests of his constituents, untainted by the strategic bargaining possibilities offered by the operation of the rule itself.

In such a setting, the representatives for the damaged apple growers might have proposed State action ordering the cutting of diseased trees near apple orchards. Those legislators representing the cedar landowners would, of course, have opposed any such proposals unless compensations were paid to their own constituents. In order to meet these objections, the apple-interest legislators would have then put forward alternative schemes which would have necessarily included taxes levied on their own constituents as the means of financing the compensations required to secure the acquiescence of the cedar tree growers, or, in this situation, their legislative representatives. The required compensations become, in this instance, and under the existing set of property rights, the cost of providing the collective or public good, defined as the reduction or elimination of cedar rust damage to the apple crops. As Wicksell emphasized, some such combined proposal (taxes and compensation payments) must have commanded the assent of all members of the assembly if the apple damage exceeded the damage from premature cutting of cedar. This provides the *only* test for efficiency that can be institutionalized politically. If the efficiency gains should have been significant, there might have been, of course, many possible sets of taxes and compensation payments which could have secured unanimous support in the legislature. The particular proposal adopted would have depended, in part, on the simple order of presentation of the alternatives, which may, of course, have been quite arbitrarily determined.

Considered as an isolated political decision, therefore, the action of the Virginia legislature in allowing the condemnation of diseased cedar trees, *without* compensation, and hence without taxes imposed on the prospective beneficiaries, the apple growers, violated the Wicksellian-Paretian precepts. In no way could such legislative action be interpreted as a surrogate for a voluntarily negotiated settlement among the parties at issue, with the collectivization made necessary only by the free-rider, transactions-cost considerations noted. There is no means of determining, from the historical record, whether the action was or was not efficient.

V

Our interpretation of *Miller et al. v. Schoene* is not complete, however, precisely because the action of the Virginia legislature cannot be considered as an isolated political event, nor can it be evaluated as such. Political choice takes place over many time periods and over several sets of alternatives in each period, covering widely divergent subject matter. Many "public goods" are supplied and financed; many proposals for collective supply and financing are rejected. As we noted above, any strict requirement of unanimity in legislative decision-making would generate costly delays in reaching agreement on anything, if indeed, agreement is reached at all. Historical evidence suggests that unanimity is the exception rather than "the rule," and legislative bodies are constitutionally empowered to act on less-than-unanimity rules, often under some version of majority voting as embedded in a complex structure of procedure and often with certain rights of executive veto. Any departure from strict unanimity provides an opportunity for collective choices that fail to meet the Pareto efficiency criterion. This must be acknowledged. Nonetheless, at some "constitutional" stage of decision on the structure of collective decision rules themselves, the prospective inefficiencies generated by less-than-unanimity voting may be less than those predicted to be generated by the decision-making inefficiencies which the more restrictive voting rule would insure.[14]

In this more realistic setting for legislative decision-making, however, any evaluation of a single choice action becomes much more difficult. In the Virginia case discussed, the absence of compensation to the owners of red cedar trees cannot, in itself, now be taken as clear evidence that the political process did not serve as an indirect and complex surrogate for the negotiation and settlement process among the parties. In a constitutional sense, we might think of both apple and cedar growers as having acquiesced in the continuing operation of a legislative process embodying constrained majority voting in the recognition that on occasion the economic interests of any particular subgroup in the community might be damaged, and perhaps severely. In this broader conception of collective decision-making, the delib-

14. For a general discussion of the theory of rule-making, see James M. Buchanan and Gordon Tullock, *The Calculus of Consent* (1962).

erations and choices made in a democratically selected and representative assembly may be interpreted as the only practicable institutional means of reconciling differences, or implementing "bargains" or "trades," in the presence of those conditions that are requisite for collective action. Those whose interests were potentially damaged, in our case the cedarmen, could have exercised their voting power on issues about which they were relatively indifferent in order to register their intensity of opposition to the tree-cutting statute. If, in fact, the damage to red cedars should have exceeded those of apple-crop infestation significantly, logrolling interaction in the Virginia legislature might have insured against passage of the statute in question.

As we know, however, the statute was enacted, and the cedar owners appealed to the courts, first at the state and then at the federal level. In this setting, the only role of the judiciary should have been one of determining whether or not the decision taken by the legislature was made constitutionally. This should have involved, first, an examination of the decision rule itself, about which there was apparently no issue. Secondly, the decision might have been evaluated in terms of the precepts of the "fiscal constitution" that were implicitly if not explicitly in being.

The taxing powers of the State allow the taking of private property for public or general purposes. If we interpret the statute that allows the condemnation of trees without compensation as a tax-in-kind on owners of such trees, in disregard of the offsetting side of the budget account, there might have been plausible grounds for the courts to uphold the legislative action. The critical element here should have concerned the nondiscriminatory nature of the tax. Formally, however, since the "tax" was imposed on all owners of red cedar trees in two-mile radii of apple orchards, an argument could have been made that such action was nondiscriminatory over a sufficiently broad class of persons. In this context, such a "tax" on the owners of red cedar trees, on the landowners, might have been legally interpreted as no different from a tax on the owners of pool tables, playing cards, or any other of the many narrowly specified bases observed in the real world.

If the offsetting or balancing side of the budget account should have been treated in isolation, the courts might have also found legitimate grounds for upholding the legislation. Representative assemblies have been empowered, constitutionally, to provide benefits to specific subgroups in the community, whether these be occupationally, geographically, industrially, or otherwise classified. Indeed, the nondiscriminatory or uniformity requirements generally held applicable to the tax side of the budget have never been applied to the public spending side.[15] Interpreted, therefore, as a specific subsidy to apple growers whose trees had been diseased, the "outlay" could have been held constitutionally valid.

On the other hand, if the two sides of the conceptualized fiscal account should have been joined in the court's deliberations, the constitutionality of the Virginia legislature's action might have proved highly questionable. In this light, the action seems similar in many respects to that which evoked the Supreme Court rejection of the original Agricultural Adjustment Administration on constitutional grounds. In *United States v. Butler* (1936), the Court held that the levy of a specific tax for the specific benefits of one subgroup was not a valid exercise of state power.[16]

Regardless of the Court's verdict in *Miller et al. v. Schoene,* Samuels' interpretation of the Court's action seems contrary to that which would seem appropriate under the alternative approach that I have tried to develop. It would have been illegitimate for the "Court, as part of the state, ... (to) make a judgment as to which owner would be visited with injury and which protected,"[17] or "decide which party would have what capacity to coerce another." The judicial role should have been limited strictly to a determination as to the constitutionality of legislative action, and this should not have included any attempt at making a judgment as to the economic efficiency or inefficiency or to the equity or inequity of the legislative choice actually made.

---

15. Recent court decisions with respect to educational spending differences among differing communities within states indicate some change in legal interpretation. For a thorough discussion of the historical asymmetry in legal treatment here, see David Tuerck, "Constitutional Asymmetry," in *Papers on Non-Market Decision-Making* 2 (1967), 27; for a more comprehensive treatment, see "Tuerck's Uniformity in Taxation, Discrimination in Benefits: An Essay in Law and Economics" (Ph.D. diss., in Alderman Library, University of Virginia, 1966).

16. 297 U.S. 1 (1936). Consider the hypothetical case in which cedar rust proved beneficial to apple crops, but in which the rust required investment on the part of cedar tree owners. Would the Court have upheld legislation that required that such investment be made without compensation? Presumably not, yet, analytically the setting seems identical with that which prevailed.

17. Samuels, "Interrelations," 438–39.

In its actual judgment, it is not clear that the Court exceeded the bounds of judicial propriety. The Court said that "the state does not exceed its constitutional powers by deciding upon the destruction of one class of property in order to save another which, *in the judgment of the legislature,* is of greater value to the public."[18] In this statement, the Court does not seem to have considered itself to be doing what Samuels' interpretation suggests; it apparently did not attempt to inject its own standards of value measurement in determining the constitutionality of the legislation. The Court's decision may have been in error in terms of consistent constitutional principles, but the error did not necessarily lie in the Court's misconception of its own functional role in a democratic governmental process.

VI

Old arguments are important only if they shed light on matters of modern relevance. Disagreements between Warren Samuels and James Buchanan on the interpretation of *Miller et al. v. Schoene* might be privately but not publicly interesting if comparable conflicts are anticipated infrequently and/or those that arise are economically insignificant. The major thrust of Samuels' paper, however, concerns the continuing ubiquitousness of such conflicts along with their economic importance. In the vision of collective action that I have imputed to him, Samuels envisages an activist State, ever ready to intervene when existing rights to property are challenged, ever willing to grasp the nettle and define rights anew, which once defined, immediately become vulnerable to still further challenges. This projects an awesome role for the State in an environment that is subjected continuously, and necessarily, to the exogenous shocks resulting from natural phenomena, from technological change, from growth itself. Broadly conceived, something akin to cedar rust must appear every day, and, in Samuels' paradigm, the State must never rest. The structure of rights, as of any moment, is subjected to question, and away goes the "white knight" to decide whose claim shall be favored and whose rejected.

What if Mr. A simply does not like long-haired men? The presence of such men in the community harms him just as much as cedar rust harmed the

18. *Miller et al. v. Schoene,* 276 U.S. 272, 279 (1928).

apple growers. Is Mr. A then empowered to challenge the existing structure of rights that allows men to wear hair as they please? It matters not that "reasonable legislative-cum-judicial authorities" should always or nearly always decide in favor of the long-haired defendants. In Samuels' model, the challenge itself must be appropriately processed, and each instance resolved on its own merits, with no apparent prejudice in favor of the "previously existing rights."

My own approach is sharply different. There is an explicit prejudice in favor of previously existing rights, not because this structure possesses some intrinsic ethical attributes, and not because change itself is undesirable, but for the much more elementary reason that only such a prejudice offers incentives for the emergence of voluntarily negotiated settlements among the parties themselves. Indirectly, therefore, this prejudice guarantees that resort to the authority of the State is effectively minimized. It insures that an efficiency basis for collective action emerges only when a genuine public-goods externality arises and persists. Furthermore, this prejudice allows for a distinct and categorical separation between the legislative and judicial roles, something that is strangely absent in Samuels' vision.

Unfortunately, the theory of politics, property, and the law that is implied in Samuels' interpretation of *Miller et al. v. Schoene* reflects the conventional wisdom of our time. This causes the number of bills passed to be the criterion of legislative excellence, a criterion that is implanted in the spirit of every aspiring politician. Much more seriously, this wisdom also involves an activist Federal judiciary, a judiciary that is now acknowledged to legislate, and which accepts, and is seen to accept, this role as such. Indeed, in Samuels' argument we may locate an apologia for the omnipresent hand of the State in all our lives, an omnipresence required by the necessary uncertainty of legal rights in a world subject to exogenous shocks. The State must adjudicate all conflicting claims, must take on all challenges to this and that, and in the process achieve the "unknown passing through the strange," a politico-legal setting that itself contributes to "future shock."

In Defense of *Caveat Emptor*

As interpreted by McKean, legal experience suggests a gradual and perhaps accelerating shift toward strict liability on the part of manufacturers of products. My discussion is limited to predicting the economic effects of this movement.

It is useful to note at the outset that *accidents cannot be prevented*, in the sense that the probability of occurrence cannot be reduced to zero. We live in an uncertain world, whether we like it or not, and the working properties of either human or material agents cannot be completely specified. Any discussion of products liability, therefore, involves only the possible modification in the probability distribution of accidents.

Two categories of events may be distinguished: those which involve pure accidents and those which involve probably preventable accidents. A pure accident occurs stochastically in a sequence of possibilities, but the probability distribution of occurrence cannot be modified by personal behavior aimed at changing the quality or use of the product, whether this be the behavior of the manufacturer, seller, user, or non-user. A probably preventable accident occurs stochastically in a sequence of possibilities and the probability distribution of occurrence can be modified by behavior on the part of manufacturers, sellers, users, or non-users aimed at changing the quality of

From *University of Chicago Law Review* 38 (Fall 1970): 64–73. Reprinted by permission of the publisher.

My assignment was to write a critical comment on McKean's monograph. I am interpreting this assignment to mean that I should not develop an editorial criticism of the manuscript, either in general or in its particulars. Instead of this, I shall use McKean's discussion as the basis for extending certain aspects of the economic theory of products liability.

the product or its use. When any given accident occurs, there remains only some positive probability that it could have been prevented with precautionary behavioral adjustments.

I. The Shift toward Strict Producer Liability under Pure Accidents

It is difficult to think of good examples of pure accidents. In almost all circumstances, adjustments in the product or its use can modify the probability distribution of accidents. Despite this, discussion will be clarified by treating the pure accident case independently. This allows examination of the economic effects of alternative liability arrangements without consideration of the possible *functional* influence of such arrangements on behavior. If it is known that no behavioral adjustments can modify the probability of accidents, then it follows that regardless of who bears the liability for damages when an accident does occur behavioral changes will not take place within the restricted product quality under consideration. As later discussion shows, however, even in this highly restricted case, alternative liability arrangements will generate differing final results, and economic analysis allows us to place some relative evaluation on these.

A. A HYPOTHETICAL EXAMPLE

I shall construct a highly artificial example. Assume that there are two kinds of coal available. Each kind is produced competitively by a large number of firms under conditions of increasing costs, or at least can be so produced if demand conditions warrant. The sole distinction between these two kinds of coal is as follows: for one kind, which we shall call "low quality," it can be predicted that one lump in one thousand will violently explode, causing possibly severe damage to surrounding objects; with the other kind, which we shall call "high quality," it can be predicted that one lump in one million will similarly explode. In all other respects the two qualities are identical. In order to make the example fit perfectly within my pure accident classification, I assume that there exists no possible means of determining in advance which lump will explode. We also assume that all persons have full knowledge as to the characteristics of the two qualities of product.

The simple economics of this industry may now be examined. Initially, assume that *caveat emptor* prevails; buyers-users are responsible for damages that might occur and they have no claim against producing-selling firms in the event of accident and subsequent damage. (We leave third party non-users out of account at this stage.) In order to sell any low-quality coal at all, sellers must offer it at a price per ton that is differentially lower than that for high-quality coal. At equal prices and given full knowledge as to quality by all potential buyers, no one would demand low-quality coal. If the costs of producing either quality of coal should be constant over varying quantities and both qualities could be produced at equal cost, no sellers would find it advantageous to sell low-quality coal at differentially lower prices. Competition would insure that the price of high-quality coal would tend to cover costs plus normal return on investment. Any differentially lower price for low-quality coal would not cover costs for producing firms. In order for this quality to be supplied at differentially lower prices necessary for sale, differentially lower costs of producing the low quality must be present.

Why should anyone demand the low-quality product, even at a differentially lower price? A person will demand such a low-quality product if he places a lower value on risk aversion than the demanders of the high-quality product. For illustration, let us suppose that the equilibrium price for the high-quality coal is $10 per ton. Let us suppose that the equilibrium price for the low-quality coal is $2 per ton. Let us further assume that the cost per ton of an insurance policy which would fully bring the protection of the low-quality user up to that received by the high-quality user is $8 per ton. With the purchase of insurance for the low-quality product, the two qualities become economically identical. Those demanders who purchase the low-quality coal at $2 per ton, without insurance, are those who are willing to take the differentially higher risk that this quality embodies. These are the buyers who place a lower valuation on risk avoidance (relative to money) than their fellows. They are unwilling to pay $8 per ton in risk avoidance. For the most part, but not exclusively, demanders of the low-quality product will be poor people who can ill afford to purchase a high degree of risk avoidance. Their effective alternatives may be those of buying coal at $2 per ton and buying no coal at all.

The simple description of the economic regime under *caveat emptor* is straightforward. Let us now assume that legal rulings begin to make producing-selling firms fully liable for all damages arising from the usage of either quality of the product. In order to absorb the increased costs of this new liability arrangement, the market price for both qualities of coal will increase, but the market price for the low-quality coal will increase much more dramatically. The imposition of strict liability will effectively prohibit firms from marketing a quality of product that inherently involves a relatively larger buyer-user risk. In our example, the low-quality product will disappear from the market in an economic sense. It will be impossible for demanders to purchase a quality of product that does not embody full insurance as a part of the price.

B. Who has benefited from the change in liability? who has suffered?

To answer these questions, we may classify persons or firms into four groups: (1) previous buyers of the high-quality product; (2) previous buyers of the low-quality product; (3) previous sellers of the high-quality product; (4) previous sellers of the low-quality product. It is clear that the change in liability has little, if any, effect on the buyers or the sellers of the high-quality product, groups (1) and (3). By the nature of our example, the product traded is inherently "safe"; hence, relatively little effect is produced by modifying liability for accidents. For group (4), the previous sellers of the low-quality product, there may be significant losses, but these are confined to the short term. To the extent that these firms have fixed investments in producing the low-quality item, losses will occur. But these will disappear as fixed facilities wear out and investment is shifted into other outlets. Over the long run, and given time for such shifting, this group will not be differentially affected. The lasting effects of the change in liability will be to damage those in group (2), those persons who were the buyers of the low-quality product under *caveat emptor*. Their effective range of choice has been narrowed. They can no longer bear the risk that they indicated a willingness to bear under the earlier regime. The shift in liability closes off mutually advantageous exchanges between these demanders and those firms that would arise to supply their expressed desires for the low-quality product.

The effects on economic welfare are clear and unambiguous. The change in liability arrangements reduces economic welfare generally, and this reduction is concentrated on the poor. On grounds of both efficiency and equity, the shift can be condemned. In economists' language, the change in legal arrangements from *caveat emptor* to strict producer liability is non-optimal. Conceptually, it would be possible to make some persons better off, by their own accounting, and no one worse off by returning to the regime of *caveat emptor*.

II. Shift toward Strict Producer Liability under Probably Preventable Accidents

The analysis is not significantly changed when we modify our example to allow for probably preventable accidents. We may stick with our same basic illustration, modified only as necessary for the discussion. Instead of two distinct qualities of product, as determined by nature, let us now assume that only one quality is naturally determined. If no quality controls are imposed, there exists a one in one thousand chance that a lump of coal will violently explode, the equivalent of the low-quality case earlier. It is now assumed, however, that a reduction in this probability of accident can be secured by specific quality-control behavior. By using available technology, the producing firm can reduce this probability, in the extreme case to the one in one million chance of explosion. Within the two extreme limits, however, the behavior of the firm can determine the quality of the product that it markets. Any given accident could, therefore, probably have been prevented with a high-quality, superior, safer product. As higher qualities of product are marketed, however, costs of the supplying firms increase since quality-control devices cost something, and the more reliable devices are, the higher these costs.

Under full *caveat emptor*, we should, as before, expect buyers-users to demand varying qualities of final product, this variation being limited in our illustration to varying degrees of riskiness. Attracted by ordinary profit motives, firms would supply differing qualities of product all along the safety-riskiness spectrum, with competitively determined price differentials established among the different qualities. These differentials in price would reflect the market's evaluation of the riskiness differentials.

If legal rulings change so as to make producing firms fully liable for damages, we can predict that the relative prices of the low-quality, high-risk products will increase dramatically. Firms which previously may have produced coal of all qualities at differing prices will modify their behavior so as to install high-intensity, high-cost quality controls for all production. There will be a reduction in the number of varieties offered for sale, and a discernible bunching of production among high-quality classes.

The effects are identical to those traced earlier. Over the long run, those who suffer are those demanders who are unable or unwilling to pay for the risk aversion that high-level quality offers.

III. Risk Aversion, Producer Liability, and the Coase Theorem

The conclusions of this analysis may seem at variance with the Coase theorem to which McKean refers. Coase argues that in the absence of transaction costs the assignment of liability as between two parties to a potential transaction will not modify the final allocative result. In apparent contrast to this, we have shown that the shift of liability to producing firms from buyers has a predictable and detrimental effect. The purpose of this section is to reconcile this apparent contradiction.

In my view, the Coase theorem is not directly applicable to situations where varying qualities of product may be marketed. There are essentially two separate but related issues of public policy that arise here, and McKean's discussion does not seem to distinguish them carefully. They are: (1) what degree of riskiness are buyers-users to be allowed to bear? and (2) what is the specific assignment of liability to be? If (1) is answered, the Coase theorem may be applied, and it says that the specific assignment of liability does not matter in the absence of transaction costs. Under normal circumstances, however, question (1) is not specifically answered separately from question (2), and, therefore, a shift in the assignment of liability may indirectly determine the solution to question (1). Hence, the assignment of liability may indirectly exert significant allocative effects.

Consider once again our example of the two kinds of coal. If it is decided, in advance and independently, that buyers-users should not be allowed to have access to the low-quality product, this product will then be eliminated from the market. Within the defined high-quality product, it then matters not at all to the final result whether producing firms are made liable for damages for the occasional accident or whether buyers-users must bear these damages. There will be only one most-efficient means of producing this specific product quality, and if we ignore transaction costs, this means will be found regardless of the legal arrangements. And, of course, buyers will bear the final incidence of the quality control in all cases so long as the industry is competitively organized.

If no such decision as to high-quality restriction is made independently, however, the same results may be achieved by the specific assignment of liability. There are two separate institutions that will accomplish this. As indicated in our analysis, producing firms can be made fully liable for damages. The low-quality product will disappear, with the effects noted. The same results could be achieved if buyers-users were required compulsorily to buy insurance against accidents. In this latter case, the high insurance premium on the low-quality items would remove them from the market, having the same effect as the differentially increased purchase price under the alternative arrangement. In either instance, buyers in the net pay for the differentially higher quality that they are forced to receive, and those buyers who are unable or unwilling to expend funds for this higher quality are harmed by being excluded from all transactions.

Professor Armen Alchian has suggested a somewhat different means of reconciling the analysis of this comment with the Coase theorem. To be fully applicable, the Coase theorem requires the assumption that there be no prohibitions on any mutually advantageous exchanges that may be made as between potential buyers and potential sellers. The shift of strict liability to producers-sellers amounts to imposing such prohibitions. Potential buyers of the low-quality product are effectively forced to purchase risk aversion; they are prevented from "buying risk." Or, in slightly different language, transaction costs become prohibitively high for such potential exchanges.

IV. Is There an Economic Rationale for the Shift to Strict Producer Liability?

With the standard economic models, I have shown that the shift away from *caveat emptor* can be condemned on both efficiency and equity grounds. The question now becomes one of examining these standard models to see if there are qualifying features which serve to make recent legal history less violative of criteria for economic rationality.

A. THIRD-PARTY OR NON-USER EFFECTS

The standard models concentrate on contractual arrangements between buyers and sellers, and they must be amended to take into account the potential interests of third parties. If it can be argued that, as product technology has developed, products increasingly exert effects on third parties in the event of accident, a plausible case can be made for the shift away from *caveat emptor*. As we have shown, this shift removes low-quality, high-risk products from the market despite the expressed willingness of potential buyers-users to assume the risks of accidents that these products embody. If third parties are not affected by possible accidents that may occur with usage of these products, the shift toward stricter producer-seller liability stands condemned without qualification. But even if potential buyers-users stand willing to assume a high degree of risk, their behavior in so doing may not be desired if accidents cause harm or do damage to third-party non-users.

The automobile is, of course, the familiar example here. If, in fact, technology could insure that damages to life and property were concentrated on the driver of the vehicle, there would be little or no argument for legislating safety features or for shifting legal arrangements toward stricter producer liability. For the reasons noted, poor users should be allowed to purchase unsafe automobiles under such conditions. By their own expressions of preference, they are better off with unsafe automobiles than with no automobiles at all. However, as we all recognize, the technology of both the automobile and the highway is such that no concentration of damage on drivers is possible. There is, therefore, a logic in imposing generalized standards of riskiness that should not be exceeded, even if agreed to by parties to a particular contract. Strict producer liability does indirectly accomplish this and is closely analogous to the direct legislation of safety requirements.

The question at issue for general liability arrangements is whether or not more and more products are coming to be like the automobile, where third-party effects are admittedly important. To the extent that this is true, some plausible justification for a general shift toward strict producer liability can be made. As the discussion should make clear, however, no generally applicable argument can be established, even on these grounds. The introduction of third-party effects points strongly in the direction of adjusting the legal liability arrangements to the particulars of the product technology. A discriminating approach is required, and courts should proceed on a product-by-product basis, taking into account the relevant economic criteria. Precedents applicable to one product category should clearly not be extended blindly across product lines. A sharper distinction must be made between those products which are likely to involve third-party effects and those which are not.

To the extent that producing-selling firms can be made liable for damages to third parties without being made fully liable for damages to direct users, some of the advantages of *caveat emptor* might be retained. The same conclusion applies to the more direct legislation of safety requirements. There is little or no argument for compulsory safety requirements when damage is concentrated on the buyer-user. There is an argument for imposing safety requirements that reduce probabilities of damages to non-users. These have not been carefully distinguished in the recent discussions of automobile safety legislation.

B. COMPLEX MODERN TECHNOLOGY AND INFORMATION

A second argument is sometimes advanced for modern safety legislation which could be equally well applied in defense of the shift toward stricter producer liability. If it could be empirically shown that the information required for buyers-users to make rational judgments as to product quality has increased over time, a case is established for some shift from strict *caveat emptor*. There seems little point in disputing the facts here; the complexities of modern technology are overwhelming, and rational purchase of even simple products requires great knowledge and discrimination on the part of buyers.

Does this justify the indirect means of securing some reduction in riskiness, or increase in safety, that the shift toward strict producer liability represents? I shall argue that it does not, although some expanded governmental role in information supply is perhaps necessary. The complex information required in discriminatory choices among product qualities is costly to produce, and individuals, as independent buyers, may not be willing to purchase such information in optimally preferred quantities. There is, or so it seems to me, a "public good" argument for collective, governmental supply of information about product qualities. Once produced, such information may be supplied to consumers. This need not reduce the range of products on the market at all, nor should it remove high-risk, unsafe products. If individuals are willing to purchase such items in the full knowledge of their dangers, they should be allowed to do so when third-party effects are not deemed important. The government's role can be restricted to the supplying of information. In terms of a practical example, there was, I think, a strong case for the requirement that the "hazard to health" notice be placed on cigarette packages. There was, and is, no economic basis for making cigarette producers liable for damages due to lung cancer.

V. The Essential Trade-offs between Quality and Quantity

As an economist who studies market processes, disciplinary prejudice alone suggests to me that departures from *caveat emptor* should be carefully scrutinized and accepted only after specific argument accompanied by convincing evidence. As an individualist, who places a high value on freedom of exchange, any limitations on the exchange process, either directly or indirectly, arouse my initial skepticism. As I have argued in this comment, *caveat emptor* encourages the maximum range of products geared to meet all variations in demand. For a commodity or product category considered as a whole, that is, for a commodity group, only by allowing quality variations within a wide range can the maximum quantity be produced and exchanged. Limitations on the quality range result in some restriction on the total quantity. The essential trade-off is that between a larger quantity with lower average quality and a smaller quantity with higher average quality.

Too much uninformed discussion proceeds as if higher average quality of product can somehow be achieved without sacrifice in quantity and indeed without cost, which indirectly amounts to saying the same thing. If my analysis is correct, the shift toward stricter producer liability tends to reduce the overall quantity of products produced and exchanged. This reduction in quantity is the cost; it is offset, in part, by the higher average quality of product that is guaranteed under the modified legal arrangements. If we think of this basic trade-off in gross and very general terms, the defense of *caveat emptor* seems strong indeed. Not only are more efficient results generated, but equity objectives are also more effectively secured.

If we shift from very general treatment to the specifics of each product category, selective departures from *caveat emptor* may well be justified. The law, as the law, tends to be general in applicability. If it is not, it ceases to be law in a certain sense. But the economics here varies from product to product. The normative rule to be applied seems to be: "Commence with some prejudice for *caveat emptor* and be sophisticated in the application of departures from this principle."

Notes on Irrelevant Externalities, Enforcement Costs and the Atrophy of Property Rights

In an earlier paper, a Pareto-irrelevant externality was defined to exist in a two-person context when there is no way that an activity which enters as an argument in each person's utility function can be modified so as to improve the position of one party without worsening the position of the other party.[1] In other words, there are no potential gains-from-trade that remain to be secured, even though the well-being of one party may be affected by the activity which is under the control of the other. Pareto-irrelevance implies that the value of the "internal economy" enjoyed by the acting party equals or exceeds the value of the loss that his action imposes externally on the affected party.[2] My purpose in these notes is to apply this concept of Pareto-irrelevant externalities to explain one basis for modifications in property rights, modifications which amount to atrophy in the basic structure.

I

By way of introducing the more interesting and more complex issues, I shall first apply the notion of irrelevant externality to the now-famous Coase the-

From *Explorations in the Theory of Anarchy,* ed. Gordon Tullock (Blacksburg, Va.: Center for Study of Public Choice, 1972), 77–86. Reprinted by permission of the publisher.

1. James M. Buchanan and W. C. Stubblebine, "Externality," *Economica,* 29 (1962), 371–84.

2. Note that both external economies and external diseconomies can be brought within this context by considering the failure to extend an activity that exerts economies as an external diseconomy.

orem.[3] This states that in the absence of transactions costs and income effects the assignment of property rights or claims does not affect resource allocation. As normally interpreted, this theorem proves the invariance of the allocative solution under alternative directions of exchange or trade between the parties to an interaction. In the context of Coase's familiar example, the final resource allocation is the same whether the ranchers hold rights that allow their cattle to roam at will over the surrounding croplands or whether the wheat farmers hold rights which allow them to exclude the straying cattle or to exact payment for damages from ranchers. In the first case, trade takes the form of compensations or "bribes" paid by the farmers *to* the ranchers, if indeed trade takes place at all. In the second case, trade involves the payment of "charges" to the farmers *by* the ranchers in exchange for straying privileges, if trade takes place at all. The differing initial assignment of rights will produce differing initial positions from which internalization through trade might commence; the differing positions attained under strictly unilateral behavior bracket the efficient allocative outcome that will tend to be established through trading.[4]

Consider now an example in which an externality may be Pareto-irrelevant under one set of rights and Pareto-relevant under the other. One assignment may generate trade; the other may not do so. If the rancher holds rights that allow his cattle to roam freely over the croplands, there may be no acceptable trade or exchange that the farmer who is damaged can offer once the rancher attains his position of independent-adjustment equilibrium. Suppose, for example, that in this position, the marginal value of free straying to the rancher is $70 per steer, while the marginal damage or loss imposed on the farmer is only $60 per steer. No internalization through trade can take place in this setting. But consider the alternative assignment of rights. Suppose that the farmer holds exclusion rights in the croplands and that these rights

---

3. See R. H. Coase, "The Problem of Social Cost," *Journal of Law and Economics,* 3 (1960), 1–44.

4. One of the controversies stimulated by the Coase theorem was the alleged symmetry between "bribes" and "charges." The result of this discussion seems to have been that the symmetry depends critically on the proper definition of the starting point.

On the general effect of institutional structure on allocative outcomes, see my "The Institutional Structure of Externality" (Center for Study of Public Choice, VPI&SU: Research Paper No. 808231-2-2A, January 1971), forthcoming in *Public Choice.*

may be enforced *without cost.* In this situation, the private-adjustment equilibrium will be characterized by Pareto-relevant externalities. To remove these, and to attain the position that he reached unilaterally under the alternative assignment, the rancher must purchase straying rights from the farmer. The Coase theorem, as such, is not modified. The initial position unilaterally selected by the rancher is Pareto-efficient under one set of rights; by definition, no internalization through trade or otherwise is required for Pareto-irrelevant externality. Under the other set of rights, trade is necessary to shift from an initial inefficient position produced by unilateral or independent adjustment to the efficient allocative outcome that would be attained without trade under the alternative assignment.

II

The analysis may be extended while remaining within the context of the rancher-farmer example. I want to concentrate on only one of the two assignments discussed above, that in which the farmer holds rights of exclusion in the croplands. As suggested, if these rights are enforceable at no cost, the farmer can prevent all damage from the rancher's straying cattle, either by requiring his prior agreement upon compensation or by collecting the full value of damages incurred, as such claims are ideally adjudicated by a third party or agency.[5] In either case, the arrangement will embody an income transfer from the rancher to the farmer.

If, however, the exclusion rights nominally held by the farmer are enforceable only at some positive cost to him, some damage or loss may be tolerated without reaction. These costs can be measured in bother, time, or monetary outlay. Everyday routines are interrupted by seeking legal relief; relationships with others in the social group may be made less pleasant; lawyers can only be hired for money; time delays involved in legal proceedings may be signifi-

---

5. It is important to distinguish rights to exclude from rights to claim for damages. In the first, agreement of the potentially affected party must be secured before action is taken; in the second, the affected party may not forestall action but he may claim damages if and after the action is taken. For a discussion of this distinction between "property rules" and "liability rules," see Guido Calabresi and A. D. Melamed, "Property Rules, Liability Rules, and Inalienability: One View of the Cathedral," *Harvard Law Review,* 85 (April, 1972), 1089.

cant. When this is recognized, the farmer may find that any attempt to enjoin or prevent external damage from the rancher's cattle or to make claims for damages after it is done may cost more than the damage itself. In the numerical illustration, the value of the loss is $60 per period per steer. We may assume that the loss function is linear; each steer destroys $60 worth of potentially marketable wheat regardless of the number that stray. By contrast with this plausibly realistic linearity in the damage or loss function, the farmer is likely to encounter severe lumpiness in his enforcement cost function. The costs of enforcing his nominal property rights to the croplands are likely to depend only indirectly if at all on the size of the damages incurred, at least over some initial ranges of damage. For purposes of illustration here, assume that the farmer anticipates a fixed outlay of $360 to be required to insure full enforcement of his property rights. For this sum, he knows that he can collect full damages from the rancher.[6] In this situation, so long as the rancher keeps the number of straying cattle below six, the farmer maximizes his profit by accepting the external loss without reaction. The situation becomes equivalent to that which is observed when the rancher rather than the farmer holds the nominal rights in the croplands. The effect is as if the external diseconomy is Pareto-irrelevant. The enforcement cost threshold of the farmer allows the rancher to behave as if the assignment of rights is the reverse of those which are nominally in existence. The property rights that may be inferred from external observation are, in this setting, sharply different from those which are nominally defined and which may, upon a sufficient outlay, be legally enforced.

The quantity limits must be recognized as critical in generating this no-reaction outcome. If the private, profit-maximizing adjustment of the rancher, subject to the internal constraints that he confronts, should dictate that he allow *more than six* steers to wander onto the cropland, the farmer will find it advantageous to enforce his nominal exclusion rights. The rancher will be required to pay damages for losses to the farmer, and possibly a share of the enforcement costs in addition. Whether or not the rancher's private, profit-maximizing behavior, considered separately from the interaction with the farmer, results in less than or more than six straying cattle will depend on

6. This must be the estimated outlay over and above that part of total enforcement costs that might be imposed on the rancher in any legal proceedings.

cost-revenue arguments that are internal to his own decision calculus. The point to be emphasized here is that, under some conditions, this behavior may violate nominally accepted property-rights assignments without setting off enforcement reaction from the affected party or parties.

If the rancher should recognize the decision-making setting that the farmer confronts, his own behavior may, of course, be modified in a strategic sense. He may find it profitable to restrict his action so as to keep within the predicted allowable limits of counteraction. In our illustration, suppose that the pure profit-maximizing behavior of the rancher, treated as exogenous to the interaction with the farmer, should involve eight steers who damage croplands. In other words, this number would be allowed to stray if the rancher held full rights to the croplands. If the farmer holds exclusion rights, and if his costs of enforcement are known to be lumpy and in the amount of $360, the rancher will try to keep damage below this level to forestall claims for damages. If all eight steers stray, and action is taken, the rancher will be required to pay a minimum of $480 to the farmer (eight times $60). In the conditions of the Coase theorem, he would, if necessary, pay this total and continue to allow all eight animals to damage crops.

Let us suppose, however, that the rancher knows the payoff structure facing the farmer. He finds that, by reducing his herd to five, he may forestall a certain outlay of $480 and perhaps more. If the benefits per animal are constant at $70 each, as we have postulated, the rancher loses only $210 by reducing the herd from eight to five. It will, therefore, be in his interest to reduce the size of the herd. Whether for such strategic reasons or whether private behavior involves such restriction naturally, if the quantity limits dictated by the enforcement-cost threshold of the farmer are not overrun, the result is that the nominal assignment of rights is eroded or undermined. The behavioral pattern that is observed departs from that pattern which would be observed under strict adherence to the rights that are nominally assigned to the parties and which, ultimately, would be legally enforced.

III

The possible divergence between nominal property rights and actual or effective rights, as observed in behavior patterns, takes on added significance when we shift to a dynamic setting. It is possible to analyze the effects of enforcement or nonenforcement behavior in one period on the decision calculus of each party to an interaction in subsequent periods.

We have assumed specifically that in Period One the assignment of rights is acknowledged by all parties; these rights are enforceable with certainty once the damaged party makes the required investment in enforcement. The costs of making this investment represent the only barrier to enforcement. This offers a starting point for a sequential modelling of rights enforcement. In periods subsequent to this base period, t_1, I shall assume that the delineation of property rights that will ultimately be enforced by the courts depends on two elements rather than one. There is the initial acknowledged assignment of nominal rights, the certain basis for the enforcement in Period One. In addition, the ultimate enforcement in later periods will depend on the observed pattern of rights reflected in behavior during earlier periods of time.

In Period One, we know that the probability of effective enforcement of nominally defined property assignments is one, upon the initiation of legal action by the damaged or potentially damaged party. That is,

$$P(E)t_1 \ = \ \frac{N}{N} \ = \ 1, \tag{1}$$

where $P(E)$ refers to the probability, (E) to the enforcement of nominal rights in the period indicated by the subscript, and N defines an index of the nominal rights assignment. In Period Two, however, we get,

$$P(E)t_2 \ = \ \frac{(N \ - \ O_{t1})}{N} < 1, \tag{2}$$

where O defines an index for the divergence between the observed patterns of rights and nominally assigned rights in the subscripted time period. Hence, we see that if the farmer in our illustration takes action in Period One to enforce fully his nominal rights the situation in Period Two becomes equivalent to that which he faced in Period One. If, however, he rationally refrains from taking enforcement action, because of the quantity threshold limits and the lumpiness in enforcement costs, the probability of securing nominal rights enforcement in Period Two is less than unity. The benefits expected from legal action in Period Two must be discounted by this reduced probability factor in any rational comparison with costs. That is, for enforcement to become rational in Period Two, (3) below must be satisfied:

$$P(E)t_2 \int_{s=0}^{s=s^*} D > C. \tag{3}$$

The total damage or loss, represented by the integral over the interval determined by the externally imposed quantity limits, discounted by the appropriate probability factor must be less than the expected total cost of initiating legal action. To this point, we have assumed that this cost is independent of the quantity of damage incurred. For generality, however, the condition represented in (3) could be rewritten as:

$$P(E)t_r \int_{s=0}^{s=s^*} D > f(D), \tag{4}$$

where the subscript, r, refers to any time period subsequent to the base, and where total cost, C, is written as a function of the damage or loss, f(D).

The effects are clear. The quantity threshold in Period Two is widened over that of Period One if the probability of successful enforcement falls below one. Having rationally acquiesced in the external intrusion into his nominal property rights in Period One, the farmer in our illustration finds that his enforcement task is even more difficult in Period Two.

It is relatively easy to extend the analysis by incorporating additional periods of adjustment. Consider period, t_m, where we might have,

$$P(E)_{t_m} = \frac{N - \sum_{t=1}^{t=m-1} O}{N}. \tag{5}$$

This could be rewritten so that more weight could be given to periods close in time to t_m.

$$P(E)_{t_m} = \frac{N - \sum_{t=1}^{m-1} w_t O}{N}, \tag{6}$$

where w_t allows for differential weights for specific time period observations.

This formulation allows us to define a situation where nominal property rights have completely atrophied. This is a situation where the holder of such nominal rights will not find it rational to enforce these regardless of the quantity of damage that is actually or potentially inflicted on him externally. This condition is defined to be present when (7) below is satisfied:

$$P(E)_{tr} \int_{s=0}^{s=\infty} D < f(D), \text{ where } C = f(D). \tag{7}$$

This states that regardless of the number of units of external damage, straying steers in the Coase illustration, the costs of effectively enforcing nominal rights remain greater than the expected benefits.

IV

Objection may be raised to the analysis sketched on the grounds that it fails to allow for a recognition of the intertemporal relationships in the decision calculus of the potentially damaged party. That is to say, the model assumes implicitly that decisions about enforcement or nonenforcement are made in each time period on a cost-benefit comparison relevant for that period in isolation. It may be argued that a more comprehensive definition of rationality would include the intertemporal interdependence. As the model indicates, the benefit-cost ratio from investment in enforcement in future periods is increased by positive action in the present. Rational behavior should be based on a recognition of this; it would seem that enforcement efforts would be strengthened.

This should, however, be considered with some caution. Suppose that in Period One, the anticipated external damage is less than expected enforcement cost. That is,

$$\int_{s=0}^{s=s^*} D < C. \tag{8}$$

In the rancher-farmer illustration, only five steers are observed to stray onto the croplands. For this period alone, enforcement response on the part of the farmer is not economically rational. Let us assume, however, that he fully recognizes the interdependence between what he does in Period One and his choice situation in subsequent periods. On the basis of this recognition, let us suppose that legal action toward enforcing Period One rights is instituted.

As Period Two arrives, the potentially damaged party is once again confronted with an *ab initio* setting. If the estimates of enforcement cost and potential damages again indicate that (8) is satisfied, the farmer faces precisely the same calculus as he did in Period One. In this manner, we could demonstrate that, if intertemporal interdependence effects dictated protective legal action in Period One despite present-period irrationality, the same would hold for Period Two and for each subsequent period. Hence, the potentially damaged party would be acting against his single-period interest in each period over an infinite sequence. The conclusion is inescapable that incorporation of this effect will do nothing toward removing the possible threshold-induced atrophy in property rights. So long as the condition defined in (8) holds in some initial period, the rational course of action for the potentially damaged party remains one of nonenforcement.

V

If the nominal assignment of rights is to be strictly enforced in a world where enforcement must involve cost, the damage threshold of the externally affected party must be reduced. This can be accomplished either by (1) increasing the benefits of enforcement, or by (2) reducing the costs of enforcement. We may discuss these alternatives in turn.

In the expressions of Section IV, the benefits from enforcement action are measured in recoverable losses. Implicitly, we have assumed that the affected party, by taking legal action, can forestall damages, or if *ex post*, can collect in full for losses suffered, but that he cannot collect from the acting party *more* than these losses, accurately estimated. The benefits from undertaking successful legal action to the affected party could be increased only if he could, somehow, collect more than the explicit damage that he suffers from the external diseconomy in itself. This excess-of-damage prospect is not, of course, completely foreign to existing legal systems (e.g., triple damage suits under American anti-trust statutes).

Consider the illustration at hand. If the farmer is allowed to collect, say, double damages from the rancher, or $120 per steer on the croplands, he will be motivated to initiate legal action if he observes, say, five animals, whereas he would not do so if only direct damages are possible of collection. In this new situation, he would stand to collect $600 for an outlay of $360, for a net gain of $240. Let us suppose, however, that the offending rancher recognizes the double indemnity aspects of the external diseconomy, as well as the pay-off structure faced by the farmer. If he simply adjusts his behavior so as to keep within a newly defined and more restrictive threshold, the same analysis applies. If, for example, only two steers are allowed to stray now, even double assessment of damages will not provoke the farmer's rational response in defense of his property. In order to insure that the damaged party will act as if enforcement costs are zero, the potentially recoverable claims from the acting party must equal actual losses *plus* the full costs of enforcement. For initial quantity ranges this might well involve some multiple of the estimated losses imposed. To an extent, the charging of all legal fees and court costs to the party that is found liable for damages accomplishes the purpose here. But this device, even if it is fully utilized, fails to insure adequate enforcement if the potentially or actually damaged party suffers nonpecuniary costs in the form of personal discomfort, inconvenience, and time. To my knowledge, direct compensation is rarely allowed for these very real costs of property-rights enforcement. To the extent that they are not, however, some erosion and ultimate atrophy of nominal or assigned rights must be predicted to occur.

In the illustration, the familiar rancher-farmer interaction, we could, of course, assume that the potentially damaged farmer might conceivably collect from the rancher claims sufficient to cover all estimated losses plus all enforcement costs, including subjective costs. A different and more difficult problem emerges, however, when we impose financial constraints on the rancher's ability to pay claims in excess of the gains that his action secures if uninhibited. Suppose that the rancher simply cannot pay more than $70 per steer. In this case, there is no way that the farmer can be insured a collection of $360 plus $60 per quantity unit, the offer schedule that we have demonstrated to be required to insure that he will effectively enforce his nominally assigned rights. Consider a situation where the struggling rancher earns a bare subsistence income unless he allows his cattle to roam on the croplands. If he is not prosecuted, he earns $70 per animal above subsistence but no more. In such case, the farmer can, at most, collect this total, and in the process reduce the rancher back to subsistence income.[7]

If the affected party cannot, for any reason, be allowed to expect collection of claims sufficient to offset all costs, including those that are purely subjective, an alternative approach might involve explicit reduction in such costs. It is clear that, if the affected party can, in fact, enforce his property rights at or near zero costs, the argument for excess-of-damage claims disappears. The processes of enforcing assigned rights that have been or may be externally violated involve genuine costs, both in resources and in personal utility. Consider only the resources cost, reflected in necessary monetary outlays on legal proceedings, lawyers, courts, clerks, etc. For our purposes, let us assume that these are supplied at competitive rates. If the costs of enforcement measured by such necessary outlays are to be reduced for the externally affected party to an interaction, they must be increased for someone in the community. The implication is that these costs, or at least a portion thereof, might be shifted to the general public, to the taxpayers as a legitimate expense of government.

In vague statements, several public-finance scholars may have referred to law enforcement as a "public good." And there seems little question but that some general structure of law fulfills many of the necessary technical characteristics for a "public good." But the analysis here forces us to be more specific with respect to the community's role in financing the enforcement costs that are incurred in defending nominally assigned property rights. As the analysis demonstrates, a shift in such costs away from the party whose nominal rights are threatened will tend to increase his willingness to initiate enforcement action. Is this, in itself, sufficient justification for governmental assumption of these costs? To make out a positive argument here, we must be able to show what will happen when enforcement response is

---

7. Note that in our whole analysis concentration is placed on the decision calculus of the affected party. This is appropriate when we are concerned with positive action toward enforcement of assigned property rights. We have explicitly left out of account the decision calculus of the acting party who must, in one sense, violate either legal or ethical norms or both in imposing or threatening to impose the external diseconomy on the other party. To the extent that the reward-punishment structure can be manipulated so as to reduce external intrusion into established or assigned rights, the danger or erosion and atrophy stemming from a failure to react by the affected party is, of course, reduced.

taken promptly and effectively. To this point, we have not gone beyond an implicit assumption that effective enforcement of nominal rights is a desirable attribute of social order. But why? The answer seems to be that only with effective enforcement can the efficient allocative outcome be achieved and, at the same time, the socially unnecessary costs of litigation minimized.

We may return to the rancher-farmer illustration. If, either by allowing claims sufficient to cover all litigation costs plus estimated damages, or by reducing costs of litigation for the farmer, effective enforcement of nominal rights is insured, and promptly, uncertainty is reduced. The basis is laid for genuine contractual negotiations between the interacting parties, and agreements can be anticipated that will fully internalize the potential externality. If the farmer's exclusion rights to the croplands are enforced, and are known to be enforced, the rancher will find it advantageous, regardless of his income-asset position, to negotiate from the assigned status-quo. Mutual gains-from-trade can be exploited; all parties can be placed in improved positions and without erosion and atrophy of property rights, and without unnecessary resource outlay on lawyers and litigation.[8] The presence of major efficiency gains suggests that the productivity of public investment in absorbing these costs may be large indeed, even if the standard "public-goods" rubric does not seem fully appropriate.

If the taxpayers, generally, are to be charged with the costs of enforcing property rights, there remains the issue "which taxpayers"? How are the tax costs for such outlays to be distributed? In this sense, there may be both equity and efficiency arguments for relating such taxes directly to measured values of nominal asset ownership.[9] That is to say, the costs of enforcement still might properly be borne by the owners of property threatened by external intrusion. The institutional arrangements dictated by the analysis involve a possible shift of these costs from the specifically damaged or potentially damaged party in an interaction to the community of potentially damaged

8. I have advanced roughly these arguments in quite a different context. See my "Politics, Property, and Law," *Journal of Law and Economics* (forthcoming). Gordon Tullock has elaborated in some detail on the social gains that might be secured from institutional rearrangements that minimize or eliminate the resources costs that are invested in pure conflict resolution, widely defined. See his *The Social Dilemma* (mimeographed).

9. For the efficiency argument, see Earl Thompson, "Taxation of Wealth and the Wealthy," UCLA Working Paper, March 1972.

owners of property. The important element is to break the direct linkage between the incurring of personal cost and the initation of enforcement action. Even though the affected party may, indirectly, bear most of the resources cost of enforcement, he may be motivated to act *as if* these costs are low.

Conclusions

This paper should be interpreted as a set of provisional notes rather than definitive conclusions. My concern is to open up discussion of the economic calculus that may be involved in the enforcement of nominally assigned property rights. There are many elements of this calculus that are not developed fully in this paper, and notably the "public-goods" aspects. As indicated, the paper concentrates on the calculus of the nominal owner in protecting and enforcing rights. The calculus of the other party is equally significant for any comprehensive analysis, that is, the party or parties who choose deliberately to violate nominally existing property rights.

PART SIX

Law, Money, and Crime

Gold, Money and the Law

The Limits of Governmental Monetary Authority

James M. Buchanan and T. Nicolaus Tideman

I. Introduction

Effective in January 1975, American citizens can own and exchange gold in any form, something that they have not been able to do for almost forty-two years. These four decades commenced with a series of events that raised many issues of "law and money," events that aroused a flurry of discussion among lawyers and economists before fading away in a general acquiescence to the constitutional revolution that the New Deal implemented. Significant modifications were made in the basic monetary structure of the United States in the 1930s, and these deserve reconsideration. Specifically, the government's initial action in forbidding the private ownership of and trading in gold and in abrogating the gold clauses in contracts is worthy of modern analysis and interpretation. By concentrating on the actions through which the government swept away these protective devices, we can discuss a defined historical sequence and, at the same time, examine still relevant issues that involve the fundamental limits of government's monetary authority.

"Law and money" offers one of the most challenging interfaces between

From *Gold, Money and the Law,* ed. Henry G. Manne and Roger LeRoy Miller (Chicago: Aldine, 1975), 9–70. Reprinted by permission of the publisher.

We are indebted to our colleagues Gordon Tullock and Warren Weber for helpful comments on early drafts of this paper. We are also indebted to our formal critics, and especially to Professor Milton Friedman, for detailed comments on the draft circulated for the conference.

law and economics, an interface that is worth exploring in the generalized revival of interest in legal constraints on economic behavior. The challenge here is enhanced by the demonstrable failures of modern governments to control inflation, failures that prompt searches for means of adjusting to this acknowledged feature of modern economic life. What legally viable means of protecting and preserving real value are available to individual citizens? Cost-of-living wage contracts, escalator clauses, index-clause bonds and notes, indexed income tax brackets, index contracts generally—these protective instruments generate controversies once again over the whole set of issues concerning the legal boundaries of governmental monetary authority. The constitutional limits of governmental monetary power in relation to the institutional instruments designed to protect persons against abuses of this power must be reexamined.

To avoid misunderstanding, it will be useful to set out our own conceptual framework. We are not legal positivists, historical determinists, or strict constitutional constructionists. On the other hand, we make no claim to a superior wisdom that makes our version of the "good society" more deserving of attention than the next man's (if indeed we could agree between ourselves on such a version). This leaves us with the contractarian framework, the only conceptual schema that is consistent with an individualistic-democratic value structure. This implies that normative justification for potentially coercive governmental actions, past or present, is located only in putative contractual agreement that might emerge from a rational decision calculus of free individuals, treated as equal participants in some constitutional stage of deliberation.

We shall use this framework to evaluate the changes in the monetary order of the United States that were made in the 1930s. We shall, directly or indirectly, raise the following questions. What is the role of the State in monetary matters? What monetary agreements might emerge from genuine social contract in which persons choose the constitutional rules under which they are to carry out their everyday economic interchanges? How did the monetary rules and institutions in existence before 1933 match up to such contractually derived criteria? Had the United States government, before 1933, met its own constitutional obligations? What might citizens have reasonably expected from government in the 1930s? How and to what extent were reasonable expectations violated by the restrictions on gold dealings and by gold-clause abrogations? What should have been the implications, legal and economic, of these governmental actions? Finally, what is the relevance of that period's history for problems in the 1970s and beyond?

These are among the questions that we shall try to answer in this paper. Section II provides a brief historical sketch of the monetary system prior to the Great Depression, along with the necessary analysis for understanding the vulnerability of this system and the situation that confronted the government in 1933. Section III discusses the policy measures actually taken by the New Deal. Section IV concentrates on the issues of constitutional law raised by the set of governmental actions, and notably, the abrogation of the gold clause in contracts, public and private, and the judicial confirmation of this action. Section V shifts to a discussion of the overall structure of a contractually derived monetary constitution, and here we look at the observed historical record in the light of contractual criteria. Section VI continues the discussion with attention to the alternative monetary arrangements that might emerge from genuine social or constitutional contract. Section VII represents a necessary detour into the realm of welfare economics to examine the grounds for possible governmental intrusion into voluntary private contracts among persons. Section VIII looks at the record of past failures on the part of government and at the implications of these events for constitutional interpretations of monetary powers in the post-Depression period. Section IX applies the whole analysis to the situation facing us in 1975, trapped in continuing and apparently uncontrollable inflation. We discuss the relevance of the interpretation of the monetary constitution to indexation of contracts in the modern economy. Section X offers summary conclusions.

II. Before the New Deal

Permanent modifications were made in the monetary rules and institutions in the 1930s; the monetary constitution was changed, with effects that continue to be felt forty years later. The nation experienced economic disaster in the 1930s. Understanding this, much can be excused. The confusion and contradiction among separate policy instruments, the haste with which actions were taken, the apparent disregard for long-run consequences, the failure of orderly political process—these deserve sympathetic explanation.[1] An appreciation of the setting for the policy choices of the 1930s does not, however, absolve the modern scholar from his duty of examining these institutional changes independently. We must look at the events of the 1930s, not in their own terms, but interpreted as permanent amendments to the nation's monetary constitution, changes that help to define the monetary *status quo* of the 1970s.

Before 1933, the United States monetary system was an integral part of an international monetary order widely referred to as "the gold standard." In fact, however, neither the international nor the domestic monetary system adhered closely to the classical gold standard rules. Up until Great Britain's departure from the gold standard in 1931, a shaky semblance of international monetary order was maintained, but this was largely due to the fair-weather cooperation of central banks superimposed on a single national system, that of Great Britain, which inspired worldwide trust and confidence. But a fatal deficiency in both the international and the domestic monetary systems was the fractional reserve base for monetary issue, a characteristic which made the whole edifice, national and international, dependent for its viability upon widespread confidence.

Nonetheless, there were features of the pre-1933 monetary constitution that appear extremely attractive, especially when set against criteria of individual freedom. The value of the dollar was defined by a specific gold content, $20.67 per fine ounce, a value that had not changed significantly since 1972, although inconvertible currencies circulated from time to time during the 19th century. The currency issue of the Federal Reserve System was limited to a defined multiple of the gold base. Currency was freely convertible into gold, both domestically and internationally. There were no restrictions on the ownership, purchase, and sale of gold in any form. The prevailing mythology of "sound money" exerted significant constraints on the behavior of individuals, in both their private-choice and their public-choice capacities.

---

1. For an *un*sympathetic but interesting summary description of the New Deal monetary measures, see Henry Mark Holzer, "How Americans Lost Their Right to Own Gold—and Became Criminals in the Process," *Brooklyn Law Review,* 39 (Winter 1973), 517–59.

Individuals, firms, and governmental units could enter into voluntary contracts that provided for deferred payments of specified amounts of gold, or of currency equivalent to specified amounts of gold.[2]

All of this was swept away by a series of New Deal actions in 1933 and 1934.

We shall summarize these actions in Section III, but in order to discuss the monetary situation of the 1930s adequately, and especially to evaluate alternative remedial measures, the conceptual underpinnings of the "gold standard" must be summarized. This requires the application of some fundamental elements of monetary theory. We begin at a very basic level, with apologies to informed readers.

Consider first a country with no international trade in which only gold is used as money. For simplicity, assume that there is a fixed quantity of gold for monetary use; gold is neither being mined nor used for nonmonetary purposes. In this setting, as real income (and product) changes, due to productivity shifts or otherwise, the price level will tend to adjust in an opposing direction. If real product increases, more goods and services will be available, and in order to maintain employment and output, sellers will find it necessary to lower the prices of nonmonetary goods. With the fixed money stock, turnover of the increased supply of real goods at unchanged prices would require an increase in the velocity of money, or, to put the same thing differently, would require a decrease in the ratio of monetary assets to income. Behaviorally, individuals would seek to adjust away from such a disequilibrium, if indeed they should find themselves in such a situation. When the level of prices falls by roughly the same percentage as real income has increased, the initial ratio of money (gold) to income would be restored.[3]

The same process also works for a decrease in real income or product, of course in the opposite direction. If a smaller quantity of real goods and services is available, and if prices do not change, people will find themselves

2. During the Greenback period, the United States Supreme Court had upheld the validity of specific gold clauses, even when these had the effect of distinguishing classes of monetary obligations. *Bronson v. Rhodes* (1869), 74 U.S. (7 Wall.), 229.

3. Prices and wages may, of course, be sticky, and there may arise quantity and employment adjustments during the period between an initial change and a subsequent monetary equilibrium. It is precisely for this reason that monetary and macroeconomic theorists have objected to monetary systems which require that the price level fall secularly with increasing productivity in the economy.

with excessive holdings of gold. They will want to spend more money on goods because aggregate gold holdings will become excessive. This willingness will be implemented through a higher level of demand which will induce a rise in prices, an increase that will restore the desired ratio of gold to real income.

Let us now consider a country that uses only gold as money, but with an economy that is linked by international trade (conducted in gold) to the economies of other countries. The domestic adjustment mechanism described above will be available, but if the country holds a relatively small part of the world's gold, much of the adjustment will now occur through international gold flows. To a first approximation, one may say that so far as a single small country is concerned, the price of gold in terms of other commodities is determined in world trade markets. At the market price, a single country can have as much gold as it wants. If real income in one country rises, prices need not fall to maintain the ratio of money to income, because additional gold can be imported to accomplish the same result. A slight decline in the price levels of all countries provides the additional gold to satisfy the demand of the one country. The maintenance of equilibrium in international trade requires that the adjustment take this form, because the price of gold relative to other commodities must be the same in all countries. While the international linking of countries reduces the price level adjustment that a country must undergo in response to a change in its real income, it also forces any country whose currency is linked to gold to share in the price level response to income changes throughout the world.

Let us consider what happens when a country uses as money a combination of gold and paper currency that is backed by and freely convertible to gold. If people are confident that the paper currency will not lose its value, they will find it convenient to hold most of their money in currency, because it is easier to store and to transport than gold. But gold will be demanded by people engaged in international trade, by people who like the look and feel of gold, and by people who think that there is a nonnegligible probability that paper currency will lose some or all of its value. If the system is not disturbed by fluctuations in confidence, a gold-linked paper currency for a single country will be superior to a monetary system that relies exclusively on gold. Not only will the economies of storage and transport associated with paper be achieved, but also the country will be able to obtain the money for its system without having to buy gold from the rest of the world. (From the perspective of the world as a whole, the latter economy is illusory, for it merely reduces the value of the stock of gold.) To a first approximation, a single country's price level will be the same whether it uses only gold as money or a combination of gold and a gold-linked currency. Equilibrium in international trade will require that the prices of internationally traded items in the one country, expressed in gold, be the same as their prices in other countries. The only difference that the use of a paper currency makes is that it reduces the demand for gold, which is equivalent to saying that the world price level expressed in gold will be higher to the extent that countries supplement gold with paper currency.

If one makes the more realistic assumption that the quantity of gold is not fixed but rather is augmentable at increasing cost, there will be little difference in the response to sharp shifts in the demand for gold, because the stock of gold will be many times the annual production. However, in the long run the stock of gold will increase whenever there are deposits that can be mined at a cost below the monetary value of gold, which value will depend on the extent to which paper augments gold as money. The long-run equilibrium and the adjustment to it are susceptible to the traditional economic analysis of supply and demand with stocks and flows.

As a final elaboration of the monetary system, consider the consequences of supplementing paper currency that is partially backed by gold with demand deposits in banks that have fractional reserves of currency and gold. This institutional change will further reduce the ratio of gold to the total supply of money, which has both advantages and disadvantages.

The profit from substituting paper and demand deposits for gold will accrue to the entities (whether governments or private firms) that have exclusive permission to issue currency and demand deposits. The issuer receives valued goods or promises for mere pieces of paper it prints or for bookkeeping entries. The issuer may promise to reexchange the currency or deposits for gold, but unless it pays interest on its liabilities or keeps reserves equal to 100 per cent of its liabilities, the issuer is receiving an interest-free loan of indefinite duration, in an amount equal to that part of its currency or deposits that is not backed by reserves. If the issue of currency and demand deposits is not restricted, and issuers are allowed to compete, they will offer their customers enough extra services so that investment in this activity will yield the same return as in other activities.

The quantity of currency and deposits (as measured by their gold value) is in any case limited by the demand for cash balances. If there is more currency and deposits than people wish to hold, they will try to spend their excess holdings. This will drive domestic prices up. People will begin to find foreign purchases more attractive than domestic ones, and will convert some currency and deposits to gold for international trade. To check the gold drain, issuers will have to reduce the amounts of currency and demand deposits, until domestic prices fall to a level that restores equilibrium in international trade. If the demand for gold continues to the point that an issuer's reserves are threatened with exhaustion, more drastic measures are required. One solution that has often been applied is a suspension of convertibility. The issuer says, in effect, "I'll give you gold when I can; in the meantime you'll just have to be satisfied with paper." Sometimes convertibility is reestablished when the bank (by selling assets) or the treasury (by raising taxes) acquires enough gold from the rest of the world; sometimes banks go bankrupt and treasuries simply renege by devaluing their currencies.

To guard against the need to suspend convertibility, a conservative government or private bank would try to keep a target level of reserves, often in some ratio to outstanding currency. If people demanded gold from its reserves, the bank would cut back its currency and deposit issue by some multiple of the size of the gold drainage. If people supplied the bank with additional gold, it would expand the currency and deposit issue, again by a multiple of the change in gold holdings. A bank would achieve the desired change in currency and deposit issue by changing its lending: To expand the issue, more loans would be made; to contract, fewer new loans would be made and old loans would be called or not renewed. Currency and deposit expansion would be associated with lower than average interest rates, and contraction with higher than average rates.

Beginning in about the 1870s, the quasi-public central bankers felt that it was not necessary for them to transmit every shock that they experienced to the domestic economy. They felt that they could successfully "lean against the wind." If an accumulation of reserves was seen as temporary, a central bank might refrain from expanding its lending. If a depletion of gold reserves was predicted to be short-lived, it might not contract loans outstanding. To the extent that bankers could be successful in such efforts, domestic interest rates would be somewhat more stable than under a regime in which the conservative gold-standard rules were strictly observed.

If international events provoke an outflow of gold that does not reflect a basic excessive supply of money, but rather a short-term fluctuation that will be reversed in a few months, then by permitting reserves to absorb all of the fluctuation rather than transmitting the fluctuation to the money supply through the banks, the monetary authorities can save the economy the costs of an unnecessary contraction and expansion. When bankers are required to contract their lending, businessmen must reduce their operations. Some firms will lay off workers. Other firms may face bankruptcy because they cannot raise funds to meet their obligations to creditors. The bunching of layoffs into a single period makes it all the more difficult for individual workers to find new jobs.

Furthermore, the reduction in the money supply associated with the credit contraction will generate a reduction in the equilibrium price level. Unemployed workers will typically find that they can obtain work only by accepting money wages lower than those that they expect to be able to secure. Some employed workers may find that they can hold their jobs only if they accept reduced wages. If workers do not perceive the possibility that the whole price level may be falling, so that lower money wages may retain the same real purchasing power as before, they may decide to keep looking for jobs that pay more acceptable wages. Similarly, people with products to sell may accumulate substantial inventories before offering the price discounts needed to move their merchandise.

An unanticipated expansion will have opposite effects. Employers will be unable to find workers as easily as usual and will raise wages. Inventories will be unusually depleted and shortages will develop until prices are raised. These processes depend critically on expectations about the rate of changes of prices. If people generally believe that prices are rising at 4 per cent per year, they may regard circumstances that limit the rise in the prices and wages that they receive to 2 per cent as just as unacceptable as a fall in wages and prices. If they perceive prices to be generally falling, they may find a corresponding fall in the prices and wages that they receive just as acceptable as stability in their own prices when prices are generally stable.

One more element of monetary theory is needed to complete the picture, and that is the role of money as a standard of deferred payment. When two people make a contract that involves payment of a definite amount of money at a time after the contract is made, there is some risk that the money will not be worth what they think it will be worth when delivery occurs. The contract implicitly assigns this risk. The payer risks the possibility that money will be worth more at the time of payment than he had anticipated when agreeing to the contract, so that he would be paying more in real terms than he had anticipated. The payee risks the possibility that prices will rise unexpectedly, so that he would be receiving less than he anticipated. In a system in which gold is the only money there is a rough symmetry in the treatment of debtors and creditors; neither is protected against waves of hoarding and dishoarding and against long-term swings in gold production, but both are substantially protected against short-run disruptive and unpredictable changes in the supply of money. The supply of money is jointly determined by the behavior of all persons producing and using money, and not by any governmental authority.

When a gold reserve system is substituted for the idealized gold coin standard, and when a commercial banking system organized on a fractional reserve basis is superimposed on this, the relatively modest, symmetric uncertainties of a commodity market are replaced by the more complex uncertainties of confidence swings and political processes. There is first the political risk of a change in the gold value of the monetary unit. Excessive expansion of paper currency will put central bankers in a position where they must choose between the painful unemployment generated by monetary contraction and the embarrassment of a devaluation. Political expediency often lies with the latter. If the gold value of paper currency could somehow be made inflexible (or if creditors are permitted through gold clauses to insure against the possibility of devaluation), and if the central bank or treasury is required to maintain a stable ratio of paper currency to gold coin or bullion, then the individual creditor is substantially protected against significant inflation. But the potential debtor is not comparably protected against deflation, because wholesale conversion of currency into gold can result in a multiple contraction in the money supply as bankers seek to maintain the ratio of reserves to currency. This vulnerability of a gold reserve system is aggravated when a fractional reserve deposit banking system is superimposed on the currency issue authority. As individuals begin to doubt the soundness of the system and seek to exercise their rights of convertibility, they exchange bank deposits for currency (which serves as a reserve for bank deposits) and/or gold (which serves as a reserve both for currency and for bank deposits). Dramatic reductions in the effective supply of circulating media result in this way, due solely to changes in expectations.

If such a crisis of confidence affects only a single country that represents just a small part of the world gold system, the consequence need not be prolonged monetary distress. The rest of the world will offer a relatively elastic supply of gold, imports of which will permit banks to pay gold to anyone who wants to hold it.[4] The only cost is an increase in other exports or a decrease in other imports. However, a world monetary system built in such a way on fractional reserves is vulnerable to a rapid succession of bank failures and currency devaluations in major countries. A combination of such confidence-shattering events makes it impossible to satisfy the worldwide public demand for currency and gold, given a low level of confidence in banks and national currencies, without a substantial contraction in income. The accompanying reduction in the price level drastically increases the real burden of deferred payments, to the financial ruin of debtors.

III. The New Deal Monetary Actions

With the above theory as background, the crisis that Roosevelt faced when he began his term in office in March 1933 can be more readily understood, and we can explore more fully the alternatives for action along with the measures actually taken.

Commencing in late 1930, the United States suffered through a series of banking crises. Many banks failed during each crisis, and the Federal Reserve System did little or nothing toward restoring liquidity in the economy. The most severe of these crises took place in February 1933, just before Roosevelt's inauguration. On March 5, 1933, one day after assuming office, President

---

4. See Milton Friedman and Anna J. Schwartz, *A Monetary History of the United States, 1867–1960* (Princeton University Press for the National Bureau of Economic Research, Paperback Ed. 1971), 108–10, 158–62, on the panics of 1893 and 1907 for examples.

Franklin D. Roosevelt, invoking the questionable authority of a 1917 Trading with the Enemy statute, declared a national bank holiday. All banks were closed, and they were prohibited from paying out gold or dealing in foreign exchange. This executive action was confirmed by Congress on March 9, 1933. Banks were allowed to reopen gradually, but the prohibition on dealings in gold and foreign exchange remained in force, apparently based on a fear that both an internal and an external gold and foreign exchange drainage would accompany convertibility. One month after the bank holiday, the President issued an executive order that forbade the hoarding of gold and required all banks to deliver gold stocks to the central banks, at the parity of $20.67 per fine ounce. In June 1933, Congress passed a joint resolution abrogating gold clauses in all contracts, past and future, and in February 1935, the Supreme Court upheld this action by Congress, at least with respect to all private contracts.

In January 1934, the Gold Reserve Act was passed, authorizing the President to reestablish a gold value of the dollar at a level between 50 per cent and 60 per cent of its former value, and President Roosevelt immediately announced that the dollar was to be redefined by a new gold price of $35 per fine ounce, representing a reduction in the gold value of the dollar to 59 per cent of its former level. In effect, the United States returned to a gold related monetary system after this date, but the restrictions on private ownership and trade in gold were retained, along with the prohibitions on gold-clause contracts. Gold was bought at the new price only by governmental authorities, and, as a result of international agreement in 1936, sales restricted to cooperating foreign central banks were made. The devaluation insured that for the succeeding thirty years the domestic monetary structure would be divorced from the internal and external discipline imposed by the operation of a gold standard. Nominally, external gold movements could exert feedback effects on internal monetary policy, but these were not relevant for the United States until the 1960s.

In 1933, continued adherence to the international gold standard, as it was then operative, might have prevented or substantially delayed the internal monetary expansion that was so urgently required. The time was ripe for dramatic shifts, but in one sense, problems were created by the failure of political leaders to act boldly enough. A shift from a gold-based currency to a national fiat currency could have been accomplished readily. Convertibility could have been suspended, with respect to both gold and currency, and new currency could have been issued that was explicitly divorced from gold. Had these steps been taken, an independent monetary standard would have been born. In this case, there would have been no need to call in gold held outside the government, to prohibit ownership and trade in gold, or even to abrogate contracts made in gold. The market price of gold in the United States could have been allowed to find its own level, and sale of the government's stock of gold might have made the price relatively low, so that gold clauses might not have been burdensome.

Instead the government suspended convertibility while keeping gold out of everyone's reach. It is not clear whether this was done as a prelude to devaluation, or out of deference to a gold mythology that presumed a currency to be sound because it had gold backing, even if no one could have the gold.

So long as the link between the dollar and gold was to be retained there were several pragmatic political reasons for the accompanying restrictions. But these must be separated into two sets. The initial prohibitions on convertibility could have been justified by a belief that individuals and firms, both domestic and foreign, had lost confidence in the United States monetary structure and that they would have, if given the opportunity after March 1933, attempted to increase their holdings of gold. The suspension of convertibility was, however, accompanied by the prohibition on trade in gold among private persons and firms and on private contracting in gold, along with the abrogation of former contracts that contained gold clauses. This set of restrictions can most readily be rationalized on the basis of an intent to return to gold at a higher parity. And it is in this respect that the whole policy framework of the early New Deal seems most suspicious. By calling in all gold stocks in exchange for the dollar equivalent in currency at the old parity, the government put itself in a position to secure 100 per cent of the profits from any devaluation that it might introduce. To the extent that private persons held title to gold, devaluation would have provided them with windfall gains. In fact, through its policy of asserting title to all gold stocks, and by calling in all gold at the preexisting parity, the government made a profit of almost $3 billion on the dollar devaluation.[5]

5. In the political temper of the times, this was probably more widely acceptable than a policy that would have allowed "speculative" profits to be made by private persons. Pol-

Essentially the same rationale can be extended to the initial actions which abrogated the gold clauses in contracts that existed in 1933. The holder of a deferred claim expressed in gold was in a position equivalent to the holder of gold itself. And windfall gains would have been secured if the dollar price of gold had been increased. Windfall gains would have accrued to creditors holding contracts with gold clauses, while windfall losses would have accrued to debtors in this set of agreements. The distributional consequences could have been prevented only by an abrogation of such clauses, insuring that contractual obligations would be met in units of current currency value.

With the intent of devaluation understood, the government's action in restricting gold ownership, trading, and contracting in 1933 can be explained. But a different question emerges after the January 1934 devaluation. Once the dollar had been redefined at its new and higher gold content, what was the basis for continuing the restrictions on voluntary contract? There seem to be three possible explanations. First of all, during the 1920s central bankers had come increasingly to the view that internal or domestic circulation of gold was not desirable. This position was based on a desire to maximize the monetary potential of gold by confining it to central banks and on an unwillingness to allow the existing gold standard to be opened up to the internal discipline and possible instability that individual ownership of gold would impose.[6] The shift toward gold bullion and gold-exchange standards found ample support in the pre-1933 discussion. A second possible reason for the failure to remove restrictions on gold ownership and use following the devaluation was probably insecurity about the effects of devaluation itself. As the subsequent gold inflow amply demonstrated, there need have been no fear that the new value of gold was set too low, but Roosevelt Administration officials and advisers may not have predicted this effect. Hence, the restrictions may have been held on in the possible anticipation of still further devaluation for the same reasons as those that prompted the initial actions. Finally, and most importantly, the restrictions on individuals' dealings in gold may have been viewed as one means of preventing the multiple con-

---

iticians were successful in shifting much of the blame for economic conditions away from government and onto private decision-makers.

6. See Gustav Cassell, *The Downfall of the Gold Standard* (New York: Augustus M. Kelley, 1966), 15–18. (First published in 1936.)

tractions in aggregate money stocks that had produced the banking crises. Even if nothing was to be done about fractional reserve banking, and hence the inherent instability involved in potential shifts between high-powered and low-powered money, there may have been the feeling that removing the prospects for conversion into very high-powered money would tend to generate confidence in the dollar currency itself. The administration decisionmakers did not foresee the importance of Federal Deposit Insurance in reducing this type of instability in the total system.

In retrospect, it seems clear that full convertibility into gold could have been restored in 1934, at the $35 price. Domestic ownership and trade in gold could have been reintroduced without any of the fears coming true, at least for the years before World War II. The policy mix as it was implemented offered the worst of both worlds in a sense. Individuals could not avail themselves of the protection, the predictability about monetary matters that the traditional gold standard had possessed, or at least had been thought to possess. At the same time, they were not allowed to make ordinary private contracts in gold, as would have been possible under a truly independent national fiduciary standard.

The monetary constitution, as it emerged from the New Deal, was a makeshift affair, consistent with no single conceptual framework. The international adjustment mechanism, tied as it was to gold as a special commodity with a defined dollar price, seemed to justify the prohibition of possession, purchase, and sale of gold by Americans. As a result, changes that might have been temporary aberrations from the country's long-standing traditions of free voluntary contract and free markets were cemented into the legal order, bringing with them the precedent-setting potential for still other interventions with freedom of contract.

IV. The New Deal and Constitutional Law

We have deliberately referred to the New Deal monetary changes as "constitutional," and we have used this word in its generalized meaning. A "constitutional" change is one that modifies the "rules of the game," the institutional framework within which both public and private decisions are made and actions taken. A "constitutional" change is intended to be, and is understood to be, quasi-permanent; it is expected to remain in force over some indefinitely long time period. In this most general usage of "constitutional," there is no explicit reference to constitutionality in a specific legal or historical setting. Nonetheless, the generalized conception must offer the principles upon which constitutional law is normally distinguished from other branches of law.

We should have expected that monetary changes that were understood to be "constitutional," in the generalized sense of the term, would have aroused controversy in constitutional law per se in the United States. This controversy was concentrated in a series of cases that challenged the constitutionality of the abrogation of the gold clauses in contracts. The Supreme Court considered these cases as a group, and explicitly addressed itself to the legality of the Joint Resolution passed by Congress on June 5, 1933, the resolution that abrogated gold clauses in all contracts, public and private, past and future. In February 1935, the Supreme Court, in a set of five-to-four decisions, upheld the legality of the gold-clause abrogations with respect to all private and local government obligations, and hedged on its judgment with respect to the obligation of the federal government itself.[7] In this section we shall examine the judgment of the Court, both with reference to criteria of monetary and economic theory and with reference to the conception of contract.[8]

Initially, it is necessary to stress that money is different in its legal characteristics from other aspects of "law" even when ideally considered. The written Constitution of the United States gives to the Congress the power to regulate the value of money, and constitutional law applicable in other countries has been interpreted as giving to national governments comparable

7. See *Norman v. Baltimore and Ohio Railroad Co.*, 294 U.S. 240; *Nortz v. United States,* 294 U.S. 317; *Perry v. United States,* 294 U.S. 330.

8. These events stimulated a flurry of discussion among constitutional lawyers, and the law journals and reviews published numerous papers in the months immediately preceding and following these decisions. A selected listing of these papers is as follows: John P. Dawson, "The Gold Clause Decisions," *Michigan Law Review,* 33 (March 1935), 647–83; John Dickenson, "The Gold Decisions," *University of Pennsylvania Law Review,* 83 (April 1935), 715–25; Henry M. Hart, Jr., "The Gold Clause in United States Bonds," *Harvard Law Review,* 48 (May 1935), 1057–99; Arthur Nussbaum, "Comparative and International Aspects of American Gold Clause Abrogation," *Yale Law Journal,* 44 (November 1934), 53–89; J. Roland Pennock, "The Private Bond Case as a Postponement of the Real Issue," *University of Pennsylvania Law Review,* 84 (December 1935), 194–211; Russell Z. Post and Charles H. Willard, "The Power of Congress to Nullify Gold Clauses," *Harvard Law Review,* 46 (June 1933), 1225–57.

powers to those that were explicitly delegated to the United States federal government. In the United States and elsewhere this has been interpreted to mean that the legislative branch of government has the authority, as constituted, to make genuine changes in the "constitution" with respect to money.[9] Legislatures can, effectively, change the fundamental "law" in this area, something that they cannot do in the more general setting of rulemaking, or at least, they were not considered to be able to do in the period of the New Deal.[10] (One problem in examining the whole set of policy measures and the court decisions from the vantage point of 1975 is that of overcoming the profound differences in constitutional attitude that have taken place over the forty-year period.) What this means is that "amendments" to the effective monetary constitution can be made by ordinary legislative majorities of national governments. This power to modify the real constitution was explicitly set out in the written legal Constitution in the United States, and comparably interpreted in other nations.[11]

This explicit delegation of power to the Congress, and through Congress to the Executive, removed from the Judiciary any seriously considered legal issue as to the legitimacy of most of the New Deal monetary measures. The prohibitions on the ownership of gold were subjected to only minor legal challenges because gold was acknowledged to be the basic monetary commodity.[12]

---

9. Persons with a more conservative view have maintained that the only power delegated to Congress was the power to specify a meaning of the dollar in terms of gold or some other commodity, but this view has not prevailed. See John Sparks, "Notes on the Legal Aspects of Gold Ownership" (Mimeographed), Hillsdale College, Hillsdale, Michigan, 1974.

10. As Gerald T. Dunne notes, the absence of more specific definition of the monetary authority in the written Constitution of the United States has been one element that has allowed governmental authority to be expanded, perhaps beyond all limits foreseen by the Founding Fathers. See Gerald T. Dunne, *Monetary Decisions of the Supreme Court* (New Brunswick: Rutgers University Press, 1960), 1.

11. The Principle of "nominalism" has been adopted as the basis for the "law of money" in most Western nations. This principle states that a monetary unit (a dollar or pound) is what the national government declares it to be. Hence, monetary obligations are fulfilled by payment in monetary units, as defined at the time of repayment. For a detailed discussion, see F. A. Mann, *The Legal Aspect of Money*, 3d ed. (Oxford: Clarendon Press, 1971), 76–96.

12. For a discussion of the unsuccessful challenges, along with citations, see Henry Mark Holzer, "How Americans Lost Their Right to Own Gold—and Became Criminals

Hence, any policy directly relating to gold was held to be within the explicit delegation of power to regulate the value of money. The federal government would have been successfully challenged in 1933 had it prohibited the private ownership of any nonmonetary metallic commodity, say copper or zinc. (Once again, we must concentrate on the legal situation of the early 1930s. After the personnel and the attitude of the Court changed in the direction of the legal position represented by Justice Felix Frankfurter, the Supreme Court became much more reluctant to find any legislative action to be outside constitutional powers.)

Those groups and interests who opposed the New Deal monetary measures were limited, in their potential constitutional challenges of import, to the abrogation of the gold clauses in contracts. These challenges were made with the explicit acknowledgment that the Congress had the power to regulate the value of money. The challenges were reduced to the subsidiary question of whether or not the abrogation of the gold clauses was necessary to the acknowledged power to regulate the value of money. In its ruling, the Court held that this action was a necessary part of the larger set of actions in the exercise of this acknowledged legal power of the Congress. It is this basis of the Court's decision that we must evaluate. In so doing, we must apply both modern monetary theory and monetary theory as this was understood by the Court at the time of its decision.

We must begin by an examination of the purpose of the monetary measures of the New Deal, considered as a combined package. Why was it necessary to take drastic action in 1933? The banking structure was in chaos; confidence in the security of bank deposits had nearly disappeared; and individuals were seeking to convert deposit claims into currency. To the extent that *some* individuals were successful in this, a multiple contraction in the nation's stock of money was required. But without additional high-powered money, *all* persons could not accomplish this, because of the fractional reserve basis for the commercial banking system. The attempt by many persons to liquidate deposits was, literally, producing insolvency for the whole financial system. The epidemic of bank failures might have undermined confidence in currency itself, producing attempted conversion of currency into

---

in the Process," *Brooklyn Law Review,* 39 (Winter 1973), 517–59. These challenges were not accepted for review by the Supreme Court.

gold. The first requirement of any policy was, therefore, to stop the attempted shifts into high-powered money and to restore confidence in the system, as it then existed. The suspension of convertibility was a reasonable step, and this clearly seemed to lie within the authority of the government.

Having suspended convertibility, however, did it follow that all trade in gold should be prohibited, and that subsequently all gold be called in and private ownership forbidden? It might be plausibly argued that, so long as gold was allowed privately to circulate, individuals would not reattain confidence in using currency or bank deposits, that confidence in the system would be restored only if the private circulation of gold, independent of the convertibility privilege, could have been prevented. For purposes of this analysis, let us accept this argument as one that was empirically justifiable.

This would have provided the basis for the calling in of gold held privately, and the prohibition of private ownership.[13] In this action there need have been no confiscation of value, however, and no redistribution of wealth from one class to another. It is only when we move to the next step beyond this that such questions arise. The economy desperately needed an increase in aggregate demand, in purchasing power. Deflation had occurred; prices were much lower than 1929 levels. Inflation was positively, indeed urgently, needed, at least to the extent of reattaining 1929 levels of incomes and prices. Monetary means of promoting this inflation required that the aggregate supply of money be expanded.[14] The Thomas Amendment to the Agricultural Adjustment Act, passed in 1933, authorized the issue of new currency, but the idea of devaluing the dollar in terms of gold was widely interpreted as the most effective means of securing an expanded monetary base for inflation. Only a month after the suspension of convertibility there were indications of an intent to raise the dollar price of gold. And, of course, suspension of convertibility itself created speculation concerning future devaluation. It is at precisely this point that profound issues of equity as well as contract were

13. There was an existing legal justification for these actions. In its 1869 decision upholding the constitutionality of a tax on state bank notes, the Supreme Court stated that Congress could restrain the circulation as money of anything that it had not specifically authorized. *Veazie Bank v. Fenno*, 8 Wall 533 (1869).

14. In retrospect, the need for expansion of the money supply seems clear, although at the time there was also a fear of excessive inflation, as in Germany in the early 1920s, so that measures to expand the money supply encountered considerable opposition.

introduced. If the dollar price of gold was to be arbitrarily increased, and if private holders of gold were to be required to turn in all holdings to the Treasury, what price did they "deserve" to get for their stocks: The old parity of $20.67, or the new parity of $35 per fine ounce? In the first case, the private holders of gold would have suffered an opportunity loss in the amount of more than $14 per ounce, although they need not have suffered historical losses in any accounting sense. The government would have gained all of the profits on the revaluation of gold, and not only the profits on the revaluation of its own holdings. In the second case, all persons and units, including the Treasury, who happened to hold gold stocks at the moment of the depreciation would have secured windfall gains. We know that the first of these two alternatives was chosen; by calling in all gold and paying for this at the old parity, the government tried to secure *all* of the profits from devaluation of the dollar.

We shall return to these alternatives, but let us now look at the relevance of the gold clauses in outstanding contracts at the time of the change in the gold price. The private owner of an ounce of gold was required to turn this in to the Treasury at the old parity. He gained nothing from the depreciation. As a matter of simple equity, it might have seemed that the holder of a deferred claim to gold, a creditor holding an obligation containing a gold clause, should not have been differentially favored over the holder of the monetary commodity itself. To call in gold at the old parity while, at the same time, continuing to honor the letter of contract through the gold clauses might have seemed contrary to justice and to law. Some such attitude might have informed the thinking of the Roosevelt Administration when the Joint Resolution was passed and also that of the majority of the Supreme Court when this resolution was upheld.

The critical questions should have been raised, not on the gold clause contracts in isolation, but on the distribution of the gains or profits from dollar depreciation. The holder of gold and the holder of deferred claims to gold might have been treated equitably by paying *both* at the new parity, that is by paying holders at $35 per ounce and honoring all gold clauses in obligations outstanding. The dissenting minority of the Court held a weak reed when they limited themselves to the gold-clause abrogations while acknowledging the authority of the government to pay holders of gold coin or bullion at the old parity. Had the minority stood willing to bring the latter into dispute and to question the government's power in this respect, they could have constructed a more convincing argument.

Let us return to the alternatives noted above. In one sequence, holders of gold coin and gold bullion are paid at the newer and higher price, set at the time of the devaluation. All gold clauses in contracts are honored. In the other, and historically descriptive sequence, holders of gold coin and gold bullion are paid at the old, and lower, price, and all gold clauses in outstanding contracts are abrogated. The question that we must ask is whether or not this sequence was necessary if the government, in the situation confronting it in 1933, was to fulfill its constituted authority to regulate the value of money. If we answer this specific question affirmatively, we must conclude that the majority opinion of the Court was correct, despite its apparent negation of long-standing principles relevant to the sanctity of contract. If we answer this specific question negatively, we must conclude that the majority of the Court erred in its judgment on its own grounds and that serious and wholly unnecessary harm was wrought to long-standing constitutional principle, due either to a misunderstanding of monetary theory or to a concealed attempt to achieve distributional objectives that could not have been embodied in the monetary clause of the Constitution.

What did the Roosevelt Administration, and its rubber-stamp Congress, seek when it went beyond the suspension of convertibility to devaluation? As we have already noted, one plausible objective would have been that of generating a domestic inflation in prices and incomes.[15] As suggested above, this would have required that the supply of circulating medium, currency and bank deposits, be increased. We must, therefore, examine the potential effects of devaluation in this respect. Our question becomes: Would the alternative sequence have prevented this increase in the supply of circulating medium and, hence, have interfered with the accomplishment of this basic governmental purpose? Analyzed in this way, in the context of the sequence historically followed, we reach an interesting, and somewhat surprising, conclusion. As we shall try to demonstrate, the objective sought by devaluation

15. A more traditional reason for currency devaluation has been deterioration in a nation's gold and foreign exchange reserve position. But the United States devaluation was almost unique in this respect; there was no danger to the nation's foreign reserve position prior to the devaluation. On this, see M. Palyi, *The Twilight of Gold, 1914–1936* (Chicago: Henry Regnery, 1972), 280.

could have been better achieved by the alternative than by the actual scenario. That is, domestic prices and incomes might have been boosted more promptly and more effectively if holders of gold coin and bullion had been paid at the new and higher parity and if all gold clauses had been honored.

Consider the following possible chain of events. Suppose that, in 1933, the government should have suspended convertibility and, simultaneously, raised the price of gold to $35 per fine ounce, while calling in all gold coin and bullion at the higher price and outlawing subsequent private ownership. In order to purchase gold, the government would have drawn from its deposit balances in the Federal Reserve Banks; checks drawn on these balances would have been transferred to private parties in exchange for gold. To cover these withdrawals, the government would have issued gold certificates on the newly acquired stocks, and these certificates would have been transferred to the Federal Reserve Banks in exchange for newly created government deposits, just sufficient to replace those used up in the initial gold purchases. In the gold-purchase transaction, as such, the Treasury would have neither gained nor lost. As private parties deposited these government checks in their own commercial banks, these banks would clear these through their Federal Reserve Banks. And, since these government checks were drawn against a Federal Reserve account, commercial banks would find that their own reserves had been increased, while deposits had increased by only some fraction of this amount. This would have provided the basis for a multiple expansion in the quantity of bank deposits.

Under ordinary circumstances this would, in itself, have been sufficient to generate inflation. But banks already possessed excess legal reserves, and although some pressure toward expansion in deposits would have been generated by an increase in reserves, there is no guarantee that the overall effect would have been sufficiently great. But there is a second and more direct force that would have been at work to spark an inflation in domestic prices and incomes. Persons and firms who had profited from holding gold at the time of devaluation would have found themselves holding more assets in the form of currency and bank deposits ($35 for every $20.67 held earlier) than they desired to hold. They would have attempted to shift out of monetary assets into nonmonetary assets. As a result, prices of nonmonetary goods and services would have increased.

To the extent that these two forces operated fully, and that the government maintaining the predevaluation ratio of money to gold, there would have been an increase in money income roughly proportional to the devaluation. In this setting, the holders of gold-clause obligations would not have gained relative to debtors. Since incomes would have been increased generally throughout the economy, the burden of payment of a gold-clause obligation would have been the same as before the devaluation and subsequent inflation. To the extent that the inflation in incomes and prices was not proportionately so large as the devaluation, debtors who had to meet gold-clause obligations would have suffered in real terms, whereas creditors would have gained. In this case, creditors would have been in the same position as those who held gold coin or bullion at the time of the devaluation.

We are not defending this alternative scenario in the sense that it is advanced as an "ideal" policy package for the setting of 1933. It seems unlikely that incomes and prices would have increased proportionately with the devaluation; supplementary measures toward expanding the supply of circulating medium would surely have been required. But we have constructed this alternative scenario in some detail here for comparative purposes. This scenario, had it been followed, would have generated *more* of the desired effects than that sequence of policy measures that were enacted and put into force by the Roosevelt Administration. Let us now examine the latter in more detail.

Convertibility was suspended; dealings in gold were prohibited; individuals were required to turn in all gold to the Treasury; private ownership was forbidden. But the price for gold coin and bullion was set at the old rather than the new parity. The government tried to guarantee to itself all of the profits from the devaluation. Distributionally, this might have been questioned, but this distributional difference, in itself, need not have prevented the attainment of the desired inflation in incomes and prices had not the government effectively sterilized the gold purchases. For gold purchased from private persons, the Treasury issued gold certificates and transferred these to the Federal Reserve Banks in exchange for federal deposit accounts. These accounts were drawn down to pay for the gold, as in the alternative scenario, but a profit was left over. If the government had utilized these profits to expand its rate of spending in the economy, the desired increases in incomes and prices might have taken place. Instead of this, however, the Treasury set aside $2 billion of the $2.8 billion profits in a special exchange stabilization fund, while $645 million was used to replace national bank notes. Of the total of $2.8 billion, less than $200 million was made available for general fund outlays by the federal government.[16] For the bulk of the paper profits, the disposition made effectively insured that this potential purchasing power could not be returned to the domestic economy and could not, therefore, become reserves of the banking system. The forces that would have been at work under the alternative sequence were, therefore, largely nullified. Private parties who previously held gold found themselves with the same share of their assets in monetary form and hence had no incentive to expand spending rates. And the government did not use the profits to expand its own spending rate. In effect, the devaluation effort per se was "wasted" almost completely; the opportunity to increase the money supply in 1933 directly through devaluation was missed, although the quantity of money did begin to increase rapidly in 1934.

Events moved swiftly in the dramatic years of the 1930s. By the time that the Supreme Court considered the arguments in the gold-clause cases, during the October 1934 term, it probably was clear that the restoration of pre-Depression incomes and prices was not imminent. As an inflationary measure, devaluation seemed to have failed. In this setting, and quite apart from the equity as between holders of gold and deferred payment obligations, the enforcement of gold clauses in contracts would have seriously damaged debtor interests. Estimates as to the quantity of gold-clause obligations outstanding ranged up to $100 billion. Debtors under these contracts would have been required to increase payments in real terms by some 69 per cent over what they might have legitimately expected to pay in the absence of the devaluation. The real burden of debt would have been increased rather than decreased by the enforcement of these clauses. Recognition of this was surely one influence on the Court's majority opinion.

In a sense, the revalued price of gold was wholly arbitrary in the setting that actually occurred. Since the potential expansionary effects of revaluation, which would have increased incomes throughout the system and reduced the burden of debt designated in nominal dollars, were largely nullified by the actions of the Treasury and the Federal Reserve Banks, the arbitrary price set on gold was divorced from the domestic economy. In subsequent

16. See Friedman and Schwartz, 471n.

years, this price did generate an inflow of gold which was then allowed to provide a basis for gradual monetary expansion, but this was not the setting within which the Court's decision was made.

How do we answer the question posed above with respect to the Court's findings? Were the actions taken in 1933–34 necessary if the government was to fulfill its constituted authority to regulate the value of money? The analysis suggests that abrogation of gold clauses in contractual obligations was not a necessary complement to the authority of government to regulate the value of money in the setting of 1933, *provided* that the government itself should have acted consistently in furtherance of its announced objectives. But, as we have indicated, the government was far from consistent in its set of policy actions, and it effectively nullified the potential results of devaluation. In this situation, what could the Court have decided? The Court could not, itself, instruct the government in monetary theory, nor could it force the government to take the positive action that might have been required to accomplish its declared objectives. (Again, it is necessary to emphasize the difference in the presumed power of the Supreme Court in the 1930s and in the post-Warren years when the Court commenced to take initiatory action in the absence of legislative action, as, for example, in the apportionment decisions.)

There was one important element in the situation confronting the Court that we have not explicitly discussed, although it is, of course, related to the objective of the New Deal measures. In reading the opinion of the majority of the Court, it seems clear that the gold-clause abrogations would not have been upheld in a situation where the government devalued the currency from a stable basis with the purpose of securing profits for itself. As the Court stated, the purpose of the gold-clause obligations was to protect the creditor against declines in the real value of the obligation, that is, against monetary inflation subsequent to the initiation of the contract. But few, if any, holders of gold-clause obligations would have suffered reductions in real value through abrogation. The domestic economy had undergone significant deflation in incomes and prices in the crisis years after 1929. Inflation was required, and desired, in order to get back to a pre-Depression *status quo ante*. In advancing their claims for increased real value under the gold clauses, creditors were forced to argue that they should gain distributionally as a result of fortuitous economic circumstances, that they should be immune from general economic loss because of the particular structure in which contracts were written, and which was introduced for quite different reasons. Interpreted as protective devices against reductions in real value, the gold clauses were, in a sense, redundant in the circumstances of the early 1930s. Real values of all monetary obligations had increased substantially; enforcement of the gold clauses after devaluation would have added yet another increment to the real value increase accruing to holders of such claims. This element strengthened the judgment of the Court's majority. Perhaps more importantly for our purposes, the Court's decision cannot be read as legitimizing subsequent prohibitions on index contracts, whether in gold or other commodities or in some composite, that are designed solely to protect citizens against inflation from a stable or even increasing price level.[17]

V. Contractual Origins of Monetary Rules

Article I, Section 8 of the United States Constitution gives the Congress the power to "coin money, regulate the Value thereof, and of foreign coin, and fix the Standard of Weights and Measures." As we have noted, the problem faced by the Supreme Court in the gold-clause cases, as well as in earlier judgments, was one of determining whether the actions taken by Congress fell within this designated monetary authority. For the gold-clause legislation in particular, this included the determination as to whether specific contractual agreements (the gold-clause obligations) interfered with Congress's exercise of this stipulated monetary authority. If congressional action was explicitly taken within this authority, and if the Court upheld the Congress's factual assertion to this effect or made this factual finding on its own, the legal issue, strictly speaking, was settled. There was no need for the Court to go behind the actual statement in the written Constitution, no need for the Court to examine the appropriateness of the stipulated monetary authority, to analyze the possible meaning of the constitutional statement itself.

In this section, we shall attempt to look critically at the monetary compo-

---

17. B. Nowlin Keener suggests that this emphasis in the Court's majority opinion, written by Chief Justice Charles Evans Hughes, possibly reflects Hughes' sympathetic awareness of the ideas of Irving Fisher. In support, Keener mentions the interesting fact that in the early 1920s, Hughes had been an honorary vice-president of Fisher's Stable Money League. See *Transcript of Keener vs. Congress with Explanations* (Privately circulated, 1973), 22.

nent in the political constitution with the objective of deriving a delegation of monetary authority to legislative bodies from the idealized constitutional-choice calculus of persons in a constitutional convention. Once we have taken this step, we can then return to the language of the stipulated power in the United States Constitution, as written, and to the interpretations that have been placed on this power.

Consider a hypothetical setting for constitution-making. A group of persons is assembled for the purpose of agreeing on rules under which subsequent private and public behavior can take place. To the extent that individual economic positions in subsequent periods are predictable in advance, there would be little prospect of securing genuine agreement on rules, on "a constitution." In order to construct a setting within which genuine constitutional attitudes may inform individual behavior, we can take either one of two possible alternatives. First, we can postulate that the rules to be chosen are to apply over a sufficiently long time sequence to insure that individual positions in specific subperiods remain uncertain.[18] Second, we can postulate that the individual adopts a normative attitude in which he places himself behind a "veil of ignorance," where he "thinks" himself equally probable of occupying any position in the society.[19] In both of these logical idealizations of a choice setting, the persons will be led to evaluate alternative rules and/or institutions on the basis of their general applicability and working properties, rather than in terms of the potential furtherance of any identifiable self-interest. "Fairness" and/or "efficiency" become plausibly acceptable criteria for judgment here, judgment which is applied to the procedure or process rather than to the particular outcomes generated.

We shall not elaborate on an analysis of the constitutional-choice setting, since adequate treatment of this can be found elsewhere. What we want to do here is to apply this conceptualized contractual decision-making to monetary rules and institutions specifically. We want to ask: What sort of a "monetary constitution" might be predicted to emerge from a genuine social contract, hypothesized in the manner that we have indicated? Not knowing

18. This is the choice setting postulated by Buchanan and Tullock in their analysis of constitutional decisions. See James M. Buchanan and Gordon Tullock, *The Calculus of Consent* (Ann Arbor: University of Michigan Press, 1962).

19. This is essentially the choice setting used by John Rawls. See his *A Theory of Justice* (Cambridge: Harvard University Press, 1971).

whether he will be rich or poor, creditor or debtor, banker or butcher, gold miner or wheat farmer, economist or lawyer, how would the individual, at this true constitutional level, evaluate alternative monetary arrangements that might be suggested or proposed?

To our knowledge, this question has not often been specifically addressed.[20] Beyond an initial definition of rights and the establishment of instruments to enforce these rights, the "fair" or "efficient" constitution would include some specification of the rules for reaching collective or governmental decisions, rules that would also include a definition of the range over which governmental action might operate. With respect to monetary institutions, we must first examine the objectives to be served. What would be desired from a set of monetary rules, a monetary framework?

We may answer this question in terms of two separate functional objectives. There are genuine "public good" characteristics of money; agreement among persons concerning the thing to be used as money will greatly facilitate economic exchange. The delegation of the authority to *define* the monetary unit to the government seems to be a plausible outcome of a constitutional contract. The definition of what is to be treated as money in the society does not seem much different from the definition of what shall be the ordinary standards of measure, and it is no surprise that the power to fix weights and measures is found in the same sentence of the United States Constitution that provides for regulating the value of money. The definition of the monetary unit does not, however, directly imply anything about the value of money through time. A second functional objective that should plausibly emerge from constitutional contract is *predictability* in the value of money, or reciprocally, in the absolute level of prices. It is difficult to see how anyone should object to this attribute as a desirable feature of monetary order, and, if government is to be granted any authority beyond the definitional, regulation with a view toward insuring predictability seems the minimal attribute upon which all persons should agree. To the extent that

20. In L. B. Yeager (Ed.), *In Search of a Monetary Constitution* (Cambridge: Harvard University Press, 1962), the authors of the separate essays were explicitly requested to analyze and present alternative monetary frameworks or constitutions. However, there was little specific treatment of the consistency of selected arrangements with an initial contractual settlement. Buchanan's essay provides a partial exception here; his discussion was implicitly based on the contractual model described above.

persons and organizations, in their ordinary capacities as economic decision-makers, can predict the value of money, they need not introduce this extraneous element of uncertainty into their decision calculus.

We note that predictability, as an objective, does not prejudice the constitutional process toward going further and selecting monetary arrangements that will produce either *stability* or *change* in the level of absolute prices through time. There remains the prospect of disagreement among those who mutually accept predictability as an objective. Some may seek a secular decline in prices; others, a secular rise; still others, stability through time. Potential differences here suggest that predictability defines the limits of consensual agreement at any genuine constitutional stage of choice. It is quite difficult to imagine why any persons would prefer uncertainty to predictability here.

If monetary arrangements are to be agreed on at the constitutional stage,[21] if monetary rules are to be among the set of quasi-permanent institutions of social order, the governmental power "to coin money," which means that of selecting and defining the monetary unit, and to "regulate the Value thereof" seems conceptually appropriate, *provided* that the regulation is understood to have as its objective the insurance of predictability in value. That is to say, the second part of this should be modified to read "regulate the Value thereof so as to insure predictability in this Value." This appears to be a meaningful derivation from genuine social contract. It would be difficult to imagine a constitutional statement that was intended to provide legislatures with powers to regulate the value of money for open-ended purposes, which might include the self-interest of the members.

We emphasize that these are minimal constitutional limits. Individuals may disagree sharply as to the instrumental means through which predictability might best be furthered. Even if there is general agreement on the working properties of alternative structures, disagreement may remain as between the two major sets, those of automatic and those of managed monetary systems. As we have defined the contractual or constitutional setting, it is not possible for us to discriminate between these two broad alternatives for

---

21. Libertarian anarchists might argue that no role for government with respect to monetary arrangements need emerge from a true constitutional process. Implicitly, they are assuming that individuals would agree on a money commodity and that this spontaneous system would do more toward insuring predictability than one that provides to government any powers at all over money.

monetary order. Either one or the other, in any one of a large set of subvariants, might emerge from a deliberative constitutional assembly, or, as in the United States, the constitutional specification may not include more than a broad statement of governmental powers.

Let us now examine the United States monetary and legal history with these two plausible contractually legitimate objectives of a monetary framework in mind. We find that there has, indeed, been ample recognition of the first, or definitional, purpose. The general benefits of having the central government define the monetary unit have been recognized in much of the historical and constitutional development. By contrast, we find little or no recognition, or even much discussion, of the second contractually derivable purpose, that of predictability in the value of money. As noted, the written Constitution leaves this authority unspecified, and we can only speculate on the reason why the Founding Fathers agreed to include the phrase "regulate the Value thereof." In practice, before 1933 (and after) the government has done little that was identifiable as falling within this regulatory power, as interpreted here. In the exertion of its power to define the monetary unit, in the exercise of the delegated definitional authority, the government has, of course, exerted spillover effects on the value of money. The silver question, which generated much political controversy during the closing decades of the 19th century, was, on the surface, one of using the government's authority to define the monetary unit. Should gold be the only money commodity? The settlement of this question was known, however, to have a major impact on the value of money, on the absolute level of prices in the domestic economy. The silver interests wanted inflation in the monetary base; the gold interests did not. Nonetheless, because the issues were discussed largely in definitional terms, there seems to have been little or no attention paid to the objective of regulation of monetary value.

On balance, it seems fair to assert that the United States government, in the exercise of its duly constituted authority, might be judged to have defaulted in its contractually justifiable purpose of regulating the value of money with a view toward insuring predictability and hence toward enhancing the overall efficiency of social order.[22] We can make this judgment with-

22. Congress's failure to carry out its specifically designated role of regulating the value of money was the basis of B. Nowlin Keener's legal action. His suit was dismissed in fed-

out at this point choosing sides between the managed and the automatic monetary systems, or among the many subvariants within each category, not to mention the mixtures. We need look only at the historical record to ascertain that the value of money has fluctuated widely and unpredictably through our history.[23] Regardless of the descriptive characteristics of the set of monetary rules and institutions that were in existence, the regulatory objective was not met. The changes in the basic monetary constitution that were implemented in the 1930s must, therefore, be evaluated against historical failure rather than success, failure of the government to meet its constitutional authority to regulate money's value, if this authority is interpreted or defined in a way that might make the delegation of regulatory power contractually legitimate.

VI. Managed versus Automatic Monetary Systems

The constitutional authority to regulate the value of money is sufficiently unspecified in the United States Constitution to allow the Congress to adopt almost any organizational structure. The Constitution does not discriminate between a managed and an automatic monetary system, and, as we have suggested in the preceding section, either of these basic forms might emerge from a genuine constitutional contract. This failure of precision may have served, in part at least, to generate the failures noted above. The monetary system of the United States, both before 1933 and after, has been neither a wholly managed nor a wholly automatic system.[24] It has represented a peculiar mixture of both forms, producing what may have been the worst features of both.

It is helpful to an understanding of the constitutional events of the 1930s to engage in some imaginary history. Let us suppose that the Constitution

---

eral district court and his appeal denied on the grounds that the court lacked jurisdiction. See *Transcript of Keener vs. Congress with Explanations.*

23. See Chart 62, p. 679, in Friedman and Schwartz, for a convenient summary of the record.

24. Since 1971, when gold sales and purchases by the Treasury were abandoned, and the dollar allowed to float vis-à-vis foreign currencies, the United States comes closest to being "pure." With these changes, it is perhaps fair to say that, finally, the system has been transformed into a pure managed system.

delegated to Congress the power "to issue fiduciary currency in sufficient quantity to insure predictability in the value thereof." This would have amounted to an explicit direction to organize and to operate a system of national fiduciary money, without relationship to any commodity, such as gold, and without implications as to the relationships between the national system and those of other nations. Let us suppose that this "pure greenback" system, with a fractional reserve banking component appended,[25] had performed in roughly the same fashion over time as that system that we did have. That is to say, assume that this pure fiat system has failed to prevent dramatic deflation in incomes and prices in the Great Depression.

In such a setting, any desired increase in the amount of circulating medium could have been produced by straightforward currency issue at relatively little cost. There would have been no constitutional barriers in the way, and individuals could have claimed no violations of legitimate expectations in such governmental actions. Suppose, however, that some persons had made specific debt contracts which contained protective clauses that required the repayment of principal in terms of the value of a designated commodity or an index of commodity prices. These contracts, if existent, should have remained fully valid, since they would have borne no direct relationship to the governmental action in increasing the quantity of fiat currency. Under a system of fiat issue, therefore, there should have arisen no question about the abrogation of private contracts in furtherance of the government's power to regulate the value of money. Freedom of private contract could have remained inviolate, at least in this respect, and the Court need not have been placed in the position of choosing between competing basic principles of constitutional law.

Let us now change our imaginary history and suppose that the written Constitution delegated to Congress the power "to define a monetary com-

---

25. Strictly speaking, there would be no basis for allowing fractional reserve banking in such a model. Since the issue of paper currency is relatively costless, there would be no need to economize on scarce monetary resources through fractional holdings of high-powered money. If, however, the fiduciary issue is limited, fractional reserve banking may emerge as an institutional means of exploiting the "publicness" efficiencies inherent in high-powered money. In a pure fiat system, therefore, fractional reserve banking may be tolerated, not because it is intrinsically efficient, but because its prohibition may prove to be costly.

modity and standard units thereof," with no further specification as to the regulation of value. This would have instructed the Congress to select a commodity, say gold, and to set a price for this in terms of dollars. This would, in turn, have implied free coinage, that is, a willingness of the government to mint and to certify units of the commodity.

Why would anyone, at a constitutional stage of deliberation, prefer a commodity to a fiat standard, an automatic to a managed monetary system? We need to go back to the predictability objective emphasized above, which we identified as one of the two objectives that might plausibly emerge from genuine contractual agreement among persons. The automatic or commodity system, whether the commodity be gold or something else, could only be preferred on the basis of some prediction that this would embody greater certainty about the value of money than would a fiat or managed system. Reasonable men may disagree here, and those who opt for a commodity standard do so because they predict that governmental decision-makers will not, intentionally or inadvertently, hold to the guidelines that are necessary for a managed or fiat system to yield a predictable value of money. That is to say, an operative commodity system works *independent* of governmental action or interference once the definitional step has been taken and the price of the commodity settled. The primary attractiveness of a commodity system lies in the limits that are imposed on the power of nation-states, on national governments, to debase the value of money by arbitrary increases in supply. The predictability that such a system guarantees is based on some assessment of the behavior of those large numbers who use and produce the monetary commodity. Such a system, if operating, insures against the unpredictability that stems from overt governmental interference, against the errors of explicit "management" attempts.

If a commodity standard is to operate within its own "principles," however, governments cannot intervene to offset the system's own internal discipline. Governments cannot allow inflation of the monetary base by encouraging the economizing of the monetary commodity, by legalizing and encouraging a fractional reserve base for note and deposit issue. Nor can central banks use the monetary commodity stocks in their possession to stabilize fluctuations in domestic price levels. Such attempts at management subvert the principles upon which the commodity system stands or falls, and they act to forestall, delay, and possibly prevent the predictability that the system can embody if left to its own inherent logic, however un-compromising.

A commodity standard, as an automatically adjusting monetary consti-tution, is effectively subverted once government so much as begins to super-impose management efforts. In the years between World War I and 1933, the so-called international gold standard, and its United States component, was not a commodity standard at all. Because persons could convert dollars into gold, they were led to believe that the value of money was protected against wildly erratic fluctuations by the automatic adjustments that a commodity system embodied in principle. Individuals did not realize that national gov-ernments, and especially their central banks, had long since moved to in-terfere with the adjustment mechanism. As we look now at the pre-1933 monetary world, the breakdown is easy to understand; it is more difficult to understand why the system worked so long as it did without collapse. It was internally contradictory, a "managed commodity" system, which in-cluded neither the predictability inherent in the automatic adjustments of a commodity standard independent of governmental interference nor the predictability that direct governmental responsibility for monetary value might have induced.

What about the legitimate expectations of those persons who entered into monetary agreements under this system? What entitlement did the holder of a gold-clause bond properly claim? What was his basic property right? If we impose rational wisdom about monetary theory on such contractors, the limits of such claimed property rights become apparent. The person who en-tered into a gold-clause contract for deferred payment should have recog-nized that because gold was the defined commodity base for money issue and because the system was not really based on the automatic adjustment process almost anything might happen, including collapse of the whole monetary edifice. Pervasive uncertainty should have entered rationally into all deferred payment contractual negotiations.[26] The fact that such uncer-tainty was not more widespread suggests the quasi-fraudulent nature of the

26. This was recognized, to an extent, in the opinion of Chief Justice Hughes, for the Court majority, in one of the gold-clause cases, where he noted that such contracts "have a congenital infirmity." (*Norman v. Baltimore and Ohio Railroad Co.*, 294 U.S. 240 at 307–8.)

monetary framework. From our vantage point in history, the era seems to have been characterized by monumental confusion.

In such a setting, the parties who sought to make deferred payment agreements independent of the inherent uncertainty in existing monetary arrangements should have selected an agreed-on nonmonetary commodity or commodity bundle which could have served as a standard or index for deferred payment.[27] Governmental attempts at abrogation of such contracts would have clearly violated basic constitutional principles, at least as we have interpreted them. And we cannot infer from anything in the historical record that the Supreme Court would have, then or later, explicitly upheld either abrogation or prohibition of purely private contracts in a designated non-monetary commodity employed as a standard of value.[28]

VII. Governmental Restrictions on Private Contract

We now digress somewhat from our main discussion to the more general question concerning the possible bases for governmental power to restrict private contracts among persons, either explicitly or by refusal to enforce. The traditional economic argument for such possible governmental restrictions on voluntary trades or exchanges lies in the presence, or presumed presence, of third-party effects, of "externalities." If the carrying out of an agreement between parties affects the interests of third parties adversely,

---

27. For a discussion of legal aspects of such contracts, see John P. Dawson and Will Coultrap, "Contracting by Reference to Price Indices," *Michigan Law Review*, 33 (March 1935), 685–705.

28. It might be argued that obligations containing multiple currency options exercisable at the discretion of the obligee were logically equivalent to those in a nonmonetary commodity or index and that on grounds similar to those advanced here such obligations should have been held valid, even in the face of the gold-clause abrogations that had been upheld by the Court. Nussbaum takes this position with respect to a New York decision that upheld the refusal of the obligor to meet an obligee's claim for payment in Dutch guilder, although this was a specifically designated option under the terms. Since guilder had not been devalued, the obligee was, of course, rational in trying to exercise this option as opposed to his dollar claim. See Arthur Nussbaum, "Multiple Currency and Index Clauses," *University of Pennsylvania Law Review*, 83 (March 1936), 569–99. The decision under discussion is *City Bank Farmers Trust Co. v. Bethlehem Steel Co.* (244 App. Div. 634, 280 N.Y. Supp. 494).

there may be grounds for governmental restrictions on the initial agreement. An "economic" theory of state or governmental action may be derived from this externalities approach, a derivation that is potentially consistent with contractual origins of governmental powers.[29] Examples are omnipresent in the discussion of applied economic policy, and notably in modern treatments of governmental policies relating to environmental quality. An individual purchaser of a new automobile cannot reach a voluntary agreement with his dealer for the removal of the pollution-control devices because of the alleged effect on overall environmental quality, which affects all persons and not only those who may be parties to the contract in question.

We need not either elaborate the analysis or extend the examples. We need to relate this externality basis for possible governmental restriction on private action to the monetary events of the 1930s. It is not surprising that in a fractional reserve note and deposit issue system the action of any person in converting or attempting to convert low-powered money (commercial bank deposits) into high-powered money (currency and/or gold) exerts potential external damage on others who hold and use money and claims to money in the economy. By the nature of a fractional reserve system, all persons are linked closely in an interdependent relationship which is highly vulnerable to behavioral changes. There has always been, and remains today, a possible contractual basis for governmental limitations on the set of institutional developments (from private unconstrained contracts) that produced the fractional reserve system of commercial banking. This is not, however, the position where the government of the 1930s chose to intervene. *Given* the institutions of fractional reserve note and deposit issue, there is an "economic" argument for granting government powers to inhibit the exercise of conversion privileges by private parties.

It is essential to distinguish between the government's exercise of its legitimate constitutional power to restrict trades or contracts among private persons in the presence of significant external effects and the extension of governmental power into an area where freedom of trade and contract had been hitherto protected by law. In the latter case there arises the issue of just compensation for those whose expectations are upset, whose property values

---

29. See William J. Baumol, *Welfare Economics and the Theory of the State*, 2d ed. (Cambridge: Harvard University Press, 1965).

are reduced or destroyed. These issues arise even when the new intrusion of governmental restriction may be justified on plausible contractarian grounds.

The freedom of persons to convert deposits and currency into gold at a long-established parity and to make contracts in gold was of value. As we have noted, there may have been a good contractarian argument for the suspension of convertibility because of the externalities inherent in any fractional reserve system. But since the suspension does destroy value should persons have been compensated for the losses suffered? This question is more easily raised than answered, but the closing off of valued options that could not have been exercised by all potential participants would not have been considered legal grounds for the payment of compensation.

We do not, however, need to answer this question here. We must, instead, go beyond the suspension of free convertibility and examine the possible externalities presented by the continued private ownership and contracting in gold, the basic monetary commodity. How would an individual's decision to hoard gold affect adversely the position of others in society? How would voluntary exchanges in gold impose external diseconomies? We have suggested an answer in our earlier discussion. If the suspension of convertibility does not fully destroy the mythology of the commodity as money, of gold as the standard of long-term value, individuals might have rejected national fiat money and they might have searched out ways to base exchanges on gold, even in the absence of governmental definition. A dual or even multiple money circulation might well have developed in 1933, and with this the destruction of some of the "public good" benefits of a single and unified monetary structure.

We find that, perhaps not surprisingly, welfare economics leads us to roughly the same point that our more general discussion did. There seems to be no externalities argument that can go beyond suspension of convertibility and restriction on ownership and trade in gold. There is no justification in the theorems of modern welfare economics for the government's failure to pay holders of gold and claims to gold at the new, rather than at the old, parity. Since the government would have lost nothing in the transaction, there could have been no adverse distributional consequences in a direct sense.

A somewhat different argument must, however, be applied to the gold-clause contracts between *private* parties. After devaluation, should the gold clauses have been honored, or was there an externalities argument for abrogation? As we have noted, in the absence of the anticipated increase in incomes and prices, debtors would have been distributionally harmed by enforcement of these clauses. Here we need to return specifically to our contractual setting for the selection of constitutional rules. Suppose that persons are behind a genuine "veil of ignorance" and/or uncertainty concerning their own roles as debtors or creditors in future periods. Are there any conditions under which they would choose to grant governmental authority to abrogate contracts among private persons? It seems plausible to suggest that some such authority might be granted for interference during periods of unforseen emergencies when the relative positions of debtors and creditors are exogenously and unexpectedly shifted. Both potential debtors and potential creditors might have conceptually agreed on such a grant of extraordinary authority to government, an authority which the abrogation of gold-clause contracts between private parties represents.[30] In this way, we can locate a more plausible argument for this particular step in the whole New Deal package of monetary changes than we can for the confiscation of values by the calling in of gold coin and bullion at the old parity, and by the failure of government to honor the gold clause in *its own* contracts.

VIII. The Record of Government Failure

We emphasize that the monetary history of the United States is one of failure rather than success, failure of the government to accomplish, even tolerably, the objectives that seem to us to have been implicit in the constitutional delegation of monetary authority. The Great Depression merely dramatized this failure; the failure did not emerge suddenly and full blown in 1929. By 1933, the whole monetary structure was in disarray; basic changes in the rules were desperately required and were seen to be required by almost everyone. The

---

30. In an analogous discussion, Mann introduces the "general doctrine of frustration," and he cites Viscount Simon in a British judgment to the effect that the event of a "'wholly abnormal rise or fall in prices, a sudden depreciation of currency' . . . does not in itself affect the bargain but the true construction of the contract may show that the parties never agreed to be bound in a *fundamentally different situation* and that, accordingly, 'the contract ceases to bind at that point.'" (Italics supplied.) Mann points out that there is no United States decision on this point. See F. A. Mann, *The Legal Aspect of Money*, 3d ed. (Oxford: Clarendon Press, 1971), 120.

New Deal actions did not destroy a previously existing monetary system in any meaningful sense. The system was already in shambles. This point must be understood before any assessment of New Deal policies.

Ideally, the reconstruction of a new set of monetary rules should have commenced with the establishment of consensual agreement on the relative entitlements possessed by individuals and groups in the then-existing "monetary anarchy." But there was no time for attaining consensus and for the genuinely constitutional deliberations that might have followed. The New Deal changes were imposed with little or no attention either to the distribution of entitlements or to the possible long-run consequences. There was, of course, distributional motivation behind the whole dollar devaluation package of legislation; one of the expressed purposes was surely that of reducing the burden of debt and this could only have been accomplished by potentially damaging creditors, at least in one opportunity-cost sense. But creditors themselves could scarcely have expected to secure gains from continued banking crises, from continued erosion of confidence in the whole monetary and economic system. Had the New Deal changes been effective in securing the purposes for which they were intended, almost all individuals and groups would have benefited relative to the absence of such changes. The tragedy of the 1930s lies not in the New Deal's destruction of a long-standing, revered, and tolerably efficient monetary order. Such monetary order simply did not exist. The tragedy of the 1930s lies in the New Deal's own failure to "seize the day" and to institute those reforms that might have fulfilled the meaningful constitutional objectives for monetary order.

The pre-1933 monetary structure involved internal contradiction between its putative commodity-convertibility base and its vulnerability-exposure to misguided attempts at management in furtherance of domestic short-term goals. The New Deal's only prospect for change was toward more effective management, toward the establishment of an independent fiduciary standard, divorced from gold and from fixed foreign exchange parities. Unfortunately, the steps taken in this direction were fumbling and unsure ones, and the return to gold in January 1934, even in the limited sense of international convertibility only, became the device that seemed to justify carrying forward most of the unnecessary restrictions on individual freedom that the gold-based system had seemed to justify in the emergency.

As gold was gradually demythologized, there was less and less excuse for the continuation of the restrictions on private ownership of gold and on private trade in gold. As the economy recovered from the Depression, and as prosperity returned with World War II, the threat that individuals would, if given the opportunity, establish gold as a second circulating medium became remote indeed. The argument for continuing the restrictions in the late 1940s, 1950s, and 1960s shifted to a wholly different base. The restrictions came to be supported on the grounds that it was necessary to economize on the world's gold stocks in order to facilitate and encourage international trading adjustments. To allow private trading and ownership in gold would have increased the so-called crisis of international liquidity. Had the Supreme Court accepted a challenge to the constitutionality of the prohibition of a gold-clause bond or of gold ownership in, say, the early 1960s, the continued restriction could have been justified within the same structure of argument as that used in 1935. The government's authority to continue the prohibitions first imposed in the 1930s could have been held to be required to prevent interference with the power to regulate the value of money, this time the value of the dollar with respect to "foreign coin."[31]

Since August 1971, or, more emphatically, since December 1971, this basis for a legal justification of the gold restrictions could not have been sustained. Once the dollar was fully divorced from gold, in international adjustments as well as domestic transactions, gold has become basically equivalent to any other commodity. Unless it could have been shown that gold continued to carry with it important aspects of the mythology that surrounded it as a

---

31. Indeed it was precisely this argument that the government took in an effort to justify the continuation of the gold-ownership restrictions in 1962. The authority of the government in this respect was successfully challenged in a single case in the Southern District of California. *United States v. Briddle and Mitchell,* 212 F. Supp. 584 (S.D. Cal. 1962). This decision was not appealed by the government under stipulation by the parties pursuant to a Supreme Court Rule. However, the decision was effectively reversed in the same district by another federal judge in 1965. *Pike and Brouwer v. United States,* 340 F. 2d 487 (9th Cir. 1965). In both of these cases, however, the government's authority was challenged, not in relation to the connection between the restrictions on gold dealings and the monetary authority of government but, instead, on the more legalistic point regarding the continued presence of "national emergency." In the context of modern legal history, any such challenge seems basically frivolous, since it seems clear that the Supreme Court would always defer to the Congress and the Executive in the definition of "national emergency." For a full discussion of the legal history, with citations, see Holzer, op. cit.

monetary metal, and, because of this, would greatly interfere with the monetary structure if freely allowed to circulate among persons, there would have been no constitutional basis for continuation of the restrictions on private ownership of gold, on private dealings in gold, and on the insertion of gold clauses in contracts. In more specific terms, the Supreme Court could not, in 1974, have upheld the validity of the Joint Resolution of June 5, 1933, on the same grounds that were used in reaching its 1935 judgment. The Court, of course, might have simply deferred to a congressional judgment, delegated to the Executive, in the determination of just what actions fall within the broad constitutional grant of monetary authority.

In this case, or in the absence of an opportunity for a clear judicial ruling, restrictions on the ownership of, and dealings in, gold and, presumably, on the insertion of gold clauses in private contractual agreements depend on the action of the Executive and the Congress. Although the President was given discretionary authority to remove the restrictions on gold ownership and exchange by legislation enacted in 1972, the Nixon Administration did not exercise this authority. Congress took additional action toward mandatory removal of the restrictions in late summer 1974, with the effective date set for December 31, 1974. President Gerald R. Ford signed the bill on August 14, 1974, although press reports indicated continuing administration misgivings.[32]

Over the early 1970s, the growing prospect that the restrictions on gold ownership would be removed undoubtedly exerted an influence on the free-market price of gold. This price was surely higher than it would have been had the removal of the ownership restrictions not been anticipated. Over the long run, and especially if domestic inflation continues at the rates of the early 1970s or even accelerates, there might possibly be some development of institutions that would, in effect, utilize gold as a money competitive with the dollar, even if there is no governmental valuation of gold at all. In our view, this seems to be a highly unlikely prospect,[33] and it is certainly not one that

32. As late as December 1974, there were strong expressions of opposition to the removal of restrictions on gold ownership. Arthur Burns, Chairman of the Board of the Federal Reserve System, specifically suggested a six-month delay in the effective date of the legislation.

33. Our colleague Gordon Tullock dissents somewhat from our prediction here, and he places a considerably higher value on the probability that such a usage of gold would

would warrant reimposition of restrictions on private ownership of gold comparable to those imposed between 1933 and 1974.

IX. Inflation, Indexation, and the Monetary Authority of Government

By necessity, we look retrospectively at the monetary changes implemented by the New Deal in the 1930s. Considered solely as a subject of economic and legal history, those years hold their own intrinsic fascination. But the issues raised in that sequence of events contain relevance for the 1970s and 1980s, and it is this which motivates our inquiry. Begrudgingly, we are increasingly being forced to acknowledge that ours is an inflationary era, and that continued and possibly accelerating decline in the value of the dollar is the most likely course of economic events. Once this recognition is made and accepted, we are led to search for ways and means of adjusting to, of living with, inflation. If inflation is characteristic of our time, we can at least try to alleviate the burdens that it generates and to reduce the dislocation that it causes. (We shall not discuss why this setting has evolved or why a governmental policy aimed at stopping the inflation is not likely to emerge from political process. These would require separate papers, or books, in themselves.)

If the value of the monetary unit is to fall through time, how can individuals who seek to hold claims for deferred payment (potential creditors) protect themselves? How can individuals who seek current funds (potential debtors) secure these funds in sufficient quantity? How can long-term wage and salary contracts be negotiated in monetary units, in dollars, when the real value of these units is predicted to fall through time? How can real tax rates be set by Congress when tax brackets are denominated in money units?

During 1973 and 1974, there was mounting discussion of indexation as a means of adjusting to the uncertainty in the rate of inflation. Contracts may be drawn in a nonmonetary standard of value, in terms of some index for prices, in order to insure some meaningful relationship between the real

---

emerge, especially over a long period. He does not, of course, use this as an argument in support of restrictions on private property and contract.

terms on which an initial bargain is struck and the real terms on which the deferred obligation is to be met. Institutionally more and more wage and salary contracts contain cost-of-living or index clauses. Social Security benefits, and maximum payroll tax bases, were indexed in 1973. Senator James L. Buckley, with wide bipartisan support, introduced legislation in early 1974 that would require indexing of progressive income tax brackets, a step already taken in Canada, Denmark, and Holland. In May 1974, Senator Mike Mansfield called for the indexing of all wages and salaries. In July 1974, corporations began issuing long-term securities with interest rates linked to the short-term Treasury-bill rate.

In this inflationary setting, the constitutional monetary authority of government may once again be challenged. At first glance, an index clause in any contract is similar in many respects to a gold clause. Each of these may represent an attempt by participants in an exchange involving a deferred payment to define their respective contractual obligations independent of the nominal monetary unit, the dollar in the United States. Having upheld the constitutional authority of the Congress to abrogate all gold clauses in contracts, would a modern Supreme Court uphold an attempt by the Congress, or the Executive, to abrogate or to prohibit the making of index contracts? This could become a critical economic and legal issue, especially if the government chooses to oppose the widespread proliferation of voluntary indexing institutions, a course of action that seems quite probable.[34]

There is, of course, a major legal distinction between possible governmental action in prohibiting future contracts between private parties and the abrogation of existing contracts. Congress might well be confirmed in its authority to prohibit all index contracts in the future but held to be powerless to abrogate existing index contracts. However, if indexing becomes more and more prevalent, the interest of the federal government in preventing future contracts may merge with its interest in abrogating then-existing indexed agreements. For our purposes, we may discuss these two actions at the same time.

The government's authority, if claimed here, would have to be based on

34. Legislative and/or administrative attempts to restrict indexation seem much more likely to occur in the late 1970s and 1980s than do any attempts to reimpose the restrictions on gold dealings that were eliminated in 1974. Index clauses, rather than gold clauses, may well become the focus of legal attention.

the interference exerted by such indexed contracts on the constitutional power to regulate the value of money, fully analogous to the gold-clause issues. There are differences as well as similarities present between the two situations, however. The situation confronted in 1935 was, in many respects, quite different from that which might confront the Court in 1976 with respect to index clauses. Abrogation of the gold clauses was upheld, at least in part, because gold was the accepted monetary commodity, because the contracts embodying these clauses were monetary contracts, because the ownership and trading in gold had previously been prohibited under an acknowledged constitutional authority. In all these respects, index clauses would be quite different. Deferred claims would be computed in a standard of value that remains independent from the medium of exchange, and there would be no side trading in the "index" as such.[35] The Supreme Court, should it decide to do so, could locate sufficient dissimilarities to reach a judgment contrary to those reached in 1935.

Nonetheless, there are also grounds upon which a court could confirm a governmental authority to abrogate index contracts and to prohibit further indexing. Widespread resort to such contracts would reduce the ability of the government to issue its own debt without itself adding index clauses.

And the employment-generating effect of unanticipated inflation would be weakened significantly in an economy where indexing was widespread. The government's ability to secure real resources for itself by expanding the money supply might also be hampered. Some persons might call these effects interference with the regulation of the value of money.

A court should not, however, blindly support governmental authority to abrogate index contracts and to prohibit the making of these by private parties under the guise of the constitutional power to regulate the value of money. It should go behind this delegation of power in the Constitution and examine the possible objectives or purposes of governmental regulation of money's value. As our earlier discussion has suggested, regulation toward insuring greater predictability seems to be a plausibly meaningful interpretation of genuine constitutional agreement. If viewed in this light, there should

---

35. Mann places considerable emphasis on a 1957 French decision in which a contract for repayment in wheat was specifically held not to interfere with the monetary authority, a decision which, apparently, reversed a series of earlier judgments. Mann interprets this as validating gold clauses in France in the absence of legislation to the contrary. See F. A. Mann, *The Legal Aspect of Money*, 3d ed. (Oxford: Clarendon Press, 1971), 152–53.

be no grounds for upholding a governmental authority to prohibit or to abrogate index-clause contracts. Such contracts are designed to insure, to debtors and creditors alike, predictability in the real value of the claims that are
exchanged, predictability that would allow ordinary economic intercourse to
proceed with minimum uncertainties about fluctuations in monetary values.

A question may be raised at this point, however, concerning the gold
clauses that were abrogated in the 1930s. When contracts embodying these
clauses were negotiated, were not debtors and creditors also attempting to
insure predictability in the real values of the claims that were exchanged?
This question requires a complex answer. In the first place, there seems to
have been less-than-universal consciousness of an indexation basis for the
inclusion of the gold clauses. In many such contracts, these clauses seemed
to have been the result of rhetorical flourish on the part of bond lawyers,
rather than consciously chosen instruments to insure stability in real value.[36]
Second, the gold clauses were not, and could not be, treated as instruments
that would effectively divorce the real value of claims in particular contracts
from fluctuations in the value of money. This follows, of course, from the
fact that gold was the monetary commodity.

In a world of widespread indexing, the medium of exchange would continue to be the national fiduciary currency. The standard of value would be
the designated index, which might, of course, vary from one contract to another. Obligations would always be paid in dollars, not in some other medium. The number of dollars required to meet any specific claim would, of
course, depend on the change in the index, which would, in turn, depend on
the change in the value of dollars in terms of some set of prices. Predictability
in real value would replace predictability in nominal monetary units. But
surely this would represent a change in the effective monetary constitution
upon which all participants might possibly agree, save for the self-serving
politicians and bureaucrats who might seek to maximize their prerogatives
in resorting to the governmental money-creation powers.

Finally, and most importantly, index clauses would work quite differently
from the gold clauses, despite the apparent similarities. The existence of in-

36. The French gold clauses were abrogated in the 1930s on the basis of the argument
that parties to contracts containing such clauses were not really aware of their existence.
See Arthur Nussbaum, "Multiple Currency and Index Clauses," *University of Pennsylvania
Law Review*, 84 (March 1936), 576.

dex clauses would protect the parties against all shifts in monetary values and not just those reflected in a shift of a single price. This point may be emphasized by supposing that, in 1929, debt contracts should have contained index clauses rather than gold clauses. There was, between 1929 and 1933, roughly a 40 per cent decline in wholesale prices, and let us assume that this was the index used in the debt contracts. In this instance, the number of dollars that debtors would have had to pay creditors on obligations maturing in 1933 would have *fallen* by 40 per cent. The index clauses, in themselves, would have served to accomplish much of the debtor relief sought by the set of New Deal monetary measures. In sharp contrast, before devaluation the presence of a gold clause did absolutely nothing to relieve the increased real burden of debt obligations. And, after devaluation, enforcement of the gold clauses might have subjected debtors to a doubly increased burden, one from the decline in prices and incomes, the other from the increase in the money price of gold. There could be no way in which index clauses could have generated such a burden on debtors in deflation.

The deflation in prices and in incomes that had occurred during the Great Depression was recognized by the majority of the Supreme Court in 1935. It seems clear from the argument in the gold-clause cases that these clauses would not have been abrogated if creditors could have demonstrated that they had suffered losses in real value due to inflation. There is nothing in the judgments of the Court that suggests an open-ended authority on the part of government to inflate the economy and to prohibit contracts that represent individuals' attempts to protect their real values against such governmental behavior.

IX. Conclusions

It would be pleasing to be able to conclude this paper with a statement to the effect that concerns such as those expressed in the preceding section are misplaced, and that modern governmental decision-makers will insure that inflation will be brought under control and depression prevented. Even if this optimistic prognosis cannot be made, it would be satisfactory if we could predict that a modern President, and Congress, would not deliberately seek to prohibit indexation or the abrogation of existing indexed contracts, that if such attempts were made a modern Supreme Court would declare such action to be unconstitutional, that the removal of the restrictions on gold ownership signals a permanent change in governmental attitude. Unfortunately, sober assessment allows no such prediction.[37] On monetary matters, present and future politicians do not seem likely to be more "enlightened" than past ones, and, if anything, they may be less so. The danger is great that modern governments, armed with the additional knowledge about the instrumental uses of money-creation powers and less fearful of challenging traditional mythologies about metallic-based money and balanced government budgets, may seek to secure an ever-increasing share of the economy's resources through continued inflationary financing.[38] To the extent that political decision-makers recognize the threat that widespread indexation poses for these objectives, they might well try to prevent such contracts and to abrogate existing ones.[39]

The modern Supreme Court has assumed powers of ultimate legislative authority.[40] The Court could protect persons from the ravages of government-created inflation. But it could just as readily do the opposite. The existence of legal precedent one way or the other would probably matter very little in the balance. We have moved a long way since 1935, when judges seemed to take "the law" more seriously.[41]

37. An informed source has indicated to the authors that an official administration policy against indexation was laid down by Secretary of the Treasury George Shultz in late 1973. Further evidence of the government's opposition to indexation was provided in July 1974 by the reaction to Citicorp's highly successful issue of notes with flexible interest rates tied to the Treasury bill rate, setting the pattern for similar issues by other corporations. Arthur Burns, Chairman of the Federal Reserve Board, stated that such a note issue was contrary to the "public interest," and Congressman Wright Patman opened hearings on legislation possibly aimed at regulating such note issue.

38. As Robert Triffin emphasizes, "Man cannot unlearn the knowledge that man-made and man-controlled money gives to him." The mythology of gold could not be restored, even if this were desired. See Robert Triffin, "The Case for the Demonetization of Gold," *Lloyds Bank Review* (January 1974), 3.

39. As Mann notes, it is precisely during periods when index clauses would provide protection that governments would be most likely to prohibit and/or abrogate them. See F. A. Mann, *The Legal Aspect of Money*, 3d ed. (Oxford: Clarendon Press, 1971), 160−61.

40. "Constitutional anarchy" seems to be the most appropriate description of the legal disorder in which we live. For a more general discussion, see James M. Buchanan, *The Limits of Liberty: Between Anarchy and Leviathan* (Chicago: University of Chicago Press, in Press).

41. For those who dispute the dramatic shift in the attitude of the courts, we suggest that they read Macklin Fleming, *The Price of Perfect Justice* (New York: Basic Books, 1974).

A Defense of Organized Crime?

> ... we should try to make the self-interest of cads a little
> more coincident with that of decent people.
>
> —Samuel Butler

I. Organized Crime as Monopoly Enterprise

Monopoly in the sale of ordinary goods and services is socially inefficient because it restricts output or supply. The monopolist uses restriction as the means to increase market price which, in turn, provides a possible source of monopoly profit. This elementary argument provides the foundation for collective or governmental efforts to enforce competition. Somewhat surprisingly, the elementary argument has rarely been turned on its head. If monopoly in the supply of "goods" is socially undesirable, monopoly in the supply of "bads" should be socially desirable, precisely because of the output restriction.

Consider prostitution. Presumably this is an activity that is a "bad" in some social sense, as witness the almost universal legal prohibitions. (Whether or not particular individuals consider this to be an ill-advised social judgment is neither here nor there.) For many potential buyers, however, the services of prostitutes are "goods" in the strict, economic sense of this term; these buyers are willing to pay for these services in ordinary market transactions. From

From *The Economics of Crime and Punishment,* ed. Simon Rottenberg (Washington, D.C.: The American Enterprise Institute, 1973), 119–32. Reprinted with the permission of The American Enterprise Institute for Public Policy Research, Washington, D.C.

I am indebted to Thomas Borcherding for helpful comments.

this it follows that monopoly organization is socially preferable to competitive organization precisely because of the restriction on total output that it fosters. It is perhaps no institutional accident that we observe organized or syndicated controls of that set of illegal activities that most closely fits this pattern (prostitution, gambling, smuggling, drug traffic). In journalistic discussion, the concentration of organized crime's entrepreneurs in these activities is explained by the relatively high profit potential. The supplementary hypothesis suggested here is that monopoly is socially desirable and that this may be recognized implicitly by enforcement agencies who may encourage, or at least may not overtly and actively discourage, the organization of such industries.

The monopolization thesis can be extended and developed. Significantly, elements of the analysis can be applied to those criminal activities that involve nonvoluntary transfers. In this paper, I shall present first the simple geometry of the relationships between law enforcement and criminal effort. This allows me to discuss, in abstract and general terms, the social advantages that may be secured from effective monopolization of criminal activities. Following this, I shall discuss some of the possible objections to implications of the simple economic argument.

II. The Geometry of Crime and Law Enforcement

The geometry of crime and law enforcement may be presented in a model that is familiar to economists. We may apply a reaction-curve construction quite similar to those that have been developed in several applications such as international trade theory, duopoly theory, voting theory, or public-goods theory.[1] Consider Figure 1. On the horizontal axis we measure resources devoted to the enforcement of law. On the vertical axis we measure resources devoted to criminal activities. We want to develop two separate and independent functional relationships between these two variables. If there were no criminals, if no resources were devoted to criminal activities, society would

---

1. For an application that perhaps comes closest to this paper, see my "Violence, Law, and Equilibrium in the University," *Public Policy,* vol. 19 (Winter 1971), 1–18. Also see Gordon Tullock, "The Welfare Costs of Tariffs, Monopolies, and Theft," *Western Economic Journal,* vol. 5 (June 1967), 224–32.

not find it useful or advantageous to apply resources that might be used to produce goods of value in wasteful law enforcement effort. If no one breaks the law, there is no need for policemen, who could be trained instead as plumbers or carpenters.[2] This establishes the origin as the base point for one of the two functional relationships, the one that we may call the "enforcement response" or reaction curve. As resources are observed to be applied in criminal activity, society—that is, the collectivity of citizens acting through organized political units, governments—will find it advantageous to invest resources in law enforcement. Passive acquiescence to crime is rarely advocated, even among Quakers.[3] Furthermore, there are acknowledged to be major advantages from organizing law enforcement publicly rather than through private and independent action.[4] We should, therefore, expect to find the enforcement response curve sloping upward and to the right from the origin in geometrical representation, as indicated by the curve L in Figure 1. The precise shape of this curve or relationship need not concern us at this point. The general upward slope indicates only that the public will desire to devote more resources to law enforcement as the observed input of resources into criminality increases.

A second relationship, independent of the first, exists between criminal activity and law enforcement effort, with the first now being the dependent and the second the independent variable. To derive the L curve, we made the enforcement response depend upon the observed level of resources in criminality. To develop the separate "criminal response" relationship, drawn as

2. For a generalized account of the "social dilemma" that law enforcement represents, along with numerous applications, see Gordon Tullock, *The Social Dilemma* (forthcoming).

3. At minimal levels of criminal activity, acquiescence may be the efficient course of action. The formal properties of an efficient or optimal position will take into account both the amounts of criminal activity and the costs of enforcement activity. See Winston Bush, *Income Distribution in Anarchy* (forthcoming), for an attempt to specify these formal properties.

4. Law enforcement qualifies as a genuine "public good" in that there are major efficiency gains from joint, as opposed to individual, provision. All persons secure benefits from the same policeman on the beat simultaneously. This need not, of course, imply that private supplements to public law enforcement may not also be advantageous. And there is nothing in the argument for public organization of law enforcement that suggests explicit governmental production. A collectivity may well secure efficiency gains from hiring the services of a private policing firm, as opposed to hiring its own municipal policemen.

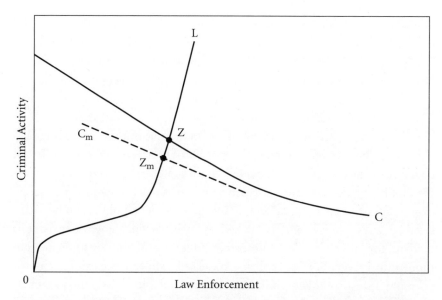

Figure 1. Relationship of resources devoted to criminal activity and law enforcement

the C curve in Figure 1, we make criminal resource input depend on the level of law enforcement that is observed. It is reasonable to hypothesize that the C curve slopes downward and to the right throughout the range of enforcement effort. If no resources were devoted to enforcement, if there were no policemen, we should predict a relatively large investment in criminal activity. This locates the left-hand intercept high on the vertical axis. As more resources enter enforcement, investment in crime becomes less and less profitable.[5] At some relatively high enforcement levels, it seems reasonable to think that a minimal level of criminality would be realized and that further enforcement would have little or no effect. This is indicated by the flattened portion of the C curve in its rightward extremities in Figure 1.

Some care must be taken to define just what the C curve represents. For any observed level of law enforcement effort, a level of investment in criminality will be generated. This will be the result or outcome of the private and

5. For those who adopt a pathological interpretation and explanation of crime, the C curve would be horizontal. This would indicate that the number of criminals and the amount of criminal effort are not influenced by enforcement at all.

independent behavior of many persons, potential criminals all, and there is no implication that the response is deliberately controlled by anyone or by any group. Hence, we may qualify or restrict the C curve by the adjective "competitive" if we assume that entry into criminality is open and that the industry is not centrally controlled, cartelized, or monopolized.

Given the two independent relationships as depicted, we can readily demonstrate convergence of the system to a stable equilibrium position at Z, provided that the L curve exhibits a steeper absolute slope value over relevant adjustment ranges than the C curve.[6] Given any starting point, under these conditions the two response or reaction patterns will lead through a succession of adjustments to Z. At such point, no further responses will be forthcoming unless the system is shocked by external forces. At Z, the public demand for inputs into law enforcement is adjusted properly to the level of input into criminality that is being observed, while at the same time, the criminal industry finds itself in equilibrium under the law enforcement effort that it confronts. There is no observed net entry into or net egress of resources from either criminality or law enforcement. Furthermore, as noted, the equilibrium is stable; if an external force shifts the system from Z, a response mechanism will come into play to return the system to a new equilibrium.

III. The Predicted Effects of Criminal Monopoly

We may now move beyond this elementary adjustment model and consider the effects to be predicted from the effective replacement of a fully competitive criminal industry by a monopolized industry. For this purpose, it will be necessary to distinguish two types of activity. The first, referred to initially in the introduction, covers those activities that are deemed "socially bad," but which involve the sale of goods and services that are considered to be economic "goods" by some potential buyers. Prostitution is the example used

---

6. If the society's law enforcement reaction to changes in the level of criminality should be highly elastic relative to the converse reaction of criminal effort to enforcement, the simple system depicted in Figure 1 would generate an explosive cycle. One implication of this suggests that the enforcement response, that which is under society's collective control, should not be overly sensitive. On this, see my paper "Violence, Law, and Equilibrium in the University."

before, and it may be taken as a typical case. In the absence of legal prohibition, activities of this sort would amount to nothing more than ordinary exchange or trade, with mutual agreement among contracting parties. Journalistic discussion often labels these as "victimless crimes," although this terminology seems misleading.

The second type of criminal activity involves no such mutual agreement, even in the complete absence of legal prohibition. We may think of burglary as an example of these so-called "crimes with victims." Here the legal structure proscribes involuntary transfers of "goods" among persons rather than the voluntary transfers proscribed under activities of the first type. As the analysis below will indicate, there are three possible sources of an argument for monopolization or cartelization of criminal industries fitting the first category, but only two of these remain applicable to those criminal industries falling within the second category.

Consider a "Type I" industry, exemplified here by prostitution. Initially, we may assume that inputs are available to this industry at an invariant supply price that is determined by the resource returns in alternative employment. Under competitive organization of the industry, there will be a tendency for each productive service to be employed so long as this exogenously fixed input price (or wage) falls below marginal value product, MVP, of this input. The necessary condition for competitive equilibrium in the employment of a particular input, I, is:

$$W_I = MVP_I = MPP_I \cdot P_0. \tag{1}$$

As noted in equation (1), the marginal value product is made up of two components, the value of the output, represented by the price, P_0, and the actual change in total quantity of output consequent on the change in the supply of inputs, MPP_I. Elementary price theory suggests that when we replace competition by monopoly, the necessary conditions become:

$$W_I = MVP_I = MPP_I \cdot MR_0. \tag{2}$$

Marginal revenue replaces output price as a component of marginal value product of input. The reason for the change is that under monopoly, rational decision-making (profit-maximizing behavior) will take into account the fact that price varies with total output placed on the market. Even if the monopolist acts as a pure price-taker in the market for inputs, as he does under our assumptions, he cannot assume the role of price-taker in the output market. In setting output, he also sets price. Hence, he will take into account not only the actual price that an incremental unit of output can command but also the effects that this addition to supply will exert on the potential selling price of all inframarginal units. Total revenues are a multiple of price times quantity, and it is the change in this total that is relevant to the monopolist's decisions.

From this element alone it is clear that a monopolist will find it profitable to reduce total output in the industry to some level below that which would be observed under competition. This straightforward, price-induced output effect may be identified as the first of the three parts of an argument for the effective monopolization or cartelization of a Type I criminal industry,[7] provided, of course, that the legal prohibition of this type of activity is itself a welfare-increasing policy rule.[8]

This effect is not directly applicable to industries embodying the second type of criminal activity, that which involves no potential contractual agreements or arrangements among willing buyers and sellers. Monopoly control in these "Type II" industries, exemplified by burglary, could not exploit a price-induced, output effect. This requires us to look more carefully at the basic economic model for a Type II activity, again taking burglary as our example.

Output here is presumably measured by the value of the loot that is stolen.

---

7. The argument holds so long as anything less than perfect discrimination is available to the monopolist. If perfect discrimination were possible, the output under monopoly would be identical to that under competition. Note particularly that the complete absence of discrimination is not required for the argument, and, in fact, some less-than-perfect discrimination might be expected to take place in industries of Type I. Buyers' information about alternatives would presumably be less than with noncriminal industries, and transaction costs involved in retrading would probably be significantly higher.

8. The welfare of participants in the voluntary exchanges, considered as a subset of the total population, would be maximized by an absence of legal prohibitions. In the presence of such proscriptive rules, furthermore, restrictions on industry output would be welfare-reducing. Hence, for this subset of the population, monopoly control is less desirable than competition. For the inclusive community, this welfare-decreasing effect of monopolization must be more than offset by welfare gains of nonparticipants if the legal proscriptions are, themselves, socially desirable. There is, of course, no means of determining by simple observation whether or not this condition is fulfilled. For purposes of analysis here, I shall assume that it is.

Since, however, this material is not different in kind from that which remains in the possession of legal owners, modifications in the rate of supply of loot by the burglary industry will not affect price significantly. In this respect, a potential monopolist of this industry would remain in the same position as the single member among the many members in an openly competitive structure. This point can be seen clearly if we treat the theft of money as an illustration. Units of money are indistinguishable, and the price of a dollar is invariant at a dollar.[9]

In this initial model, there is no incentive for the monopolist to restrict output in a Type II activity because of the effects on output price. But there may exist an *input-price effect,* applicable for both Type I and Type II activities, that would offer the monopolist an incentive to restrict total supply below that which would be observed under open competition. Initially, we assumed that resource inputs were available to the industry in question at constant supply prices. This amounts to assuming that the resources are unspecialized, that criminality generates no differential rents. If we drop this assumption and allow for this possibility, then an expansion in output of the industry may increase the prices of inputs. If a monopolist (monopsonist) is unable to discriminate among different owners of specialized inputs, he will have an incentive to reduce total inputs hired (and hence total output produced) below that generated under competitive organization.[10]

There remains the third source of the argument for monopolization, and this part also carries over for both Type I and Type II criminal activities. Note that in our discussion of either the output-price or input-price effect, we did not find it necessary to introduce law enforcement effort or investment as a

---

9. When we consider the theft of real goods, such as items of clothing, jewelry, plate, and automobiles, some elements identified as characteristic of Type I industries may enter. The value of stolen items here is determined by the ability to market them through indirect and illegal channels. To the extent that the supply of "fence" services is not, itself, highly elastic, the monopolist might face a downsloping curve of effective "demand price." In this case, the argument developed above would, of course, hold and marginal revenue would fall below price. My purpose is not to deny the real-world relevance of this situation, but to develop a pure Type II model in which, by assumption, final purchasers do not distinguish stolen from nonstolen goods and in which there are no institutional or supply barriers to resale.

10. Discrimination among suppliers of inputs may be considerably easier to accomplish than discrimination among purchasers of outputs. See Footnote 7 above.

determining variable. Regardless of the public's attitudes toward law enforcement and the total investment in enforcement determined by such attitudes, if the conditions described are present, monopolization will tend to reduce total social investment in criminality below that which would be forthcoming under competitive structure. This conclusion holds when society does nothing at all toward law enforcement as well as when society expends a major share of its annual treasure to this end. Furthermore, the shape of the relationship between law enforcement and the level of criminal activity, the enforcement response, or L curve, in Figure 1, is not relevant. Indeed, we could have dispensed entirely with any L curve to this point in the analysis.

Things become different when we examine the third part of the monopolization argument. Here the ability of a potential monopolist to observe the *shape* of the enforcement-response relationship distinguishes the monopoly outcome from the competitive one. If the L curve should be vertical, indicating that there is no enforcement response to changes in the level of investment in criminality, the monopoly situation becomes identical to the competitive. For almost all other configurations, however, strategic behavior by the monopolist in recognition of anticipated enforcement response will generate lower levels of criminality than those predicted under competitive organization.

In order to isolate this effect, which we may call the "internalization of externality" effect, we shall assume that the output of the criminal industry is marketed in a fully competitive setting, and, furthermore, that inputs are available to the industry at constant supply prices.[11] This means that producers must remain price-takers in both output and input markets whether the industry is organized along competitive or monopolistic lines. Despite the invariance in input prices, however, average costs of engaging in criminality would increase with an expansion in the output of the industry. This increase in the costs would be directly caused by the shape of the L curve in Figure 1, that is, by society's expressed response to the aggregate level of criminality. The effect is to increase the average cost of a unit of criminal output, or, to state the same thing differently, to decrease the marginal (and average) pro-

11. These assumptions are not fully consistent with a general equilibrium setting. They may be made plausible by assuming that the industry is small relative to the total economy. They are made here, however, solely for purposes of exposition.

ductivity of an input into criminality. The supply curve for the criminal industry would slope upward, despite our assumption that input prices are invariant.

The individual firms in a competitive organization of the industry will not recognize the effects of expanded industry output on average costs. The enforcement response generated by expanded industry output acts to place such firms in a position of imposing reciprocal external diseconomies, one on the other. In considering its own output decisions, the individual firm will act as if it has no influence on total industry output and, hence, on the change in costs as industry expands. In making a decision to produce an additional unit, the competitive firm will impose costs on other firms in the industry.

It is precisely the existence of this enforcement-induced external diseconomy that provides the third argument for monopolization. The replacement of competition by monopoly has the effect of internalizing the diseconomy. The monopolist can take into account the relationship between aggregate industry output and the predicted enforcement response, and he can control total industry output so as to increase profits above those forthcoming under competition.

Both the price-induced and the enforcement-induced effects work in the same direction; both provide opportunities for the rational monopolist to secure gains from reducing output below competitive levels. For any given enforcement level, we could, therefore, predict that monopoly output would fall short of the competitive. We may return to Figure 1 and depict monopoly output as a function of enforcement effort, as indicated by the curve C_m in the diagram. This curve falls below C at all points. The equilibrium toward which the system converges under monopoly or cartel control of the industry is shown at Z_m.

If the enforcement-response depicted in Figure 1 is assumed to be socially efficient, then a position at Z_m is clearly preferable to one at Z. The level of criminality is lower, and this must be evaluated positively unless crime itself is somehow considered to be "good." Furthermore, at Z_m the total amount of enforcement effort is lower than that at Z. Resources involved in enforcement may be freed for the production of alternative goods and services that are positively valued; the taxpayer has additional funds that he may spend on alternative publicly provided or privately marketed goods and services.

IV. Possible Objections to Criminal Monopolies

We should examine possible counterarguments or objections to the monopolistic organization of criminal industries. Are there effects of monopolization that are socially undesirable and which have been obscured or neglected in our analysis?

Distributional objections may be considered at the outset. Monopolization offers opportunities for profits in crime over and above those forthcoming under competition, and this, in itself, may be deemed socially "bad." It must be noted, however, that profits are made possible only because of the reduction in total criminal activity below fully competitive levels. Furthermore, the possible monopoly profits do not represent transfers from "poor deserving criminals." Under open competition, in the absence of specialization, owners of inputs into crime secure returns that are roughly equivalent to those that could be earned in legitimate, noncriminal activities. Monopolization has the effect of shifting a somewhat larger share of these inputs into noncriminal pursuits. For some of these services, transfer rents may be reduced, but these reductions are offset by increased transfer rents received by other owners of services. It seems difficult to adduce strictly distributional objections to the monopolization of crime.

A second possible objection may be based on the presumed interdependence of the several types of criminal activities. In the analysis above, I have implicitly assumed that the separate criminal industries are independent one from another. If we should assume that potential criminals constitute a noncompeting group of persons, distinct and apart from the rest of society, monopolization of one or a few areas of criminality may actually increase the supply of resources going into remaining and nonorganized activities. This sort of supply interdependence provides an argument for the extension of monopolization to all criminal activities. It does not, however, offer an argument against monopolization per se. Under full monopolization or effective cartelization, the allocation of resources among the separate criminal activities may not be equivalent, in the proportional sense, to that which would prevail under competition. The crime syndicate that effectively controls all criminal activities will equalize the marginal return on its resources in all categories, but the returns captured will include portions of "buyers' surplus" not capturable under effective competition. The mix among crimes will probably be different in the two cases; there may be more burglars relative to bank robbers under one model than under the other. There will, however, be fewer of both under monopoly except under exceptional circumstances.

A third possible objection to the whole analysis must be considered more seriously and discussed in more detail. To this point, I have implicitly assumed that resource inputs are transformed into criminal output with equal efficiency in competitive organization and in monopoly. This assumption may not be empirically appropriate. It seems plausible to argue, at least under some circumstances, that a monopolized or cartelized criminal industry can be more efficient than competition. For any given output, the monopoly may require fewer resource inputs. If this is the case, the C curve of Figure 1 cannot be allowed to represent resource input and/or criminal output interchangeably as we have implicitly done in the discussion. The nonstrategic monopoly-response curve will not be coincident with the competitive C curve if the former is defined in terms of output. The nonstrategic monopoly-response curve will lie above that which describes competitive criminal response. The strategic monopoly-response function will lie below the nonstrategic function, as depicted, but there is no assurance that it need lie below the competitive-response function as shown in Figure 1. To the extent that there are significant economies of large scale in crime, monopoly organization will tend to be relatively more efficient. Even if this hypothesis is accepted, however, the advantages of competitive criminal organization are not clear. Consider an example in which a fully strategic monopoly response, given a predicted enforcement-response function, generates a criminal output valued at X dollars, which is the same as the output that would be generated under competition. Assume, however, that the latter industrial organization uses resources valued at X dollars in alternative uses, whereas the monopoly uses up only X/2 dollars in generating X. The social "bad" represented by crime is identical in the two forms; law enforcement investment is the same. But resources valued at X/2 are freed for the production of valued "goods" under monopoly whereas these "goods" cannot be produced under competition.[12]

---

12. The media sometimes become confused in assessing the comparative efficiency of organized and unorganized crime. In June 1971, attention was focused on the theft of

A possible misunderstanding of the whole analysis rather than an explicit objection to it may well emerge. Emotions may be aroused by the thought that one implication of the whole analysis is that governments should "deal with the syndicate," that law enforcement agencies should work out "accommodations" or "arrangements" with those who might organize central control over criminal effort. I should emphasize that there is nothing of this sort implied in the analysis to this point. In its strictest interpretation, the analysis carries no policy implications at all. It merely suggests that there may be social benefits from the monopoly organization of crime. Policy implications emerge only when we go beyond this with a suggestion that governments adopt a passive role when they observe attempts made by entrepreneurs to reduce the effective competitiveness of criminal industries. In practice, this suggestion reduces to an admonition against the much-publicized crusades against organized crime at the expense of enforcement effort aimed at ordinary, competitive criminality.

I do not propose that explicit "arrangements" be made with existing or potential criminal syndicates. If this approach were taken, the solution to the system depicted in Figure 1 would not be at Z_m, but would, instead, be located to the southwest of Z_m, embodying even less criminal output and less enforcement effort. At Z_m, "gains from trade" between a monopoly syndicate and the community may be exploited only by moves in the general southwesterly direction.[13] There are compelling arguments against this approach. In the first place, even if the persons in potential control of criminal activity could be identified in advance and a bargain struck with them, the governmental agency involved would find that the "trading" solution lies off the community's enforcement response, or L, curve. This would bring pressure on politicians to break the agreement. A government agency, precisely

---

stock certificates from brokerages. On consecutive evening news broadcasts, one TV network reported (1) organized crime *exploits* the actual thieves by giving them only 5 percent of the face value of the stolen certificates, and (2) the increase in theft is facilitated because organized crime provides a *ready market* for the securities.

13. Economists familiar with ridge-line or reaction-curve constructions will recognize that the C_m curve depicts the locus of vertical points on the series of indifference contours representing the preferences of the monopolist. Similarly, the L curve is the locus of horizontal positions on the community's set of indifference curves, assuming away all difficulties in interpersonal amalgamation. The preferred position of the monopolist lies high along the ordinate, and the preferred position of the community lies at the origin.

because it acts on behalf of, and is thereby subject to review by, the whole community, cannot readily behave monolithically, whether this behavior is unilateral strategic response to, or explicit bilateral dealing with, a syndicate. The community enforcement-response function necessarily describes outcomes generated by the interaction of many behavioral components; in many respects such responses are more closely analogous to competitive, than to monopoly, behavior.

Perhaps an equally important technical difficulty with this approach involves the question of identification itself. Even if the enforcement agencies could act monolithically, independent of community political pressures, the question would remain: If the criminal syndicate could be identified with sufficient predictability to allow bargains to be struck, why should "trade" be necessary? The community's preferred position is the reduction of criminal activity to zero, allowing for a comparable reduction in enforcement effort. The enforcement-response function, shown by the L curve in Figure 1, is based on the implicit assumption that there are technological limits to the productivity of police effort. These limits may rule out the full identification of the organizers of crime, even if monopoly is known to exist and to be effective. Passive acquiescence in the syndication of crime is a wholly different policy stance from active negotiations with identified leaders.

If "arrangements" are ruled out on technological, ethical, or contractual bases, however, a subsidiary question arises concerning appropriate policy norms to be followed when and if positive identification of the monopolists becomes possible, either fortuitously or as a result of search effort. Suppose, for example, that a municipality that is initially in a Z_m equilibrium finds it possible to identify leaders of the local syndicate. Should the community prosecute these leaders and break up the monopoly? Failure to prosecute here is quite different from the arrangement of explicit trades or deals. Breakdown of an existing control group may loose a flood of entrants and the competitive adjustment process might converge toward a new equilibrium at Z. If such a pattern is predicted, attempts at breaking up even those criminal monopolies whose leaders are positively identified should be made with caution.

The law enforcement response that this analysis implies is no different in detail from that which might be followed under competitive organization of the criminal industries. Enforcement units and agencies are presumed to make normal efforts to apprehend criminals of all sorts, and community or public pressures will insure that these efforts are bounded from both sides. Indeed, the monopolist's response function has been presumed to be based on the expectation that community response would be as noted. The analysis does nothing toward suggesting that enforcement agencies should not take maximum advantage of all technological developments in crime prevention, detection, and control. To the extent that new technology increases the cost of criminal output, the relevant C curve, competitive or monopolistic, is shifted downward. To the extent that court rulings increase the expected productivity of investment in criminality and/or reduce the productivity of enforcement effort, the relevant C curve is shifted upward. The whole analysis has been presented on the assumption that the public's "tastes" for enforcement remain unchanged. This is merely a convenient expository device, and there is no difficulty in incorporating shifts toward the right or left in the L function.[14]

V. Criminal Self-Interest as a Social "Good"

The genius of the eighteenth-century social philosophers, notably Bernard Mandeville, David Hume, and Adam Smith, is to be found in their recognition that the self-interests of men can be made to serve social purpose under the appropriate institutional arrangements. They sought reform in the organization or the institutions of society as an instrumental means of accomplishing more specific social objectives. The philosophical foundations of competitive economic organization are contained in Adam Smith's famous statement about the butcher whose self-interest, rather than benevolence, puts meat on the consumer's supper table. So long as attention is confined to the production, supply, and marketing of pure "goods," as evaluated both by direct purchasers and by the members of the community in their "public" capacities, competition among freely contracting traders, with open entry

14. The situation in the United States in the early 1970s may be interpreted in terms of the analysis of this paper. Adverse court rulings since the middle 1950s have continually shifted the relevant C curves upward. This has created a disequilibrium in the whole system that is reflected in the observed increases in enforcement effort.

into and egress from industry, furthers the "public interest" in a meaningful sense of this term. There is no argument for monopolistic restriction in this setting, whether this be done via governmental agencies, as in Smith's era (and, alas, all too commonly in our own) or by profit-seeking private entrepreneurs. The preservation of free entry and egress, the prohibition of output-restricting, price-increasing agreements among sellers, the control of industries or groups of industries by one or a small number of persons and/ or firms—all of these are genuinely "public goods" and, as such, their provision warrants the possible investment of governmental resources.

Things become somewhat different, however, when it is recognized that "goods," which individuals value positively in their private capacities, may be mixed variously with "bads," which individuals value negatively in their capacities as members of the community. To the extent that the "goods" element is isolated, restrictions on competitive supply are socially undesirable. If the "bads" necessarily accompany the production-sale of the "goods," however, some balance must be struck, and some reductions in the output of "goods" below openly competitive levels may be in the social interest. If the "bads" are internal to an industry, monopolization will cause these to be internalized and taken into account in decision-making. In this case, profit-seeking behavior of the monopolist will reduce the output of "goods" below socially optimal levels. In this case, it becomes impossible to determine, a priori, which of the two organizational forms, competition or monopoly, is socially more efficient. If the "bads" are external to an industry, wholly or partially, monopolization will at least shift the total supply of "goods" in the direction indicated by social optimality criteria, but profit-induced restriction may fall short of or overshoot the mark. Aside from this, there may also be highly undesirable distributional consequences of monopolization. In general, no straightforward organizational or institutional principles can be deduced for the cases where "goods" and "bads" are mixed. The choice between competitive and monopoly organization, if these are the only effective alternatives, must be made on the basis of pragmatic considerations in each case.[15]

---

15. Economists, in their roles as social reformers, constantly search for alternatives that will accomplish the explicit objectives more directly, without basic modifications in or-

Unambiguous organizational-institutional guidelines re-emerge, however, when we examine activities that are unambiguously "bads" in the social or public sense. Here the argument advanced by Mandeville and Smith becomes applicable in reverse. If it lies within the self-interest of men to produce "bads" without accompanying and compensating "goods," this same self-interest may be channeled in a socially desired direction by encouraging the exploitation of the additional private profit opportunities offered in explicit restraint of trade. Freedom of entry, the hallmark of competition, is of negative social value here, and competitiveness is to be discouraged rather than encouraged. These principles become self-evident once we recognize, with the eighteenth-century philosophers, that institutional structures are variables that may be used as instruments for achieving social purpose, in this case, the reduction in the aggregate level of criminality along with the reduction in resource commitment to law enforcement. It is not from the public-spiritedness of the leaders of the Cosa Nostra that we should expect to get a reduction in the crime rate but from their regard for their own self-interests.[16]

---

ganizational structure. For example, witness the current popularity of schemes to correct for "public bads" exemplified in air and water pollution by placing charges or fees on the production and sale of marketable goods and services, while maintaining competitive structure as the organizational form.

It will be recognized that the content of this paragraph covers, in extremely brief form, many parts of modern welfare economics. Earlier works of my own have discussed some of the points made. See my "Private Ownership and Common Usage: The Road Case Reexamined," *Southern Economic Journal*, vol. 22 (January 1956), 305–16; "External Diseconomies, Corrective Taxes, and Market Structure," *American Economic Review*, vol. 59 (March 1969), 174–76; and "Public Goods and Public Bads," in *Financing the Metropolis*, ed. John P. Crecine (Beverly Hills: Sage Publications, 1970), 51–71.

16. Only upon reading another paper delivered at the conference did I see the reference to the paper by Thomas Schelling on the economics of organized crime. Upon subsequent examination, I find that Schelling explored some of the issues touched on in my paper but that he did not explicitly discuss the central principle that I have emphasized. See Thomas C. Schelling, "Economic Analysis of Organized Crime," Appendix D in *Task Force Report: Organized Crime*, Annotations and Consultants' Papers, Task Force on Organized Crime, The President's Commission on Law Enforcement and the Administration of Justice (Washington, D.C.: Government Printing Office, 1967).

Name Index

Subject Index

Agricultural Adjustment Act (1933):
Thomas Amendment, 403;
unconstitutionality of, 355
anarchy: constitutional, 182; Hobbesian,
175
anti-federalism, 75
anti-Federalism: in development of U.S.
Constitution, xiii–xiv, 103
Articles of Confederation, American,
102–5, 146–47
autarky, extra-market, 236–38
autonomy: efficacy under competitive
federalism, 72–76, 86–88; range and
scope of individual, 106; for sub-units
of federal system, 95–96

bargaining: in political exchange, 186
Bronson v. Rhodes (1869), 389 n. 2
buyers: rent-protecting interests of, 210;
substitute, 203–4; value of liberty for,
205

central banks: monetary expansion by
national, 124–25; in nation-states, 124;
in proposed European Union, 112
centralization: under competitive
federalism, 72–76, 86–88; of control
over economic activity, 91–92; of
political power, 134–37; pressures in
European Union for fiscal, 139
central place theory, 28–29

choice: economy constrains individual,
268–69, 274; exit options as, 97;
expectational, 295; in market economy,
268–70; in political action, 82–85;
politicization of, 68; in radical
subjectivism, 294–96. *See also* exit
option; freedom of choice; individual
choice; social choice
choice, collective: within limiting rules,
170; in socialist philosophy, 106–7
*City Bank Farmers Trust Co. v. Bethlehem
Steel Co.*, 419 n. 28
clubs: in absence of locational fixity,
47–48; formation of fiscal, 63
Coase theorem: applicability, 363;
assignment of liability under, 363;
Pareto-irrelevant externality applied to,
369–73; required assumption of, 364;
statement of, 370
commons, the: interdependence with
shared, 217; liberties of access to, 210–11;
rule of law with partition of, 222–26;
tragedy of, 216, 220–22
competition: demand side of, 239;
disciplinary pressure of, 93; among
European central banks in federal
union, 112; linkage between individual
liberty and, 258; in market economy, 69;
among nation-states in federalism,
123–30; in proposed European federal
union, 109–10; to protect

This book is set in Minion, a typeface designed by Robert Slimbach specifically for digital typesetting. Released by Adobe in 1989, it is a versatile neohumanist face that shows the influence of Slimbach's own calligraphy.

This book is printed on paper that is acid-free and meets the requirements of the American National Standard for Permanence of Paper for Printed Library Materials, z39.48-1992. ♾

Book design by Louise OFarrell, Gainesville, Fla.
Typography by Impressions Book and Journal Services, Inc., Madison, Wisc.
Printed and bound by Worzalla Publishing Company, Stevens Point, Wisc.